*John Donne,
Coterie Poet*

John Donne, Coterie Poet

ARTHUR F. MAROTTI

WIPF & STOCK · Eugene, Oregon

Wipf and Stock Publishers
199 W 8th Ave, Suite 3
Eugene, OR 97401

John Donne, Coterie Poet
By Marotti, Arthur F.
Copyright © 1986 by Marotti, Arthur F.
ISBN 13: 978-1-55635-677-3
Publication date 8/1/2008
Previously published by The University of Wisconsin Press, 1986

COVER ILLUSTRATION:
Portrait of John Donne c. 1595 (oil on canvas)
by English School (16th century).
Copyright © National Portrait Gallery, London, UK/
The Bridgeman Art Library.

For my parents

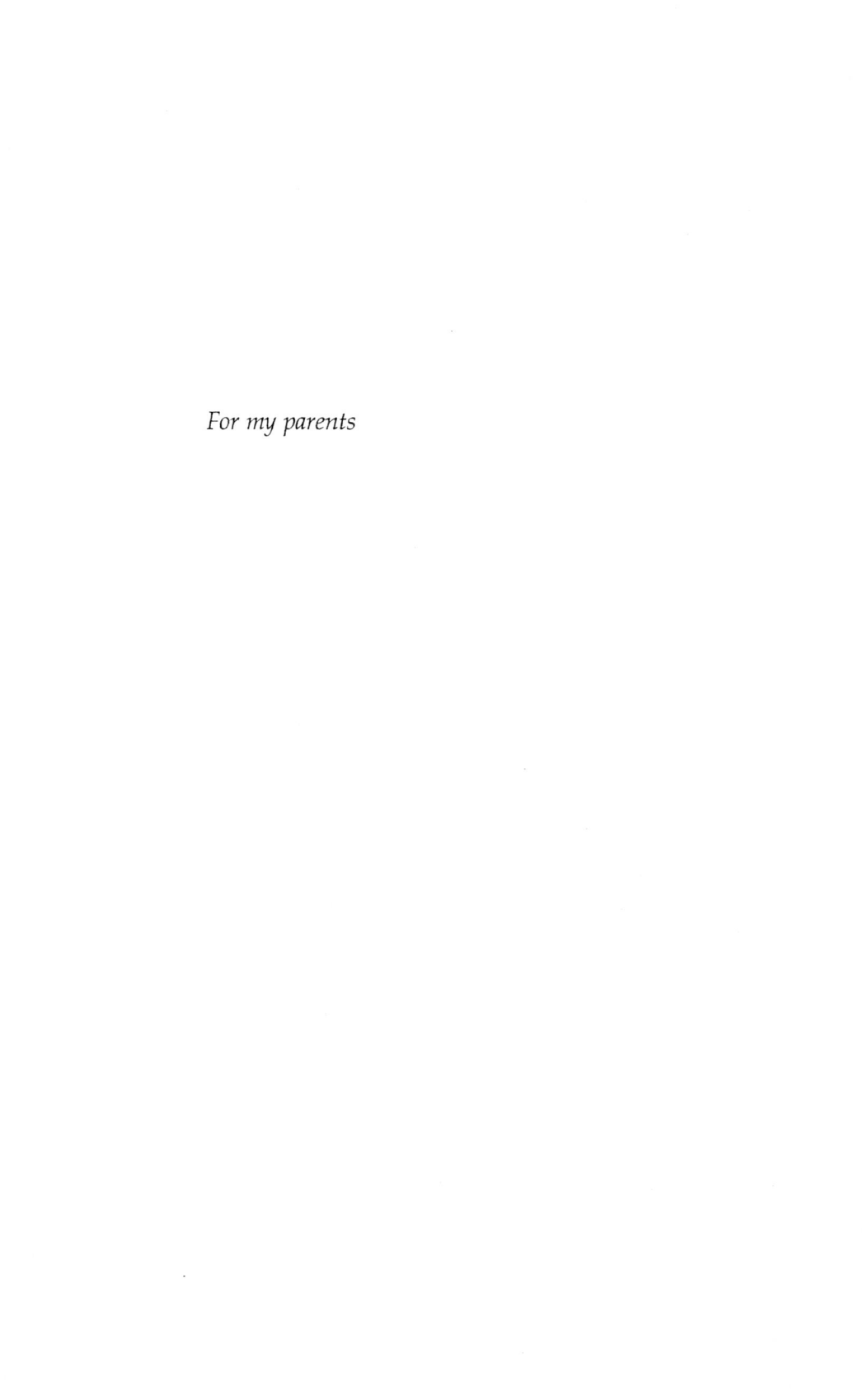

Contents

PREFACE TO THE 2008 REPRINT ii

PREFACE ix

A NOTE ON TEXTS xvii

INTRODUCTION: DONNE AND THE CONDITIONS OF COTERIE VERSE 3

1. DONNE AS AN INNS-OF-COURT AUTHOR 25
   The Inns of Court as a Socioliterary Environment 25
   Donne at Lincoln's Inn: The Early Verse Letters and First Three Satires 34
   The Paradoxical, Ovidian, and Dramatic Elegies 44
   The Art and Conditions of Donne's Early Lyrics 66
   Libertine Poems and the Art of Writing "Feelingly" 71
   Courtly and Anticourtly Lyricism 82

2. DONNE AS A YOUNG MAN OF FASHION, GENTLEMAN-VOLUNTEER, AND COURTLY SERVANT 96
   Early Poems of Valediction and an Anticourtly Satire 97
   Courtly Lyrics of Compliment and the Poetry of Disillusionment 106
   The Writing of the Employed Courtier 116
   The Poetry of Courtship 133

3. DONNE AS SOCIAL EXILE AND JACOBEAN COURTIER 152
   The Love Lyrics of the Married Man 152
   Donne's Writing and the Jacobean Environment 178
   Donne's Politics and His Early Jacobean Prose 183
   The Verse of Poetic Exchange: Donne and Sir Edward Herbert 195
   Donne, Lady Bedford, and the Poetry of Compliment 202
   "A Nocturnall" and the *Anniversaries* 232

Contents

The Religious Verse and Prose of the Secular Man 245
The Final Secular Poems 269

EPILOGUE: DONNE'S LAST POEMS 275

NOTES 291

INDEX 351

Preface to the 2008 Reprint

In the quarter century since I wrote this book much has changed in the academic study of early modern literary texts and in Donne scholarship and criticism. In the 1970s it was unusual to emphasize the sociohistorical coordinates of literary texts, to read poetic texts politically. The New Historicism and cultural-materialist criticism were yet to exert their powerful influence and scholar-critics were only beginning to write in opposition to anti-historical formalist criticism as well as to old-fashioned intellectual-historical approaches, which dealt little or not at all with social, economic, and political processes. Donne had, in Merritt Hughes's words, been "kidnapped" by that form of modernist formalism, whose American practitioners were ideologically conservative and, when Donne's work was contextualized, it was done mainly with reference to the world of ideas, a sphere meant to float above quotidian realities. The image of Donne as an author was that of the solitary craftsman or passionate intellectual, writing works that would transhistorically reach an audience of exquisitely sensitive and intelligent readers, if only finally in the twentieth century. Even though revisionist historians such as Lawrence Stone and Conrad Russell were starting to have a strong impact on literary studies, there was little work on Donne that emphasized the social embeddedness of his poetry, much less its political valency.

I knew by highlighting Donne's burning ambition in this study, rather than his emotional sensitivity or serious religious struggles (both of which I do not deny), I would displease readers fond of idealizing Donne. I was aware that, in reading Donne's love poetry as well as his religious verse in terms of their relationship to his sociopolitical aspirations, I would be presenting an authorial image that many Donne scholars would find uncongenial. The wealth of contextual material found in R. C. Bald's biography of the poet, *John Donne: A Life* (New York and Oxford: Oxford University Press, 1970), enabled me to situate the verse in the various social environments in which Donne found himself over the course of his poetic career and to construct a narrative of Donne's activities with which the poems were aligned. Although I read it after most of my book was written, John Carey's provocative *John Donne: Life, Mind, and Art* (New York: Oxford University Press, 1981) confirmed my own inclination to de-idealize Donne and to read his work in relation to his biography. There are psychoanalytic assumptions undergirding my interpretations of Donne's behavior: some rise to the surface of my prose, but most are implicit in the exposition. I was strongly influenced by mainline psychoanalytic writing, especially by the "object-relations" and "psychology of the self" traditions in psychoanalytic theory and they shaped my understanding of Donne. So too did psychoanalytic theories of communication, about which I wrote in a separate essay, "Countertransference, the Communication Process, and the Dimensions of Psychoanalytic Criticism" (*Critical Inquiry* 4.3 [Spring 1978]: 471–89).

While I was in the midst of composing this study, I wrote an essay representing the kind of sociocultural analysis I was attempting in it, "'Love is not love': Elizabethan Sonnet Sequences and the Social Order" (*ELH* 49.2 [Summer 1982]: 396–428). In this (now much cited) piece, I examined the language of love as it was used in the poetry of late Elizabethan England as an expression of ambition and the desire for patronage. In another essay that adumbrated the argument of this book, "John Donne and the Rewards of Patronage" (in *Patronage in the Renaissance*, ed. Guy Fitch Lytle and Stephen Orgel [Princeton: Princeton University Press, 1981]; 207–34), I ranged through Donne's writings to delineate his persistent pursuit of place, preferment, and patronage. In all this work, my primary intention was not primarily to do intensive close readings of poetic texts, though here and elsewhere, as in the case of my reading of "The Canonization," I did this very thing. Instead, aware of all the formalist and intellectual-historical explications of Donne's poetry that had been written over the previous half-century, I felt it unnecessary to explicate each poem I examined, for I took for granted intelligent readers' abilities to interpret and appreciate the verse well. What I wanted to do is introduce and emphasize

Preface to the 2008 Reprint v

contextual meanings that had not sufficiently been acknowledged in previous Donne scholarship and criticism. They are not the whole story—after all, no critical analysis can be exhaustive—but they are an essential part of it.

What came to be a crucial element of *John Donne, Coterie Poet* emerged in my research and writing as I examined some of the many manuscripts in which Donne's poetry survives, the connection of Donne's writing and the system of manuscript transmission of literature in which he chose to function. I came to see Donne as a coterie poet or coterie author, directing almost all of his verse and much of his prose to select, and known, audiences whose responses he could imagine and whose knowledge of him enabled them to bring the kind of interpretive nuances to the understanding of his work that a broad, anonymous readership might not have brought. I wrote the Introduction to his book last and realized, when I had finished it, that I needed to pursue a much more ambitious study of manuscript poetry and of its relation to the printing of verse in the sixteenth and seventeenth centuries. And so, Donne's coterie activities led me to the explorations of over two hundred manuscript miscellanies and poetical anthologies I undertook in order to write my second book, *Manuscript, Print, and the English Renaissance Lyric* (Ithaca and London: Cornell University Press, 1995). Between the time *John Donne, Coterie Poet* was published and the writing of this other study (completed in 1993), Peter Beal's volumes of the *Index of British Literary Manuscripts* appeared, the annual *English Manuscript Studies, 1100-1700* began its life under his co-editorship, and some of Harold Love's essays, which were incorporated into his 1993 book, *Scribal Publication in Seventeenth-Century England* (Oxford: Clarendon Press, 1993), were published, greatly facilitating my own work and confirming my belief that manuscript research was still a little-explored territory for literary scholars, except for those textual editors using manuscripts in a limited way for their particular purposes. Today, of course, archival manuscript research is no longer on the margins of literary scholarship.

Donne has remained a major focus of scholarly attention over the past quarter century. The establishment of *The John Donne Journal*, the annual conference of the John Donne Society, and the ongoing *Donne*

Variorum all testify to this fact. There has been a notable increase in the quality and quantity of feminist interpretations of Donne, which have, of course, addressed some topics I ignored or did not highlight in my study and corrected at least one omission in my study I regret making, that of the poem "Sappho to Philaenis." Following Helen Gardner's lead, I put this piece outside the canonical Donne texts I was discussing, but I should not have been so ready to accept her opinion about a poem that obviously made her uncomfortable to acknowledge as Donne's. Feminist scholars such as Janel Mueller and Elizabeth Harvey have written well about it as they and other feminist critics have, also, of the rest of his poetry, providing some correctives and supplements to my own analyses. Other scholars, some of whose work I included in my collection, *Critical Essays on John Donne* (New York: G. K. Hall, 1994), which concentrates on work done from the late 1970s to the early 1990s, have offered valuable historically contextualized readings of Donne's poetry and prose. Were I to write a comprehensive book on Donne's poetry now, it would, of course, have to be different and have different emphases than this one, acknowledging as well the many contributions made by intelligent readers of Donne over the past two decades.

In recent years two specific developments in the scholarly conversation in the field have affected Donne scholarship: the turn to religion in early modern English Studies (about which Ken Jackson and I have written in *Criticism* 46.1 [Winter 2004]: 167–90) and the resurgence, with a difference, of formalism or, as Michael Clark names it in his edited collection, *The Revenge of the Aesthetic* (Berkeley, Los Angeles, London: University of California Press, 2000). New historicist and cultural materialist criticism are not dead, but much of the work they set out to do has been accomplished and the perspectives they introduced have been assimilated into general scholarly and critical discourse. Their tendency to treat religion as false consciousness or as a code that needs to be translated into social, economic, and political realities and their avoidance of aesthetic issues as contaminated by bourgeois and upper-class interests have, ironically, provoked some of the new serious attention to religion and the neoformalist rereadings of literary texts. But scholars and critics can no longer be innocent of the politics of literature and of the social dynamics of literary production and reception, two focuses of the New Historicist and cultural materialist work of an earlier generation. Whether they write about religion and literature or do close readings of poetic texts, whether they are anxious or not, they feel the influence of this earlier work. I hope my study of Donne, which was published originally at a different historical moment in literary studies, can still affect the ways new generations of scholars and readers view this fascinating poet and his work. My own scholarship has moved on to other topics and methods and has involved much more archival work with primary manuscript and print texts from the early modern period, but I would still stand behind almost all I have said in this study, even while acknowledging its inevitable incompleteness. I believe that its examination of Donne's poetry within the contexts of coterie social transactions and of manuscript literary transmission is still valuable and timely.

I have taken advantage, in this reprint of the original 1986 edition to correct some fourteen errata in the text. I am grateful for the opportunity to do so.

Detroit, Michigan
September 26, 2007

Preface

In a letter he wrote in 1619 as he was about to leave for the Continent with Viscount Doncaster on what he thought was a dangerous diplomatic mission, John Donne presented his friend Sir Robert Ker with a manuscript of his poems along with a copy of the unpublished prose work *Biathanatos*, referring to the latter in the following way: ". . . it is a Book written by *Jack Donne*, and not by *D. Donne*: Reserve it for me, if I live, and if I die, I only forbid it the Presse, and the Fire: publish it not, but yet burn it not; and between those, do what you will with it" (*Letters*, p. 22). In expressing his wish that his work exist in limited manuscript circulation somewhere between the extremes of book publication for a general audience and destruction of the text itself, the ecclesiastical Donne defined a set of socioliterary circumstances he had consistently desired for most of his writing, particularly for his poetry. Even before he became a minister Donne thought of almost all of his verse and much of his prose as coterie literature. Although at least twice, in 1614 and in 1619, Donne collected his poetry with the idea of publishing it, he could not bring himself to commit the body of his verse to print.[1]

When Donne was preparing for taking orders by providing for the payment of his outstanding debts, he wrote (in 1614) to his close friend Sir Henry Goodyer, who was staying with Lucy, Countess of Bedford, the poet's patroness for the previous six or seven years:

. . . the going about to pay debts, hastens importunity. . . . One thing I must tell you; but so softly, that I am loath to hear my self: and so softly, that if that good Lady were in the room, with you and this Letter, she might not hear. It is, that I am brought to a necessity of printing my Poems, and addressing them to my L. Chamberlain. This I mean to do forthwith; not for much publique view, but at mine owne cost, a few Copies. I apprehend some inconruities in the resolution; and I know what I shall suffer from many interpretations: but I am at an end, of much considering that; and, if I were as startling in that kinde, as ever I was, yet in this particular, I am under an unescapable necessity, as I shall let you perceive, when I see you. By this occasion I am made Rhapsoder of mine own rags, and that cost me more diligence, to seek them, than it did to make them. This made me aske to borrow that old book of you, which it will be too late to see, for that use, when I see you: for I must do this, as a valediction to the world, before I take Orders. (*Letters*, pp. 196–97)

It is perhaps surprising that Donne did not have copies of all his poems in his possession and that he should have had to borrow a manuscript collection of them from a friend in order to produce a text for publication.[2] He poses as a gentleman-amateur whose expected scorn for the medium of print is related to his treatment of his poems as trifles as well as to the embarrassment at the prospect of publishing them. In becoming, as he says, "Rhapsoder of mine own rags," Donne tried to protect his precarious social status and to conceal what he was doing from the noblewoman who was his patroness. He thought to minimize the disgrace by not selling his work to a printer, but publishing it at his own expense in a limited edition for use as presentation copies to "persons of . . . rank" (*Letters*, p. 197) from whom he expected financial assistance.

In any event, fearful caution, good judgment, snobbery, and/or belated help from Lady Bedford kept Donne from following through with his plan.[3] His collected verse was not published until 1633, two years after his death. Except for the *Anniversaries*, the Prince Henry elegy, and the few lyrics that found their way into songbooks,[4] Donne's poems did not appear in print during his lifetime. He remained a literary amateur, treating poetry as an avocation, part of a life and career whose main goals, even for some time after his ordination, were social status and advancement.[5] Though seriously committed to the life of the mind, Donne did not consider himself primarily a man of letters. His verse was not composed for a wide literary audience but rather for coterie readers—for his friends, acquaintances, patrons, patronesses, and the woman he married. We know, from manuscript evidence and from the poet's own letters, that copies of single poems or groups of poems reached the hands of such friends as Sir Henry Goodyer, Rowland Woodward (the compiler of the authoritative Westmoreland Manuscript), Sir Henry Wotton, George Garrard, and Sir Robert Ker (the cousin of the man who became the Earl of Somerset). Particular works were addressed at the time of their composition or afterward to Christopher Brooke, Sir Edward Herbert, Magdalen Herbert, Sir Robert Drury, the Countess of Bedford, and the Earl of Dorset (among others).[6]

Donne's restriction of his contemporary readership was a deliberate act. For the most part, he designed his poems specifically for a succession of social environments in which he functioned between his arrival in London in the early 1590s and his ordination in 1615, for himself and for the individuals with whom he chose to associate at the Inns of Court and in the urbane and courtly circles to which he belonged in both the Elizabethan and Jacobean periods. In the few years following his unauthorized marriage to Ann More and his consequent dismissal from Sir Thomas Egerton's service, he used letters and poems to help maintain contact with the social world from which he had been virtually exiled, but his literary production, like his social activities, flourished best when he was in close proximity to people he knew. To varying degrees, Donne consciously controlled the dissemination of his writing. At least initially, he apparently did not release some of his work into circulation at all, reserving it for himself. In the verse letter to Mrs. Herbert, "Mad paper stay," he entertained the possibility of keeping the piece in his own possession "here to burne / With all those sonnes whom my brain did create" (1–4). In sending his prose paradoxes to a friend in 1600, he demanded an "assurance . . . that no coppy shalbee taken for any respect of these or any other my compositions sent to you" (*Selected Prose*, p. 111). Although he professed a willingness to show his friend a large body of writing ("I mean to acquaint you with all myne" [*Selected Prose*, p. 111]), as he evidently did to Goodyer and to Sir Robert Ker,[7] he tried to foreclose the possibility that it would travel further by the normal means of manuscript transcription. The gentleman editor of the Elizabethan miscellany *A Poetical Rhapsody* (1602) listed under "Manuscripts to get" the "Satires, Elegies, Epigrams, etc."[8] of Donne, but, like most other contemporaries, Francis Davison could not gain access to the poet's work. It was easier for him to obtain privately circulated poems of the Court than to lay his hands on Donne's verse. Generally, only close friends, patrons, and patronesses had limited access to the poetry Donne wrote.

In this book, I analyze Donne's poems as coterie literature, as texts originally involved with both their biographical and social contexts. After setting Donne's practice in the framework of sixteenth-century literary manuscript transmission, I discuss the verse chronologically and according to audience, paying particular attention to the rhetorical enactment of the author's relationships to peers and superiors through the conflicting styles of egalitarian assertion, social iconoclasm, and deferential politeness. I relate the poetry to the contemporary prose Donne wrote either for private circulation or for publication. I deal with his choice of different literary forms in terms of both his changing sociopolitical circumstances and the shift from Elizabethan to Jacobean rule that brought about a realignment of genres within the culture's literary system. I examine the social coordinates of Donne's formal satires, humanist verse letters, erotic elegies, and complimentary epistles, and define the markedly different contexts within which his libertine, courtly, satiric, sentimental, complimentary, and religious lyrics were originally set. I proceed more or less chronologically, dividing the discussion roughly into the following parts: (1) Donne's Inns-of-Court period (1592–95), (2) the time of his involvement in public life through military service and employment by the Lord Keeper (1596–1602), and (3) the period of his brief social exile followed by his reemergence as an active courtier seeking preferment (1602–14). Donne's entry into the ministry in 1615, the outcome of his decision to seek ecclesiastical, rather than secular, advancement, marks a convenient stopping point, for, in effect, he abandoned verse when he was ordained, and subsequently wrote only a few poems (treated in my Epilogue). He began to invest most of his creative literary energies in the composition of sermons.

This chronological arrangement necessitates disintegrating some of the traditional generic groupings of Donne's verse such as the *Satires*, *Elegies*, *Verse Letters*, and *Songs and Sonnets*. It most affects the last, a body of temporally disparate occasional verse composed in different situations for different readers. Rather than designing these poems as parts of a poetic sequence or collection, Donne wrote some for Inns-of-Court colleagues and friends, some for a mixed male and female courtly audience, some in the context of poetic competition and exchange, others for the woman he married, and still others as complimentary verse to a patroness. Those who have discussed the *Songs and Sonnets* as an aesthetically unified whole have missed many of the interesting features of Donne's artful response to the poems' particular contexts of composition and reception. After all, as social verse, these pieces functioned differently than they have as a collection of texts whose literary canonization was facilitated by the 1633 edition. The lyrics were written for known readers who could receive them as the social, as well as the literary, gestures of a person whose life and behavior were incorporated in their complex autobiographical discourse. In subsequent literary history, intrinsic and extrinsic issues are more easily separated, but in the original historical circumstances of these works, neat formalist distinctions between poet and persona, fictive listener and real reader break down in interesting ways.

Though, in the following pages, I am indebted to formalist critics as well as to scholars who have viewed Donne's verse in the light of literary or intellectual history, my reexamination of this major Renaissance author is grounded in revisionist history, psychoanalytic theory, and some of the heuristic methods of poststructuralist criticism. I simultaneously emphasize social-historical and psychological perspectives, but, in pointing to both social and biographical determinants of Donne's poetry, I wish to avoid having to choose between what seem, to me, equally unacceptable and reductive alternatives: that of dissolving individual authorship into the larger cultural "language" or that of treating it as prior to or radically separate from the sociocultural system to which it necessarily belongs. My psychoanalytic assumptions lead me to relate the individual writer to his or her own social environment and culture, but also to resist viewing the "self" as a phantom or bourgeois illusion.[9] Although I question some of the features critics have attributed to Donne's artistic "uniqueness," I treat this author as having a characteristic personal style manifested in both his behavior and his writing. At the same time, I relate some of the attitudes and language traditionally ascribed to Donne's individual temperament to social beliefs and idioms shared with contemporaries. To communicate with his original readers, Donne had to express himself in familiar language. The very existence of a large body of dubiously or wrongly ascribed verse on the fringes of the Donne canon attests to this social dimension of his work.

This book is at once a particular argument and a comprehensive rereading of Donne's verse. Instead of looking only for selective evidence to support my central thesis that Donne's poetry needs to be read historically as coterie literature, I have decided to discuss virtually all of the poems. I do this for three reasons. First, I am convinced that it is time for a reexamination of Donne's poetic canon. Although there have been many studies of single poems and groups of poems, there have been surprisingly few books on the poetry as a whole. J. B. Leishman's *The Monarch of Wit* (1951)[10] is perhaps the last substantial work of that kind—one, of course, based on critical and scholarly assumptions quite different from mine. Second, a general discussion allows me to consider and reevaluate some of Donne's lesser-known work, the verse letters to Lady Bedford, for example, which critics concentrating on the more familiar poems have largely ignored or, unaware of contextual complexities, have failed to appreciate for their artistry. Third, because the evidence for my argument is basically circumstantial, it is useful to provide a wealth of varied examples, rather than to rely on representative poems. Individual readers may find parts of my exposition more or less convincing. After all, I am conjecturally assigning a chronology to poems for which solid evidence for dating is difficult or impossible to find. I offer mostly internal evidence to define social circumstances of individual poems, using Donne's habitual practices (and those of some of his contemporaries) to deduce contexts from the generic and rhetorical signals found in particular works. Such hermeneutic circling is often repeated both to demonstrate how my rereading of Donne's verse works in a large number of cases and to make what I am arguing seem progressively more plausible.

I hope this book is useful not only for its general argument and its particular interpretations, but also for some of its observations about amateur authorship and the dynamics of manuscript-circulated literature, for what I say applies, with necessary modifications, to works written in similar social circumstances by a number of Donne's predecessors, contemporaries, and successors. It makes sense historically, for example, to view much lyric poetry from the early Tudor through the Stuart periods as coterie literature, especially poems composed in courtly and satellite-courtly environments. Though some professional and quasi-professional writers of the time publicly attempted to invest authorship with social and political as well as intellectual and literary authority, many authors, like Donne, chose to function as literary amateurs, submerging their writing in their social lives. While the former no doubt helped to create modern conceptions of authorship and literature, the historically embedded work of the latter presents us with the clear challenge of rediscovering the vital connections between less literarily isolated texts and their immediate social, economic, and political contexts. My new historicist reinterpretation of Donne's poetry is offered, then, not only as a rereading of an important poet, but also as a model for the kind of inquiry that might be undertaken into the work of many other writers from the late medieval through the early modern eras. In redefining the historical specificity of Donne's texts, I mean to question some traditional humanist assumptions about the cultural position of literature and to contribute to the current scholarly analysis of the processes by which literature was defined and institutionalized in the modern world.

I am grateful to the John Simon Guggenheim Foundation for support for my research. I also thank Wayne State University for providing two summer Faculty Research Awards and a publication subvention. I benefited from the hospitality and assistance provided by the staffs of the Folger Shakespeare Library, the Houghton Library of Harvard, the A. S. W. Rosenbach Museum, the New York Public Library, and the Wayne State University Library (especially George Masterton). I thank Princeton University Press for permission to use portions of "John Donne and the Rewards of Patronage," which appeared in *Patronage in the Renaissance*, edited by Guy Fitch Lytle and Stephen Orgel, copyright © 1981 by Princeton University Press. Reprinted by permission of Princeton University Press. And I also thank The University of California Press for use of portions of "Donne and 'The Extasie,'" which appeared in *The Rhetoric of Renaissance Poetry*, edited by Thomas O. Sloan and Raymond B. Waddington, copyright © 1974 by The University of California Press. My greatest personal and collegial debts are to Stanley Fish, Annabel Patterson, Joseph Summers, and Marilyn Williamson. For their interest in and support of my work I am indebted as well to many other colleagues and friends both at Wayne State and other universities, particularly to Jackson Cope, Philip Finkelpearl, Suzanne Ferguson, Jonathan Goldberg, Jacob Lassner, Naomi Lebowitz, Stephen Orgel, and Leonard Tennenhouse. Marvin Schindler and the Romance and Germanic Department at Wayne State deserve special thanks for providing me with the office in which this book was written. I owe a lot to my typist Margaret Maday, whose patience and alertness were remarkable. My wife Alice and sons Bill and Steve have sustained me emotionally.

A Note on Texts

Unless otherwise noted, quotations from Donne's works are from the following editions:

Biathanatos, A modern-spelling edition, with introduction and commentary by Michael Rudick and M. Pabst Battin. Garland English Texts, no. 1. New York and London: Garland Publishing, 1982.

The Courtier's Library, or Catalogus Librorum Aulicorum. Ed. Evelyn Simpson, with a translation by P. Simpson. London: Nonesuch Press, 1930.

The Divine Poems of John Donne. Ed. with introduction and commentary by Helen Gardner. 2nd ed. Oxford: Clarendon Press, 1978.

The Elegies and The Songs and Sonnets. Ed. with introduction and commentary by Helen Gardner. Oxford: Clarendon Press, 1965.

The Epithalamions, Anniversaries, and Epicedes. Ed. with introduction and commentary by W. Milgate. Oxford: Clarendon Press, 1978.

Essays in Divinity. Ed. Evelyn M. Simpson. Oxford: Clarendon Press, 1952.

Ignatius His Conclave, An edition of the Latin and English texts with introduction and commentary by T. S. Healy, S.J. Oxford: Clarendon Press, 1969.

Letters to Severall Persons of Honour (1651), A facsimile reproduction with an introduction by M. Thomas Hester. Delmar, N.Y.: Scholars' Facsimiles & Reprints, 1977. (Cited as "*Letters.*")

Paradoxes and Problems. Ed. with introduction and commentary by Helen Peters. Oxford: Clarendon Press, 1980.

Pseudo-Martyr, A facsimile reproduction with introduction by Francis Jacques Sypher. Delmar, N.Y.: Scholars' Facsimiles & Reprints, 1974.

The Satires, Epigrams and Verse Letters. Ed. with introduction and commentary by W. Milgate. Oxford: Clarendon Press, 1967.

The Sermons of John Donne. Ed. George R. Potter and Evelyn Simpson. 10 vols. Berkeley and Los Angeles: Univ. of California Press, 1953–62. (Cited as "*Sermons.*")

In addition the following works are cited within the text:

Bald, R. C. *John Donne: A Life.* New York and Oxford: Oxford Univ. Press, 1970. (Cited as "Bald, *Life.*")

John Donne, Selected Prose. Chosen by Evelyn Simpson, ed. by Helen Gardner and Timothy Healy. Oxford: Clarendon Press, 1967. (Cited as "*Selected Prose.*")

The Poems of John Donne. Ed. . . . with introductions and commentary by Herbert J. C. Grierson. 2 vols. Oxford: Oxford Univ. Press, 1912. (Cited as "Grierson.")

Gosse, Edmund. *The Life and Letters of John Donne.* 2 vols. 1899; repr. Gloucester, Mass.: Peter Smith, 1959. (Cited as "Gosse.")

Simpson, Evelyn. *A Study of the Prose Works of John Donne.* 2nd ed. Oxford: Clarendon Press, 1948. (Cited as "Simpson, *Prose.*")

*John Donne,
Coterie Poet*

Introduction: Donne and the Conditions of Coterie Verse

To understand Donne's context-bound verse historically, it is important to recognize its place in the dominant system of manuscript transmission of literature to which the poetry of courtly and satellite-courtly authors belonged. In the Tudor and early Stuart periods, lyric poetry was basically a genre for gentleman-amateurs who regarded their literary "toys" as ephemeral works that were part of a social life that also included dancing, singing, gaming, and civilized conversation. Socially prominent courtiers like the Earl of Oxford, Sir Edward Dyer, and Sir Walter Ralegh, like Sir Thomas Wyatt and the Earl of Surrey earlier, as well as other less-important figures like George Gascoigne, essentially thought of poems as trifles to be transmitted in manuscript within a limited social world and not as literary monuments to be preserved in printed editions for posterity. For most sixteenth-century poetry the book was an alien environment. Gentlemen-amateurs avoided what J. W. Saunders has called the "stigma of print" by refusing to publish their verse, publishing it anonymously, or (accurately or inaccurately) disclaiming responsibility for its appearance in book form.[1] Sidney's poems, for example, particularly the carefully restricted songs and sonnets of *Astrophil and Stella*, were coterie works, intended for an audience of close friends, clients, and family members. Shakespeare, despite his professional status as theatrical shareholder and playwright, at least initially followed the gentlemanly custom in limiting the circulation of his sonnets to his patron and his "priuat frends."[2] Philip Rosseter's introduction to the published version of Campion's airs refers to the lyrics as "made at his vacant hours, and privately emparted to his friends."[3]

In Epigram 424 Sir John Harington proudly asserts a poetic amateurism not unlike that practiced by Donne and many of his contemporaries:

> I near desearvd that gloriows name of Poet;
> No Maker I, nor do I care who know it.
> Occasion oft my penn doth entertayn
> With trew discourse. Let others Muses fayn;
> Myne never sought to set to sale her wryting.
> In part her frends, in all her selfe delighting,
> She cannot beg applause of vulgar sort,
> Free born and bred, more free for noble sport.
> My muse hath one still bids her in her eare;
> Yf well disposd, to write; yf not, forbear.[4]

In such circumstances, poetic "discourse" was deliberately adjusted to the "Occasion," written sometimes to please an audience of friends and, supposedly, always to please oneself.[5]

Saunders describes the system of amateur versifying in which Greville, Dyer, Sidney, Harington, and others participated: "Whether poetry was produced in isolation, in the quiet of a study, in prison, in idleness or 'furtive hours,' on guard in a lonely outpost, or in melancholy solitude, or whether it was produced as the direct result of companionship, competition, social communion and group suggestion, it found its first audience in the circle of friends. And whether it was communicated orally, or through the mutual exchange of scripts, or by correspondence, the recognized medium of communication was the *manuscript*, either in the autograph of the author, or in the transcription of a friend."[6] Professional authors like Thomas Nashe and Michael Drayton, from their socially inferior positions, criticized the exclusiveness of such literature. Nashe introduced an edition of Sidney's *Astrophil and Stella* in a way that reveals his pleasure that such coterie verse has escaped its social confines: "although [such poetry] be oftentimes imprisoned in Ladyes casks & the president books of such as cannot see without another man's spectacles, yet at length it breakes foorth in spite of his keepers, and useth some private penne (in steed of a picklock) to procure his violent enlargement."[7] Drayton complained about the difficulty in getting access to such poetry: "Verses are wholly deduc't to Chambers, and nothing esteem'd in this lunatique age, but what is kept in Cabinets, and must onely passe by Transcription."[8] When Campion finally introduced his own verse to a book audience, he defended himself against those who objected to publication, referring scornfully to those contemporaries who "taste nothing that comes forth in Print, as if *Catullus* or *Martials* Epigrammes were the worse for being published."[9]

The transmission of poems in manuscript "by transcription" took a number of forms. As Saunders has explained, "The story proper begins when a poet, either in solitude or in company, either acting on his own inspiration or the instigations of friends, writes down a poem on *loose papers*."[10] Although the author himself may make a *"fair copy* . . . for a patron,"* if not even "a special presentation copy,"[11] the next steps in the process occurred when transcriptions of the verse were made either by friends, by friends of friends, or by professional scribes. Also, frequently "fair copy of loose papers circulating among friends might . . . gather appended commendatory verses or glosses."[12] These added poems were often "answer poems" to individual lyrics.[13] The whole procedure was one in which authorship could dissolve into group "ownership"[14] of texts: Saunders is right in calling "the poem . . . a public document shared by the circle," for "more pens than the author's might share the same paper."[15] This, of course, is to say nothing of the unconscious and conscious rewriting that occurred when poems were transcribed from memory, a practice, as J. B. Leishman has shown,[16] that accounts for some of the most striking alterations in texts of individual poems, if not for the production of virtually new texts.

Beyond the uncertain circulation system involving loose papers, "quires" of poems and large manuscripts of individual poets' work, two related practices, in particular, throw light on the system of manuscript literary transmission: the keeping of manuscript commonplace books of poetry (or of poetry and prose) and the related, markedly Elizabethan, phenomenon of the published poetical miscellany. The first is a holdover, albeit a socially respected one, from a pre-Gutenberg era, and is a custom that persisted well into the seventeenth century. Standing midway between manuscript-circulated verse and professional publications like *The Works of Beniamin Jonson* (1616), the second is a part of the cultural transformation of the literature of social occasion into the (more aesthetically isolated) literature of a book culture.

The dozens of manuscript poetical miscellanies that survive from the sixteenth and early seventeenth centuries belonged to different social environments and represent different forms of collecting by individuals, families, and social groups. Men and women at Court and in aristocratic households as well as men and youths at the university and Inns of Court both gathered and composed verse in commonplace books for their own pleasure and edification. The famous Devonshire manuscript (which contains many poems of Wyatt's) was owned successively by several women connected with the Howard family and includes poems transcribed by them, by the men with whom they associated at Court, and by friends to whom the volume was lent.[17] John Harington of Stepney, the pre-Elizabethan client of Protector Somerset who found courtly service under Queen Elizabeth, began a collection of Tudor verse in a book whose blank pages his son, Sir John Harington, used to record verse from the second half of the Elizabethan period.[18] John Finet, who later became one of Sir Robert Cecil's secretaries, served King James, and was appointed Master of Ceremonies by King Charles, compiled a miscellany in the late 1580s while at Court and at Cambridge (Bod. Rawl. Poet. MS. 85),[19] a volume that contains as rich a collection of courtly poems as almost any published Elizabethan anthology. Another courtly academic collection is to be found in BL Harl. MS 7392, a volume L. G. Black calls "an Oxford counterpart to the Cambridge RP 85."[20] One of the most interesting manuscript miscellanies, Cambr. Univ. Lib. MS Dd. 5.75, is a collection compiled by Henry Stanford, who moved from Oxford to service in several noble households, and who not only composed verse himself and collected courtly poems, but who also transcribed the novice poetry of the young boys he tutored in the Paget and Berkeley families.[21] Some volumes were associated particularly with the milieu in which Donne wrote many of his poems, the Inns of Court: both the Farmer-Chetham MS, which has the largest surviving manuscript collection of John Hoskins's poems, Rosenbach 1083/15 and Bod. Add. MS B.97, large portions of which contain the epigrammatic verse of which Inns and university students were fond, include much Inns-of-Court verse.[22]

Those volumes that are classified as manuscript miscellanies constitute a range of texts bounded, at one extreme, by the system of circulating loose poems and sets of poems and, at the other, by the carefully arranged published volume. Black has noted that BL Add. MS 28253 begins with thirteen folios made up of "a number of sheets which were at one time loose and folded separately (like a letter), and each has been inscribed on the back with the description of its contents. These sheets are apparently a little collection made by Edward Bannister of Putney between 1583 and 1602 (each sheet is dated)."[23] Bod. MS Rawl. poet. 172 is a collection "of loose sheets of different sizes in different hands."[24] The small Ann Cornwallis miscellany (Folger MS V.a.89), which I have examined, appears to be a similar collection of loose poems on different-sized paper.[25] Other commonplace books are composites of separate parts, often in different hands. Most manuscript miscellanies, however, began with the purchase or gift of a blank book or "table book" in which poems or poems and prose were meant to be transcribed by its owner—usually without a governing plan or arrangement. Shakespeare's Sonnet 77, in fact, seems to have been written to accompany just such a gift to his patron.[26] Other manuscripts represent systematic efforts to collect poems by author, by genre, or by topic. Some volumes, like BL Harl. 6910, record the texts of published poems, reversing the movement from manuscript to print.[27]

In format, some manuscript miscellanies resemble published anthologies or, it would probably be more accurate to say, some published miscellanies resemble manuscript anthologies. As Ruth Hughey has observed, those portions of the Arundel-Harington Manuscript transcribed by John Harington of Stepney constitute a midcentury poetical miscellany comparable to the famous one printed by Richard Tottel in 1557.[28] Although some published miscellanies are further than others from the social situation of manuscript-circulated verse, there is a continuum from, rather than a sharp boundary between, commonplace-book anthologies and those printed volumes that disseminated coterie literature to a wider readership. Tottel's *Miscellany* (1557), Hyder Rollins argues, was probably based on a single courtly manuscript collection that fell into the hands of a printer, who then added poems he obtained from other sources.[29] The most popular Elizabethan miscellany, *The Paradise of Dainty Devices* (1576) is a printed version of the commonplace book compiled by Richard Edwards, the courtier-dramatist who served as Elizabeth's Master of the Children of the Royal Chapel until his death in 1566.[30] *The Phoenix Nest* (1595) and *A Poetical Rhapsody* (1602) were edited by gentlemen who probably had better access than commercial printers to the verse that circulated in manuscript in polite society. The first collection is an anthology compiled by an Inns-of-Court man who addressed his collection to his peers, printing a number of poems that originated, no doubt, in the Inns environment as well as in the Court itself. The second volume was edited by Francis Davison, a former Gray's Inn man who had just lost his government position as secretary to Sir Thomas Parry. Both collections are addressed to an audience of gentlemen and include previously unpublished poems by gentlemen-amateurs.[31]

Although published miscellanies clearly came into being as products of the information explosion caused by the invention of movable type, they actually presented themselves as a kind of compromise between two coexistent systems of "publication," the circulation of literature in manuscript to restricted audiences and the printing of individual authors' works for different (narrow or wide) readerships. Even as they helped to bring about a more modern conception of literature as a (supposedly) distinct order of discourse set apart from the culture-specific languages of social, economic, and political transactions, they affirmed the primacy of poetic amateurism, associating literary merit with the social prestige of aristocratic and genteel authors, and emphasizing the connection between literary works and the social milieus in which they were written.

When George Gascoigne decided to publish a collection of his various literary works in order to relieve his financial distress, he chose the miscellany form as a way of protecting his courtly amateurism even as he sought, in print, the kind of laureateship he imagined for himself in the picture of his presentation to Queen Elizabeth of his manuscript text for the entertainment "Hemetes the Hermit."[32] In *A Hundreth Sundrie Flowres*, Gascoigne disguised his prose and poetry as a courtly commonplace-book manuscript collection of works by a number of authors rather than offering it, as he did two years later in *The Posies*, as a compilation of the literary productions of a single writer. A fictional editor "H. W." explains to the reader the supposed source of the volume:

In *August Last* passed my familiar friend Master G. T. bestowed uppon me ye reading of a written Booke, wherin he had collected divers discourses & verses, invented uppon sundrie occasions, by sundrie gentlemen (in mine opinion) right commendable for their capacitie. And herewithal my said friend charged me, that I should use them onely for mine owne particuler commoditie, and eftsones safely deliver the original copie to him againe, wherein I must confesse my selfe but halfe a marchant, for the copie unto him I have safely redelivered. But the worke (for I thought it worthy to be published) I have entreated my friend *A. B.* to emprint: as one that thought better to please a number by common commoditie then to feede the humor of any private parson by nedelesse singularitie.[33]

In the letter of "G. T." to "H. W." that follows, the book is identified as a courtly anthology, partly because of the social prestige such volumes possessed for gentlemen readers. Gascoigne created the illusion that the literary works contained in *A Hundreth Sundrie Flowres* passed through the normal stages of manuscript transmission, but he obviously set up a situation in which he could enhance his own literary fame through print. G. T.'s letter offers an explanation for the orderly arrangements of the supposedly miscellaneous works in the collection and pretends that it is not intended to be made "common" (i.e., transmitted further either in manuscript or in print), even as it announces the existence of other meritorious works of "one" of the authors represented, copies of which have not yet been obtained.

After Gascoigne has dropped the mask of anonymity midway through the collection, the fifty-seventh through sixty-first poems are introduced as works associated with an Inns-of-Court environment not unlike that in which Donne functioned a generation later:

> *I have herde master Gascoignes memorie commended by these verses following, the which were written uppon this occasion. He had (in middest of his youth) determined to abandone all vaine delights and to retourne unto Greyes Inne, there to undertake againe the study of the common lawes. And being required by five sundrie gentlemen to wrighte in verse somwhat worthy to be remembered, before he entred into their felowship, he compiled these five sundry sortes of metre uppon five sundry theames which they delivered unto him, and the first was at request of Francis Kinwelmarshe who delivered him these theame.* Audaces fortuna juvat. *And thereupon he wrote thys Sonnet following.* (p. 152)

The practice of composing verse on set themes, a holdover from the grammar school and university, was a common one in both courtly and satellite-courtly environments, like the Inns of Court, a coterie game especially suited to the system of manuscript transmission of literature with which Gascoigne affiliated his book.[34]

Like the genuine manuscript and published anthologies, Gascoigne's counterfeit miscellany creates the impression that poetry was properly a social activity. We can see from both manuscript and printed evidence that poems, for example, were enclosed in letters, handed to people personally, read orally before select groups,[35] given as gifts at times such as New Year's day, passed to women as complimentary trifles (like Ralegh's poem put into Lady Laiton's pocket), composed at the request of a mistress or at the challenge of a competitor, written on set themes agreed upon by both authors and audiences, and designed as response or answer poems to other lyrics. In *A Hundreth Sundrie Flowres*, the elaborate editorial-narrative comments prefixed to the lyrics provide social contexts for poems, sometimes producing, in effect, a "title" that is longer than the work that follows it. After a particular poem and answer set, for example, Gascoigne provides the following heading for a nine-line poetic riddle:

> *And for a further profe of this Dames quick understanding, you shall now understand, that soone after this answer of hirs, the same Author chaunced to be at a supper in hir company, where were also hir brother, hir husband, and an old lover of hirs by whom she had bin long suspected. Nowe, although there wanted no delicate viands to content them, yit their chief repast was by entreglancing of lookes. For G. G. being stoong with hot affection, could none otherwise relieve his passion but by gazing. And the Dame of a curteous enclination deigned (now and then) to requite the same with glancing at*

him. Hir old lover occupied his eyes with watching: and hir brother perceyving all this could not absteyne from winking, wherby he might put his Sister in remembrance, least she should too much forget hirself. But most of all hir husband beholding the first, and being evill pleased with the second, scarse contented with the third, and misconstruing the fourth, was constreyned to play the fifth part in froward frowninge. This royall banquet thus passed over, G. G. knowing that after supper they should passe the tyme in propounding of Riddles, and making of purposes: contryved all this conceipt in a Riddle as followeth. The which was no sooner pronounced, but she could perfectly perceyve his intent, and drave out one nayle with another, as also enseweth. (pp. 117–18)

Whether or not the poems Gascoigne included in his collection were actually ever part of the contexts he constructed for them, the act of social-narrative articulation in which he engaged is found, in shorter or longer form, in prose works like his own novella "A Discourse of the adventures passed by Master F. J.," Sidney's *Arcadia*, and Thomas Whythorne's *Autobiography* as well as in a miscellany like Tottel's.[36]

From such evidence we can perceive some of the distinctive features of courtly and satellite-courtly verse and understand what happened to such work once it left its original environment. Most poems written by gentlemen-amateurs were occasional in nature, their production and reception strongly involved with their biographical and social contexts. Whatever its conventional literary features, such verse was attuned to the personal circumstances of the authors and to the social, economic, and political milieus they shared with their chosen audiences. Inevitably, contextual particularity was lost when such work passed to a wider audience both within and beyond the writers' own times.

Sir Philip Sidney's *Astrophil and Stella* provides a good example of coterie literature and of the fate of such work beyond its original readership.[37] Read by modern critics as the literary masterpiece of an English Petrarch, a man of letters whose powerful dramatic lyrics were aesthetically more sophisticated than the work of his contemporaries, received by a general Elizabethan audience as the love poems of a martyred culture hero whose artistic achievements (supposedly) compensated for his lack of political success, the *Astrophil and Stella* poems were far more historically particularized for Sidney's primary readership. Friends like Sir Edward Dyer and Fulke Greville brought to their experience of the sonnet sequence a knowledge of the precise personal and sociopolitical contexts that were involved in the poems and manipulated by Sidney with ironic wit. They knew the author as a politically, economically, and socially disappointed young man—someone who had recently lost his prospects of inheriting the Leicester and Warwick estates when his aging uncle, the Earl of Leicester, had a son by his mistress-turned-wife, a woman who also happened to be the mother of the person fictionalized as "Stella" in the sequence, Penelope Devereux, Lady Rich. They saw Sidney, despite his impolitic intervention in the French marriage negotiations, as unfairly neglected or rejected by the Queen after his prodigious beginning in national and international politics and diplomacy. They could, therefore, perceive the way Sidney made Lady Rich, as Wyatt had Anne Boleyn, into a symbol of his unattained social, economic, and political goals.[38] They understood this poet's disavowals of ambition in the sonnets as disingenuous ones and saw that he was using erotic desire for the sexual favors of a Petrarchan mistress as a metaphor for his worldly aspirations. For example, in Sonnet 64 they knew how to interpret the amorous protestations of Astrophil, whose fictional identity merges with the actual one of the poet in the following amorously self-sacrificial words to Stella:

> I do not envie *Aristotle's* wit,
> Nor do aspire to *Caesar's* bleeding fame,
> Nor ought do care, though some above me sit,
> Nor hope, nor wishe another course to frame,
>   But that which once may win thy cruell hart:
>   Thou art my Wit, and thou my Vertue art.
>   (64.9–14)

Aware of Sidney's passionate love of learning, of his attraction to the kind of military heroism that led to his bravely foolish death, and, especially, of his sensitivity about his relatively inferior social status, the coterie audience could see in these amorous protestations a witty irony meant to be appreciated by a knowing readership. Disengaged from their coterie context, particularly when read by post-Renaissance readers, such lines lost the precise biographical and social matrices that enlivened their meaning, becoming conventional Petrarchan attitudinizing.

But this kind of decontextualization occurred in stages for all coterie literary works that passed beyond their original social contexts. The historical vicissitudes of Sir Thomas Wyatt's poetry also illustrate the process. As Patricia Thomson, Stephen Greenblatt, and others have argued, Wyatt's verse reflects his fortunes as an ambitious courtier and government servant in the Court of Henry VIII.[39] But the conventional literary language Wyatt used to express what were probably, in context, quite specific personal responses to social and political circumstances came across to later readers as peculiarly contentless.

Something was lost that had particularized the meaning of individual poems for their coterie readers. As Jonathan Kamholtz has shown, when some of Wyatt's obviously political lyrics were printed in Tottel's *Miscellany* with titles emphasizing amorous themes, the way they were read changed as they were absorbed into the tradition of poetic amorousness running from the troubadours through Petrarch to the High Renaissance.[40] They lost most of their witty topicality and artful self-dramatizing as they were converted into typical utterances of the poetic lover.

Manuscript and printed miscellanies often give the impression that they retain a sense of the social environment of the verse they collect. They usually present courtly or satellite-courtly poems written on particular (if conventionalized) social occasions. They insist, if only on their title pages and in the printers' or editors' prefatory letters or introductions, on the importance of the poetry's originating environment and of the contributors' social prestige.

Some manuscript miscellanies incorrectly name the author and occasion of particular works: for example, Dyer's lyric, "The lowest trees have topps," a poem whose amorous language argues for a system of reward based on merit rather than on privilege, is identified in Stephen Powle's commonplace book as "Sr Walter Rawleigh's verses to the Queen Elizabeth: in the beginninge of his fauoures"[41]—a misattribution that has a certain historical appropriateness given the courtly uses of such verse. The letters by prominent courtiers like Ralegh and Essex in some manuscript poetical miscellanies preserve some sense of the social atmosphere of both the epistolary and the poetical texts.[42] Finally, the grouping in both manuscript and printed anthologies of poems by authors who either belonged to the same coterie or wrote in the same social environment preserves some sense of the original context of their poems. One section of *The Phoenix Next* contains series of lyrics associated with Ralegh, which (Helen Sandison argues) includes poems by his cousin Sir Arthur Gorges, with whose verse his own circulated.[43] Poems by Sidney and Dyer appear together in Finet's miscellany. Donne's verse is preserved in a number of manuscripts alongside the related work of John Hoskins, Sir John Roe, Sir Henry Wotton, and others from the social circles to which he belonged. In both manuscript and printed collections, answer poems, parodies, and other forms of competitive versifying testify to the status of poetry as a kind of social currency.

Despite all this, the texts in manuscript and printed miscellanies lost touch with their original contexts, as the very act of anthologizing dislodged poems from their place in a system of transactions within polite or educated social circles and put them in the more fundamentally "literary" environment of the handwritten or typographic volume. An extreme example of decontextualization is found in one seventeenth-century manuscript anthology, Rosenbach MS 243/4, in which there is a section of poems by a number of different authors (including Donne) presented anonymously as though they were a continuous narrative sequence written by a single individual describing stages of a love affair. To keep the fictional frame intact, the compiler entitled or retitled specific lyrics to fit them into the series. For example, Donne's poem "The Message" is headed "Shee continuing in her disdainfull behauiour hee desires to bee released" and the next piece, Donne's "Breake of Day," is discursively identified "At last they enioye one the other, but his business enforseth him to make an early hast. Her lines upon it."[44] Authorship and original contexts both disappear in a "new" text written, in effect, by the compiler. Such literary recontextualization, however, occurs in any formalist or ahistorical literary reading. It is visible in the Petrarch commentaries that simply paraphrase the fictional situations that can be inferred from the poems themselves, in Tottel's situating of some of the pieces he printed in a framework of traditional literary amorousness, as well as in the very act of collecting what were often aesthetically ephemeral utterances within the pages of a printed book that designated both them and other texts as monuments of "literature."[45]

The coterie poems that found their way into manuscript or printed miscellanies were, to some degree, written in the culturally encoded language of the time by the occasion that generated them. Writers in particular courtly or satellite-courtly milieus adopted socially sanctioned or coterie-specific styles that marked their texts as part of a shared language. Many sixteenth-century English poems were anonymous and still remain unidentified, despite the efforts of scholars to detect the unique stylistic features of such authors as Ralegh and Sidney, which indicates that writers produced just this kind of literature. Foucault's notion of authorless discourse[46] is useful for approaching certain literary works as the articulation of (often conflicting) cultural codes, the product less of romantically conceived individual geniuses than of the language of social life at a particular historical moment. Manuscript-circulated poetry, subject as it was to reader emendation, to answer-poem responses, to parody, to unconscious and conscious revision, approaches the condition of such authorless discourse, especially for an audience beyond the original coterie: in a sense the published miscellanies echoed back to a general readership the language they were already speaking.

At the same time, however, coterie work circulated in manuscript was often essentially self-advertising, deliberately part of the social performance of an individual who could play the sometimes-bland generalities of poetic conventions against perceived particularities of his personality and personal situation: authors like Wyatt, Ralegh, and Sidney were masters of this art. Like them, Donne used the literary and cultural languages of his time to fashion a self-reflexively autobiographical discourse, calling his coterie audience's attention to his implication in both the text and contexts of his writing: he consistently exploited his readers' knowledge of his personal style and social circumstances to fashion distinctive utterances from literarily and culturally familiar material.

Given the various circumstances in which poems could be transmitted in manuscript to more or less private readerships, Donne's work had quite a wide range of possible forms of limited circulation short of the author's having his verse printed. The various manuscripts containing Donne's poetry, including those that also contain the work of other authors, offer some help in defining the different situations in which Donne's verse was communicated either to primary readerships or to secondary (but still restricted) audiences. Those editors who have most carefully examined the manuscripts in which Donne's verse appears, however, have done so basically to produce authoritative modern editions of this poet's work, not necessarily to place it in its social contexts. Herbert Grierson's and Helen Gardner's analyses of the complex manuscript situation of Donne's verse throw light on the early stages of literary circulation through which various poems or groups of poems passed—but their main interests lay in the establishment of texts, not in the definition of the social circumstances of the works' primary or secondary transmission.[47] Nevertheless, from what they and others have discovered we can reach some conclusions about the poems' socioliterary situations. By combining their information about the textual vicissitudes of the poems with other social-historical and literary-historical information, we can get some sense of the social conditions of Donne's coterie art.

The results of Donne's efforts in 1614 to gather his verse for publication, Gardner argues, was "X," that ancestor of the surviving Group I manuscripts.[48] Margaret Crum has shown, however, that, rather than a single large manuscript, this probably comprised "a collection of books and extra sheets which was used by the poet and the scribes."[49] It represents, then, as the letter to Goodyer indicates, a collecting effort undertaken *after* the original times of composition and initial circulation of individual poems or groups of poems. Alan Mac-

Coll has suggested that the Group II manuscripts descend from the collection of papers Donne gave to Sir Robert Ker in 1619, which Ker arranged to have transcribed, along with some subsequently composed works, by 1623.[50] In both of these lines of manuscript transmission, then, we are dealing with a stage of circulation at least one step removed from the poems' original circumstances.[51] Even in the case of the Westmoreland Manuscript, in the first part of which, Gardner claims, "we should expect to find the text [of Donne's poems] that circulated in the 1590's,"[52] there is little indication about original groupings of poems, since Woodward was arranging poems and prose in the collection by genre and, like some other copyists, transcribing texts that were scattered among loose sheets and sets of poems.

We need, I think, to postulate several stages of circulation for Donne's poems. The *Problems* might serve as a model for the primary and secondary forms of transmission: Donne gave these works first singly, then in groups, to particular readers.[53] So too there was probably, first, an original private circulation of individual poems or small groups of poems—the passing on to a single person or to small groups of known readers of, for example, individual verse letters (like "The Storme" and "The Calme") or the first one, two, or three satires, or a particular elegy or single lyric (like "The Curse," "A Jeat Ring Sent," "The Extasie," "Twicknam Garden," or "Loves Infiniteness"[54]). In some cases, there probably followed the gathering of certain poems, like the *Satires*, the *Elegies*, or *La Corona* and/or the *Holy Sonnets*, into sets to be circulated in "books" or quires.[55] At Jonson's urging, for instance, Donne sent the five-poem version of the *Satires* to the Countess of Bedford.[56] Some of the manuscripts indicate that earlier sets of three or four satires might have circulated, while some of the manuscript evidence points to the circulation of the *Satires* along with the two verse letters to Brooke ("The Storme" and "The Calme") and with Sir John Roe's (?) "Sleep, next society"—a Jacobean poem sometimes passed off as a sixth satire of Donne's.[57] This last type of transmission, in effect, constitutes another form of circulation in which Donne's poems were mixed with other work by contemporaries who may or may not have been writing in the same socioliterary environment.

The *Elegies*, which eventually were gathered into the collection represented by the group of poems found in Woodward's manuscript in this generic division, were probably first circulated individually or in small sets: lacking a consistent poetic persona, they are not, as I argue, a "book" even in the loose definition of the term used by the classical poets who composed in this form. Although Gardner does not claim that the *Songs and Sonnets*, composed over a greater time span than the *Elegies* and *Satires*, circulated as a single collection of poems, she gives the impression that the initial manuscript circulation of these pieces was in the form of groups of poems.[58] But, since these lyrics were, demonstrably, associated with a wide variety of social circumstances, this characterization is misleading—more accurate, in many cases, for situations of transmission subsequent to their initial ones. The presence of a single lyric in the Westmoreland manuscript, the appearance of a few others in songbooks, the pointedly occasional character of several others, all point to the probability that some *Songs and Sonnets*, like the *Verse Letters*, were initially transmitted as individual poems rather than in groups.

We can see eventually that there were different degrees of privacy to Donne's poetry. Setting aside the atypical case of the *Anniversaries*, those patronage poems whose publication Donne regretted, one can distinguish between the freer circulation of the *Satires* and *Elegies* and the more restricted transmission of most of the *Songs and Sonnets*, the poems that Helen Gardner claims Donne "kept . . . especially for the eyes of friends."[59] In a Latin letter to Goodyer written in 1611 before his departure for the Continent, Donne indicated that some works existed in "copies . . . which have crept out into the world without my knowledge," the "originals having been destroyed by fire . . . condemned by me to Hell." Others were obviously circulated with his consent: he calls these "virgins (save that they have been handled by many)," while still others were kept to himself, "so unhappily sterile that no copies of them have been begotten." These last he foresaw as destined for "utter annihilation (a fate with which God does not threaten even the wickedest of sinners)."[60] The omission of all of Donne's *Songs and Sonnets* save one ("A Jeat Ring Sent") from the important Westmoreland manuscript may point to the particularly private character of the lyrics, copies of which did not even come into the possession of a fairly close friend like Rowland Woodward.

Francis Davison's wish to get copies of "Satyres, Elegies, Epigrams &c. by John Don"[61] for publication indicates those poems by which Donne was known beyond his immediate social circles: the absence of the lyrics from this list (even though they may have been covered by the "&c." in Davison's statement) is probably due to their having been less widely known than the poet's other work. Donne nevertheless probably treated some of his early *Songs and Sonnets* more casually than others in allowing them to circulate fairly freely in the social environments in which he functioned in the 1590s: this is suggested by the setting to music of such poems as "Breake of Day," "The Message," and "Song: Sweetest love"—a fate about which the poet himself seemed to complain in "The Triple Foole." But, generally, Donne kept those lyrics he composed between about 1593 and 1610 quite close, only allowing them to begin to circulate more freely quite some time after their original composition: had they traveled beyond a restricted readership earlier, they would have appeared regularly in manuscript collections before the 1620s and 1630s. Even when the lyrics began to show up in commonplace-book anthologies, notably absent were such poems as "A Nocturnall upon S. Lucies Day," "The Primrose," "The Relique," "The Dissolution," "Negative Love," and "Farewell to Love," pieces that, I shall argue, either were especially private works or were designed for particular individuals (like Sir Edward Herbert).[62]

Aside from "The Storme" and "The Calme," the verse letters generally were sent to particular readers in circumstances of privacy similar to those of the familiar letter—although, in the case of certain encomiastic pieces to Lady Bedford, Donne may have shown what he wrote to a friend like Sir Henry Goodyer. Crum has argued that *La Corona* and the *Holy Sonnets* circulated together as a set of poems,[63] but this probably happened some time after their original composition and initial transmission. Their absence from some of the earlier manuscripts of Donne's poetry was probably due to Donne's careful restriction of their circulation and to their consequent coming before a wider audience at a later time than, for example, the *Satires* and *Elegies*. The *Epigrams* present an interesting case of survival and transmission. The poems do not show up at all in the Group I manuscripts and thirteen appear in the later Group II manuscripts, and still more in the Group III manuscripts, but the fullest collection of these poems appears in Rowland Woodward's manuscript—which suggests that the poems were available to Donne's friends in the 1590s and that the author himself, like Sir John Davies, did not keep in his own possession a full set of his exercises in this form.[64]

If we look at the manuscripts that textual scholars have used to produce modern editions of Donne's poetry, we discover an interesting—though, in light of the usual processes of manuscript transmission, an unsurprising—fact: that Donne's work is frequently found in the company of that of other poets, many of whom were socially connected with him in some way. For example, the Group I manuscript BL Harl. 4064 (*H 40*), like Bod. Rawl. Poet. 31 (to which it is related), includes poems by Harington, Wotton, Campion, Jonson, and Beaumont along with those of Donne.[65] The Group II manuscript BL Lansdowne 740 (*L 74*), a manuscript Gardner claims was copied out at different times by a single individual, contains sacred and secular poems

Donne wrote before 1610 along with poems by Sir Thomas Overbury, Sir Thomas Roe, Sir John Roe, and John Hoskins.[66] Of the Group III manuscripts, the Haslewood-Kingsborough manuscript (Hunt. Lib. MS HM 198) represents the combining of two different compilations: as Gardner has shown, "each contains solid blocks of poems by Donne and so is, strictly speaking, a miscellany containing a Donne collection."[67] Although Gardner only mentions the presence in *HK*, part 2, of one other author's poems, Sir John Roe's epistles to Ben Jonson, it is clear that the compiler(s) associated Donne's work with that of others from the same social environments, a common practice. BL Add. MS 25707 (*A 25*) presents Donne's pre-1610 verse, in Grierson's words, "interspersed with poems by other writers."[68] Margaret Crum believes the volume originally started out as a collection of Donne's poems but then was expanded to include poems by other authors identified only by their initials (a frequent method in both manuscript and printed miscellanies).[69] The Hawthornden MS (National Library of Scotland MS 2067) and the recently rediscovered Wedderburn MS (National Library of Scotland MS 6504) both record texts of poems by Hoskins, Sir John Roe, Wotton, Overbury, Pembroke, and Rudyerd along with Donne's.[70] The Burley manuscript, a commonplace book kept by Donne's friend Sir Henry Wotton, contains transcriptions of poems by Jonson, Pembroke, and others, along with those of Donne.[71] Some Donne poems appear in the Farmer-Chetham manuscript miscellany as well as in Rosenbach 1083/15, both collections associated with the Inns-of-Court environment in which Donne wrote much of his early verse. Of course, the further away chronologically the manuscript miscellanies got from the times of the poems' composition, the less useful for social-historical purposes their juxtaposition of poets. Nonetheless, the presence of Donne's verse in the company of work of authors with whom he was socially connected or who wrote in the same social environments points to its coterie character.[72]

The mixture of Donne poems (often without identification of authorship) with the work of other poets has led, however, to certain problems of ascription. As is the case with courtier poets like Ralegh, Oxford, and Sidney, in some manuscripts and in some early printed editions Donne is identified as the author of verse written by others. For generally good reasons, Gardner has placed in the category of "Dubia" such pieces as "Sapho to Philaenis," "The Expostulation,"[73] "His Parting from Her," "Julia," "A Tale of a Citizen and his Wife," "Variety," "The Token," "Self Love," and "Song: Stay, O sweet, and do not rise," most of which were probably written within the same environments in which Donne composed verse.[74] This group of works should probably be added to the much longer list of spurious poems attributed to Donne in various sources, works that include Sir John Roe's "Sleep, next Society," the lyric "Dear Love, continue nice and chaste" (ascribed to J[ohn] R[oe] in *L 40*), Lady Bedford's "Death be not proud, thy hand gave not this blow," and Hoskins's famous lyric "Absence." To a certain extent, such works represent not just the poetic "influence" of Donne, but also the sharing of certain styles of communication—a fact underscored by the games of exchange and answer poetry in which Donne and his friends participated. The very fact that some verse by other authors can be mistaken as Donne's indicates the distinctiveness of a coterie—as well as of a personal—style of writing.

It may be difficult for modern readers to view Donne's poems as coterie social transactions, rather than as literary icons, but this, I believe, is necessary since virtually all of the basic features of Donne's poetic art are related to its coterie character. His creation of a sense of familiarity and intimacy, his fondness for dialectic, intellectual complexity, paradox and irony, the appeals to shared attitudes and group interests (if not to private knowledge), the explicit gestures of biographical self-referentiality, the styles he adopted or invented all relate to the coterie circumstances of his verse. Donne was obviously most comfortable when he knew his readers personally and they knew him. Ideally, the social relationship with a known audience made possible the kinds of "intercommunication"[75] Donne found congenial. He defined this creative cooperation between poet and reader in the opening lines of his epistle to Christopher Brooke, "The Storme":

> Thou which art I, ('tis nothing to be soe)
> Thou which art still thy selfe, by these [lines] shalt know
> Part of our passage; And, a hand, or eye
> By *Hilliard* drawne, is worth an history,
> By a worse painter made; and (without pride)
> When by thy judgment they are dignifi'd,
> My lines are such: 'Tis the preheminence
> Of friendship onely to'impute excellence.
>   (1–8)

Donne was doing more than simply appealing to his addressee's goodwill or alluding to the epistolary convention of the friend as an alter ego. In the specific context of their friendship and common social and political aspirations, Donne clearly knew that Brooke was aware of his personal motives for serving as a gentleman-volunteer on the expedition to which the poem refers. Donne could thus feel confident that his primary reader could make do with relatively few aesthetic cues to read this verse letter perceptively. The "lines" of the poem, like those of the skillful painter, suggested much to a knowledgeable perceiver: this is, of course, the basic assumption behind the Renaissance idea of connoisseurship,[76] but the notion took on a special definition in the case of coterie art like Donne's.

Donne expected certain intellectual, aesthetic, and social knowledge or sophistication of his readers—the capacity to understand the nuances of his witty manipulation of literary conventions, genres, cultural codes, and specific social and rhetorical circumstances. "I would have no such Readers as I can teach," he proclaimed in the preface to *Metempsychosis*, expressing a wish for what Ben Jonson called an audience of "understanders,"[77] the admission to which was not simply a matter of moral and intellectual qualifications, as it was for Jonson. It was probably the coterie character of Donne's audience that led Jonson to postulate that "Done himself for not being understood would perish,"[78] a statement that has proved accurate enough in predicting *some* of the historical vicissitudes of Donne's verse. Many readers have found the poems perplexingly difficult, "a continued Heap of Riddles" as Lewis Theobald[79] called them—a consequence not only of the general changes in cultural conditions from the Renaissance to more recent periods, but also of the loss of the special contexts in which they were originally set. Dryden's famous comment that Donne "affects the Metaphysicks, not only in his Satires, but in his Amorous Verses . . . and perplexes the Minds of the Fair Sex with nice Speculations of Philosophy"[80] reveals the later poet's unawareness of the primarily male readership of most of the love lyrics and of the shared background they would have brought to an understanding of the verse.

If we approach Donne's poetry in terms of the kind of text-context interaction implied by courtly and satellite-courtly verse, we can perceive some of the pointedly witty ways he handled his poetic materials as he adjusted his rhetoric to specific audiences, occasions, and milieus. This context of interpretation, however, is one in which we need to play down the importance of explicit discursive statements in the poems and attend more closely to the metacommunicative (or metapoetic) level of discourse.

As defined by Gregory Bateson, "metacommunication" is that (usually implicit) form of communication in which "the subject of discourse is the relationship between the speakers."[81] It constitutes, he writes elsewhere, "all exchanged cues and propositions about (a) codification and (b) the relationship between the communicators."[82] The basic fact that Donne's verse was originally coterie literature, of course, increased its metacommunicative power, for author and reader had a social relationship apart from the text that could be evoked as a context of composition and of reception/interpretation.[83] In fact, all the contextual messages of Donne's verse have metacommunicative implications, since they refer back to and further define the relationship of writer and reader in a particular social milieu. Donne highlighted his relationship with his coterie readers both explicitly and implicitly. Often he put self-reflexive statements in his poems—e.g., "Sooner then you read this line" ("The Storme," 29); "*Venus* heard me sigh this song" ("The Indifferent," 19); ". . . by these hymnes, all shall approve/Us Canoniz'd for Love" ("The Canonization," 35–36); "Be this my Text, my Sermon to mine owne" ("Hymne to God, my God, in my sicknesse," 29). But, in fact, Donne's whole rhetorical manner is generally self-reflexive, manifesting an acute consciousness of language and style as well as of the socioliterary circumstances of individual works. Donne often depicted or fictionalized the poet-reader relationship within the inner rhetorical space of particular poems in the interaction of poetic speaker and fictive listener (or implied reader). Any time he suggested by direct or indirect means that he knew that his reader knew or that he knew that his reader knew that he knew something, he emphasized the metacommunicative aspect of his verse.

In his letters, Donne set forth a model of communication with his coterie reader that he sought, I believe, in most of his poetry. He told his close friend Goodyer in one missive that he conceived of letters as "conveyances and deliverers of me to you" (*Letters*, p. 109): the interpersonal relationship, then, not the circumstantial content, was what mattered. He wished for or fantasized a perfect mutual understanding with his correspondent-friend: "Angels have not, nor affect not other knowledge of one another, then they list to reveal to one another. It is then in this onely, that friends are Angels, that they are capable and fit for such revelations when they are offered" (*Letters*, pp. 109–10). In another letter, Donne emphasized the metacommunicative aspect of epistolary communications, telling Goodyer, "I have placed my love wisely where I need communicate nothing" (*Letters*, p. 115)—by which he meant that he felt that the letters' information content was much less important than the friendship they mediated. Defending the absence of "news" from his prose epistles, Donne said that "their principall office . . . [is] to be seals and testimonies of mutuall affection, but the materialls and fuell of them should be a confident and mutuall communicating of those things which we know" (*Letters*, p. 121). He regarded the content of his correspondences as "nothing" (*Letters*, p. 121), but such "nothing" was the rhetorical space in which the interpersonal transaction with his reader could take place. This negation or absence of discursive meaning is that condition toward which all Donne's writing moves—not only his poems, but also his prose, especially his *Sermons*. For example, in a letter he wrote to accompany a copy of a sermon requested by the Countess of Montgomery, he used a theological language to portray the kind of contextual relationship of preacher and congregation the written text only partially captures:

> I know what dead carkasses things written are, in respect of things spoken. But in things of this kinde, that soul that inanimates them, receives debts from them: The Spirit of God that dictates them in the speaker or writer, and is present in his tongue or hand, meets himself again (as we meet our selves in a glass) in the eies and eares and hearts of the hearers and readers: and that Spirit, which is ever the same to an equall devotion, makes a writing and a speaking equall means to edification. (*Letters*, p. 25)

Donne's dream of communication was one in which the reader or audience or congregation repeated, or mirrored in their responses, the thoughts and feelings of the author who made the text. In the letters, as in the poetry, personal psychological struggles were used as a medium of communication with a sympathetic reader.

As a consequence of his communicative purposes, Donne often undid or aborted the discursive lines of development in his writing, making his works often virtually "self-consuming artifacts."[84] But this was one of his habitual ways of fostering intuitive understanding he felt he could share with his chosen audiences. In particular lyrics, the failure or subversion of rationality often makes possible both emotional closure and complex forms of understanding that transcend the bounds of narrow logic. Critics like Joan Webber and Donald Friedman recognize that, in both his *Sermons* and some of his best poetry, Donne enacts a process of discovery that necessitates such witty destruction of rational discrimination and control for the sake of emotional and intuitive apprehension of complex or mysterious subject matter.[85] To this end, Donne used a strategy of deliberate confusion to clear the way, in his own and in his reader's minds, for higher understanding.[86] Donne used many means to produce such creative discordance in his works, including the deliberate clashing of vehicle and tenor, the noncongruence of statement and tone, the witty misalliance of dramatic situation and actual speech performance, the opposition of rhetorical manner and stylistic decorum. The wit of many of Donne's poems depends on his awareness of his readers' responses to his manipulation and conflation of generic expectations: in his love lyrics, his unfinished *Metempsychosis*, the *Anniversaries*, and the encomiastic epistles, he made use of his audience's expected reactions to different literary genres and modes as he altered the literary coordinates of his works, creating a lively metacommunicative intraction between poet and reader that was self-conscious for both.

Problems arose for Donne's readers, no doubt, when the complexities became so difficult that they reached the limits of their competence, unable to maintain social and intellectual contact through the medium of a relentlessly perplexing text. Donne's elegists (who were, for the most part, removed from the original literary circumstances of his verse) point to the combination of competence and incapacity in those who read this poet's work. Carew, who proclaimed Donne "a King, that rul'd as hee thought fit/The Universall Monarchy of wit"[87] recognized this poet's intellectual advantage over his readers. Jasper Mayne, himself one generation younger than Donne's original audience, called the *First Anniversarie* "so farre above its Reader . . . that wee are thought wits, when 'tis Understood." "What was thy recreation turnes our braine," Mayne wrote, "Our rack and paleness, is thy weakest strain."[88] Though Mayne's confusion may have exceeded that of Donne's primary readers, what he says, I think, points to some of the difficulties they probably encountered. Donne's metacommunicative affirmations of his bonds of feeling, of understanding, and of social intimacy with his readers, may have been designed partly to counteract some of the effects of the deliberate difficulties of his work. Donne thus seems to have created a kind of double relationship with his readers, alternately adversarial and intimate, sometimes to the point of being insulting and complimentary at the same time. Perhaps it was necessary for him to feel both distance and immediacy in the coterie circumstances in which he wrote.

To read Donne's verse as coterie poetry, one must not only interpret it in terms of its immediate biographical and social matrices, but also locate it more generally in the Elizabethan and Jacobean sociocultural contexts that encoded the literary genres, modes, conventions, and languages that Donne used. Like Spenser, Shakespeare, or Jonson, Donne played with the rich cultural resources of his time, as well as with the intellectual and aesthetic materials of Renaissance Europe. Those who have interpreted his poems in terms of intellectual and literary history have discovered much that has gone into Donne's creatively revisionary art, but it is equally important to read his work in relation to the general and specific social, economic, and political contexts within which he lived, acted, and wrote. Both the general and the specific social milieus of the verse determined Donne's choice of literary forms, modes, conventions, and idioms, his decisions to observe and/or subvert decorum, the choice of literary forms, modes, conventions, and idioms, his adoption of styles of address and of self-presentation, and his exploitation, within the constraints they imposed, of contextual resources. It is obvious that the different socioliterary circumstances of "The Indifferent," *Metempsychosis*, "The Extasie," "Twicknam Garden" and "Goodfriday, 1613. Riding Westward" greatly affected the composition and original reception/interpretation of these works. Donne's poems were products less of the study than of a series of social relationships spread over a number of years. The special character of this verse with its rich interplay of text and context has been falsified since its posthumous publication in 1633 as a poetical corpus.[89] This study attempts to recover some of what has been lost through the literary institutionalization of Donne's verse.

1
Donne as an Inns-of-Court Author

Donne seems to have composed his first poetry at the Inns of Court between 1592 and 1596. Both the institution of which he was a part and his audience within it affected his choice of literary forms and modes, the development of his characteristic style, and the subject matter of his verse—that is, all the artistic, intellectual, and social coordinates of his literary work. If there is some truth to Ben Jonson's statement that Donne wrote his best poems before he was twenty-five,[1] much of his most important poetry belongs to the Inns period. To understand it historically in its sociocultural context, it is necessary to examine the environment of the Inns of Court as well as Donne's motives for being there and for writing verse while he was in residence.

THE INNS OF COURT AS A SOCIOLITERARY ENVIRONMENT

In the late sixteenth century, Gray's Inn, Middle Temple, Inner Temple, and Lincoln's Inn were educational institutions for the training of young men in the common law and convenient places for the conduct of legal business. They were also "finishing schools" where gentlemen could both continue their education in a variety of subjects and acquire the civility and sophistication that would help them function successfully at Court or in other prestigious social circles. In close touch with the economic, political, and social centers of power, the Inns of Court were recognized as an avenue to opportunity and reward in the larger society. Though less distant from the heart of the society than the universities were, the Inns were nevertheless a social environment distinct from the Court, the City, and the general social system. Inns members often criticized the other institutions of society at the same time as they made persistent efforts to join the Establishment—an ambivalence reflected both in their way of life and in the literature they produced.[2]

The Inns housed a larger proportion of gentlemen than the universities. These men were concerned with maintaining or improving their social and economic status, so the fashionable forms of behavior often were implicitly designed to advertise their (sometimes tenuous) gentility.[3] When Donne, for example, had his portrait painted in 1591, he made sure that his family's coat of arms was affixed: although he came from middle-class stock as the son of a member of the Ironmonger's Company, he wished to emphasize his right to be regarded as a gentleman.[4] The antagonism to the Inns gentlemen on the part of some lower-born university men and professional writers can be attributed to the socially exclusive character of Inns life. The *Parnassus* plays performed at St. John's College, Cambridge (1597–1601), for example, portray an Inns-of-Court gentleman-amorist as a villain because he uses his wealth and social position to unfair advantage.[5] Even Ben Jonson, who pointedly dedicated *Everyman Out of his Humour* to the Inns of Court and who had many close friends there, expressed his own social resentment when he characterized Ovid in *The Poetaster* as an Inns gallant punished for his degenerate way of life, a figure morally inferior to the more socially humble Horace and Virgil. Economic and social competition lay behind such expressions: after all, the main topic of the *Parnassus* plays is the sorry career prospects available in the late Elizabethan period to able, university-trained men who did not happen to be gentlemen (professional writers like Nashe and Marlowe, for example).[6] Jonson, of course, was especially sensitive to the handicap of low birth.

Within the Inns themselves the need to struggle for place and career made the atmosphere a heatedly competitive one. Whether or not they chose to prepare themselves for the legal profession (as only a relatively small minority did), Inns men were usually extremely ambitious, sharing the desire to succeed in a world in which the rewards were genuine, but the opportunities few. In his *Directions for Speech and Style*, the Inns author John Hoskins facetiously included the following examples of that species of irony considered under the term "catachresis": 1) "I am in danger of preferm[en]t"; 2) "I have hardly escaped good fortune"; and 3) "He threatens me a good turn."[7] No matter how much Inns men appeared to be wasting their time enjoying the pleasures of City and Court, they were usually eager for advancement and employment. After all, they were the trained elite of an educational system originally expanded in Tudor England to provide large numbers of competent civil servants for a centralized monarchy's growing bureaucracy. But their numbers, by the end of the sixteenth century, far exceeded the positions available. Lawrence Stone has called attention to this virtual "educational revolution" and noted that the overproduction of trained gentlemen caused a competitive scramble for the few available places that were socially and economically attractive. In these circumstances, ambitious young men often had to endure the long wait for success or to scale down their expectations.[8]

While he was still at Gray's Inn, Francis Bacon repeatedly petitioned his uncle, Lord Burghley, for help to advance his career, taking the occasion of his thirty-first birthday to remind his powerful relative that he had been patient for a very long time:

I wax now somewhat ancient; one and thirty years is a great deal of sand in the hour-glass. My health, I thank God, I find confirmed; and I do not fear that action shall impair it, because I account my ordinary course of study and meditation to be more painful than most parts of action are. I ever bare a mind (in some middle place that I could discharge) to serve her Majesty; not as a man born under Sol, that loveth honour; nor under Jupiter, that loveth business (for the contemplative planet carrieth me away wholly); but as a man born under an excellent Sovereign, that deserveth the dedication of all men's abilities.[9]

Bacon warned his uncle that, if he did not win advancement, he would be forced to make a vocation of his philosophical avocation and "become a sorry bookmaker." The irony is that in this letter, in which Bacon boasts "I have taken all knowledge to be my province" (*Works*, 8:109) and expresses his desire to purge thinking of traditional fallacies and illusions, he should present the role of the professional writer of philosophical prose in so negative a way. But, given the traditional association of learning and poverty, Bacon's aversion to the life of living by one's wits and pen is understandable. When, a few years later, his career was again not advancing rapidly enough to suit him, he wrote *The Advancement of Learning*.

In a revealing way, many of the terms of the letter to Burghley figure in Bacon's 1597 *Essays*, a work whose topics were close to the interests of ambitious Inns-of-Court men. The original ten essays cover subjects attractive to intellectual young men concerned with the means by which they could prosper in the larger society: "Of studies," "Of discourse," "Of Ceremonies and respects," "Of followers and friends," "Of Sutes," "Of Expence," "Of Regiment of Health," "Of Honour and Reputation," "Of Faction," and "Of Negociating" (*Works*, 6:523–34).

"Of Studies" offers the model of the civic humanist, not the reclusive scholar, the man polished, learned, refined, ready for business in the world. Bacon extols the virtues of the active man: "Histories make men wise, Poets wittie: the Mathematickes subtle, naturall Phylosophie deepe: Morall graue, Logicke and Rhetoricke able to contend" (*Works*, 6:525). Knowing one's place in the social hierarchy involves the proper use of "ceremonies and respectes": "Not to vse Ceremonies at all, is to teach others to vse them againe, and so diminish his respect. . . . Among a mans Peires a man shall be sure of familiaritie, and therefore it is a good title to keepe state; amongst a mans inferiours one shall be sure of reuerence, and therefore it is good a little to be familiar" (*Works*, 6:527). One of the most interesting statements Bacon makes in "Of Followers and Friends" assumes that equals compete and "friendship" (in the older sense of benefaction) is to be found between those on different levels of the social hierarchy: "There is little friendship in the worlde, and least of all betweene equals; which was wont to bee magnified. That that is, is betweene superiour and inferiour, whose fortunes may comprehend the one the other" (*Works*, 6:528).[10] The advice on "suits" (*Works*, 7:528–29) is apposite: he particularly recommends secrecy and good timing. Inns men were usually in the position of petitioners and suitors to the powerful and great. Bacon's remarks concerning "expence" (*Works*, 6:530) have to do with tempering the social display attached to wealth with prudent economy. His advice about "Regiment of Health" (*Works*, 6:530–31) is commonplace—although he does mention conspicuously in his letter to Burghley that he is of good health, implying a comparison with his sickly brother Anthony, who was well placed in the service of the Earl of Essex.

In the essay "Of Honour and Reputation" Bacon descends from generalities to the specific social categories for those who were part of the Establishment:

Degrees of honour in subiects are first *Particepes curarum*, those upon whome Princes doe discharge the greatest waight of their affaires, their *Right handes* (as we call them.) The next are *Duces belli*, great leaders, such as are Princes, Lieutenants, and do them notable services in the wars. The third are *Gratiosi*, fauorites, such as exceede not this scantling to bee sollace to the Soueraigne, and harmelesse to the people. And the fourth *Negotiis pares*, such as have great place vnder Princes, and execute their places with sufficiencie. (*Works*, 6:532)

In Elizabeth's government, men like Burghley and Walsingham fell into the first category, Captain John Norris and Admiral Charles Howard into the second, Sir Christopher Hatton, Sir Walter Ralegh, the

Earl of Essex into the third (though the last was also an active, if unreliable, military leader), and other government ministers, in whose company Bacon wished to be numbered, into the fourth. The very next essay is "Of Faction" (*Works*, 6:532–33); the picture of the Court in Elizabethan England is incomplete without considering this topic and Elizabeth's strategy of balancing rival groups against one another. Bacon, who in 1597 was still an Essex client, articulates the principle that "Meane men must adheare, but great men that haue strength in themselues were better to maintaine themselues indifferent and neutrall" (*Works*, 6:533), marking the difference between himself and his cousin Robert Cecil (or between the greater nobility and lower-born gentlemen). The last essay of the 1597 edition, "Of Negociating," concludes with Machiavellian advice: "If you would worke any man, you must either know his nature and fashions and so leade him, or his ends, and so winne him, or his weaknesses or disaduantages, and so awe him, or those that haue interest in him and so gouerne him. In dealing with cunning persons we must euer consider their endes to interpret their speeches, and it is good to say little to them, and that which they least looke for" (*Works*, 6:534). The 1597 Essays *in toto* can be looked on as a success manual for Elizabethan gentlemen, particularly for Bacon's Inns-of-Court colleagues.

Like Bacon, other talented young men of the Inns had to be patient until the right opportunities presented themselves. The wish for a satisfying career was never very far from their consciousness, so that when Donne joked in his "Song: Goe and catche a falling starre" about the impossibility that one could "finde / What winde / Serves to'advance an honest minde" (7–9) he was voicing a common feeling of frustration. Gabriel Harvey's definition of the employed man implies some of the opposite characteristics of the restless and impatient unemployed: "An jmployed man, hath no leysure to be acowld in wynter, to thinke uppon heate in Somer, to be heauyheartid, or drowsely and swaddishly affectid, to be syck, but euer goith cheerefully, and lustely through with all his enterprizes, & affayres. He is A very swadd, & sott, that, dullith, or bluntith either witt, or boddy with any lumpish, or Melancholy buzzing abowt this, or that."[11] The discontented and the melancholic, who felt cheated or disappointed by the system, found ways of expressing their dissatisfaction in their behavior, if not in their writing. It was no accident that it was an Inns-of-Court man turned dramatist who wrote *The Malcontent*.[12] Much of the epigrammatic and satiric literature of the time rested on the same foundation, including that written at the Inns.

Writing to an audience of social familiars, John Donne called the

Inns environment one of "study and play" ("Epithalamion made at Lincolnes Inne," 30). Both of these spheres of activity reflected the competitive strivings of Inns members. "Study" embraced not only the law (which was in the usual agonistic mode of higher education), but also lectures and tutoring in disciplines not taught at the university or reading in a wide variety of areas.[13] Since most of the Inns men were quite young, they pursued intellectual interests that their successors in later times did at the university. Strictly speaking, such endeavors were a distraction from the discipline of legal studies, so it was mainly the nonlawyer majority that engaged in them. In a 1608 letter to Goodyer lamenting his lack of employment, Donne recalled that while at Lincoln's Inn he was "diverted by the worst voluptuousnes, which is an Hydroptique immoderate desire of humane learning and languages: beautiful ornaments to great fortunes; but mine needed an occupation . . ." (*Letters*, p. 51). In preaching years later to a Lincoln's Inn congregation, Donne acknowledged that the "profession [of law] . . . requires the whole man for it. It is for the most part losse of time in you to divert upon other studies . . ." (*Sermons*, 2:156). He spoke from experience.

It was, nonetheless, just such a ferment of interests that made the Inns an intellectually and literarily rich environment.[14] Inns men were both traditional and *au courant* in their study and discourse—concerned with the age-old philosophical, moral, and theological topics as well as with new concepts and discoveries (in science and medicine, for example). Religion and politics were recurrent subjects for conversation and argument. A nimble or "witty" capacity for argumentation and controversy was highly prized—a fact reflected, for instance, in the fondness for such literary forms as the prose paradox and essay. Ben Jonson praised the Inns of Court as the "nourceries of liberty and humanitie,"[15] alluding, it would seem, to their atmosphere of critical freedom and intellectual inquiry.

As Wilfrid Prest has argued, the "play" of Inns men, whether the communal forms of reveling or the private fashionable recreations of individuals, should, first, be seen, in terms of the nonlawyer majority's desire "to adopt attitudes and patterns of behavior which would clearly distinguish them from the common lawyers with whom they were nominally associated." As Prest notes, "the competitive aping of court modes in dress and taste, the cult of wit, the incessant versifying (for private circulation, not mercenary publication), even perhaps the obsessive drinking, gaming, and womanizing"[16] were part of this style of life. Sir Richard Baker's description of the young Donne as "very neat; a great visiter of Ladies, a great frequenter of Playes, a great writer of conceited Verses"[17] connects him with those who used the Inns as gentlemanly finishing schools and convenient places of access to the resources of City and Court. In one of his later Lincoln's Inn sermons, Donne identified the different "arrows" of temptation threatening the young men of the Inns, drawing, no doubt, on his own experience: "A fair day shoots arrows of *visits*, and *comedies*, and *conversation*, and so wee goe abroad: and a foul day shoots arrows of *gaming*, or *chambering*, and *wantonnesse*, and so we stay at home" (*Sermons*, 2:62). The various activities named were normal features of the "play" of Inns gentlemen.

Some descriptions of the communal recreations of the Inns have survived, such as accounts of the Gray's Inn revels of 1594–95 and the Middle Temple revels of the *Prince D'Amour* (1597–98). These ceremonials reflect not only many of the serious and recreational activities of Inns members but also their ambivalent attraction/aversion to the Establishment of which they were so conscious. The *Gesta Grayorum* is obviously an Establishment festivity—sanctioned, in fact by Lord Burghley and the Queen. In the license of holiday merriment, which lasted from Christmas to the beginning of Lent, 1594–95, the Inns men travestied the structure and rules of the Court-centered society, mocked its fashionable modes of behavior and speech, parodied its ceremonies (such as the royal procession and progress), but finally complimented the monarch. The fiction of a "Prince of Purpoole," with his royal court and kingdom, comically mirrored the actual situation of Elizabethan courtly government, exploiting the metaphor of chivalry of which Elizabeth was so fond. After the installation of this play monarch, "Then was his Privy Council assigned him, to advise of State-Matters, and the Government of his Dominions: His Lodging also was provided according to State; as the Presence-chamber, and the Council-chamber: Also all Officers of State, of the Law, and of the House-hold. There were also appointed Gentlemen-Pensioners to attend on his Person, and a Guard, with their Captain, for his Defence."[18] The published account of the revels contains a lengthy list of functionaries. As was the case for other revels in which similar play monarchs were installed, the "succession of ceremonies [that] took place," as Finkelpearl has summarized them, included "an elaborate emblazoning of the Prince's titles, a detailed description of the responsibilities of court officers, a conferring of 'knighthoods,' a declaration of laws and edicts for the Prince's realm,"[19] activities associated with the normal conduct of royal government. On one of the days of the *Gesta Grayorum* six "Counsellors" made formal speeches of advice to the Prince of Purpoole on such serious subjects as warfare and conquest, learning and philosophy, building and the support of educational institutions, finances, legal reform, and the art of political compromise and balance. One speaker recommended that the prince "advance Men of Vertue, and not of Mercenary Minds,"[20] a formula for preferment to which most Inns men would have paid lip service no matter how deliberately they sought special favors and influence. The evidence suggests that it was Francis Bacon who composed the speeches,[21] which are in the traditional form of advice to the monarch.[22] Although the last of the six orations undoes the serious purpose of the previous five with its facetious defense of the values of license and festivity, the whole performance reinforced the connections between the Inns and the royal court, the participants demonstrating their interest in and knowledge of their culture's central political institution. The proceedings concluded on Shrove Tuesday with a masque and barriers at Elizabeth's court complimenting the Queen as a magnetic power of "attractive vertue,"[23] highlighting the intentions of Gray's Inn revelers as aspiring courtiers who looked to the monarch and to her officers for preferment.

In such circumstances there were real limits placed on the satiric and iconoclastic tendencies of Inns wits. Finkelpearl should not have been surprised in his invaluable discussion of the *Gesta* that there was little "overt satire" in the presentation of "speeches filled with hyperbolic courtly language, metaphoric cliches, Ciceronian periods, and rhetorical flourishes."[24] These revels, and others like them, were not the right occasion for Inns men to dissociate themselves too aggressively from the courtly system. Rather, they were an opportunity in the largest possible social "theater" (the Inns, the City, and the Court all served as stages) to exhibit a familiarity with the Court-centered social system and a mastery of its behavioral and literary vocabularies. The revelers engaged in forms of self-satirization—mocking the foibles of Inns gallants, expelling, at one point, allegorical figures representing their own worst qualities, "*Envy, Male-content,* and *Folly.*"[25] But, like Jonson in *Cynthia's Revels*, they would not mount a frontal assault on the institution of courtly government.

Given what we know of the intellectual and recreational activities of the Inns members, it is possible to define the Inns-of-Court style, that complex of common interests, values, attitudes, tastes, and modes of behavior that marked this social environment as a distinctive subcultural milieu. This is important to do because this style is implicit in the writings of many Inns authors, including John Marston, Sir John Davies, and Donne himself.[26]

Since the Inns were virtual "suburbs of the court,"[27] it is not surprising that Inns men learned and practiced the modes of behavior, speech, and writing appropriate in the Court itself. John Hoskins wrote of himself and his fellows: ". . . we study according to the predominancy of courtly inclinations" (p. 39). Although he refers primarily to the fads in conversational idioms, his remark applied more generally to that large sphere of activity in which Inns men learned both the polite and the devious ways of the Court to prepare themselves for successful careers. While they often resisted or satirized it, they learned the nuances of "complement," that language of deferential courtly transactions broadly defined by Hoskins as the "performance of affected ceremonies in words, looks, or gesture" (p. 44). Their culture-heroes were courtly figures like Sir Philip Sidney and the Earl of Essex, their gossip was often "court news," and much of the literature published for their consumption, such as the printed poetical miscellanies, was courtly literature. They collected courtly verse and prose in commonplace books as both literary and behavioral models. They acquired the courtly skills of dancing, singing, and the writing of love lyrics.[28]

At the same time there was a strong anticourtly impulse shared by many Inns men, reinforced by their common frustration in their search for preferment. Like disappointed courtiers, they attributed the envied success of others to the whims of Fortune or to influence-peddling, and viewed their own condition as that of injured merit. This led to a kind of moral or satiric disengagement from the courtly world, a stance of (sometimes openly cynical) criticism of its rules, of its styles, and of its (deliberately exaggerated) corruptions, the typical reaction of what Mark Curtis has called the "alienated intellectuals"[29] of Elizabethan England. The verbal medium for such an attitude was a linguistic style sharply distinguished from that of "complement," a form of plainspeaking with roots in the egalitarian mode of humanist literary exchange, noncourtly literary genres like the epigram and the Ovidian elegy, as well as the native English traditions of moral prose and poetry. The features of this style Hoskins articulated in his *Directions*, a work intended to instruct a young Inns-of-Court man in the proper language of social transactions. Against such a model of affected gesturing as the following—"Have you leisure to descend to the remembrance of that assurance which you have long had in me, and upon your next opportunity to make me happy with any employment you shall assign me" (p. 4)—Hoskins sets the virtues of a plain style that is brief, clear, and lively. This simpler language was connected with the Inns tradition of "liberty" in speech, the freedom to state criticisms openly and boldly, with sometimes socially iconoclastic effect. As Finkelpearl has argued, this license in speech lay behind some of the Parliamentary opposition that developed to the policies of James I, demonstrated, for example, in the 1614 ("Addled") Parliament in which some former Inns men found themselves thrown into prison for their overbold criticism of their monarch's policies.[30] They included, incidentally, Richard Martin, Sir Walter Chute, and John Hoskins himself, all friends of Donne. In his letter to his wife from the Tower, Hoskins characterized himself as having been imprisoned because "greate ones" were hypersensitively offended by his "witt,"[31] a quality cultivated in the Inns and associated with a plainspeaking manner.

Under more careful control, however, plainspeaking was a kind of ideal of frank, businesslike communication—Bacon knew this full well,[32] and he was, after all, an Inns-of-Court man. It was an antidote to the stylistic convolutions of courtly compliment and flattery. John Marston, an Inns author, portrayed it this way in *The Fawn*, a play (like so many other satiric comedies) intended for an audience largely composed of Inns men:

> Freeness, so't grow not to licentiousness,
> Is grateful to just states. Most spotless kingdom,
> And men, O happy born under good stars,
> Where what is honest you may freely think,
> Speak what you think, and write what you do speak,
> Not bound to servile soothings.
> (I.ii.318–23)[33]

Free, plainspeaking honesty could be adopted to advantage as a rhetorical style in complimentary verse and prose—in, for example, a letter requesting patronage such as Wotton's to Robert Cecil[34] or in encomiastic verse epistles where it could serve to verify the truth behind the worn clichés of praise—but basically it advertised itself the mode of communication between (male) equals. When Inns authors wrote love poetry for an audience of peers, it was marked by the plainspeaking, somewhat conversational style favored in the Inns environment.

DONNE AT LINCOLN'S INN: THE EARLY VERSE LETTERS AND THE FIRST THREE SATIRES

John Donne entered the world of the Inns of Court in 1591 as a young man who, because of his Catholicism, had been unable to pursue his studies to a degree at Oxford or Cambridge.[35] At the Inn of Chancery,

Thavies Inn, he continued his education under tutors as he prepared himself for admission to Lincoln's Inn, which was granted in 1592.[36] Though his commitment to the law was, evidently, not a wholehearted one,[37] he fulfilled the residence requirements at Lincoln's Inn and learned enough about legal matters to serve him well in his later government employment. Donne's program of nonlegal self-education was more ambitious: he read widely in many fields, including "the whole body of Divinity, controverted" (*Selected Prose*, p. 50) between Catholic and Protestant polemical writers. Though scholarly in temperament (he left, at his death, notes on some 1,400 to 1,500 authors), Donne lived the life of the fashionable gallant and wit, acquiring the urbanity and courtliness necessary for entry into sophisticated social circles. He made strong and close friendships at this time, many of which lasted the rest of his life, associating himself generally with a group of young gentlemen eager for social and political or professional advancement. Restless, ambitious, and gregarious, he thrived in the rich environment of the Inns as he familiarized himself with City and Court.

While at Lincoln's Inn and during that period before his employment with Sir Thomas Egerton, when he lived as a London gentleman and aspiring courtier, Donne tried his hand at various traditional and revived literary genres, viewing this writing as part of his social life, intending it for an audience of friends and acquaintances whose literary and sociocultural competence resembled his own. He composed epigrams, verse letters, formal satires, love elegies and libertine lyrics, and prose paradoxes—all genres fostered by the social circumstances of the Inns[38] and that male social group that developed out of this environment into those courtly and professional circles with which Donne was later connected. He imitated and wittily recreated literary forms associated with the Court, such as the love complaint, the Petrarchan complimentary lyric, and the art-song, utilizing the literary language of love sanctioned in Elizabethan England as a fit medium for certain patron-client transactions and other polite relationships in the hierarchical social system. In almost all of these works, his point of view was that of the Inns-of-Court wit who could self-critically and ironically examine the social institutions and environments with which he was involved as well as his own ambivalent feelings about them. In handling different genres, Donne self-consciously reformulated their rules and conventions, sometimes mixing or conflating separate literary kinds and modes, thus questioning the social coordinates of literary forms in interesting ways;[39] he evolved a characteristic style that was both distinctively personal and, at the same time, congenial to his immediate audience of Inns gentlemen.

Although Donne regarded poetry only as an avocation, not the main business of his intellectual, moral, social, or professional life, soon after his arrival at Lincoln's Inn he wrote a number of verse letters to friends, expressing the desire to foster epistolary composition as a communal enterprise. These poems are probably not only his first literary works but also his earliest effort to define the kind of coterie audience with whom he wished to communicate. The classical and humanist models of the verse epistle determined, of course, many of the ideas he expressed in them, but he seems to have wished to relate his epistles particularly to the circumstances of his life and social relationships at the Inns of Court.[40] R. C. Bald has argued that these early verse letters, in effect, establish a "coterie of ingenious young men assiduously cultivating the Muse and warmly applauding each other's efforts" (*Life*, p. 74).[41] The rhetorically familiar manner of these epistles has, in Finkelpearl's words, "the easy intimacy of someone speaking to an audience of equals."[42] Donne and most of his addressees shared a background of university education, common experiences in London and at the Inns, and a social familiarity that included visits to one another's homes or estates. Thus, Donne wrote to Samuel Brooke, the brother of his chambermate at Lincoln's Inn, advising him to write poetry while he was still at the university (*To Mr. S. B.*, "O thou which"); in the epistle *To Mr. E. G.* ("Even as lame things"), he assumed his reader shared his gentleman's attitude of not taking legal study seriously, alluding to the London scene to which they were both accustomed, then changed by the plague; the letter *To Mr. I. L.* ("Blest are your North parts") was sent to a friend whose estate the poet's "Mistress" was visiting. In another poem to the same addressee (*To Mr. I. L.*, "Of that short Roll of friends"), he teasingly reprimanded his friend for neglecting the "duties of Societies" (7) in being too preoccupied with a new wife. Although in another poem (*To Mr. C. B.*, "Thy friend, whom thy deserts") he expressed a more balanced attitude toward male friendship and heterosexual love—"Strong is this love which ties our hearts in one,/And strong that love pursu'd with amorous paine" (7–8)—he treated I. L.'s marriage as a threat to relationships between men (interestingly, the position of the antagonist in the later, more famous poem, "The Canonization").

These verse epistles make sense in terms of the aesthetics of poetic exchange, and Donne thought of them this way. In *To Mr. T. W.* ("All hail sweet Poet"), he acknowledged the reception of some verse from the addressee, as he did in another piece to the same man ("Pregnant again with th'old twins Hope, and Feare"). The Westmoreland Manuscript, in fact, records one of T. W.'s poems to Donne written in response to the receipt of both verse and prose epistles: "Thou sendst me prose & rimes, I send for those / Lynes, w^c beeing nether, seeme or verse or prose."[43] The writer's reference to the unpoetic character of his own verse letter matches Donne's own characterization of his epistles as "harsh verse" (*To Mr. T. W.*, "Hast thee harsh verse") that is more prosaic than poetic: "'Twill be good prose, although the verse be evill" (*To Mr. T. W.*, "All haile sweet Poet," 27). Donne and his correspondents adopted the style of intimate plainspeaking that was both practiced in the Inns-of-Court environment and expected in the humanist verse epistle.

At the same time, Donne employed another mode in some of these poems, the language and manner of courtly Petrarchanism, using it to maintain a level of well-bred politeness proper to the style of a gentleman. In *To Mr. T. W.* ("At once, from hence"), Donne portrayed his absence from his friend as a lover's melancholy suffering. But, more typically, he used this vocabulary to refer to his relationship with a woman known to his friends as his beloved. In *To Mr. I. L.* ("Blest are your North parts"), he referred to her as "My Sun" (2), asking the addressee, who was her host, to report to her his "paine" (22)—i.e, to give her his regards. The letter *To Mr. C. B.* ("Thy friend, whom thy deserts") refers to the same woman, whom Donne had left at Brooke's house, as the "Saint of his Affection" (3), and describes his behavior as a lover in strictly conventional terms:

> . . . loves hot fires, which martyr my sad minde,
> Doe send forth scalding sighes, which have the Art
> To melt all Ice, but that which walls her heart.
> (12–14)

In *To Mr. R. W.* ("Zealously my Muse doth salute all thee"), Donne asked whether his friend had withdrawn to the country to act out the role of the pining lover: ". . . is thy devout Muse retyr'd to sing / Upon her tender Elegiaque string?" (9–10). At this point in his career, at least, Donne thought of the love elegy in old-fashioned terms as the medium for Petrarchan complaint, a form congenial to the gentleman-amorist. In expressing affection for a friend or a mistress, he therefore used the formulas proper to formally polite social relations, adopting a manner that clashed with his intention of plainspeaking familiarity. He had not yet successfully integrated these two rhetorical modes.[44]

Donne seems, however, to have experienced a breakthrough in the rhetorically more consistent formal satires, poems that have both generic and socioliterary affinities with his verse epistles. In these longer poems, particularly in the first two, he addressed himself with stylistic boldness to a receptive audience of peers, articulating more fully than was possible in the verse epistles some of the features of the social world in which they lived. Outside the codes of complimentary politeness, he freed his wit, his language, his critical impulses, and his feelings in the kind of verse that the Inns's atmosphere of "liberty" encouraged. In context, these poems proclaimed not only the values and attitudes poet and readers shared, but also the primary audience's personal knowledge of Donne's experience and behavior. They rested, like the verse letters, on the guarantee of intimate communication provided by their coterie circumstances. It is not surprising, then, that these poems are found in several manuscripts alongside "The Storme" and "The Calme," two ambitious epistles to Christopher Brooke, Donne's closest friend at Lincoln's Inn, the man who might also have been the addressee of *Satire 2*.[45]

Donne composed his first four satires before he entered government service, the first two clearly belonging to his early Inns period.[46] All these poems are the work of a man eager to become a part of the Establishment but angry about the forms of self-abasement necessary to succeed in a world of social, economic, and political power relationships. They were written for an audience of men similarly impatient for preferment and fond of asserting their intellectual, moral, and social autonomy. They assume common attitudes toward City and Court as well as a sophisticated knowledge of the way the social system worked. Reflecting the special interest of Inns men in such topics as religion, literature, and the social skills necessary for advancement in a competitive society, they strike a critical and self-critical stance, satirizing the various routes to success followed by Inns men, including those of the professional lawyer and the gentleman-courtier. The sins and follies that Donne attacked in these poems were part of the daily life of many Inns members. Later, in one of his sermons, he wrote: "We make *Satyrs*; and we looke that the world should call that wit; when God knowes, that that is in a great part, self-guiltinesse, and we doe but reprehend those things, which we ourselves have done, we cry out upon the illnesse of the times, and we make the times ill" (*Sermons*, 7:408). Both he and his readers knew that the stark contrasts of satire obviously distorted their world. Neither Donne nor his readers were scholar-saints, addicted as they both were to the pleasures of City and Court, to some of the very things criticized in these poems—amorous adventuring, fashionmongering, courtly ceremonies of "complement," swaggering and quarreling, and all the other vices of the Inns gentleman. One has only to look to the other satires and to the epigrammatic literature popular at the Inns in the 1590s to see how typical these targets were and how they characterized the life of the Inns residents.

The usual approach to satire by way of intellectual and literary history has obscured the social coordinates of this genre in Elizabethan England.[47] Donne and his contemporaries knew full well that satire was less a way of expressing one's devotion to moral ideals or one's condemnation of worldly vice than it was the literary form practiced by those whose ambitions were frustrated and who yearned to involve themselves more deeply in the social environments they pretended to scorn. The satirist, as Bosola puts it in *The Duchess of Malfi*, "rails at those things which he wants" (I.i.25).[48] Hence, the motive of envy is habitually associated with the satiric urge.[49] Ingenioso, in the *Parnassus* plays, a university wit resembling Thomas Nashe, attacks the world satirically because he cannot find a satisfactory career.[50] Sir John Harington explained the composition of *The Metamorphosis of Ajax* as the product of his unwilling rustication and of the need to be noticed by the Court in which he sought preferment: "I was the willinger to wryte such a toye as this, because, I had layne me thought almost buryed in the Contry these three or fowre yeere; and I thought this would give some occasion to have me thought of and talked of."[51] The subtext of most satiric literature, including Donne's, is the strong attraction to the very world being criticized.[52] Both the sociocultural encoding of this genre and the particular coterie context of Donne's Inns-of-Court audience confirmed this fact.

Of his five satires, the first two especially reflect the Inns-of-Court setting in which they were composed: Donne advertises in them his knowledge of the environment in which he and his audience lived. Sir Isaac Walton's description of Donne's life at Lincoln's Inn as arranged around a regimen of study from four o'clock to ten o'clock each morning, followed by less respectable activities in which he "took great liberty,"[53] seems to be reflected in the poet's splitting of himself in the first satire into the scholar-moralist and the inconstant fool addicted to the fashions of Court and City. In holding up to ridicule the pathetic gull who "Sells for a little state his libertie" (70), Donne expressed his feeling of revulsion for some of the follies in which both he and his peers indulged, particularly their imitation of some of the features of subservient courtly behavior. This antagonist figure in the first satiric poem resembles Sir John Davies' epigrammatic definition of the gull as the man who "feares a velvet gowne, / And when a wench is brave, dares not speake to her" (Kreuger/Nemser, p. 130), a strutting gallant who is really a coward ready to endure "Knockes about the eares" (11), a fashionmonger who speaks nonsense. Donne's gull apes the manners of fashionable gallants and courtiers, bowing and scraping to "men of sort, of parts, of qualities" (105), attracted by every "many-colour'd Peacock" (92). Though he thinks he can "command" (109) at least his mistress, he competes unsuccessfully with rivals and is defeated in a duel (or "quarrel"), finally turned out of doors. His failures in the sophisticated world of social and economic power relations are an object lesson in the dangers that lie beyond the Inns's precincts. Thus, the boundary between self-satirization and satiric attack on the outside world is blurred in such a poem. Just as the satiric persona's intellectual and moral complacency is disturbed by his socially irritating association with the inconstant fool who has befriended him, so too Donne and his readers were, no doubt, morally, intellectually, and emotionally ambivalent about their own attraction to the world outside their chambers.

In the second satire, Donne expressed the Inns gentleman's snobbish hostility to professional lawyers, those "men which chuse / Law practise for meere gaine" (62–63).[54] The target of the attack is a lawyer-poet whose verse is a crass parody of true poetry, but whose real crime is his naked greed, which poses an economic threat to social superiors with whom both Donne and his readers wanted to identify. In fantasizing that this man will use his legal maneuvers to increase his real-estate holdings to the point that "Shortly . . . hee'will compasse all our land" (77), the speaker of the poem treats land as the gentleman's natural possession that should not fall into the hands of ruthless middle-class entrepreneurs—an attitude reflected in the drama of the period, especially in those private theater plays of the first decade of the seventeenth century that formulated similar class conflicts.[55] But the satirist's ethical posture and his social status are portrayed in this poem as precarious. His moral outrage is compromised by his envious resentment of the very man he criticizes. Despite the affirmation of the genteel values he shared with his readers, Donne communicated the frustration of the man whose wish to be a powerful part of the Establishment and to punish socioeconomic abuses was a futile one: ". . . my words none drawes / Within the vast reach of th'huge statute lawes" (111–12). Both this and the previous poem reflect the vulnerability of the Inns gentlemen who scorned the less-dignified kinds of legal and business careers available to them, but who felt unrewarded or rejected by the corrupt, but more socially prestigious, courtly establishment.

In this satire, Donne expressed an aversion to various forms of poetry, an attitude consistent with the harshly unpoetic stance of the formal satirist. He mocked not only hack playwrights and plagiarists, but also those who wrote complimentary verse to beg for money: ". . . they who write to Lords, rewards to get, / Are they not like singers at doores for meat?" (21–22). He objected to those who slavishly followed the literary fashions of the day, including the courtly practice of composing Petrarchan lyrics. The man who "would move Love by rimes" (17) is foolish because he is not aggressive enough: "Rammes, and slings now are seely battery, / Pistolets are the best Artillerie" (19–20). Here as elsewhere, Donne rejected the polite courtly idiom of love poetry, preferring instead a less-delicate assertion of erotic desire, the form of active pursuit of sexual conquests found in those elegies and lyrics he wrote in a deliberately anti-Petrarchan and anti-courtly literary idiom.

Although it has been read primarily in the context of intellectual history,[56] *Satire* 3 takes on a pointed meaning in relation to the steps Donne took to enter the world of political involvement. Given his background as a Catholic and the limitations this placed on his opportunities for advancement, this poem is, at once, both a personal and political statement.[57] In its refusal to adopt a stance of faithful Catholicism, it constitutes a necessary gesture in preparation for the pursuit of a courtly career, but, in its skeptical, even iconoclastic attitudes, it is the kind of dangerous statement whose disclosure outside his coterie Donne feared. In a letter to a friend accompanying some manuscript copies of his prose paradoxes, Donne later expressed his concern about the wider social exposure of the satires and his other verse: ". . . to my satyrs there belongs some feare and to some elegies, and these [paradoxes] perhaps, shame. . . . Therefore I am desirous to hyde them with out any over reconing of them or their maker" (*Selected Prose*, p. 111). It is not difficult to understand how Donne might have been embarrassed about the dissemination of his libertine elegies and lyrics beyond the young male audience of the Inns of Court: their ribaldry and rebelliousness belonged more to the world of the undergraduate or of the rambunctious termers than of the world of adult seriousness. But the "feare" about the satires was probably another matter, related to their socially or politically sensitive subject matter, features that led to the authorities' suppression of the form in 1599.[58]

In the *Satires*, Donne criticized harshly some of his society's central institutions—the Crown, the Court, the Church, and the legal system. This is apparent in many of the boldly irreverent similes that abound in these poems. For example, Coscus the poet-turned-lawyer in the second satire can "to'every suitor lye in every thing, / Like a Kings favorite, yea like a king" (69–70).[59] Referring to this character's vices, the speaker remarks:

> Bastardy'abounds not in Kings titles, nor
> Symonie'and Sodomy in Churchmens lives,
> As these things do in him.
> (74–75)

The treatment of the Court in the fourth satire is merciless. But in the third satiric poem Donne came close to the treasonous and seditious. He did not merely criticize England's foreign adventurism (17–19) and satirize uncritical adherence to the established Church, but he also carefully, if indirectly, rejected the Elizabethan Oath of Allegiance, placing man's responsibility to his conscience and obedience to the laws of God above submission to a merely human law:[60]

> Foole and wretch, wilt thou let thy Soule by ty'd
> To mans lawes, by which she shall not be try'd
> At the last day? Will it then boot thee
> To say a Philip, or a Gregory,
> A Harry, or a Martin taught thee this?
> (93–97)

Under the guise of speaking about all kinds of legal coercion of one's conscience, whether from Catholic or Protestant sources, Donne seems to have directed his fire at the contemporary requirement that all Englishmen, including Roman Catholics, take the Oath. The issue is put finally in terms of the qualified obedience to secular power—a subject someone like Robert Southwell had tried to handle in *An Humble Supplication to Her Maiestie*:[61]

> That thou may'st rightly'obey power, her bounds know;
> Those past, her nature and name's chang'd; to be
> Then humble to her is idolatrie;
> As streames are, Power is; those blest flowers that dwell
> At the rough steames calme head, thrive and prove well,
> But having left their roots, and themselves given
> To the streames tyrannous rage, alas, are driven
> Through mills, and rockes, and woods, 'and at last, almost
> Consum'd in going, in the sea are lost:
>   So perish Soules, which more chuse mens unjust
>   Power from God claym'd, then God himselfe to trust.
> (100–110)

Donne not only stated that subscribing to the Oath of Allegiance was an act of idolatry, but that the power that demanded such compliance was "tyrannous," a dangerous term to use in this context, since it charged the (basically moderate) Elizabeth with the unjust or excessive use of power in the treatment of Catholic subjects.

Even the intellectual and religious idealism of this satire had dangerous implications. By placing Mistress Truth at the moral center of the world, Donne, in effect, ideologically displaced the idealized Queen Elizabeth, who had herself appropriated some of the features of an older Catholic Mariolatry to enhance her power.[62] Of course, by having the satiric speaker withhold his allegiance from secular authority—by refusing to endorse the Oath of Allegiance or the Queen whose power it supported—and by privileging the individual's autonomy of conscience and personal search for truth, Donne not only adopted the stance of intellectual independence favored by him and his associates but also refused to subordinate his beliefs to the demands of political expediency. As he explained in the preface to *Pseudo-Martyr*:

> ... I used no inordinate hast, nor precipitation in binding my conscience to any locall Religion. I had a longer worke to doe than many other men; for I was first to blot out, certaine impressions of the Romane religion, and to wrastle both against the examples and against the reasons, by which some hold was taken; and some anticipations early layde upon my conscience, both by Persons who by nature had a power and superiority over my will, and others who by their learning and good life, seem'd to me justly to claime an interest for the guiding, and rectifying of mine understanding in these matters. And although I apprehended well enough, that this irresolution not onely retarded my fortune, but also bred some scandall, and endangered my spirituall reputation, by laying me open to many mis-interpretations; yet all these respects did not transport me to any violent and sudden determination, till I had, to the measure of my poore wit and judgment, survayed and digested the whole body of Divinity, controverted betweene ours and the Romane Church. (*Selected Prose*, pp. 49–50)

In the third satire Donne refused to defend or reject either Catholicism or the Established Church. He dealt with religion, a subject of intense interest to Inns-of-Court gentlemen,[63] specifically highlighting the political dimension of religious commitment. Donne was all too aware of the sociopolitical dangers and handicaps resulting from his Catholicism, yet, as he explained, he would not abandon the religion of his youth until he had satisfied himself intellectually and morally that it was the right thing to do. In any case, the discussion of the topic in the third satire was not meant for a general audience and Donne probably had very good reasons for fearing the transmission of such a poem beyond its restricted readership.

THE PARADOXICAL, OVIDIAN, AND DRAMATIC ELEGIES

Donne probably wrote the majority of his *Elegies* while he was in the Inns-of-Court environment. Although, as Gardner argues, they were finally gathered for circulation as a set of poems,[64] I think it is inaccurate to define them as a "book" of elegies according to the classical model, for these heterogenous poems really lack the minimal unity necessary for such a collection. Anthony LaBranche, whose essay on them is probably the best general study,[65] mistakenly perceives a single dramatic speaker in all the poems, even though the Ovidian *praeceptor amoris* of "Natures lay Ideot" obviously differs from the courtly lover of "Oh, let mee not serve so," the gentleman-volunteer of the epigrammatic "His Picture," and the emotionally sensitive lover of the valedictory poem "On his Mistris." It is best to approach these works, like the lyrics, as separate compositions rather than as parts of a unified collection, relating them to their coterie circumstances as well as to their antecedents in literary history.

According to both classical and Renaissance humanist tradition, love elegies were young men's poetry,[66] which doubtless influenced Donne's choice of the form. Thomas Campion, Donne's Inns-of-Court contemporary who claimed to be the first Englishman to produce a book of elegies on the Roman model, opened his Latin collection with the warning: "Ite procul tetrici, moneo, procul ite severi, / Ludit censuras pagina nostra graves" (1–2; "Go far away, gloomy men; I warn you, go far away stern men, our page makes sport of serious judgment").[67] In his elegies, Donne displays a youthful iconoclasm, sometimes a cynicism, as he adjusted his pieces to the interests and attitudes of his peers, replacing Ovid's Rome with Elizabethan London[68] and the mythological metaphors of Roman elegies with multiple allusions to contemporary social, economic, and political realities.[69] Individual features of the traditional elegy appealed to him—such as the formal curse, the surprise ending, and the irony of the love-expert tricked by his pupil-mistress.[70] Certainly in turning to this poetic form, Donne was competitively engaged in the practice of producing modern versions of classical genres, a sport in which other Inns authors indulged.[71] But it is misleading to view Donne, as Roma Gill does, as basically "a scholar engaged in the respectable academic pursuit of imitating Ovid."[72] After all, Ovid's *Amores* were never respectable literature in academic environments: Quintilian banned them from the curriculum[73] and Marlowe's translation of them while he was still at Cambridge looks like a characteristic act of impiety.[74] The presence of erotic elegies in commonplace-book miscellanies kept by University and Inns-of-Court students suggests that it was the energetic disrespectfulness of the form that made it fashionable.[75] Nashe's defense of "amorous *Elegies*" as the source of "precious knowledge" for "discerning" readers looks like special pleading.[76] The very fact that Donne, unlike Campion, chose the more accessible vernacular medium for his erotic elegies, breaking the tradition of Neo-Latin poetry with which the genre had been associated,[77] suggests a conscious attempt to take the form out of its academic humanist setting and put it into his contemporary social world.

Donne's *Elegies* generally take the London of the 1590s as the sphere for young men's amorous adventuring,[78] setting an Inns-of-Court sophisticated style against the dominant social and literary modes of the Court, substituting plainspeaking directness for polite compliment, sexual realism for amorous idealization, critical argumentativeness for sentimental mystification, and aggressive masculine self-assertion for politely self-effacing subservience. By replacing the Petrarchan mistress of courtly verse with the less socially and aesthetically elevated creatures of libertine fantasizing and antifeminist invective, Donne imaginatively articulated a set of socioeconomic relationships in which the lover could be portrayed as enjoying independence, scope, and success in his adventures. But, in the light of the actual constraints and frustrations experienced by Inns-of-Court gentlemen hungry for status, preferment, and the other rewards sought for in their Court-centered society, these love poems attempted to satisfy, as John Carey has observed, the need for "the repair of self-esteem . . . a convenient literary compensation for the actual economic, political, and, later, military insufficiency"[79] of Donne and his readers. The manner and matter of the poems, like those of the *Satires*, were grounded in attitudes and circumstances proper to their specific socioliterary environment.

Some of Donne's *Elegies* are verse paradoxes rather than imitations of the classical erotic model. Although the Renaissance paradox, in both its prose and poetic versions, influenced Donne's secular poetry generally, among the *Elegies* one should distinguish pieces like "The Anagram," "The Comparison," "Loves Progress," "The Autumnall," and "Change" from such clearly Ovidian elegies as "Jealousy," "Natures lay Ideot," "Loves Warre," and "Going to Bed," and such dramatically realized pieces as "The Bracelet," "The Perfume," "On his Mistris," and "His Picture." As verse paradoxes, they draw on different literary antecedents and relate to the prose paradoxes Donne composed at the same time.[80] And yet, both they and most of the other *Elegies* grew out of the same Inns-of-Court environment, which provided the social coordinates as well as the primary audience for the poems.

Critics have turned to Donne's prose paradoxes to discover some of the stylistic and aesthetic habits that mark his early poetic compositions, and this is a useful strategy for considering both kinds of work as coterie literature.[81] The ten prose paradoxes are found, for example, along with complete sets of the *Satires* and *Elegies*, in Rowland Woodward's manuscript, which contains a good collection of Donne's early work (with the exception of the early lyrics). Like the *Satires* and *Elegies*, the prose paradoxes evidently circulated among Inns-of-Court readers and found their way, for example, into John Manningham's *Diary* in 1602, where excerpts from Paradox 2 (*"That women ought to paint themselves"*) and Paradox 7 (*"That a wise man is knowne by much Laughinge"*) are alternated with parts of two other paradoxes by another writer (or writers) (*"Hee that weepeth is most wise"* and *"To keepe sheepe the best lyfe"*).[82] The four paradoxes by Sir William Cornwallis found in Sir Stephen Powle's commonplace book[83] and the piece that was part of the 1610 Middle Temple Revels, "A Defence of Womens Inconstancy,"[84] suggest that the prose paradox, like the essay, was popular at the Inns as fashionably iconoclastic literature.

Like the *Elegies* and early lyrics, the prose paradoxes present themselves as youthfully witty performances. Adopting the stances of fashionable gallantry and iconoclastic skepticism, they mock the rigidity and hypocrisy of (older) authority figures,[85] they use the libertine amorist's antifeminism to criticize women,[86] they mock court fops as well as the "colerique firebrands" (p. 16) who braved it through the City, and they demonstrate an ability for humorous self-criticism.[87] They stress group solidarity through the use of first person plural forms and refer to the "nourishing of Civil Societies and mutual Love amongst men" as "one cheife end why we are men" (p. 12). Paradox 9, *"That by Discord things increase,"* contains an exaggerated, but valid, intellectual and aesthetic rationale for much of Donne's writing, portraying discord, dialectic, conflict as the creative conditions with which he felt comfortable.[88] Generally, "arguing, and differing in opinion" (p. 20) produce the result Donne hoped for from these wittily heterodox prose pieces, an increase of sophisticated understanding. In a letter later written to accompany the sending of his paradox collection to a friend, he characterized the works as light recreations "made rather to deceave tyme then her daughter truth" but functioning as intellectual stimuli to the knowledgeable reader: "If they make you to find better reasons against them they do their office: for they are but swaggerers: quiet enough if you resist them. . . . alarums to truth to arme her than enemies" (*Selected Prose*, p. 111). Both they, and the seriocomic verse paradoxes, called for intellectually lively responses from a congenial readership.

Those works among the *Elegies* that are verse paradoxes are written in the iconoclastic, skeptical, anti-authoritarian manner of much of Donne's poetry and prose. They not only assault specific literary conventions and social pieties, but also assert, albeit satirically, the intellectual and critical freedom Donne felt he and his Inns audience valued. As Rosalie Colie has argued, paradoxography, even in its most seemingly trivial forms, was a serious business with broad social as well as intellectual implications.[89] "The Anagram," for example, is a paradoxical encomium cast in the form of facetious advice to a competitor-listener to marry an ugly woman.[90] The speaker and listener are both presumed to be men of wit and fashion, suspicious of beautiful women because experience has taught them that such mistresses are unfaithful—pleasant enough for "one nights revels" (33) but unreliable as mates for husbands who regularly plan to be away from home on "business" (44). This wittily illogical piece evokes a world of amorous adventuring among the sexually promiscuous women of London, but the "things in fashion" (56) in which Donne and his readers indulged are certainly not glamorized, any more than are the more courtly manners with which the poetic blazon of beauty was associated.

The poem works on its readers in a number of ways. First, it amuses them to draw their interest; then it challenges them with its false logic and the speed of its argument;[91] finally it disgusts them, but with a disgust that is consciously presented as the antithesis of elegant literary prurience. The imagery of the poem moves from the playfully innocuous to the outrageous and nauseating. Donne first rearranges "beauties elements" (9) in the facial inventory of the blazon, giving the ugly woman small eyes, a great mouth, dark teeth, rough skin, yellow cheeks and red hair: this is "an Anagram of a good face" (16), wittily compared to a piece of music that rings variations on an original melody. The conclusion to this first section of the poem is a syllogism that rests on a misuse of its key term: "All love is wonder; if wee justly doe / Account her wonderfull, why not lovely too?" (25–26). The dramatic listener is treated with a witty contempt, but the reader is hardly threatened.

The next section begins with what sounds like a cynical articulation of a truism: "Love built on beauty, soone as beauty, dies" (27), but the remainder of the poem actually verifies the statement through progressively more repugnant means. The first metaphor of fallen angels is relatively harmless, but the second, an analogy between reveling and marriage, on the one hand, and "silke and gold" (33), "cloth, and leather" (34), on the other, brings the issue into a direct relationship with the way of life of the coterie readers. The first-person-plural pronoun of line 33 alludes to the life-style the poet and audience shared.

With the metaphor of lines 35 and 36 ("Beauty is barren oft; best husbands say / There is best land, where there is foulest way") the speaker, in his discussion of the "durty fouleness" (42) that guards the woman's virtue, begins to confuse the facial and the genital (as well as the anal), referring alternately to each in a way that comically treats the psychological process of displacement upward involved in the traditional blazon of beauty even as it makes it sexuality repulsive. For example, the metaphor of lines 41–43,

> When Belgiaes citties, the round countries drowne,
> That durty foulenesse guards, and armes the towne:
> So doth her face guard her . . .

and the references to the woman's swarthy complexion (45–46) lead to a discussion of her sexual parts (47–54) that suggests a connection between the foulness of both. The woman is finally perceived as one whom "Dildoes, Bedstaves, and her Velvet Glasse, / Would be as loath to touch as Joseph was" (53–54). The mention of dildoes, especially the exotic "Velvet Glasse" (53) appliance, evokes that world of "fashion" (56) in which young gentlemen-amorists conducted their sexual adventures. The whole poem, in its blatant anti-eroticism, systematically debases this sphere of activity which was mystified by courtly Petrarchan convention as well as by fashionable prurient Ovidianism.[92] The point of the exercise is not to indulge in a virtuoso antifeminism, but to question an entire range of amorous customs and rituals.

In "The Anagram," there is, of course, a strong element of the adversarial beneath the sportive wittiness and shared cynicism. In "The Comparison," a far more scabrous poem in the tradition of festive abuse, the hostility is more explicit. In this piece, Donne unrestrainedly uses the aesthetics of disgust for antierotic purposes, provoking his reader into a critical examination of the opposed languages of idealization and debasement, both of which exaggerate. In its intertwined blazon and antiblazon, the language of vilification contaminates that of praise, revealing that both are distortions. Both also are perceived as having a sexual orientation, for the "best lov'd part" (38) of a woman is presumed to be her genitals.

In this poem Donne assaults the reader with a barrage of scato-

Paradoxical, Ovidian, and Dramatic Elegies 49

logical similes. Sex is portrayed in the most imaginatively energetic sections of the piece as nauseatingly filthy. The perspiration on the antagonist's mistress's brow is "Ranke sweaty froth" "Like spermatique issue of ripe menstruous boiles" (7–8). Her breasts are "like worme eaten trunkes, cloth'd in seals skin" (25). Her complexion has the color of "Sun-parch'd quarters on the citie gate" (31)—a grim reminder of one punishment for treason in Elizabethan England, drawing and quartering. Donne follows the comparison of her vagina to "the dread mouth of a fired gunne" (40) and to a volcano with a question that nastily confuses the oral, genital, and anal in a deliberately offensive way: "Are not your kisses then as filthy,'and more, / As a worme sucking an invenom'd sore?" (43–44). Intercourse is portrayed as "harsh, and violent, / As when a Plough a stony ground doth rent" (47–48). After this, even the contrasting image of the lovemaking of the speaker and his mistress is not without a troubling ambiguity:

> . . . so devoutly nice
> Are Priests in handling reverent sacrifice,
> And such in searching wounds the Surgeon is
> As wee, when wee embrace, or touch, or kisse.
> (49–52)

The same comic aggression underlies the depiction of the bride in the "Epithalamion made at Lincolnes Inne" as one who

> . . . at the Bridegroomes wish'd approach doth lye,
> Like an appointed lambe, when tenderly
> The priest comes on his knees t'embowell her. . . .
> (88–90)

The antifeminist brutality is not entirely disguised in either case.

The technique of the antiblazon that is used in both "The Anagram" and "The Comparison" was conventionally employed for lower-class women. This is the case in the *Arcadia* in Sidney's depiction of Mopsa[93] and in Shakespeare's *Comedy of Errors* (a play performed as part of the Gray's Inn Revels) where Dromio of Syracuse's description of Luce the kitchen wench follows hard upon Antipholus of Syracuse's polite praise of Luciana (III.ii). Sir John Davies's epigram on the "ill favored whore" (14) Gella, "the filthyest wench in Towne" (5), whose cosmetics and fine clothes largely disguise her sordid ugliness, is in the same tradition. Gentlemen, partly because of their fear of venereal disease (referred to in some of the metaphors in "The Comparison"), preferred sexual experience with the wives and daughters of London citizens to the riskier involvement with professional prostitutes:[94] this is the class snobbery that makes the final punishment of Lucio in *Measure for Measure* so appropriate. As Spenser's Duessa, some of Jonson's upper-class female characters, and the grotesque creations of Jacobean drama suggest, the kind of satiric antifeminism found in the antiblazon was used against women of higher station—notoriously in such forms as moral and satiric attacks on cosmetics, clothesmongering, and promiscuity. Donne and his readers knew not only that, according to Ovid's *Remedia Amoris*, the hideous and disgusting could serve as antidotes to superficial amorous attraction, but also that the satiric debasement of women could imply a general critique of the cult of female beauty with its prescribed forms of hyperbolic praise—found at Court in wooing an aging, rotten-toothed, cosmetically plastered Queen Elizabeth as a lovely goddess or, in more pedestrian circumstances, in complimenting mistresses. In "The Anagram" and "The Comparison" Donne crudely and awkwardly attacked not only some of the conventions of courtly amorous politeness but also the fashionable sexual adventuring in which he and his fellows indulged.

"Loves Progress" is in a similar mode, arguing that the technique of the blazon by which a lover praises his mistress's physical beauty starting with her facial features is an inefficient one, since one can reach faster the sexual fruition that is the "right true end of love" (2) by beginning with her feet: this is, incidentally, the direction Nashe's lover takes in "The Choice of Valentines."[95] There is an interesting aspect, however, to the demystifying strategy of "Loves Progress" in the way it associates what Davies called "love and lucre" (Kreuger/Nemser, p. 172). Using terms that reappear in many of his Ovidian elegies, Donne lays bare the connections between amorous and economic desires and exploits, in terms that his Inns audience could particularly appreciate.

It is clear that one of the ends of love assumed in this poem is the economic one. From the first, the sexual is defined in relation to commercial realities:

> Who ever loves, if hee doe not propose
> The right true end of love, hee's one which goes
> To sea for nothing but to make him sicke.
> (1–3)

As in Shakespeare's *Merchant of Venice*, there is an implicit analogy between erotic and commercial venturing.[96] Later in the poem woman as a sexual creature is likened to gold as an economic commodity:

> .. Preferre
> One woman first, and then one thing in her.

> I, when I value gold, may thinke upon
> The ductillness, the application,
> The wholesomeness, the ingenuity,
> From rust, from soyle, from fyre ever free,
> But if I love it, 'tis because 'tis made
> By our new Nature, use, the soule of trade.
>   All these [qualities] in women wee might thinke upon
> (If women had them) but yet love but one.
>   (9-18)

The "one thing" that this impudently paradoxical poem argues a man should value in a woman is her "Centrique part" (36), metaphorically "her India" (65), so named after the part-actual, part-fantasized goal of oceanic trading voyages. Finally, combining downward displacement with another economic image, the poem states aphoristically:

> Rich Nature hath in woman wisely made
> Two purses, and their mouths aversely laid:
> They then which to the lower tribute owe
> That way which that exchequer lookes must goe.
>   (91-94)

In unmasking the self-serving erotic and avaricious impulses behind cynical libertine attitudes, Donne suggests the less-flattering motives involved in more politely decorous forms of wooing. Raymond Southall's provocative discussion of the marked predominance of commercial metaphors in sixteenth-century love poetry[97] suggests that it was not only libertine or antifeminist verse that treated women as economic symbols. Donne invited his audience to see that Mammon was disguised as Cupid even in Petrarchan and Neoplatonic love poetry. The final effect of "Loves Progress," despite its obscenity, is antierotic.

The rhetorical, intellectual, and social coordinates of "The Autumnall" mark it as a poem addressed to the same kind of male audience Donne chose for his other verse and prose paradoxes.[98] This piece, which argues the virtues of having a middle-aged mistress, with whom love would be more a matter of "Reverence" (6) than "voluptuousnesse" (22), assumes the usual context of the gentleman's amorous adventuring: "Yong Beauties force your love" (3), the speaker says to his audience of peers, later using a simile ("Lanke, as an unthrifts purse" [38]) that refers to the prodigality of fashionable gallants. Because this poem seems to embody an argument consistent with some of the purposes of encomiastic verse, however, it has been discussed as a poem of compliment, written, perhaps, for a woman like Mrs. Magdalen Herbert (whom, some argue, Donne may have met as early as 1600).[99] But the evidence for this social context is weak and, although the statement that "Affection here takes Reverences name" (6) defines well the character of the "love" expressed in conventional complimentary poetry, this poem utilizes the form and strategies of the other verse paradoxes. Donne seems sophistically to present the case for loving a mature woman as a way of subverting some of the contemporary fashionable forms of both polite and libertine loving to which his readers were attracted. The title of the piece in the Stephens Manuscript, "A Paradox of an ould woman,"[100] is probably an accurate assessment of the poem's (sub)genre. It lacks the signs of direct or indirect complimentary purpose.[101]

Donne's Ovidian elegies reflect some of the social and economic struggles of Inns-of-Court gentlemen who were involved not only in their immediate urban surroundings but in the larger society as well. Like private-theater satiric comedies a decade later, these poems portray successful sexual adventuring among the married and unmarried women of middle-class London as young men's fantasy-triumphs over economic disadvantages, specifically as symbolic victories over a citizenry whose wealth Inns men resented. Many Inns of Court gentlemen, especially those who, as younger brothers, had little or no hope of inheriting money and property, looked to the urban merchant class to find rich wives for themselves. Donne's "Epithalamion made at Lincolnes Inne" comically celebrates an Inns man's prosperous union with a woman of the urban bourgeoisie: speaking for his peers, Donne addressed the "Daughters of London" as "Our Golden Mines, and furnish'd Treasurie" (13–14). The city woman who was "faire, rich, glad" (23) represented the gentleman's dream of economic freedom and prosperity. At the same time, as John Carey has argued, the rich middle-class woman of late Elizabethan London was regarded by Donne and his fellows as a threat, "frighteningly emancipated and self-assertive."[102] Antifeminist love poems depicting the sexual conquest of such women and a satiric attitude toward the class to which they belonged were, thus, the products of socioeconomic resentment and of larger class rivalries. When literary works dramatize the libertine lover's loss of control over the women he happily exploited, they present a phenomenon symptomatic of young men's inability to master other social, economic, and political circumstances. The Inns-of-Court prose paradox "In Defence of Womens Inconstancy" jokingly admits that women "will . . . never be tamed nor commanded by us" (*Selected Prose*, p. 6), but, behind the stance of rambunctious male libertinism implicit in this work and in much erotic poetry written in the Inns environment lay the frustrated desire to control not simply women but all those unmanageable circumstances of life in the larger society in which young gentlemen felt vulnerable and inadequate.

Such a social context is implicit in an ironic elegy like "Natures lay Ideot," a poem in which a gentleman-lover is outraged that his middle-class paramour has escaped his governance.[103] In this poem a libertine speaker criticizes his mistress morally for abandoning him after he has taught her all the sophisticated ways of adulterous love. The relationship is defined as originally one of (gentleman) master and (middle-class female) pupil: the lover has instructed his mistress in "The mystique language of the eye [and] hand" (4), the gestures of amorous deceit necessary to escape a jealous husband's detection. Before this tutelage, she was a docile, quiet wife, but, after the lover "sever'd" her "from the worlds Common" (21), and "Refin'd" her "with amorous delicacies" "into a blis-full paradise" (23–24), she left him for other lovers. The excited metaphors of the poem's conclusion underscore the libertine lover's crude possessiveness and lack of self-conscious irony:

> I planted knowledge and lifes tree in thee,
> Which Oh, shall strangers taste? Must I alas
> Frame and enamell Plate, and drinke in Glasse?
> Chafe waxe for others seales? breake a colts force
> And leave him then, beeing made a ready horse?
> (26–30)

Incensed because he has lost a valuable possession—alternately a precious object he had made or a horse he has broken—he sees no contradiction between his sexual greed and the civilized refinement of which he boasts. Donne suggests that the former is implicit in the latter and that the spectacle of the betrayal of the sophisticated libertine is ironically amusing.

The erotic elegy "To his Mistress Going to Bed" also belongs to the same social context as "Natures lay Ideot," for it specifically dramatizes an encounter between a witty young man and a middle-class city woman. John Carey has argued that the term of address used in the first line of the poem, "Madame" (1):

> . . . is a word, above all of social deference: a word into which all the social consciousness of the young Inns of Court men can be packed, all their hatred for the aspirations of the enviably rich citizen-class woman. In Donne the word is filled with sarcasm: he is savouring his triumph, relishing his humiliation of a wealthy lady as he commands her to strip. For the young men of Lincoln's Inn the poem would be a perfect vicarious readjustment of social realities. The emphasis upon the richness of each expensive garment as it is taken off . . . is important for the same reason."[104]

The differences between Donne's poem and its classical model, Ovid's *Amores* I.5, are revealing. Whereas Ovid's poem is a narrative of a past event, Donne's is set in the dramatic present, highlighting the comedy of the lover's erotically importunate commands and allowing for the surprising information that the speaker is naked to be postponed to the end of the poem. While Ovid's Corinna comes to her lover lightly dressed, the woman in Donne's poem is elaborately clothed in fashionable garb; and so, while Ovid's lover had only to snatch off his mistress's tunic, the mistress in Donne's poem goes through several steps to undress herself down to her white smock. While Corinna puts up a (sexually exciting) struggle, the mistress in Donne's poem does not—except perhaps in her hesitation in removing her last bit of clothing. Ovid's amorist takes time to describe his mistress's nakedness before he gets to the actual lovemaking, providing the opportunity for a certain degree of sensual heightening of the verse. Donne's lover plays with his mistress emotionally and intellectually more than sexually: the erotic gestures are accompanied by humorous commentary, so there is little sensuousness or prurience in the poem. Ovid focuses entirely on the erotic scene he portrays, but Donne fills his poem with metaphoric distractions, using the mistress's clothes and body as occasions for witty metaphors. While Ovid's elegy is an imaginatively excited (if brief) poem about satisfying sexual experience, Donne's is a curiously antierotic treatment of a sexual encounter.

"To his Mistris Going to Bed" celebrates wit as a way of mastering an erotic situation comically. It does not offer the kind of poetic sensuality found in the erotic epyllion of the 1590s, a literary fashion mocked tantalizingly in another Inns-of-Court literary work, John Marston's *The Metamorphosis of Pygmalions Image*.[105] Instead of passive immersion in sensual experience, Donne depicts, through the poem's brusque imperatives ("Come" [1], "Off" [5], "Unpin" [7], "Unlace" [9], "Licence" [25], etc.), through the witty metaphors and allusions, and through an aggressive (if comically self-aware) male sexuality, the kind of confident control of experience he and his audience of Inns-of-Court gentlemen desired. Phallic narcissism and economic ambition are joined in the speaker's exclamations accompanying his touching of his mistress's "centrique part":

> Oh my America, my new found lande,
> My kingdome, safliest when with one man man'd,
> My myne of precious stones, my Empiree,
> How blest am I in this discovering thee.

> To enter in these bonds is to be free,
> Then where my hand is set my seal shall be.
> (27–32)

Sexual, economic, and legal/political power are wittily confused in this apostrophe, as Donne portrays here and throughout the poem the clever young man's triumph in a familiar, if fictionalized, social world.

Like "To his Mistress Going to Bed," "Jealosie" portrays the young lover as a sexual adventurer having an adulterous affair with a middle-class woman, in this case the wife of a wealthy, older, jealous husband. This poem has love, youth, and play imaginatively triumph over jealousy, age, and money, but sex and money are connected rather than contrasted by the counterfeiting metaphor the speaker uses:

> . . . if, as envious men, which would revile
> Their Prince, or coyne his gold, themselves exile
> Into another countrie,'and doe it there,
> Wee play'in another house, what should we feare?
> (26–30)

The simile suggests that, for the young gallant, sexual success is a substitute for a wished-for economic power as anti-authoritarian bravado disguises vulnerability and "envious" resentment.

In the elegy "Loves Warre," Donne deals with military adventuring.[106] Although the mistress in the poem is technically the addressee, the speaker seems to look beyond her to an audience of understanding males who can appreciate the witty editorializing about the follies and frustrations of military exploits. Donne blurs the boundary between the internal and external audiences as, for example, he uses the first-person-plural pronoun in an ambiguous way. In one passage he writes,

> Other men warre that they their rest may gaine,
> But we will rest that wee may fight againe.
> Those warres the ignorant, these th'experienc'd love;
> There wee are alwayes under, here above.
> (33–36)

The first "we" refers to the speaker and his mistress, the second to the group of sexual and military adventurers of which the speaker (or the poet) is a part. In both its subject matter and phallic aggressiveness, the poem really seems most concerned with the male audience.

Although it was not published until 1802, "Loves Warre" is nonetheless found in the collection of elegies preserved in the Westmoreland manuscript. In its original coterie situation, this poem, one of the most Ovidian of the elegies, was more than a modish literary exercise. Since military expeditions and privateering were significant contemporary realities for Donne and his Inns audience, the subject of the poem was a topical one. Like other contemporaries, many of them looked to military service as a means to wealth, preferment, and honor, despite the fact that few prospered from the experience. Lawrence Stone, in his discussion of soldiering in late Elizabethan England, has concluded that "War did not pay its English practitioners."[107] Few men enriched themselves on privateering ventures or on military expeditions. Honor was a fragile commodity, won only at great, often foolhardy, risk. The military route to advancement was not an easy one: though, as Gabriel Harvey recommended, soldiers could win some patronage by devoting themselves "to sum ualiant especial nobleman"[108] such as the Earl of Essex, the Queen was inveterately suspicious of professional soldiers. Despite all this, young men in need of money, employment, and social prestige (including Donne himself and many of his friends), romanticized adventure and warfare, offering themselves as gentlemen-venturers and gentlemen-volunteers.[109] "Loves Warre" deromanticizes such activity through some of the strategies of the formal paradox and of the Ovidian elegy.

One of the important terms in "Loves Warre" is "service" (46), used in its pointed conclusion, but throughout this poem soldiering is defined as a public activity performed for the monarch and the state. Donne wittily subordinates military service to sexual service with typical elegiac logic—as he does later in "The Canonization" where the "Soldiers [who] finde warres" (16) are inferior to the couple who make love. In "Oh, let me not serve so" Donne uses state service and amorous service as ironic commentary upon one another, establishing a relationship between the two from the very start:

> Oh, let me not serve so, as those men serve
> Whom honours smokes at once fatten and sterve
> Poorely enrich't with great mens words or lookes;
> Nor so write my name in thy loving bookes
> As those Idolatrous flatterers, which still
> Their Princes stiles, with many Realmes fulfill
> Whence they no tribute have, and where no sway.
> Such services I offer as shall pay
> Themselves, I hate dead names: Oh then let mee
> Favorite in Ordinary, or no favorite bee.
> (1–10)

In the route to preferment taken by way of the patronage of "great men," mainly the major influential aristocrats and power brokers of Elizabethan England, complimentary rhetoric, sometimes outright flattery, was the prescribed social currency—as it was in transactions with the monarch. In a country ruled over by a Queen who sometimes encouraged her courtiers to woo her in the language of polite amorousness, it was connected with the deferential terms of Petrarchan love against whose conventions Donne rebelled in this poem.

This elegy stands apart from the Ovidian poems of urban sexual adventuring in depicting a relationship with a married woman of the Court who must be wooed with polite Petrarchan language, a mistress who enjoys having several admirers.[110] The speaker uses conventional terms in threatening to respond to her "scorne" (31) and "hate" (43) with his. He turns the point of view represented by the kind of advice found in Ovid's *Remedia Amoris* against that held by the frustrated Petrarchan amorist: he raises the possibility that he will be cured of love and, consequently, "survay" the woman with "new eyes" (39), able to "renounce" the "dalliance" (44) with her. He rejects fruitless Petrarchan wooing, involving formulaic "oathes" and "kisses" (12) and the migration of the lover's "Soule" (11) to the mistress's heart, but, with it, the whole code demanding from him subservience, passivity, and the willingness to endure long frustration. The aggressively blunt language[111] and the bawdy suggestion that sexual "services" are preferable to courtly ones connect this poem with the other elegies, but the general issues raised by it, in context, suggest that, in the experience of the Inns gentlemen who functioned in both City and Court, the socioeconomic relationships of the urban elegies are related to those of this one. Economically vulnerable in both environments, Donne and his readers knew that the kind of swagger affected in one social world was the mirror opposite of the prescribed deference of the other.

The last group of poems from the *Elegies* I would like to consider are those that might be looked upon as the most dramatic, "The Bracelet," "The Perfume," and "On his Mistris."[112] There are, of course, dramatic elements in other elegies, such as "Going to Bed" and "Jealosie," but in these particular poems Donne more fully articulates the fictional situations, portraying the kinds of complex dramatic and emotional interplay of speaker and listener that characterize some of his best love poetry. In them the woman or the beloved is a richly imagined presence and the reader's pleasure is assumed to rest partly in his ability to construct a drama of thought and feeling from subtly presented cues.

Critics have long acknowledged Donne's dramatic conception of love poetry. Leishman, for example, called him "an essentially *dramatic* poet"[113] and LaBranche identified his "full understanding and use of the dramatic speaker" as "an extreme innovation."[114] Comparing Donne with his main classical model, Leishman wrote: "While Ovid merely describes situations, Donne enacts them: the nature and details of the situation emerge, as it were, incidentally, from an overheard discourse or tirade."[115] Ellrodt argues that a confluence of influences accounts for this increase in the dramatic conception of the love elegy and the lyric: the popularity of contemporary theater,[116] the appearance of a journalistic style, the dramatic features in other important literary forms such as the satire and epigram, the "aesthetic of discontinuity" associated with the urban environment.[117] This is to say nothing of the style of dramatic self-presentation fashionable in polite society, a subject Stephen Greenblatt has discussed so well.[118] Beyond this, however, we should look to the coterie situation of the verse for the aesthetic and social coordinates of the dramatic elegies and lyrics.

Understanding this subject requires that we blur somewhat the sharp distinctions between poet and persona, internal and external rhetorical relationships, fictional and real worlds. In an essay on Donne's elegies, Alan Armstrong discusses their dramatic character in terms of "the persona's unremitting awareness of his projected image and of his audience, which creates the impression . . . of the active presence of the speaker."[119] This definition, which assumes a separation between persona and fictive listener, ought to be broadened to include the poet-reader relationship.[120] In this context, Donne expected his audience to have the literary and social sophistication enabling them to contribute cocreatively to the dramatic and rhetorical realization of his poetic texts. More generally, in late Elizabethan England, such an ability was regarded as a proper one for young gentlemen. Emotionally nuanced and dramatically suggestive poems were written for cultural sophisticates like the gentlemen with whom Donne associated while at Lincoln's Inn. They were expected to be able to exercise their sympathetic imagination to appreciate sketchily presented scenes of amorous intimacy associated with a whole range of polite and libertine erotic experience.[121] In using the theater metaphor in his introduction to Sidney's *Astrophil and Stella*, Thomas Nashe assumed that "Gentlemen" readers would value a "tragicomedy of loue . . . performed by starlight"[122] partly because they would have had the social awareness and sensibility needed to read such poems. In his dramatic elegies, as well as in his lyrics, Donne, like Sidney, left much to the imagination, believing that his reader had the social, literary, intellectual, and psychological sophistication necessary to fill out, from very few signals, the emotional drama of particular poems, an activity that was an essential preliminary to the perception of their ironies. Although we tend to regard such skills as part of the literary competence of readers generally, they were looked on in the Renaissance as the accomplishments of educated (courtly or satellite-courtly) gentlemen. Donne's chosen audience for his dramatic elegies and lyrics is only one example of a larger cultural phenomenon.

"The Bracelet," a poem singled out for praise by Ben Jonson,[123] begins not only in the midst of a love relationship, but also in the middle of a dramatic encounter that the poet invites his reader to reconstruct. The ironic tone of the first verse paragraph is the sort adopted by some the antisentimental sentimentalists in Shakespeare's romantic comedies, here used by Donne to establish a mode of intimate communication, the dramatic and emotional implications of which the reader is supposed to draw:

> Not that in colour it was like thy haire,
> For Armelets of that thou maist let me weare;
> Nor that thy hand it oft embrac'd and kist,
> For so it had that good which oft I mist;
> Nor for that seely old moralitie,
> That as those links are tyed our love should be;
> Mourne I that I thy seavenfold chaine have lost,
> Nor for the luck sake; but the bitter cost.
> (1–8)[124]

The mention of love tokens and hair-bracelets defines the love relationship as a fashionable one between social equals, not that of a witty gentleman and a less-sophisticated middle-class woman found in several of the elegies already examined. The assumption here, and through the rest of the poem, is that the fictive listener has the sophistication to understand the witty rhetorical indirections of her lover and that, beyond the frame of the fiction, the coterie reader, whose fashionable gallantry is represented in the style of the speaker, can both sympathetically and critically evaluate the social and emotional drama taking place. In these first lines the negations contradictorily assert that the lover deeply cares for his mistress and that he is only concerned about money: the emotional and discursive lines of development clash at this point and throughout the poem—as they do in the verbal encounters of Beatrice and Benedick in Shakespeare's *Much Ado About Nothing*. The antiromantic pose of the speaker cannot disguise the fact that he is complimenting his mistress's (conventionally) blond hair, noticing her every gesture, yearning for her physical affection, teasing her about her coyness, and expressing belief in, rather than cynicism about, the symbolism of the linked chain. The significant statement made by the opening of this elegy is that the lover feels secure enough about their relationship to communicate with her through affectionately ironic teasing. The anticlimactic assertion at the end of this verse paragraph that he is only worried about the "cost" of replacing the lost bracelet is a comic pretense.[125]

This elegy wittily transfers the conventional avariciousness of the elegiac mistress to the lover himself, a change that allowed Donne to reflect on some of the socioeconomic ironies of the gallantry he and his fellow Inns members affected.[126] Roman love elegists often complained about the selfish venality of their mistresses. Propertius's Cynthia goes to bed with a soldier home from the wars because he can give her expensive presents the penurious poet cannot afford (II.16); Tibullus's Delia acts similarly by entertaining the poet's rivals to his great torment. The lover in Ovid's *Amores* bitterly criticizes his mistress's greed: he objects to her request for gifts (*Amores*, I.10) and, when he writes about her going to bed with a soldier for money, he expresses ironic outrage at the avariciousness of the times. All three writers have poems cursing the materialistic bawds who ply their mistresses' souls.[127] Ovid, for example, attacks Dipsas for trying to persuade Corinna to accept a rich lover (the very advice that estranges Juliet from her Nurse in *Romeo and Juliet*). Poetry and love are both seen as threatened by money; since these poets can offer only the first two, they are bitterly angry that their mistresses should want the third.

In "The Bracelet" Donne's speaker does not analyze or directly attack the motives underlying the mistress's demand that the lost gold chain be replaced: instead he satirizes himself, then uses a scapegoat figure as the recipient of the hostile feelings evoked by the situation. With comic obliqueness, Donne ironically comments on some of the economic realities of the way of life he shared with his fellow Inns men. Like the speaker of this poem, the typical Inns-of-Court gentleman knew that money was the basis of a great many social relationships, the means not only to "gaine new friends" or "appease great enemies" (15), but also to contracting successful marriages. On the one hand, the fashionable gallant could look on it, as the speaker here does facetiously, as "my guard, my ease, my food, my all" (50), the nourisher of "hope" (51) or of career prospects as well as of "able youth, and lustyhead" (52). On the other hand, he knew that he would be unattractive to many women as a lover and potential spouse if his wealth were small: the speaker of this poem accuses his mistress of caring so much about money that she would love him "lesse" (54) when he has spent some of his precious capital to replace her bracelet. The life of fashion was an expensive activity for Inns men; Donne, we know, spent much of his £750 inheritance while at Lincoln's Inn.[128] Such financial problems underlie the wit of this poem.

This elegy, like so many of the others, digressively alludes to the larger (international) political world in which young English gentlemen functioned: many of them, after all, served in the Continental wars in France and the Low Countries. But, for example in the long section comparing (superior) English coinage with foreign currencies, Donne's speaker does not really lose sight of the dramatic center of the piece. In referring to the pride and greed of the post-Armada Spanish, who used their gold to overthrow governments and upset economies, and in alluding to the venereal disease supposedly rampant in France, the fashionably "Gorgeous" lover, who is liable to be prodigally "ruin'd, ragged, and decay'd" (40), seems to be exorcising his own base motives and degeneracy, dissociating himself from irresponsible gallantry and money-grubbing. The elaborate curse of the last part of the poem, a self-conscious set piece of wit, is a release mechanism for the speaker's aggressive feelings, which themselves are set in a social framework. After wishing a hypothetical "wretched Finder" (91) of the lost bracelet damnation and "hellish paines" (96), the curse picks up some of the themes developed earlier, suggesting that the world outside the lovers' relationship is one of political scheming, murder, "libells" (101). The public world is both vicious and avaricious. The speaker revealingly wishes his unknown enemy the very punishments appropriate to his own prodigality: "Lust-bred diseases rot thee'and dwell with thee / Itchy desire and no abilitie" (103–4). Donne breaks the rhetorical frame of the curse, however, when he has the speaker include "love and marriage" (108) in his maledictions: internally, within the dramatic frame, this is a surprise to the mistress-listener—a startling bit of antisentimental teasing that brings the situation back to the emotional relationship that the lost bracelet symbolizes. William Rockett is right to notice that the speaker's rhetoric in this poem has a deliberate "comic futility."[129] But, again, this comedy opens out into the world of the coterie readers as well. John Carey observes that the antimarriage joke here is a sign of a typical Inns-of-Court mockery of Puritan pieties about the marital state,[130] part of a stance of fashionable gentlemanly libertinism, but the humor contains an element of self-satirization: gallant libertinism is not left unchallenged here any more than it is in Donne's other ironic love poems. The shift at the end of "The Bracelet" to forgiveness, repentance, and the "heart" (114), the last word of this love elegy, dramatically reasserts the love that was disingenuously denied at the poem's outset, thus undercutting not only the stance of smug libertinism but also the wittiness associated with it, the latter a rhetorical and poetic force that seems finally to undo itself in the act of defending against the very emotional realities to which it returns. The response called for at the end of this elegy—"'tis cordiall, would 'twere at thy heart" (114)—is not expected from the hypothetical finder so much as from the mistress and, imaginatively, from the reader, a rhetorically multivalent strategy characteristic of Donne.

The word "thy" of the last line of "The Bracelet" thus has more than one referent. The whole last section of "The Perfume" (53–70) contains a similar rhetorical ambiguity. In this elegy, another witty speaker, here a perfumed darling of the *beau monde*, wittily satirizes himself and the caricatured members of his young mistress's family on the occasion of the discovery of their sexual relationship. In apostrophizing as the hated cause of his problem the perfume that revealed his presence in the house to his mistress's father, the speaker uses language that sounds as though he were attacking the mistress herself, both generally about the supposed faults of her sex and particularly about some problem in their relationship:

> . . . thou bitter sweet, whom I had laid
> Next mee, mee traiterously hast betraid,
> And unsuspected hast invisibly
> At once fled unto him, and staid with mee.
> Base excrement of earth, which dost confound
> Sense, from distinguishing the sicke from sound;
> By thee the seely Amorous sucks his death
> By drawing in a leprous harlots breath;
> By thee, the greatest staine to mans estate
> Falls on us, to be call'd effeminate;
> Though you be much lov'd in the Princes hall,
> There, things that seeme, exceed substantiall;
> Gods, when yee fum'd on altars, were pleas'd well,
> Because you'were burnt, not that they lik'd your smell;
> You'are loathsome all, being taken simply'alone:
> Shall wee love ill things joyn'd, and hate each one?
> If you were good, your good doth soone decay;
> And you are rare, that takes the good away.
> (53–70)[131]

There is a joking antifeminism implicit in the rhetorical assault on the perfume: the lines suggest that women, like perfume, are "Base excrement of earth," sexually and morally destructive to men, whom they effeminize, fair creatures who are "much lov'd in the Princes hall" but who were ritually sacrificed in ancient times, "ill things" without real "good." The implication is that it is the mistress who has, somehow, betrayed her lover and this fact underlies the antifeminist vehemence of this section.[132]

By this point in the elegy, however, Donne assumed that his reader would have picked up enough of the signals to be able to understand why such a strategy was used. In the context of the (melo)dramatic situation and the sketchy history of the love relationship the poem provides, the speaker implies that the mistress, despite the fact that she was moved by "love" to deceive her own mother for his sake, emotionally wavers in her commitment to him. Thus he insistently caricatures her family and household as hostile to youth and love, and concludes the poem with a couplet raising the possibility of her father's death. In line with the suggestion in the previous lines that the mistress has somehow "betrayed" him, these final two lines of direct address are a particularly aggressive form of teasing:

> All my perfumes, I give most willingly
> To'embalme thy fathers corse; What? will hee die?
>
> (71–72)

Given Donne's usual emphasis on endings, it is reasonable to suppose that this concluding couplet contains an issue of major significance for the whole poem. Even though the lover has characterized himself—with his "silkes" (51) and "loud perfume" (40)—as a dandified sexual adventurer, possibly a fortune hunter as well, there are suggestions that, behind the exaggerations and satiric wittiness there is a serious emotional relationship at stake in this poem.

The witty assault on the beloved's family, in whose midst the lovers had "sweet nights" (28) of secret lovemaking, is actually more than a simple attack on those who would prevent the young people from enjoying one another sexually; it is, as well, a defense against the forces of parental tyranny, mercenary values, and suspicious cynicism that would destroy young love, as they do in a play like *Romeo and Juliet*. The father's opposition to the young man as a suitor has something to do with his desire to dispose of his property ("his goods" [11]) as he sees fit in an approved marriage for his daughter. The mother's suspicions about her daughter arise from her inability to conceive of love as anything more than "ranke lustinesse" (24). Having been threatened with disinheritance (9–11), the mistress has risked much to meet secretly with her lover, so why does the speaker suggest that she has betrayed him?

In the heightened feelings of the dramatic situation, this facetious suggestion, like the whole comic strategy of the piece, is a way of displacing attention from the real problem the lovers face, that of discovery and forced separation, to, first, the past victories they shared over her father, mother, and "grim eight-foot-high iron-bound servingman" (31) and, then, to the attitude of the mistress herself. If, as I suspect, the drama of the poem requires a response on the part of the mistress that both indicates her participation in the comic self-confidence of her lover and demonstrates her renewed commitment to him, the accusation of treachery or betrayal is a witty translation of the real problem of having to cope with parental opposition into a false problem of the mistress's attitude. Thus, all that is necessary for the poem's conclusion to work is for the reader to imagine the mistress's responding to the suggestion that she is holding back on her commitment to her lover because of her attachment to her father by reaffirming both her love and her willingness to risk even more in the future. The comically blunt elements in this elegy really disguise its romantic stance toward its materials. As happens often in Shakespeare, tough-minded wit and emotional sensitivity fuse nicely.

The situation of the dramatic elegy "On his Mistris" looks like it is borrowed from romance and romantic comedy: this poem presents a scene in which the lover responds simultaneously to his mistress's unrealistic proposal that she accompany him on his journey disguised as a page and to the underlying feelings that generated the plan. He prefaces his rejection of the suggestion with a brief recital of the history of their relationship to create a framework for the strategies of consolation in this valedictory situation:

> By our first strange and fatall interview,
> By all desires which thereof did ensue,
> By our long sterving hopes, by that remorse
> Which my words masculine perswasive force
> Begot in thee, and by the memory
> Of hurts which spies and rivalls threatned mee,
> I calmely beg, but by thy parents wrath,
> By all paines which want and divorcement hath,
> I conjure thee; and all those oathes which I
> And thou have sworne, to seal joint constancie,
> Here I unsweare, and over-sweare them thus:
> Thou shalt not love by meanes so dangerous.
> Temper, oh faire Love, loves impetuous rage,
> Be my true mistris still, not my feign'd page.
> (1–14)

Paradoxical, Ovidian, and Dramatic Elegies 65

These self-reflexive lines argue that parting is necessary, but also, more significantly, that a love that has already survived threats and challenges ("spies and rivalls," parental hostility, "want and divorcement") will remain alive through the period of separation. Speaking to an obviously distraught mistress with the voice of calm consolation, the lover uses the occasion to reswear previous oaths, an act which, like the reiteration of baptismal vows at Eastertime, strengthens a preexistent bond.

On this bond of "joint constancie" the whole poem rests. But, after assuring his beloved that she is "onely worthy to nurse in [his] minde / Thirst to come back" (16–17), the lover does not elaborate the familiar constancy theme in a straightforward manner, signaling a shift in the poem's tone and manner with the antisentimental brashness of "Feede on this flatterye, / That absent lovers one in th'other bee" (25–26). Engaging in the kind of affectionate teasing we find in many of Donne's best dramatic lyrics, he disguises the idea of fidelity in the comic-satiric fantasy he creates to illustrate to his mistress the (primarily sexual) dangers she would face should she accompany him abroad. This technique of distraction not only relieves the emotional tension of the poem's initial situation, but also, by means of an implicit contrast of the speaker's behavior with that of the corrupt foreigners he caricatures, acts as an oblique assurance of his fidelity. Identifying French fashionmongering and lust, Italian homosexuality, and Dutch drunkenness as species of inconstancy (interestingly, that familiar symbol of inconstancy, the moon, introduces this short satiric catalog), the speaker explicitly argues that it is better for his mistress to stay in sturdy, virtuous England than to journey with him into the lands of the lechers, buggers, and drunkards. Between the lines he says, "I will keep myself unstained by the vices of these absurd foreigners while I am away from you."

The speaker does not, however, attempt to eliminate as decisively his beloved's other major fear, that he will die in his absence. After suggesting that she might be the one to die first (17–18), he seems, in the first part of the poem, to argue for resignation—although he may be stressing the dangers of travel partly to dissuade her from undertaking the journey with him:

> Thy (else Almighty) Beauty cannot move
> Rage from the seas, nor thy love teach them love,
> Nor tame wilde Boreas harshness; Thou hast read
> How roughly hee in peices shivered
> Faire Orithea, whome he swore hee lov'd.

> Fall ill or good,'tis madness to have prov'd
> Dangers unurg'd. . . .
>
> (19–25)

Perhaps naming her fear might serve to diminish it, but these lines clearly stress, rather than play down, the genuine dangers of travel. It is only after the speaker has argued decisively against her proposal to accompany him and has assured her of his constancy that he can return to his beloved's concern for his safety and handle it comically in reducing it to an explicit melodramatic fantasy:

> [do not] fright thy nurse
> With midnights startings, crying out, oh, oh,
> Nurse, oh my love is slaine; I saw him goe
> Ore the white Alpes, alone; I saw him, I,
> Assayld, fight, taken, stabb'd, bleede, fall, and dye.
>
> (50–54)

The poet who later wrote a treatise on suicide in the period of his greatest despondency knew that the best way to master a fear was to express it openly and fully, even comically. The allusion to Juliet-like behavior found in these lines connects the poem with the interest in romantic comedy and tragedy Donne shared with the coterie readers to whose capacities for dramatic involvement he appealed.

It is clear that Donne used the flexible form of the elegy for a number of different kinds of poetry—some more, some less faithful to classical models.[133] As works like "The Bracelet," "The Perfume," and "On His Mistris" demonstrate, he began to realize some of the dramatic possibilities of the love poem. He developed these further, however, in the rhetorically more economical bounds of the short lyric, a form of literary currency acceptable in both courtly and satellite-courtly environments, especially suited as it was to the system of manuscript transcription through which nonprofessional poetry passed.

THE ART AND CONDITIONS OF DONNE'S EARLY LYRICS

Young men at the university composed verse on set themes or produced epigrams and bawdy trifles for their own amusement. In writing lyric poetry, the Inns-of-Court termers extended these practices into a new environment in which versifying was a social activity associated with their "revelling" and a variety of other urbane and courtly activities. Preaching later in life before a congregation at Lincoln's Inn, Donne recalled the social and recreational atmosphere he knew there in his youth. In condemning his past behavior morally he gives a sense of the relationship of the fashionable gallantry of Inns gentlemen and the poetry they wrote: ". . . I was fain to sin lest I should lose my credit, and be under-valued. . . . when I had no means to doe some sins, whereby I might be equall to my fellow . . . I would bely my self, and say I had done that, which I never did, lest I should be under-valued for not having done it. . . . I saw it was thought wit, to make Sonnets of their own sinnes. . . . I sinn'd not for the pleasure I had in the sin, but for the pride that I had to write feelingly of it . . ." (*Sermons*, 2:107–8). Apart from the elegies, Donne seems to be referring both to his libertine lyrics and to those other dramatic and sentimental poems he composed while at Lincoln's Inn, "pieces," Walton reports, "that had been loosely—God knows, too loosely—scattered in his youth" and that he "wished . . . had been abortive, or so short-lived that his own eyes had witnessed their funerals."[134] These poems could not have been disseminated as widely as Walton suggests they were, else they would have shown up in the pages of commonplace-book miscellanies before the 1620s. Donne's recantation clearly associates some of his lyrics with his participation in the social life of the Inns.

The Inns-of-Court amorist is a stock figure in the literature of late Elizabethan England. If not love itself—in its most sophisticated forms—then the composition of love poetry was regarded as properly a gentleman's occupation, a sign of social status either within or outside the Court. In his preface to *Licia*, Giles Fletcher asserted that "for the matter of love, where everie man takes upon him to court exactlie . . . [gentlemen of] the Innes of Court, and some Gentlemen like[wise] students in both Vniversities . . . onlie are fittest to write of Love."[135] In his study of the manuscript poetical miscellanies of the late sixteenth and early seventeenth centuries, L. G. Black has shown how the composition and collection of love poetry was part of the education of young gentlemen.[136] Printed miscellanies and editions of sonnets and other poems were addressed primarily to an audience of gentlemen who bought such "pamphlets"[137]—a readership probably centered in the Inns of Court, where such literature was much in demand. Donne's friend, the essayist Sir William Cornwallis, defined polite amorous activity as an attractive and worthy pursuit for Inns gentlemen: "It is a pretty soft thing this same Love, an excellent company keeper; full of gentlenesse and affabilitie; makes men fine and to go cleanly; teacheth them qualities, handsome protestations; and if the ground be not too barren, it bringeth forth Rimes and Songs full of passion, enough to procure crossed armes and the Hat pulled down. Yea, it is a very fine thing, the badge of eighteene and vpward, not to be disallowed. Better spend thy time so then at Dice."[138] It is interesting to note that Donne's Lothian portrait shows him as a young man in just the pose Cornwallis describes: his hat is pulled down, his arms are crossed, and the epitaph "Domina illumina tenebras meas" wittily marks him as a fashionable lover.[139] If Sir Geoffrey Keynes is right in perceiving the figure in this portrait as "holding a book, the rough edges of which suggest that it is a manuscript [of his poems?]. . . . [whose] lower edge . . . rests on a pewter standish with an inkpot and a quill pen,"[140] then Donne is not simply posturing as a gallant, but as a lover who writes amorous verse, a true Inns-of-Court "Amoretto" (to use the term that appears in the *Parnassus* plays).

In his discussion of the *Gesta Grayorum* and the *Prince d'Amour* revels, Finkelpearl notes that they reveal Inns men's "simultaneous admiration for the code of courtly love and for the morals of an Aretino."[141] The young termers were fond of *both* Petrarchan *and* libertine or Ovidian poetical vocabularies. Their catholicity of interest is reflected in the wide variety of lyrical forms they composed and collected. While the printed miscellany edited by an Inner Temple man, *The Phoenix Nest*, contains mainly courtly poetry in the polite manner, manuscript collections like Rosenbach MS 1083/15, Bodleian Add. MS B.97,[142] and the Farmer-Chetham manuscript preserve a large number of satiric epigrams and lyrics. Campion's 1601 *Booke of Ayres* represents the tastes of the author's fellow Inns members of the 1590s: this heterogeneous collection includes six persuasions to love, an erotic epigram, Petrarchan complaints, an Anacreontic idyll, a lyric of Christian stoicism, and a simple religious poem. The sources are plainly Catullan, Horatian, Ovidian, Petrarchan, Anacreontic, and native English.

In stating "What Epigrams are in Poetrie, the same are Ayres in musicke,"[143] Campion calls attention to the briefness and plainness of his verse, naming both Martial and the poets of the Greek Anthology as models of epigrammatic poetry. In such songs as Campion's, a single dramatic voice holds center stage and sustains a clear line of poetic discourse unobscured by the denser ornamentation of the madrigal.[144] But what Campion's lyrics and the work of some of his contemporaries exemplify is really the conflation of different poetic kinds, a subject whose importance Rosalie Colie has demonstrated. In combining the subject matter, conventions, and styles of courtly verse with the strengths of the epigram and classical lyric, writers like

Campion, Davies, Shakespeare, and Donne created a new style for amatory verse. What Colie says of Shakespeare's sonnets applies as well to Donne's lyric poems: ". . . part of their power comes from the poet's capacity to enliven generic styles, to animate, confront, and intertwine lyric and epigrammatic styles in such a way as to permit the poet-figure in the poems a different kind of self-analysis from that of the sonnet genre, to permit him, indeed, to find another kind of self. The middle style between the high vocabulary of the love-sonnet and the low vocabulary of the epigram brackets a psychological and social reality between these two generic renderings of milieu."[145]

For a number of reasons, including the popularity of the form at the Inns of Court, Donne's handling of the lyric was affected by the epigram. William Drummond of Hawthornden, who claimed he read a manuscript of "Jhone Dones lyriques" in 1613, observed that "*Donne* among the Anacreontick Lyrics, is Second to none, and far from all Second. . . . I think, if he would, he might easily be the best Epigrammatist we have found in *English*. . . ."[146] There is truth to Joseph Spence's later complaint that "the majority of his pieces are nothing but a tissue of epigrams."[147] Certainly Donne's fondness for pointed or surprising conclusions marks them as epigrammatic in effect. Donne himself remarked: ". . . it is easie to observe, that in all Metricall compositions . . . the force of the whole piece, is for the most part left to the shutting up; the whole frame of the Poem is a beating out of a piece of gold, but the last clause is as the impression of the stamp, and this is it that makes it current" (*Sermons*, 6:41). In their wit, style, and forms of closure, most of Donne's lyrics are epigrammatic, but, as in Campion and Shakespeare, the epigrammatic is fused with other elements as well, depending on the social, rhetorical, and dramatic coordinates of the verse. Whether libertine or courtly, argumentative or dramatic, Donne's lyrics characteristically blend their epigrammatic features with those of other forms and modes to create the kinds of poems he and his readers liked.

The element of the epigrammatic, of course, is only one sign of the preoccupation with wit among Inns-of-Court gentlemen. The witty poet and the witty reader were assumed to be capable of sustaining both an imaginative involvement in and a critical attitude toward poems—that is, to write and read both poetically and metapoetically. In his early lyrics as well as in his more complex later productions, Donne handles the separate discursive, affective, rhetorical or dramatic, and metapoetic elements of his poems with the kind of virtuosity that gave him the reputation of being a supremely witty writer. After constructing an argument, sometimes explicitly in the form of a syllogism or enthymeme, he then dismantled it through pseudologic, semantic punning, paradox, and other techniques, including the switching from discursive to metaphoric thinking. At the same time, he sustained an emotional or dramatic argument that developed by its own logic—seemingly in conflict with the poem's intellectual content, but actually served by it. Rhetorically in some pieces and dramatically in others, he created situations in which the internal speakers and audience could interact in interesting ways, serving as the medium through which the poet and reader made imaginative contact. Employing the techniques of "serial form,"[148] these lyrics require constant shifts of attitude and attention. As Michael McCanles has put it, "the reader is . . . called upon to make continual adjustments as he looks through (i.e., by means of) the poem at what the poem is referring to, grasping this reality just as the poem itself does, by a constant realignment of individual statements in relation to one another."[149] Donne expected his sophisticated readers to understand the literary-historical vicissitudes of various genres and modes and to appreciate his inventive reformulation of them in ways that called into question both familiar conventions and their usual ideological and social affiliations.

Difficulty, even magnificently unnecessary difficulty, was a valued commodity in the Inns-of-Court environment, the opportunity to exercise an intellectual mastery that somewhat compensated for political and social vulnerability. Sir Edward Coke complained about the intellectual preciosity of some lecturers in the law in a way that suggests the kind of objections that have been leveled against Donne's verse by unsympathetic readers: Coke disliked those discourses that were "full of new conceits, liker rather to riddles than lectures which when they are opened they vanish away like smoke, and the readers [i.e., lecturers] are like to lapwings who seem to be nearest their nests when they are farthest from them, and all their study is to find nice evasions out of the Statute."[150] The kind of skeptical, riddling temperament that made for a needlessly complicated legal scholarship, however, was an advantage in the social and literary recreations enjoyed in the Inns environment.

Such sophisticated complexity also served, for Donne, a serious purpose. In one of his sermons, he expressed his lifelong preference for the "problematical" over the "dogmatical": "It has been observed amongst Philosophers, that *Plato* speaks probably, and *Aristotle* positively; *Platoes* way is, It may be thus, and *Aristotles*, It must be thus. The like hath been noted amongst Divines, between *Calvin*, and *Melanchton*; *Calvin* will say, *Videtur*, It seemes to be thus, *Melanchton*, It can be no otherwise but thus. But the best men are but Problematicall, Onely the Holy Ghost is Dogmaticall; Onely he subscribes this *surely*, and onely he seales with Infallibility" (*Sermons*, 6:301). The intellectually earnest skepticism Donne favored, pithily expressed in the phrase "Doubt wisely" (*Satire* 3, 77), is manifested in both his poetry and prose, especially in the paradoxical arguments, the witty conflicts between discursive and emotional lines of development, the disturbing juxtapositions, the problematical endings, and the arguments conducted at a speed that makes them difficult to assimilate. He had the good fortune to have as an audience a group of like-minded individuals who could appreciate such strategies.

In their self-conscious fusion of genres and modes, their deliberate difficulty and complexity, their wittily problematical character, Donne's lyrics are often "self-consuming artifacts"—works that undo their own deceptive lines of development as they become virtual metapoems, that is lyrics that are about the nature and process of writing certain kinds of verse and about the communicative relationship of poet and reader. Whether or not they reach this degree of aesthetic reflexivity, a quality that includes the self-conscious manipulation of the interaction of text and context, the metapoetic element in Donne's lyrics is usually highlighted, a function of the wittily sophisticated relationship of poet and audience in the original coterie situations. Whatever the subject matter, whatever the rhetorical and dramatic coordinates of particular pieces, Donne assumed readers receptive to highly self-reflexive verse.

In the lyrics Donne composed while he was still at Lincoln's Inn, he handled two basic stances familiar to his readership, that of the witty and iconoclastic libertine and that of the courtly sophisticate. While the two can be distinguished in terms of their social decorum and their different literary roots, they often appear in mixed form in the verse as they were, no doubt, in actual experience. The literary vocabularies appropriate to each were, respectively, those of Ovidian amorousness and of Petrarchan/Neoplatonic politeness. Donne turned his analytic intelligence on both, and on the social circumstances with which each was associated. In doing so, he often set up a creatively adversarial relationship with his audience as he engaged them in various forms of imaginative and intellectual participation.

LIBERTINE POEMS AND THE ART OF WRITING "FEELINGLY"

As those who have studied the various manifestations of "Ovidianism" in the 1590s have noted, there were various literary expressions of sexual fantasy in Donne's time, ranging from witty bawdry in a coolly libertine manner to imaginatively dramatized sensuality and decadent prurience. Gentlemen of the Inns composed and enjoyed bawdy epigrams and lyrics, works of the sort referred to and exemplified by Sir Benjamin Rudyerd's epigram "In Clara[m]":

> Clara halfe angry wth my baudy songe
> straight told her husband she had done wth mee
> fye Clara I should suffer much more wronge
> ear I would tell if I had donne wth thee.[151]

Some of the work of Inns-of-Court authors in the surviving commonplace-book poetical miscellanies associated with the Inns environment indicate clearly that there was a lively interest in erotic and sexually realistic poetry. Rosenbach MS 1083/15, for example, preserves not only a large number of satiric epigrams and libels, but also some erotic and obscene verse as well. We find poems dramatically depicting sexual encounters,[152] including an abbreviation of Thomas Nashe's famous "The Choice of Valentines," a version of the poem that omits the most comically interesting part of the original, the section in which the lover loses his erection temporarily and his prostitute-partner, whose excitement is building, decides to use a dildo to achieve orgasm. The Rosenbach version ends:

> she ierkes her legges & sprawleth wth her heeles
> No toung can tell the solace that she feeles
> w^t may be added more to my renowne
> she lieth breathles & I am taken doune
> the waues do swell the tyde oreclymbes the bankes
> Iudg gentlemen if this deserve not thankes.[153]

The mutual orgasm finally enhances male phallic narcissism—the symbolic form of self-esteem revealingly threatened in the long version of the poem and in its Ovidian model, *Amores* III.7. The man in the Rosenbach text of the poem enjoys both social and economic as well as sexual mastery: he is wealthy enough to spend the extra money to buy the services of the best whore in the bawdyhouse and potent enough to satisfy both himself and her sexually. Like the audience addressed in the last line, he is, presumably, a gentleman.

The poetry of phallic narcissism and of sexual adventure is the social, as well as the literary, antithesis of polite courtly verse. There is a stark contrast between the social subservience of the courtly lover who addresses a woman of higher station and the bravado of the gentleman recreating himself among the lower classes. In the fascinating autobiography of the musician Thomas Whythorne, a narrative framing a series of poems with their specific social occasions, it is clear that the deferential idiom of courtly verse signals the social gap between Whythorne and his wealthy or well-born female employers. He reports that a widow he served liked to flirt with and manipulate men for her amusement: ". . . her joy was to have men to be in love with her, and to brag sometimes how she would handle such as were so, and how she could fetch them in, and then how she could with a frown make them look pale, and how with a merry look she could make them to joy again."[154] In defense, the politely amorous lyrics Whythorne composed for her were carefully ambiguous. From Queen Elizabeth on down to wealthy women of the middle class, the game of Petrarchan mistress and lover was played with men whose social and economic dependence found expression in the language of courtly amorous verse.[155]

Socially, economically, and politically vulnerable Inns gentlemen, however, obviously found it pleasant to turn the tables imaginatively by composing, circulating, and collecting love poetry of another sort, literature that celebrated male social, economic, and sexual power: the roots of such verse were Ovidian, Catullan, and (in the loose sense of the term) "goliardic." It was a kind of verse distinguished from the Petrarchan, sometimes Neoplatonic, poetry of courtly and academic traditions but, in their own experience as gentlemen who often aspired to success at Court, both types of verse were related sociologically in their world.

Although Donne, like some other Inns-of-Court authors, used the style of Ovidian libertinism in some of his early lyrics to express certain iconoclastic attitudes toward the established code of deferential amorousness, he also treated the poetic mode he adopted with self-conscious irony, criticizing its social, psychological, and moral assumptions. In these works, Donne portrayed the processes by which libertine swaggering led to emotional involvement. His attitude toward libertine loving was not mainly that of traditional Christian morality, as N. J. C. Andreasen has argued,[156] but rather that of the Inns-of-Court paradoxographer and ironist who could express a critical attitude toward both the poems themselves and the forms of behavior with which they were associated.

One of the simpler libertine lyrics, "Communitie," bluntly exposes the moral insensitivity behind smug libertinism in proving, with false logic, the legitimacy of exploiting women sexually. The poem's wit rests on the willingness of the reader to appreciate the outrageous execution of a false argument that debases women to the level of indifferent objects. Yet Donne does not allow the work to end in an intellectually playful way, concluding it, rather, with a surprisingly brutal metaphor for libertine loving that takes from the social pose any mischievous charm it might have had:

> Chang'd loves are but chang'd sorts of meat,
> And when hee hath the kernell eate,
> Who doth not fling away the shell?
> (22–24)

He deliberately unsettled his reader, forcing a reexamination of the premises not only of libertine behavior but also of Ovidian poetic wittiness. This poem resembles "Loves Progress," whose final lines have a similar effect.

False logic, rhetorical bluntness, and a final arresting metaphor deromanticize literary (if not actual) libertinism in "Communitie." The use of a female speaker in "Confined Love" has similar results.[157] In this lyric the typical witty arguments for libertine naturalism are put in the mouth of a woman who finally interprets fidelity as greediness and promiscuity as generosity. "Womans Constancy" also seems to have a female speaker, whose self-conscious recitation of libertine rationalizations for betrayal converts the piece virtually into a metapoetic statement, a lyric about the making of a libertine poem: the heart of the work, lines 2 to 13, is a series of hypothetical excuses for abandonment the male lover might use, all "scapes" (14) rather than truths. The pointed conclusion suggests not only that the woman could hold her own with counterarguments—the sort of activity in which the reader of outrageous paradoxes is supposed to engage—but, as she indicates, she probably shares her lover's libertinism. In the internal rhetorical space of the lyric, then, the speaker embodies one of the reader's functions and serves as a useful means of displacing male libertinism from its privileged position by co-opting its arguments and attitudes. The emotional advantage is the woman's because she dramatically disappoints her lover's expectations that she will be hurt by abandonment. Arnold Stein says the poem is "unquestionably a display, but of whom and for what reasons?"[158] I would suggest the answer lies outside the dramatic frame of the lyric in the context of the original poet-reader relationship: the game played in the prose paradoxes is repeated here as Donne expected his audience to question not only the soundness of the arguments presented but also their own attitudes as well.

"Loves Usury" embraces a range of social experience typical of gentlemen-amorists of the Inns of Court. It also presents the ironic situation of the libertine who has fallen in love, but the dramatic speaker's attitudes and idioms securely locate him in the context of the youthful amorous adventurism romanticized by Inns men. The first stanza sounds like the performance of a classical Ovidian lover:

> For every houre that thou wilt spare mee now,
>   I will allow,
> Usurious God of Love, twenty to thee,
> When with my browne, my gray haires equall bee;
> Till then, Love, let my body raigne, and let
> Mee travell, sojourne, snatch, plot, have, forget,
> Resume my last yeares relict: thinke that yet
>   We'had never met.
>   (1–8)

"Love" is sexual experience in this formulation, an energetic activity of moving from conquest to conquest, a process mimicked by the syntax of lines 5 to 8. It is a competitive sport, the second stanza suggests, in which women of Country, Court, and City are prizes:

> Let mee thinke any rivalls letter mine,
>   And at next nine
> Keepe midnights promise; mistake by the way
> The maid, and tell the Lady'of that delay;
> Onely let mee love none, no, not the sport;
> From country grasse, to comfitures of Court,
> Or cities quelque choses, let report
>   My minde transport.
>   (9–16)

The marks of the Roman erotic elegy appear in lines 11 and 12. The bewildering speed of the poem suggests the hectic pace of the young man's sexual adventures.

The final stanza hypothetically extends the situation into the future as the lover repeats his plea to love to be allowed to seize the day while he is young:

> This bargaine's good; if when I'am old, I bee
>   Inflam'd by thee
> If thine owne honour, or my shame, or paine,
> Thou covet, most at that age thou shalt gaine.
> Doe thy will then, then subject and degree,
> And fruit of love, Love, I submit to thee,
> Spare me till then, I'll beare it, though she bee
>   One that loves mee.
>   (17–24)

The awareness of remorse, of shame and pain, somewhat undercuts the sportful attitude of the first two stanzas. But the real surprise comes in the last seven words of the poem which reveal that the speaker's plea is fundamentally a defensive one, that he is asserting libertine freedom as a weak protection against the kind of emotional involvement he already feels. Again, the responsiveness, the sensitivity to the need for reciprocating affection, ironically undoes the comical bravado of the libertine stance. The conversion of "Love" from a god of sexual promiscuity to a lord of affection signals the transformation of a libertine lyric into a love poem.

This same conversion takes place in "The Indifferent," an extraordinarily complex lyric that serves as a good example of Donne's Inns-of-Court lyricism.[159] This poem progressively changes, continually shifting its rhetorical coordinates, its attitudes, its subject matter, forcing its reader constantly to reformulate its basic situation. It begins as a rambunctiously libertine performance in the Ovidian mold, a poem celebrating, it would seem, the brash erotic adventurism of the young male lover, a man who is an expert on women and who can joke about them in a self-satisfied manner:

> I can love both faire and browne,
>   Her whom abundance melts, and her whom want betraies,
> Her who loves lonenesse best, and her who maskes and plaies,
>   Her whom the country form'd, and whom the town,
>   Her who beleeves, and her who tries,
>   Her who still weepes with spungie eyes,
> And her who is dry corke, and never cries;
> I can love her, and her, and you and you,
> I can love any, so she be not true.
>   (1-9)

The model of this catalog of possible mistresses is found in Ovid,[160] but the terms are the contemporary Elizabethan ones of the swaggering gentleman-amorist. Through the first seven and one-half lines, the poem rhetorically portrays a speaker addressing an audience of sympathetic males, but with the pronoun shift in the eighth line, he begins to speak to an audience of women.

This second rhetorical situation is extended into the next stanza:

> Will no other vice content you?
> Will it not serve your turn to do, as did your mothers?
> Have you old vices spent, and now would finde out others?
>   Or doth a feare, that men are true, torment you?
>   Oh we are not, be not you so,
>   Let mee and doe you, twenty know.

> Rob mee, but binde me not, and let me goe.
> Must I, who came to travaile thorow you,
> Grow your fixt subject, because you are true?
> (10–18)

Although this female audience is technically plural (a question like "Will it not serve your turn to do, as did your mothers?" indicates this), the impression gradually created by this stanza is that the lover is really interested in addressing one particular woman whose behavior demands of him a response he is unwilling to make. The last part of the stanza seems directed at someone whose love for him he finds disturbing in some way. The final question seems to require a singular "you" to correspond to the singular form of "I" and "subject." If this is so, the two previous rhetorical situations are really ruses: the lover addresses an individual mistress all along, not a group of men or women in general.

The most striking rhetorical shift in the poem comes, however, with the third stanza, which metapoetically frames the previous two as a self-enclosed lyric uttered at some past time, a poem within the larger poem whose new rhetorical features are ambiguous:

> *Venus* heard me sigh this song,
> And by Loves sweetest Part, Variety, she swore,
> She heard not this till now; and't should be so no more.
> She went, examin'd, and return'd ere long,
> And said, alas, Some two or three
> Poore Heretiques in love there bee,
> Which thinke to stablish dangerous constancie.
> But I have told them, since you will be true,
> You shall be true to them, who'are false to you.
> (19–27)

In the narrative space of this lyric the lover may finally be addressing all three possible audiences, men, women, and mistress. This humorous section posits a male audience similar to the one the speaker appeared to assume earlier. The emotional message of the stanza and of some of its language seems directed, however, toward the woman who loves him: to characterize the previous two stanzas as a "song" that a lover could "sigh" is to redefine them facetiously, but, in some sense, accurately as a sentimental (Petrarchan) lyric. The last line and one-half of the lyric are doubly distanced by presenting their statement as a quote within a quote spoken by a character other than the speaker, a Venus who, like Shakespeare's, is the goddess of untrammeled sexuality,[161] who now embodies the libertine attitudes to which the lover had tried to adhere. She warns the few constant women to be found in the world that they will be betrayed by the men to whom they are "true." This is a final comically ironic articulation of an issue present throughout the piece.

The question of fidelity in love does not fit into the framework of libertine naturalism, except in either an ironic or a cynical sense. The terminal line of each of the poem's three stanzas and the last two lines of the final one insist upon the term "true" as crucial. In the first stanza the word is semantically incongruous in the context of a celebration of erotic freedom: "I can love any, so she be not true" is comically nonsensical, but at the same time the note of protest here and elsewhere in the poem suggests a kind of emotional vulnerability. The speaker seems not simply to wish to avoid women who will take love seriously and to commit themselves in it, but to fear them. This anxiety is more explicit in the second stanza's final lines, in which the rhetorical question bespeaks a troubled defensiveness: "Must I, who came to travaile thorow you, / Grow your fixt subject, because you are true?" The logic here is not that of the libertine but of the emotionally and morally sensitive individual who recognizes the need for reciprocity in love. The speaker's earlier smug libertinism is threatened by the experience of actually falling in love with a particular woman. In fact, the emotional drama implicit in the poem's rhetorical turns consists of a speaker's reluctantly communicating to his mistress that he is in love with her.

Donne, I believe, assumed that his reader was able to perceive "The Indifferent" as a love poem, a piece that converts a fashionable libertine stance into one of affectionate responsiveness. He dramatized some of the ironies of the libertine's finding himself in love and reacting to it with emotional and moral sensitivity. The effect of this is to suggest, to an audience receptive to such a message, that libertine attitudes are the social defense of the emotionally vulnerable, the behavior of those who are afraid either of affectionate involvement or of the possibility of rejection. The same Inns-of-Court audience that was fond of antisentimental Ovidianism could also appreciate its ironic undoing, especially in a lyric whose rhetorical and emotional complexities were a challenge to their intellectual agility as readers. Although the poem dramatizes the speaker's ambivalence toward the situation in which he finds himself, it suggests also the kind of mutuality in loving celebrated in those Shakespearean romantic comedies for which Inns men were such an appropriate audience as well as in Donne's later lyrics of reciprocal love.

Libertine Poems and Writing "Feelingly" 79

In his discussion of "The Indifferent," Clay Hunt emphasizes the way in which it deliberately satirizes the manner and matter of contemporary Petrarchan poetry,[162] the kind of verse with which the term "sigh" could be associated. In the Inns-of-Court social world such forms of parody were popular. But more was involved than the mere mockery of a fashionable literary mode: since Petrarchan verse was associated with the Court and its rule-bound hierarchical system, and since it served as a vehicle for expressing the petitioner's stance of submission and deference, if not his pathetic frustration, it represented to Donne and his fellow Inns members the kind of social weakness they feared and eschewed. In opposing the conventions of polite Petrarchan verse, they affirmed, at least imaginatively, their own autonomy and independence in a world whose social, economic, and political realities severely limited them. More so than "The Indifferent," some of the other lyrics that might be considered libertine or Ovidian seem to oppose themselves insistently to the standard mode of the courtly Petrarchan lyric. Poems like "Song: Goe and catche a falling starre," "The Curse," and "Loves Diet" are iconoclastic male-audience performances, but they are more concerned than the simpler libertine lyrics like "Communitie," "Confined Love," and "Womans Constancy" with the genteel world of fashionable behavior—an environment in which ambition and competition reigned.

"Song: Goe and catche a falling starre," a sportful literary exercise in reciting impossibilities,[163] is a cynically libertine and antifeminist poem, but its concern with the tension between scorn and idealization, focused on the search for the "woman true, and faire" (18) is a metaphor for broader social relationships. The conflict between the Ovidian and the Petrarchan in this lyric, between the need to engage in the antifeminist devaluation of women and the urge to express devotion to them, is really subordinate to the act of sharing group attitudes toward the larger world. In the first stanza, there is a revealing shift from the list of merry impossibilities of the first five lines:

> Goe, and catche a falling starre,
>   Get with child a mandrake roote,
> Tell me, where all past yeares are,
>   Or who cleft the divels foot,
> Teach me to heare Mermaides singing . . .
>   (1–5)

to the concern with the realities of competition and ambition implied by the rest of the stanza:

> Or to keep off envies stinging,
>> And finde
>> What winde
>> Serves to'advance an honest minde.
>
> (6-9)

The search for "advancement," for which amorous courtship served as a convenient metaphor in Elizabethan England, is a topic of more genuine concern to Donne and his Inns readers than the question of women's constancy. And by locating the search for "a woman true, and faire" in the second stanza in structurally the same position as the search for advancement in the first, Donne suggests the connection between love and ambition. Finally, the tension between idealism and disillusionment which the third stanza focuses sharply is presented as the sophisticated man's skeptical attitude in a world in which ambition and love are interrelated. The point of the final lines is not simply that women are bad creatures but that the world inevitably disappoints the idealistic young: in a later verse letter to Sir Henry Wotton, Donne referred to the same idea in the phrase "Utopian youth, growne old Italian" ("Sir, more then kisses," 46).

The jauntily antifeminist "Song: Goe and catche a falling starre" has a speaker who harbors no illusions about the danger to be encountered by either the ambitious man or the lover—envy and betrayal. In "The Curse"[164] Donne sets love in the context of a competitive world of economic, legal, and political relationships and uses a harshly antifeminist statement in the epigrammatically pointed ending to freeze the poem's tough-minded attitude. This lyric begins, however, with terms belonging to the framework not of cynical libertinism, but of fashionable courtly amorousness. The lover starts by defending the secrecy of his love and concealing the identity of his mistress:

> Who ever guesses, thinks, or dreams he knowes
>> Who is my mistris, wither by this curse;
>> His only,'and only'his purse
>> May some dull heart to love dispose,
> And shee yeeld then to all that are his foes;
>> May he be scorn'd by one, whom all else scorne,
>> Forsweare to others, what to her he'hath sworne,
>> With feare of missing, shame of getting, torne. . . .
>
> (1-8)

The Ovidian curse, the traditional literary form with which Donne experiments here,[165] ill suits the Petrarchan situation evoked by the con-

Libertine Poems and Writing "Feelingly" 81

vention of courtly secrecy and the relationship of love and "scorne": a libertine iconoclasm disguises a politer form of amorous activity.

What comes through as the real subject of the lyric, however, is not the protection of a courtly mistress's identity from malicious gossip (the duty of the courtly lover) but rather the competitive concern with money and success. In the first stanza, love is related to rivalry with "foes" and being in love is a threat to one's "purse." Both "missing" and "getting" ambiguously refer to financial and amorous matters. The elaborate curse is specifically related to class and group interests of Inns-of-Court gentlemen preoccupied with such issues as inheritance, finances, competition, "Treason" (17), "Gamsters" (25), and legal "schedules" (30).

The sensibility of the poem is that of an Elizabethan Ovidian libertine. The appropriateness of this stance to the poem's original context is revealed in the lines that were probably part of an early text of the work:

> Or may he for her vertue reverence
> One, that hates him onelie for impotence,
> And equall traytors be shee and his sence.[166]
> (14–16)

In this version Donne more explicitly mocked the situation of the complimentary Petrarchan lover, whose attitude of "reverence" is, from the point of view of the anticourtly rhetoric of this lyric, one of social, as well as sexual, impotence. The opposite attitude to that of the "reverence" for women associated with courtly encomiastic verse is found, finally, in the surprising antifeminist conclusion of the poem. After wishing an inventively varied series of ills on the hypothetical male who might learn his mistress's identity, the speaker raises the possibility that a woman might be the one to discover it: "For if it bee a shee / Nature before hand hath out-cursed mee" (31–32). Having associated sexual and social impotence with the form of loving assumed by the lyric's initial situation, and having put love in the context of masculine preoccupations with competition, money, and autonomy, "The Curse" dissociates "mistressing" from the codes of courtly loving, a distinction that the antifeminist joke of the last lines only sharpens.

By mixing the languages of courtly Petrarchanism and Ovidian libertinism, "Loves Diet" creates a critical and metapoetic frame for its subject matter. Designed for the benefit of a male audience concerned with asserting its autonomy and independence, this lyric dramatizes the irony of the libertine lover's partially failed attempts to use remedies for love on a day-to-day basis as a defense against the passive dependency of the Petrarchan amorist. Like "The Curse," this poem uses the language of plainspeaking realism to deal with subject matter that normally would be expressed in more polite idioms. Although the speaker uses an aggressively masculine style and seems concerned with extra-erotic matters such as his "fortune" (8) as a counterbalance to the feared dependency of the Petrarchan lover and despite his attempt to convert polite wooing into gentlemanly sporting, this lyric dramatizes the ultimate *inadequacy* of an Ovidian libertine stance as a defense against emotional vulnerability. The lover comes across as genuinely bothered that his mistress shows favor to others and that he is losing his rakish autonomy by being in love.

The blunt language of this poem—e.g., "cumbersome unwieldinesse / And burdenous corpulence" (1–2), "she sigh" (10), "brin'd" (13), "sweat" (18), "fat" (21), "buzard love" (25), and "game kill'd" (30)—imperfectly disguises the fact that the lover does sigh, weep, write love letters, and fall in love. Although he tries to assert his control, the freedom to "chuse," his cynical Ovidianism breaks down and the last two lines of the piece syntactically enact an emotionally troubled aimlessness: ". . . I spring a mistresse, sweare, write, sigh and weepe: / And the game kill'd, or lost, goe talke, and sleepe" (29–30). Nicely fusing the vocabularies of Ovidianism and Petrarchanism, this poem seems to invite its sophisticated male readers to question the emotional realities distorted by contemporary amorous language. Like "The Indifferent," "Loves Diet" is a love poem at last, but its rhetorical path is strewn with the debris of discarded fashionable terminology.

COURTLY AND ANTICOURTLY LYRICISM

Although Inns-of-Court men were fond of libertine Ovidian verse and of a literature that satirically mocked the follies and fashions of courtly society, at the same time they were genuinely attracted to the forms and styles of courtly literature. They pointedly included courtly poems in their manuscript commonplace-book collections of verse [167] and they were the prime consumers of printed poetical miscellanies containing lyrics written by courtier poets. Although it was customary for wits like Donne and other Inns authors to satirize the "puling sighes," "aye me's," "oyle of Sonnets, wanton blandishment, / The force of teares, & seeming languishment" [168] of courtly amorists, they utilized just such literary and behavioral idioms as prestigious signs of cultural sophistication and of rhetorical and social mastery. Donne admitted in "Loves Exchange" that the Court was, after all, the proper environment for "th'art of Riming" (4) and even anticourtly love poems of the sort he and his fellows composed had to be measured against the courtly models they creatively reformulated.

Like John Davies, who could compose anticourtly epigrams and lyrics ("Gulling Sonnets," for example)[169] as well as polite courtly poems like the "Sonnets to Philomel," John Donne turned to the themes, forms, conventions, and language of fashionable Petrarchan poetry and of the other lyric styles popular in polite society. He wrote some parodic anticourtly verse and poems of literary competition but he also composed poems of compliment, plaintive poems of love, art songs, and persuasions to love—all set within the cosmopolitan context of a fashionable "civility / And Courtship" ("The Will," 21–22) he and his fellows cultivated. Donne's different handlings of amorous literary material all testify to the cultural centrality of love languages in Elizabethan England, for dramatic, fictional, and poetic works all reflected the social, economic, and political encoding of literary amorousness, particularly of Petrarchan love.[170] In manipulating love conventions, Donne self-consciously played with their larger contexts in ways his coterie readers would have understood.

In the case of Donne's courtly amorous lyrics, there is a serious problem of dating. Although they could have been written at almost any time from about 1592 to the time of his marriage in December 1601—and, in the case of those poems that were used for the purpose of complimenting patronesses, even later—I think it makes sense to associate the poems with Donne's Inns-of-Court period, when he found himself in a large group of ambitious young men whose interest in love poetry was especially pronounced. It was in this kind of environment that he probably wrote a poem like "A Jeat Ring Sent" as an answer to Davies's ninth sonnet of the "Ten Sonnets, to Philomel."[171] Davies's poem reflects the contemporary custom of writing a posy to accompany a gift of a ring;[172] Donne's answer poem critically examines the courtly practice and the literary form associated with it, commenting (metapoetically) for a socially sophisticated audience on some aspects of the love rituals practiced in a courtly environment. In parodying the kind of poem Davies wrote in his "ring" lyric, Donne criticized the casual "fashion" (8) of exchanging love tokens[173]—a practice to which he himself alludes in such pieces as "The Relique" and "His Picture." He points out the difference between a sophisticated game in which love tokens could actually be of little emotional or social consequence and the objects (e.g., "Marriage rings" [5]) that symbolize a more serious relationship. More broadly, he converts Davies's stance of refined, deferential compliment into an aggressively critical one of cynical sophistication, mocking a ritual of courtly amorousness in which others engaged supposedly with a low degree of critical self-awareness. The point of view is that of the outsider who knows the rules and assumptions of literary and social games of the Court.

This, incidentally, is the same angle of vision implicit in Donne's later satirical *Catalogus Librorum Aulicorum*. In that work Donne listed as one of the items: "The Justice of England. Vacation exercises of John Davies on the Art of forming Anagrams approximately true, and Posies to engrave on Rings" (pp. 47–48). The "anagrams" refer to the *Hymnes to Astraea*, hyperbolical compliments written to Elizabeth at a time Davies needed official pressure to get reinstated at the Middle Temple, from which he had been expelled for his violent attack on Richard Martin.[174] The second item refers to the kind of ring-posy literature represented by the Philomel sonnet Donne answered in his antiromantic piece. At the time Donne wrote the satirical catalog, he was an unemployed courtier and Davies was a secure member of the legal profession in the service of the Crown so that the joke about Inns men's writing verse instead of taking part in the legal "exercises" during the "vacations" is a snide reference back to the time when Davies was playing the Inns gallant devoted to the latest poetical fashions.

In "The Baite," Donne parodies Marlowe's "The Passionate Shepherd to his Love," a poem that circulated widely in polite circles.[175] Donne's stylistically uncharacteristic lyric self-consciously mixes the smooth manner of courtly pastoralism with the stronger language of which he was fond. Walton's comment that Donne wrote the piece "to shew the world that hee could make soft and smooth Verses, when he thought them fit and worth his labour"[176] may be an accurate explanation of this poem's genesis, but the difference between the language of the first and fifth stanzas demonstrates that Donne could not comfortably settle into such a pretty elegance:

> Come live with mee, and bee my love,
> And we will some new pleasures prove
> Of golden sands, and christall brookes,
> With silken lines, and silver hookes. . . .
>
> Let others freeze with angling reeds,
> And cut their legges, with shells and weeds,

>   Or treacherously poore fish beset,
>   With strangling snare, or windowie net. . . .
>   (1–4, 17–20)

Donne's answer to Marlowe is very different from Ralegh's. Whereas Ralegh turns to the language of both classical and Christian moral verse to shift the intellectual ground away from Marlowe's courtly pastoralism, Donne criticizes the belief that pastoral retreat can simplify emotional relationships. His comic literalization of the Petrarchan metaphor of the lady's bright eyes (stanzas 2 and 4) and of the conceit of love as a snare or hook[177] remind the reader that the participants in the make-believe are courtly sophisticates who bring the emotional complexities of their world into a landscape whose comic literalization destroys the idyllic mood of pastoral metaphor: the realistic depiction of fishing methods in stanzas 5 and 6, like Shakespeare's reminder of landlord-tenant relationships and the harshness of the rural environment in *As You Like It*,[178] deromanticizes the pastoral fantasy, just as Donne's mixed diction disturbs the smooth flow of the verse.

Both "A Jeat Ring Sent" and "The Baite" can be placed in the general category of answer poems and parodies, kinds of work that appear in academic, courtly, and other environments. Such poetry at the Inns of Court, however, was sometimes more directly the product of a game of literary competition between friends, a manifestation of a spirit of competition that permeated most of the activities of Inns members. The poems and answer poems of William Herbert (later Earl of Pembroke) and Benjamin Rudyerd preserved in the published account of the *Prince d'Amour* revels[179] are good examples of this practice. "The Paradox," which may have been composed while Donne was at Lincoln's Inn or at almost any time during the (relatively short) period during which he penned love lyrics, appears to have been a competition lyric. It is found in a number of manuscripts along with another piece, "Who so terms love a fire," to which it was either an answer or a rival handling of a set theme. Gardner speculates that the poems were "attempts by Donne and a friend to write paradoxes to prove that 'Love cannot be known,' the one arguing that, since Love slays and dead men tell no tales, nobody can know what Love is; the other that the most common description of it is plainly false but its opposite is unprovable."[180] Both texts reflect the kind of analytic examination of fashionable love conventions of which Donne and his readers were fond. They were explicit responses to contemporary poetic conventions and styles—that is, as metapoetic as well as poetic utterances.

"Who so termes Love a fire" is a conventional paradox, "proving" that the opposite of a common belief is true—that love is more justly associated with water than with fire:

> Who so termes Loue a fire, may like a Poet
> Faine what hee will, for certaine cannot showe it.
> For fire nere burnes, but when the fuell's neare
> But Loue doth at most distance most appeare.
> Yet out of fire water did neuer goe
> But teares from loue aboundantlie doe flowe.
> Fire still mounts vpward; but Loue ofte descendeth:
> Fire leaues the midd'st: Loue to the Center tendeth.
> Fire dryes, and hardens: Loue doth mollifie.
> Fire doth consume, but loue doth fructifie.
>   The powerfull Queene of Loue faire Venus came
> Descended from the Sea, not from the flame;
> Whence passions ebb and flowe, and from the braine
> Run to the heart like streames, and back againe.
> Yea Loue ofte fills mens breasts with melting snowe
> Drowning their Loue-sick minds in flouds of woe.
> What is Loue water then? it may bee soe;
>   But he saith truth, who saith hee doth not knowe.[181]

This poem assumes a high degree of "intertextual competence" on the part of readers—a familiarity with the common metaphors of Petrarchan and Neoplatonic love poetry. The attitude the writer assumes, however, is at once one of rationally critical analysis and one of amorous sophistication—the very stance found in, for example, the *Prince D'Amour* revels, that of the lover-wit. From this point of view a love discourse can be more metapoetic than poetic, a critical examination of the materials of amorous verse.

This is certainly the case with Donne's "The Paradox," which not only reflects metapoetically on some familiar Neoplatonic and Petrarchan metaphors, but also uses a more systematic antirational rationalism to create a wittily self-annihilating work—a poem that is paradoxically and metapoetically a lie:[182]

> No Lover saith, I love, nor any other
>   Can judge a perfect Lover;
> Hee thinkes that else none can nor will agree,
>   That any loves but hee:
> I cannot say I lov'd, for who can say
>   Hee was kill'd yesterday?
> Love with excesse of heat, more yong then old,
>   Death kills with too much cold;

> Wee dye but once, and who lov'd last did die,
> Hee that saith twice, doth lye:
> For though hee seems to move, and stirre a while,
> It doth the sense beguile.
> Such life is like the light which bideth yet
> When the lights life is set,
> Or like the heat, which fire in solid matter
> Leaves behind, two houres after.
> Once I lov'd and dyed; and am now become
> Mine Epitaph and Tombe.
> Here dead men speake their last, and so do I;
> Love-slaine, loe, here I lye.

Although Donne later seriously used some of the very formulations presented here with skeptical wit—in a work like "A Nocturnall upon S. Lucies Day," for example—he creates the impression that his analytic intelligence can playfully reduce all amorous hyperboles to absurdity. The strategy he adopts merges successfully the spirited skepticism of the libertine verse and prose with the fashionable pose of the sophisticated amorist: the speaker of the piece is both a lover and a tough-minded wit. Donne addressed a male audience able to see through the equivocations of paradoxical reasoning, a readership that valued, however, the ability to assume self-consciously the stance of the courtly amorist. The last line of the poem, "Love-slaine, loe, here I lye" is thus both a paradoxical undoing of the whole discourse and the striking of an admired social pose. Such a wittily self-critical assumption of the fashionable amorist's role is implicit in the contemporary Lothian portrait of Donne as the melancholy lover.[183]

By the time Donne wrote "The Triple Foole," which objects to the publicizing of his poems and the setting of them to music, he had composed enough verse to think of himself as a love poet (albeit an amateur one). What is ironic about his complaint in the lyric that "Some man, his art and voice to show, / Doth set and sing my paine" (13–14)[184] is that he himself evidently had written a number of pieces to fit existing tunes—for example, "The Message," "Sweetest love," "Communitie," "Confined love," "Song: Goe and catche a falling starre," and "The Baite."[185] This was a well-established practice in courtly circles and in engaging in it Donne played the part of the courtly lyricist. Although in "The Triple Foole" he spoke disparagingly of such "whining Poetry" (3) and of the singing of verse, the existence of manuscript musical settings for some of his poems suggests that they escaped his control and, at a time in which airs were replacing madrigals in popularity, were seized upon by composers because they were the kind of emotionally expressive lyrics that were in fashion.[186]

A number of the *Songs and Sonnets* certainly appear to have been art songs (which may or may not have been performed by their author): in particular, works like "The Message," and "The Expiration" demonstrate Donne's ability in writing in the refined courtly manner, although not always without suggestions of characteristic impiety. "The Expiration" is a separation poem that rehearses such conventional conceits as those of the soul-kiss and of separating as dying, but its diction gives it a comic bluntness: "breake off" (1), "sucks" (2), "thou ghost" (3), "cheape" (6), "quite kil'd" (7), "Ease mee" (8), "just office" (10), "murderer" (10), and "double dead" (12), for example, counterbalance the polite self-effacement of the speaker's ostensible stance. "The Message" exhibits a similar combination of conventional attitudinizing and aggressive rhetoric; the speaker is a frustrated lover who can use the metaphors of compliment as forms of attack on the mistress. By handling the role of courtly lyricist with a kind of critical daring and sophisticated assertiveness, Donne enacted a (wished-for) social autonomy even through the very literary vocabulary that signaled hierarchy and deference.

The persuasions to love Donne composed as a young man are good examples of the application of an Inns-of-Court sensibility to the practice of courtly lyricism. In order to appreciate what Donne was doing with this traditional poetic situation in such poems as "The Dampe," "The Dreame," "The Prohibition," "The Apparition," and "The Flea" it is important to locate the seduction poem in its sociocultural context. In the late Elizabethan period this poetic form was more than just a way of dramatizing erotic intimacy. Like the Ovidian elegy, it was the vehicle for expressing social and economic, as well as emotional and sexual, fantasies. Persuasion lyrics, like erotic epyllia and dramatic renderings of amorous fulfillment, enacted wishes for success in spheres other than the erotic. Given the association of Petrarchan poetry, the Elizabethan cult of chastity, and the system of social, economic, and political constraints under which ambitious young men labored in their Court-centered culture, it is not difficult to perceive the literature of erotic fulfillment as the expression of the desire for worldly satisfaction in the larger sense. Just as Donne's erotic elegies depicting the sexual adventurism of the young lover among the women of the urban middle class served as imaginative compensation for the social and economic vulnerability of Inns men in relation to the Establishment, so too the persuasions to love reverse the passivity, dependence, and frustration competitive young men normally experienced.

The persuasion-to-love poem is only one literary manifestation among several of the need to overcome the social disadvantages metaphorized in the position of the deferentially polite Petrarchan lover. The erotic epyllion, which often reverses the direction of desire by having an aggressive feminine wooer hungry for the erotic attentions of a young man, is a parallel phenomenon to the seduction lyric. In a poem that probably circulated at Lincoln's Inn in the 1580s, *Scillas Metamorphosis*, Thomas Lodge presented an ironic fable about the just punishment that awaited coy and scornful mistresses.[187] As William Keach has observed, "Emphasis falls . . . on the narrator's delight in being able to warn the 'ladies' in his fictional audience against proud, disdainful resistance to their lovers' advances, a warning which Lodge's actual Inns-of-Court audience would certainly have enjoyed."[188] The fantasy of a hierarchically superior female's sexual yielding appears in wonderfully quaint comic form in Simon Forman's dream about amorous intimacy with Queen Elizabeth:

. . . dreamt that I was with the Queen, and that she was a little elderly woman in a coarse white petticoat all unready. She and I walked up and down through lanes and closes, talking and reasoning. At last we came over a great close where were many people, and there were two men at hard words. One of them was a weaver, a tall man with a reddish beard, distract of his wits. She talked to him and he spoke very merrily unto her, and at last did take her, and kiss her. So I took her by the arm and did put her away; and told her the fellow was frantic. So we went from him and I led her by the arm still, and then we went through a dirty lane. She had a long white smock very clean and fair, and it trailed in the dirt and her coat behind. I took her coat and did carry it up a good way, and then it hung too low before. I told her she should do me a favour to let me wait on her, and she said I should. Then said I, 'I mean to wait *upon* you and not under you, that I might make this belly a little bigger to carry up this smock and coat out of the dirt.' And so we talked merrily; then she began to lean upon me, when we were past the dirt and to be very familiar with me, and methought she began to love me. When we were alone, out of sight, methought she would have kissed me.[189]

Apart from the personal material implicit in this account—its Oedipal thematics and the anal-sadistic conception of sex, for example—it is interesting that it takes amorous service to an idealized female monarch and transforms it into a fantasy of masculine sexual assertion. It substitutes for the culturally sanctioned metaphor of loving devotion to an inaccessible Queen the socially leveling relationship of seducer and seduced: as a contemporary poem put it, "to kisse & tosse & tumble / will make an empresse humble."[190] Some males responded to an oppressively hierarchical society whose rules prescribed deferential rhetoric and politely sublimated sexuality with forms of acting out or fantasizing that reduced such behavior to its original libidinal and aggressive components. Thus, in the Forman dream, "waiting on" the Queen, an image of needy subservience, becomes an aggressive sexual service "upon" her. Such a process of desublimation often took the form of deflecting desire from the Queen to her Maids of Honor or other women of the Court: the Queen's reaction to the sexual misdeeds or the unapproved marriages of courtiers like Leicester, Ralegh, Southhampton, and Pembroke was to punish masculine aggressiveness as a violation of her social prescriptions, which required subservient passive-aggressive posturing and patient devoted service.

The tension between desire and social constraint figured in the conflict between sexual need and the Petrarchan lover's painful frustration reflected the conflict between the courtier's or the ambitious man's activist assertion and the subservience or frustration demanded by the established order. This is obvious in a work like Sidney's *Astrophil and Stella*, a sonnet sequence in which the social and political aspirations of the author are transformed into the adulterous passion of a Petrarchan lover. As Richard McCoy has suggested in reference to Mucidorus's attempted rape of Pamela in Sidney's *Old Arcadia*, there is a connection between seduction and sedition, or at least between sexual solicitation and the violation of the rules of the system.[191] In an age in which birth mattered more than merit and love was hostage to the socioeconomic transactions of powerful families, romantic fictions of heroic achievement or of true love as well as sportive celebration of sexual adventurism or of successful seduction mediated the conflict between men's wishes and the social realities. In these circumstances, what Anthony Esler has called "the aspiring mind of the Elizabethan younger generation" could express its thwarted wishes, among other ways in fantasies of sexual triumph. The seduction poem, or persuasion to love, a form adjustable to courtly social circumstances, was one vehicle for such expressions.

In his seduction lyrics, Donne locates amorous experience in the social world of the Court where issues of "*Feare, Shame, Honor*" ("The Dreame," 26) refer to the dangers of extramarital or premarital sexual experience. "*Disdaine*" (11), "*Honor*" (12), "*Constancy*, and *Secretnesse*" (19), familiar features of courtly amorous experience from the time of the troubadours, point to the courtly context of the seduction attempt of "The Dampe." The game of "solicitation" (3) and "scorne" (1) of "The Apparition," like the relationship of male victim and female "conquerour" (13) in "The Prohibition," defines the social advantage the woman has in the courtly sphere of activity until she yields whereupon the position of superior and inferior are reversed.[192] These poems imaginatively assault the social rules that frustrate ambitiously importunate gentlemen by attacking the Petrarchan vocabulary and conventions that represent them.

Many of Donne's early courtly poems have a rough edge of male aggression—manifested in their insistent social and literary iconoclasm, their eroticism and bawdry, and their complex argumentativeness. A teasingly comical antifeminism permeates them and clashes with the moral and social assumptions of their Petrarchan and courtly conventions. In "The Dampe," for example, Donne seems to portray a young man's delight in exposing the fatuousness of a love game he cynically plays. Under the guise of displaying his proficiency in traditional metaphors and compliments, he writes a thinly disguised seduction lyric. As in so many of his other poems, the ending reveals what has been concealed for the major part of the piece. After the expected Petrarchan gestures and language (the speaker refers to his death by his mistress's scorn, promises "*Constancy*" and "*Secretnesse*" in return for her abandonment of her "*Disdain*" and her fastidious concern with "*Honor*"), he concludes:

> Kill me as a Woman, let mee die
> As a meere man; doe you but try
> Your passive valor, and you shall finde than,
> Naked, you'have odds enough of any man.
> (21–24)

The conversion of Petrarchan into sexual "dying" is just the sort of thing we find in Inns-of-Court erotic wittiness, the joke intended for the benefit of a sophisticated male audience.

"The Prohibition" uses pseudological paradoxical argumentation to formulate the persuasion. It assumes a politely amorous situation in which the lover has played the sighing, crying Petrarchan lover who is "dying" because his love is unrequited. When the speaker requests in the third stanza "Love mee, that I may die the gentler way" (19), he teasingly argues that the "mistress"'s sexual yielding would convert Petrarchan "love-death" into the "dying" of erotic satisfaction, the same transformation with which "The Dampe" concludes.[193]

The wit of the lyric entitled "The Dreame" lies in the tension between its dramatic situation and bawdy double entendres on the one hand and its Petrarchan and Neoplatonic language and gestures on the other. But since courtly sexual transactions can take place through the medium of politely refined language—the basis of much humor in works like Gascoigne's *The Adventures of Master F. J.* and Sidney's *Arcadia*—the effect is as much that of an unmasking as contrast of incompatible modes. The courtly context of the poem is established by the poem's gestures of complimentary Petrarchan and Neoplatonic idealization: "thoughts of thee suffice, / To make dreames truth; and fables histories" (7–8); "Thine eyes . . . wak'd mee" (12); "I thought thee . . . an Angell, at first sight" (13–14). So too the mention of "*Feare, Shame, Honor*" (26) conjures up the courtly social context with the dangers to the woman's reputation posed by sexual yielding. Donne repeats the comic situation of the sexually eager man in bed wanting sexual satisfaction from the woman who enters his room: but instead of the willing bourgeois matron of the elegy "Going to Bed," he has a courtly woman who can teasingly respond to witty sexual entreaty by leaving his presence.

The poem gradually reveals its dramatic situation, postponing the information to the second stanza that the lover's "happy dreame" (2) whose "theame [is] / For reason, much too strong for phantasie" (3–4) is an erotic one. As this section of the piece indicates, the lover has an erection[194] and his dream was about to become a wet dream: "thou knew'st when / Excesse of joy would wake me" (17–18). Hence the plea at the end of stanza 1 to "do" (10) in actuality what would have been accomplished in fantasy. The phallocentrism of this lyric, the speaker's focus on his aroused sexuality, is used as a comic assault on the polite modes and language of courtly behavior.[195]

"The Apparition" treats the persuasion to love as a dramatic situation of intimacy, not simply as an occasion for cleverness set in a vague rhetorical space. Much of the wit of the poem rests in the reader's ability to appreciate the counterpoint between the dramatic scene and the ironic language. It begins by translating generalized Petrarchan terms of appeal and rejection into sexual persuasion and denial:

> When by thy scorne, O murdresse, I am dead
>   And that thou thinkst thee free
> From all solicitation from mee,
> Then shall my ghost come to thy bed,
> And thee, fain'd vestall, in worse armes shall see. . . .
>
>   (1–5)

In this literalization of poetic conventions, sexual refusal is equated with the Petrarchan mistress's scorn that murders the vulnerable lover.

The "solicitation" of the speaker, however, is not simply polite pleading for favor, but, as the poem implies, a specific request for sex. Since the mistress is described as a "Fain'd vestall," what is at stake is her virginity: either she counterfeits being a virgin as a pretext for denying the appeal for love or she really wants to remain one (would "fain" be one) and must be persuaded to yield.

Instead of explicitly using the Catullan argument to make love before youth passes and time wastes their bodies, Donne submerges this message in a melodramatic fiction that is actually a form of affectionate teasing, not, as Donald Guss has stated, an expression of "a lover's anger at his lady's refusal."[196] The speaker facetiously converts the young coy mistress into a sexually importunate middle-aged woman whose future lover will not only be a "worse" (5) man than he but who will shrink from her (then excessive) sexual demands. The speaker pretends that his "love is spent" (15) and that he is through pleading with his beloved, interested only in a kind of witty revenge, but the whole poem is a humorous reassertion of his ongoing "solicitation." Implicitly denying that a sexual yielding on her part will mean a diminishment of her self-respect, the lover suggests that the real loss of self-respect will come in the future when she will have to settle for less-worthy lovers and when she will be demeaned by her own sexual desperation: there is no middle ground between the coy virgin and the kind of libidinous aging woman mentioned here—a figure comically represented in the contemporary erotic epyllion, Shakespeare's *Venus and Adonis*.

In the most complex of his seduction poems, "The Flea," Donne explicitly mentions marriage, a topic omitted from the conventional persuasion to love; he thus not only converts the traditional flea poem from a merry lyric of erotic exploration of the female body[197] into a playfully intellectualized poem of seduction, but also transforms the sexual seduction lyric into a more serious persuasion to full affectionate and physical loving. The result is a lyric that, like most of Shakespeare's romantic comedies, imaginatively reorders the economic, social, and moral realities that frame the love relationship. Given the customary prurience of this kind of poem, "The Flea" seems particularly unerotic in character, extraordinarily preoccupied with ethical and social, particularly marital, matters. The real task Donne sets himself in the witty argumentation of this piece is to convert an act that could imply "sinne, or shame, or losse of maidenhead" (6) into a morally and socially honorable one. He does this by outrageously sophistical means, but the real argument lies in the developing dramatic situation whose coordinates are suggested by some crucial, but subtly insinuated, pieces of information. As the poem develops it becomes clear that the coy mistress is not merely a willing and witty participant in the courtly game—she "answers" the lover's facetious arguments with gestures dramatically placed between the stanzas—but a woman whose deep-seated feelings of ambivalence are the dramatic referent for the speaker's emotional strategies. What is said to her explicitly and implicitly defines her feelings and thoughts.

Her "feares" (25) seem to be concerned with the dangers of sexual yielding—sin, shame, and the loss of "innocence" (20) and "honor" (26). But her relationship to her lover is presented as more than a casual one. In the second stanza, in facetiously proving that intercourse is legitimate because they are "maryed" (11), the speaker says that "though parents grudge, and you, w'are met, / And cloystered in these living walls of Jet" (14–15). In the progression from "parents" to "you" to "we," Donne places the woman rhetorically, emotionally, and morally between the disapproving parents and the importunate suitor. Parental grudging, in Elizabethan society, usually had to do with the social, familial, and economic issues involved in marriage arrangements made for daughters (or sons)—the realities Shakespeare repeatedly introduced into his romantic comedies and into a romantic tragedy like *Romeo and Juliet*. The mistress's grudging, in context, looks as though it is rooted in the emotional opposition between her ties to her parents and her bond with her lover, the situation suggested in "The Perfume." Donne's speaker does not attempt to solve this sort of deep-seated conflict. Instead he suggests indirectly that there is a context between competing systems of ethics in which a shame morality that views loss of virginity before marriage as a woman's greatest dishonor is set against a personalist morality that regards the intention of commitment (and marriage) as largely legitimizing the premarital intercourse of mutual lovers—issues represented in Shakespeare's *Measure for Measure*. Love authorizes sex and society frustrates love, the speaker argues. Donne tried romantically to dislodge sex, love, and marriage from its contemporary cultural matrix, an act that is possible in imaginative literature, but, as he bitterly learned in his own experience, disastrous in real life.

As Donne suggests in his various erotic elegies and lyrics, love and sex had particular economic, political, and social implications in the life and literature of his time. The different languages of amorous verse, from the libertine Ovidian to the refined Neoplatonic and Petrarchan idioms, expressed actual as well as wished-for social relationships. Donne and his readers shared a sophisticated awareness of the sociocultural encoding of literary languages, and could thus reflect on the contextual complexities of poetic texts. It is difficult to draw the line between the love poems Donne wrote while actually in residence at Lincoln's Inn and the verse he wrote soon after, since the rhetorical and social coordinates were virtually the same. Suffice it to say that the style he developed in the congenial circumstances of the Inns of Court, with its artful combining of fashionable gallantry and critical wittiness, carried over into subsequent writing. It was not only a manner obviously personally satisfying to Donne but also one that expressed for the readership he addressed strongly conflicting attitudes toward the Establishment, its rules, and the prescribed ways of achieving success in the larger society.

2

Donne as Young Man of Fashion, Gentleman-Volunteer, and Courtly Servant

There is no sharp boundary between Donne's early Inns-of-Court period and that stage of his life in which he moved out more deliberately to seek preferment in a career of government service. It makes sense, however, to look at some of his verse, first, in light of the transition he self-consciously made from the Inns world to the environment of the City and Court (1595–98) and, then, in terms of his service as secretary to the Lord Keeper, Sir Thomas Egerton (1598–1602). At this time he lived the life of a man of fashion, joined two military expeditions as a gentleman-volunteer, involved himself, with strongly ambivalent feelings, in the life of the Court and its systems of advancement and reward, and fell in love and married.

There are indications that, throughout this period, Donne kept close contact with special friends from the university and Inns of Court, men like Christopher Brooke and Henry Wotton. He wrote some of his works particularly for them, knowing that they shared similar attitudes and ambitions. At the same time some of his other compositions appear to have been directed toward a mixed or double audience rather than, as the earlier verse was, toward an all-male readership. The rhetoric of some pieces assumes the context of a performance not simply for a sympathetic group of male peers but also for sophisticated women who could appreciate their wit and manner. In the latter part of this period, Donne met, wooed, and eloped with Ann More. Some of his poems were undoubtedly associated with their relationship, during both their courtship and marriage. Because there are both chronological and thematic affiliations between those lyrics Donne probably wrote before he and Ann wed and his other love poems of the last years of Elizabeth's reign, works whose rhetorical and dramatic evolution in many ways they culminate, I shall separate these pieces from those composed after their marriage and Donne's consequent loss of employment. The later verse belongs to markedly changed biographical and social circumstances and is better discussed in relation to Donne's efforts between 1602 and 1615 to reestablish himself sociopolitically.

EARLY POEMS OF VALEDICTION AND AN ANTICOURTLY SATIRE

There is no clear evidence about the dates of Donne's departure from Lincoln's Inn to take up residence in London as a young gentleman of fashion in the mid-1590s. As Bald notes, he was last named in the Lincoln's Inn records at the end of 1594. He took a fifteen-year-old youth into his service in July of 1595[1] and he sailed on the first of two naval expeditions in June of 1596. With a modest inheritance at his disposal, Donne apparently enjoyed the pleasures of London and of the Court, although his social life probably changed little from the time of his Inns residence. He was, however, determined to find employment and so his decision to serve as a gentleman-volunteer on the Cadiz (1596) and Islands (1597) expeditions was probably the result not only of financial need, but also of a desire for advancement. Bald believes (*Life*, p. 80) that at this time, probably through his old friend from Oxford, Henry Wotton, Donne approached the Earl of Essex to offer his services. Like so many other educated and ambitious, but prospectless, young men, he looked to the Earl and to the system of patronage of which he was a part for some help in making his way in the world. In taking part in two military adventures, he participated in an activity in which his Catholic background would not have hindered him and that held the promise of financial reward to improve his economic state. Warfare was not only, as Shakespeare put it in *All's Well That Ends Well*, "nursery to our gentry, who are sick for breathing and exploit" (I.ii.16–17)—that is, a chance to win honor through (what was perceived as) manly action—but also a way to establish one's clientage to a powerful patron and to enrich oneself with spoils and booty.[2]

In the second of two verse letters to Christopher Brooke on the occasion of the Islands voyage (1597), Donne meditated on his experiences as a gentleman-volunteer and mercilessly criticized his own motives for joining the two naval expeditions:

> Whether a rotten state, and hope of gaine,
> Or to disuse mee from the queasie paine
> Of being belov'd, and loving, or the thirst
> Of honour, or faire death, out pusht mee first,
> I lose my end. . . .
>   ("The Calme," 39–43)

Here the economic and social reasons for becoming a soldier are mixed with such unflattering motives as the need to escape amorous entanglement and the urge to self-destruction. The mention of love in this context and of the poet's ambivalent feelings about being involved with a particular woman points, in an interesting way, to the epigrammatic elegy that Donne probably wrote on the occasion of one or the other of the two military adventures, "His Picture."

Donne may have actually addressed this courtly piece to a woman with whom he was amorously involved, perhaps the person to whom he alluded in a later letter to his father-in-law in which he denied the accusation that he had deceived a "gentlewoman" (*Selected Prose*, p. 116) before he became involved with Ann More.[3] Whether or not he was in love in the mid-nineties with a specific woman of fashion, it is useful to read "His Picture" as a valediction embodying, like Donne's other exercises in this form, complex feelings about love commitment. Though the leave-taking ceremony of which the poem is a dramatic part centers in the fashionable practice of giving a miniature of oneself to a mistress as a pledge of love[4] (and as an act of self-display), Donne metaphorized the situation in a way that involves broader emotional implications than those of the usual farewell ritual:

> Here take my Picture, though I bid farewell;
> Thine in my heart, where my soule dwels, shall dwell.
> 'Tis like me now, but I dead, 'twill be more
> When wee are shadowes both, then 'twas before.
> When weather-beaten I come backe; my hand,
> Perchance with rude oares torne, or Sun beams tann'd,
> My face and brest of haircloth, and my head
> With cares rash sodaine hoariness o'rspread,
> My body'a sack of bones, broken within,
> And powders blew staines scatter'd on my skinne;
> If rivall fooles taxe thee to'have lov'd a man,
> So foule, and course, as, Oh, I may seeme than,
> This shall say what I was: and thou shalt say,
> Doe his hurts reach mee? doth my worth decay?
> Or doe they reach his judging minde, that hee

> Should like'and love lesse, what hee did love to see?
> That which in him was faire and delicate,
> Was but the milke, which in loves childish state
> Did nurse it: who now is growne strong enough
> To feed on that, which to'disus'd tasts seemes tough.

This piece is in the tradition of the medieval military *congé d'amour*,[5] which moralizes the gift-giving act in the farewell ceremony as a sign of constancy and mutual fidelity. Conventionally this pledge and the promise of safe return are the two assurances the lover tries to give his beloved on such an occasion. Donne handled both of these elements of the valediction with affectionate wittiness, but not without the intimation of deeper problems.

Donne knew that, in scenes of parting, the woman being left behind could respond to separation, at least partly, as abandonment, worried that the absent lover was rejecting her by leaving or that he would not remain faithful in absence. Donne reversed the situation, however, by having the speaker take his own constancy for granted and make his mistress's the issue. Surrounded by suitors, she must (hypothetically) defend her fidelity to a lover whose military experience will have made him rougher and less handsome than the fair gallants who are his rivals. The mischievous suggestion that the mistress might find the tougher veteran more sexually attractive than less manly lovers is part of a strategy of affectionate teasing of the sort found in some of the persuasions to love, but it disguises the more serious implication that the speaker is dissatisfied with the love game in which he and his mistress are involved. The comic hyperbole of the description of his physical appearance after (naval) military experience not only mocks the mistress's fears for his safety by promising to return (if in damaged condition), but also calls into question the pretty refinement of the amorous practices and way of life the lovers shared.[6]

Instead of putting his discomfort with the relationship in which he was involved in terms of the emotional queasiness to which he refers in "The Calme," Donne used a formulation traditional in the military *congé*, the conflict between (private) love and (public) duty, an opposition he had facetiously resolved in favor of the former in the elegy "Loves Warre." In "His Picture" the issue is related to the perception of military experience as a rite of initiation into manhood,[7] an opportunity for moral maturing which the speaker urges his mistress to match in her own experience. The parodic use of the Pauline metaphor of milk for children and meat for adults[8] points to this topic, but its handling assumes a particular amorous and social context. As a fashionable Elizabethan gallant, like the figure in "The Perfume," the speaker of this poem reflects the style of Donne, whom his friend Sir Richard Baker described as "very neat; a great visiter of ladies . . . a great writer of conceited Verses," the young man who, like other fashionable gentlemen, joined the Essex, Howard, and Ralegh naval expeditions out of idleness, romantic excitement, the desire for easy wealth, and desperation for service and employment. On the face of it, the decision to participate in such activity was not obviously one of choosing a course of behavior superior to peacetime activities, even though it was formulated as such in this poem. The speaker turns his back on an amorous courtly relationship under the guise of responding to the call to duty and to the obligation to mature. Although the mistress is portrayed as having the ability to relate more to her lover's "judging minde" than to his superficial physical beauty (whose loss supposedly she would not lament), and although she is given the capacity to leave "loves childish state" for a more adult relationship that involves a fuller exercise of sexuality as well as a more spiritually and morally mature attitude, there is a strong suggestion that she is being rejected along with the way of life of which she and her lover have been a part.

As a love lyric handling the subject of departure, "Witchcraft by a Picture" may have been connected with the same personal circumstances as "His Picture." This song seems to be an earlier rather than later courtly poem, the work of a man conscious of performing as a fashionable lover: its love conventions and sophisticated manner mark it as a lyric appropriate to the beau monde.[9] Whether or not Donne restricted the readership of such a poem to his customary male coterie, it certainly bespeaks his participation in the world of fashion in which love was on a higher social level than that of the gentleman's sexual adventuring among the women of the middle class.

The wit of this dramatic courtly lyric rests largely on the friction between its separate discursive and emotional lines of development:

>   I fixe mine eye on thine, and there
>   Pitty my picture burning in thine eye,
>   My picture drown'd in a transparent teare,
>   When I looke lower I espie;
>   Hadst thou the wicked skill
>   By pictures made and mard, to kill,
>   How many wayes mightst thou performe thy will?
>
>   But now I'have drunke thy sweet salt teares,
>   And though thou poure more I'll depart;
>   My picture vanish'd, vanish feares,

> That I can be endamag'd by that art;
> Though thou retaine of mee
> One picture more, yet that will bee,
> Being in thine owne heart, from all malice free.

The dramatic context of parting is revealed no earlier than line 9, which mentions departure, and then ambiguously in a way that could indicate either abandonment or temporary separation. The final conceit suggests that the latter alternative is the appropriate one to infer, since the exchange-of-hearts metaphor implies a situation of amorous reciprocity. A coterie reader other than the woman who might have been fictionalized as the mistress in this poem would have had to guess the reason(s) for the tears Donne handles with witty conceit.[10] If the poem were to have been given to an actual mistress from whom the poet was taking leave to go abroad, it would certainly have been read primarily in terms of the emotional dynamics of the valedictory situation. Either way, the poem invited a creatively constructive reading.

Donne took the courtly Petrarchan technique of complimentary insult and utilized it for dramatic purposes. In treating the beloved as a witch, he used a conventional device—employed by Sidney, for example, in the fifth song of *Astrophil and Stella*, in which the lover calls his mistress a witch, as well as a thief, murdering tyrant, rebel runaway, and devil. But Donne turns insult to artful praise through his witchcraft metaphor: by treating weeping as a magically powerful means of detaining him, the lover acknowledges the hold his beloved has on his affections. The interstanzaic gesture of kissing the woman's tear-moistened cheeks dramatizes the affection implicit in the scene of intimacy.

Both the conceits and the sophistical argumentation, however, point to disturbances the speaker of the poem tries to control with witty persuasiveness and amorous assurances. The crying mistress is metaphorized as a witch partly to suggest that her fears about the safety of her departing lover and the durability of his love bespeak anger or hostility. Consider the combination of the following elements in the poem: parting, crying, burning, drowning, fears, and being "endamag'd." These suggest that the lover, like the man of "His Picture," is undertaking a hazardous (sea) journey during which burning, drowning, and being hurt are real possibilities. The woman therefore has some reason to be concerned about her lover's welfare. The speaker, however, by pretending that the real dangers exist not in the indefinite future but in the definable present, teasingly suggests that the woman's anger at her lover's leaving underlies fantasies of harm coming to him in absence. Here, and elsewhere in his valedictory poetry, Donne attributes to the mistress a fear of abandonment that looks, suspiciously, like a sensitivity to actual intentions of rejection of the sort mentioned in the poem to Brooke. The term "malice" in the second stanza of this poem is disturbingly strong in this context, suggesting a situation of rejection and revenge rather than one of departure and intended return that the conclusion of the lyric forecasts. The witty contrivedness of "Witchcraft by a Picture" may have represented an attempt to disguise difficulties in the amorous situation being dramatized. In this case, courtly sophistication and the rhetoric of emotional sincerity may have belied other, less noble motives.[11]

Apart from these valedictions, the only poems that can possibly be connected with the first of Donne's two naval adventures are some of the epigrams—in particular, "A Burnt Ship" and "Sir John Wingfield." Bald (*Life*, p. 83) suggests that the first piece probably refers to the burning of the Spanish galleon *San Felipe* during the Cadiz raid. The second memorializes the captain who performed heroically in the attack on the city itself.[12] In the latter poem, Donne wrote, it would seem, to an audience of fellow Essex clients, referring to "our Earle" (3). Significantly, this epigram, along with two others, is found only in Rowland Woodward's manuscript and one other, an indication that it was restricted to a small readership.

Between the Cadiz and Islands expeditions Donne had a period of about a year (August 1596 to July 1597) during which he lived in London again, probably looking for further opportunities as he continued to enjoy the life of a young gentleman. He felt particularly dissatisfied with military service as a career prospect, if the letter he wrote in hope of cultivating the friendship (i.e., patronage) of an anonymous gentleman is any indication: in it he refers to his use of "the fashion of a soldier (wch occupation for a while I professe)" (Simpson, *Prose*, p. 324), clearly stating that he thought of his military activities as temporary until better prospects of employment presented themselves.

At this time he probably wrote the longest and most pessimistic of his satires, the fourth, a poem whose intensity of criticism of the courtly world is probably a function of the frustrations of his ambition.[13] In this poem, Donne fell back on the persona of the first two satires in dramatizing the satiric speaker's nightmarish experience of the Court, but this later piece seems rooted in Donne's more deliberate search for courtly employment in the late nineties.[14] This would partly explain the speaker's insistence that, although he freely went to Court, he "had no suit there" (7). Adopting the stance of the disinterested, morally aloof observer, the satiric persona depicts his reactions to the

Court as the society's center of vice and corruption even as he recognizes it as the locus of power, authority, and opportunity. The gestures by which he separates himself morally from the inhabitants of such an environment reveal a fear of guilt by association. The speaker notes ironically that his experiences have seemed to prove that

> . . . it pleas'd my destinie
> (Guilty'of my sin of going,) to thinke me
> As prone to'all ill, and of good as forget-
> full, as proud, as lustfull, and as much in debt,
> As vaine, as witlesse, and as false as they
> Which dwell at Court, for once going that way.
> (11–16)

This satire dramatizes the process of the breakdown of critical and moral distance in the man who involved himself in the Court.

The foolish courtier chosen as the antagonist in this poem is an easy target for criticism, for he embodies familiar vices and follies. For Donne, however, he is particularly defined as a master of the "tongue, call'd complement" (44), that rhetorical medium necessary to the dependent courtly petitioner. This figure is a consummate liar, poseur, and gossip, but he is in touch with both the trivial and essential topics of concern in courtly society:

> . . . [he] tells many'a lie.
> More then ten Hollensheads, or Halls, or Stowes,
> Of triviall houshold trash he knowes; He knowes
> When the Queene frown'd, or smil'd, and he knowes what
> A subtle States-man may gather of that;
> He knowes who loves; whom; and who by poyson
> Hasts to an Offices reversion;
> He knowes who'hath sold his land, and now doth beg
> A licence, old iron, bootes, shooes, and egge-
> Shels to transport. . . .
> (96–105)

The Queen's favor and disfavor, amorous intrigues, the ruthless ambition of would-be officeholders and the importunity of spendthrift aristocrats and gentlemen who looked to licenses and monopolies to rescue them economically—all are portrayed as parts of the same corrupt system centered in royal patronage. Flattery, gossip, and libel are the abuses of language associated with such a world.

Donne consistently uses the antagonist figure in this poem as one means of calling attention to the various evils of the Court, such as the selling of offices or of their reversions and the system of licenses and monopolies. The danger of such criticism is indicated when the satiric persona worries about hearing (both true and false) gossip about courtiers and their practices:

> I more amas'd then Circes prisoners, when
> They felt themselves turne beasts, felt my selfe then
> Becomming Traytor, and mee thought I saw
> One of our Giant Statues ope his jaw
> To sucke me in. . . .
> (129–33)

Donne's soldiership at this time associated him with the activist war faction in Elizabethan England; the courtier-antagonist of this poem is assigned one of the typical attitudes of this group: "He saith, our warres thrive ill, because delai'd" (122).[15] There is good reason for Donne's satiric persona to express a fear of moral, political, and social contagion from such a man.

Once the speaker has escaped the boorish courtier and fled the Court, he reasserts the moral and social autonomy he felt was threatened or compromised in that world, formulating the issue in a way that clearly represents some aspects of Donne's aversion to the role of the importunate courtier seeking advancement:

> At home in wholesome solitarinesse,
> My precious soule began, the wretchednesse
> Of suiters at court to mourne. . . . . . .
> . . . .
> . . . Low feare
> Becomes the guiltie, not th'accuser; Then,
> Shall I, nones slave, of high borne, or rais'd men
> Feare frownes? And, my Mistresse Truth, betray thee
> To th'huffing braggart, puft Nobility?
> (155–57, 160–64)

Donne knew full well—and resented—the fact that he had to relinquish many of his pretensions to intellectual and social independence once he sought the patronage of the great.

In the nightmare vision of the Court presented in the latter part of this satire, Donne depicts the place as a theater where "All are players" (185), engaged in elaborate forms of self-display. The polite relationships between men and women in such a world are cynically artificial:

> The Ladies come; As Pirats, which doe know
> That there came weak ships fraught with Cutchannel,

> The men board them; and praise, as they thinke, well,
> Their beauties; they the mens wits; Both are bought.
> (188–91)

In addition to satirizing fashionmongering and cosmetics, Donne here reduces the verbal transactions of courtly amorousness to mere gibberish. The typical courtier

> ... enters, and a Lady which owes
> Him not so much as good will, he arrests,
> And unto her protests protests protests. ...
> (210–12)

Such a couple deserve one another: "'tis fit / That they each other plague, they merit it" (217–18).

In the imaginary passage out of the Court from the royal Presence Chamber, and "the great chamber" (231), past the oversized guards who intimidate visitors, the speaker says he "shooke like a spyed Spie" (237), a reminder that the Court was not simply an arena for harmless foolishness but a politically perilous place as well. The poem ends with a statement that unites this work with the previous satiric poems—and rightly so since, at least in the case of *Satires* 1, 2, and 4, the scholar-moralist persona is consistent and the anticourtly attitudes are the same:

> ... Though I yet
> With *Macchabees* modestie, the knowne merit
> Of my worke lessen: yet some wise man shall,
> I hope, esteeme my writs Canonicall.
> (241–44)

In 1596 or 1597, however, Donne was no longer quite the courtly novice he was in his earlier Lincoln's Inn days. The aversion to suitorship, to its proper language of compliment, and to the corruptions of the system of patronage and preferment was less that of an outsider than that of a participant. The consciousness of office and reward, of the loci of power, wealth, and authority, of the importance of the Queen's favor and disfavor, and of the influence of the aristocracy and of "rais'd men" signals a close interest in the workings of the Court on the part of someone who, despite his other feelings, wanted to succeed there. It is fitting that, in this poem, the satiric stance of distanced criticism breaks down as the speaker finds, to his horror, that he has internalized the world he has sought to flee. This phenomenon justly represents Donne's ambivalence about his own courtiership, a

106   *Young Man of Fashion and Courtly Servant*

conflict he expressed strongly in the verse and prose of the next few years.

COURTLY LYRICS OF COMPLIMENT AND THE POETRY OF DISILLUSIOMENT

Some early lyrics of compliment probably belong to this time in Donne's life between his Lincoln's Inn residence and the period of his serious involvement with the woman he married. As products of his involvement in polite society, they might have been written almost any time in the latter half of the 1590s or at the turn of the century, that is in the period in which he lived the fashionable life of a London gentleman, then that of the young courtier and secretary to the Lord Keeper. "Loves Deitie," "The Will," and "The Blossom" enact the Petrarchan style of courtly amorous compliment to a hierarchically superior mistress in ways that anticipated many of the strategies of the later encomiastic lyrics. In the case at least of the first two of these three poems, however, Donne seems to have been as much concerned with the witty presentation of the self to an audience of peers as with the stylish attitudinizing of the courtly lover performed for a woman of high society.

"Loves Deitie" humorously mocks the Petrarchan/courtly "custome" (6) prescribing adoring service to a scornful mistress. But in the bald language of the last line of stanza 1, repeated with slight changes at the end of the following two stanzas, "I must love her, that loves not mee" (7), this rule seems senseless, a distortion of the basic character of love, which Donne reduces, for comic effect, to primitive simplicity. He argues the pre-Petrarchan god of love's

> . . . office was indulgently to fit
> Actives to passives: Correspondencie
> Only his subject was.
>   (11-13)

The equation of male with active and female with passive suggests much about Donne's aversion to the passive stance of the socially deferential Petrarchan amorist. Thinking of lovers as "fitting" one another makes sexual coupling the basis of love, "Correspondencie" in a physical sense. The critique of amorous fashion is concluded in the third stanza:

> But every moderne god will now extend
> His vast prerogative, as far as Jove,

> To rage, to lust, to write to, to commend,
>   All is the purlewe of the God of Love.
> Oh were wee wak'ned by this Tyrannie
> To'ungod this child againe, it could not bee
>   That I should love, who loves not mee.
>   (15–21)

The list of behaviors associated with love in line 17 is an incongruous combination of sexual rambunctiousness and polite restraint: "To rage" and "to lust" seem so far removed from "to write to" and "to commend" it is hard to see them all included in "the purlewe of the God of Love." Donne, in effect, argues that requited and unrequited love, sexual experience and polite compliment should have different names. As in the first two stanzas, the speaker protests against the rule that he love a scornful mistress.

The last stanza suddenly reveals that the addressee, whose treatment of him the lover protests, is faithful to another commitment—perhaps as a married woman:

> Rebell and Atheist too, why murmure I,
>   As though I felt the worst that love could doe?
> Love might make me leave loving, or might trie
>   A deeper plague, to make her love mee too,
> Which, since she loves before, I'am loth to see;
> Falshood is worse then hate; and that must bee,
>   If shee whom I love, should love mee.
>   (22–28)

As in the later complimentary lyric, "Twicknam Garden," Donne suggests that the mistress's scorn is a manifestation of her fidelity. He thus converts protest into praise and the whole poem from a comically critical assault on courtly Petrarchism[16] into an encomiastic piece whose lively wit could be appreciated both by an audience of peers and sophisticated women of fashion.

A double audience of this sort might have been appropriate for "The Will," a witty mock-testament whose shift to second person address to the woman in a four-line section of the final stanza implies that the speaker (like the poet) was not simply aiming his words at a sympathetic group of male friends—the "company" receptive to his "wit" (33)—but also at a particular woman among whose admirers or courtly suitors he was numbered. Undoubtedly Donne thought of a lyric like this as a *jeu d'esprit* suitable to the kind of coterie audience with whom he shared other wittily recreative verse, a readership aware not only of the literary tradition of the mock-testament,[17] but also of the social and autobiographical contexts of the various stanzas of this lyric. This was an audience, the poem suggests, interested in cultivating the same "civility/And Courtship" (21–22) as the poet, one harboring no illusions about the world of power, but one close enough to the poet to know him as a religiously troubled (stanza 3), intellectually serious, but skeptical and witty, young gentleman (stanza 4) whose courtly amorousness was a badge of a shared sophisticated life-style. Donne refers specifically to his interests in medicine ("my physicke bookes" [38]), in philosophy ("Morall counsels" [39]), and in collecting coins ("My brazen Medals" [40]).[18] But, more important, he refers to a body of verse he has composed ("all that I in Ryme have writ" [32]), which he assumes the readership knows. The amorous mistress about whose neglect the poem's speaker complains is teasingly described as one spoiled by too much attention (stanza 1), incapable of expressing love (stanza 2), offended by his suitorship (stanza 3), attracted to "yonger lovers," and unappreciative of his "gifts" (45). The mention of "gifts" and the probable use of the word "friendship" (44) in the sense of beneficent patronage point to the kind of patroness/client relationship for which Petrarchan amorousness was an appropriate metaphor, rather than to a love relationship set in the context of social equality. In this framework, the socially superior mistress of this poem is regarded as having stimulated love in the speaker (stanza 4), but she is depicted as one who supposedly needed his poetic praise of her "beauties" (48) and "graces" (50) so they could be manifested to the world—a version of the message the poet/client Shakespeare conveyed to his patron in the *Sonnets*. The witty threat of "dying" (47) for love made in the last stanza is actually an appeal for favor and attention in what is, finally, despite its iconoclastic wit, a lyric of amorous compliment. The audience was meant to be surprised in discovering that Donne had written a lyric of compliment instead of simply an anti-Petrarchan, anticourtly poem of the sort popular with witty young men.[19]

"The Blossom" has the marks of a lyric of compliment composed, probably, as a witty thank-you note for hospitality enjoyed in the household of a woman of fashion.[20] It opens with two stanzas that enact a style of polite social Petrarchanism:

> Little think'st thou, poore flower,
>   Whom I'have watch'd sixe or seaven dayes,
> And seene thy birth, and seene what every houre
> Gave to thy growth, thee to this height to raise,
> And now dost laugh and triumph on this bough,
>   Little think'st thou

> That it will freeze anon, and that I shall
> To morrow finde thee falne, or not at all.
>
> Little think'st thou poore heart
> That labour'st yet to nestle thee,
> And think'st by hovering here to get a part
> In a forbidden or forbidding tree,
> And hop'st her stiffenesse by long siege to bow:
>   Little think'st thou,
> That thou to morrow, ere that Sunne doth wake,
> Must with this Sunne, and mee a journey take.

The situation being metaphorized, these lines suggest, is that of a happy visit of "sixe or seaven dayes" that is about to come to an end. The Petrarchan language of frustrated desire defines the limits of the decorum within which a socially deferential man must function. The complaint to the mistress whose "stiffenesse" will not allow her to reciprocate erotic affection is an oblique form of praise of her virtue, for the expression "forbidden or forbidding tree" implies not only that she is a married woman,[21] but also of a higher social rank than the poet. Figuratively a Petrarchan "Sunne" whose bright radiance holds the lover's attention, the mistress is one properly addressed in the language of amorous complaint or refined praise.

The last three stanzas of the poem, however, shift the style from the sentimental to the bluntly realistic, comically rendering a situation of debate between the soul and body (or heart and head) in a way that bespeaks a more casual social familiarity and provides a wittily critical context for the very mode with which the poem began. A return to London, to the society of men, where the speaker has other "businesse" (20), is comically portrayed as a departure occasioned by erotic frustration. From the point of view from which one sees love as a sexual as well as an emotional and intellectual experience, polite Petrarchan and Neoplatonic amorousness, love of the "heart" (24, 27, 29, 32) and "minde" (40), is incomplete or distorted—a familiar idea in Donne's lyrics. The language of these stanzas, that of libertine or iconoclastic male-audience verse, acts as a corrective to that of the complimentary initial stanzas.

What is said, however, in the context of the debate[22] in the last three stanzas, looks like sophisticated teasing—for the benefit, perhaps, of a specific female reader with whom the poet was on some terms of social familiarity. In addressing his own heart, the speaker charges the beloved with heartlessness, suggesting bawdily that she will "know some other part" (31) through "Practise" (31) or experience as he says he will turn away from her to "another friend" (39) (or mistress) willing to have a physical as well as an intellectual relationship. But such a comic assault on the decorum of complimentary verse paradoxically reaffirms the polite character of the relationship of social inequality the poem fictionalizes, expressing a reluctance to part at the termination of a visit. Clay Hunt is right, I think, when he says: "The effect of [Donne's] clowning . . . is, in the final analysis not that of destructive satire but rather of high comedy. The turnabout in the middle of the poem makes fun of the conventionalized emotion of the first two stanzas, but the ridicule is so engagingly playful that it does not actually obliterate the romantic sentiment of the opening. Its effect is rather to sophisticate that sentiment by criticism and thus to give to it a suggestion of essential genuineness which it originally lacked."[23] One has only to set this poem beside a nonironic Petrarchan handling of the same material such as Thomas Watson's "A Dialogue betweene the Louer and his heart"[24] to note the difference between naive and sophisticated complimentary lyricism.

Despite his exercises in the mode, Donne portrayed fashionable amorousness as a cynical game in two lyrics probably composed about this time, "Loves Alchymie" and "Farewell to Love." A. J. Smith suggests that the latter "was written before the great celebrations of mutual love—while that further possibility, unglimpsed here, was yet to prove. . . . We must take it as a report on experience up till then; and this indeed seems to be how Donne himself saw it."[25] It is useful to examine these renunciation-of-love lyrics, as Smith does, against the background of intellectual and literary history against which they were written and in the framework of Donne's other love poetry, but we should also recognize that poems like "Loves Alchymie" and "Farewell to Love" were also familiar political gestures. At least from the time of Wyatt, the renunciation lyric expressed disappointment and disillusionment with the game of courtly striving. This kind of poem, then, could be seen as an anticourtly act on the part of the man whose ambitions were frustrated and who had mixed feelings about entering the courtly world. Both of Donne's lyrics are palinodes. At the end of *Cynthia's Revels*, Ben Jonson arranges for the stupidly fashionable courtier-lovers to be punished by being forced to sing a palinode[26]—obviously the sort of verse that could be conceived of as the antithesis of the courtly amorous lyric and, therefore, by his comic logic, as a way of curing the characters of their foolish behavior. As in the case of the antagonist in Donne's fourth satire, what is wrong with the Court is symbolized by its amorous fashions. To reject these is to reject the rules they enacted and the environment to which they belonged.

Donne's two palinodes are exercises in an established form performed for an audience of sympathetic, knowledgeable males, gentleman-amorists, like his earlier Inns-of-Court readers, expert in the full range of libertine and polite love practices and able to entertain a critical point of view toward their own actions. These poems, like Donne's earlier amorous lyrics, are the work of a young man—mischievous, iconoclastic, self-consciously witty—yet they are presented also as the utterances of someone with considerable experience, particularly in the world of the Court where Petrarchan and Neoplatonic conventions were part of a system of deferential politeness, of patronage relationships, and of ambitious striving. As in the fourth satire and some of the verse letters of the late nineties, Donne dissociates himself from courtly practices and language partly in order to proclaim his independence and autonomy, partly to express frustration and disillusionment and he assumed a readership whose attitudes and awareness were similar to his.

The blunt rhetorical manner of "Loves Alchymie" marks it, like the libertine elegies and lyrics, as a male-audience piece.[27] Through the use of the first-person-plural pronoun in the poem's second stanza, the first stanza's personal disenchantment becomes a kind of shared cynicism. This lyric assumes that speaker and listeners have both acted the role of the fashionable lover, wasting their "ease," "thrift," "honor," and "day" (13). The contemptuous dismissal of marriage in the poem resembles the comic hostility to the institution expressed in some of the love elegies, and the critique of the courtly Neoplatonic amorist's attitude toward love looks like the easy gesture of the libertine skeptic. Like some of the earlier lyrics and some of the prose pieces of the nineties, this poem is an exercise in outrageous paradox, deliberately excessive in its statements in order to force a hard reexamination of its subject matter.

"Loves Alchymie" particularly mocks the Neoplatonic "loving wretch" (18) who views love as a spiritual or mental joining, the path to a "hidden mysterie" (5). Donne uses a kind of facile antifeminism (e.g., "Hope not for minde in women" [23]) to demythologize the *donna angelicata* of spiritual lovers, perhaps with a contemporary sonnet sequence like Spenser's *Amoretti* in mind.[28] The cynicism of the piece is far-reaching: it not only criticizes the foolishness of some forms of fashionable loving, but also the experience of love in a more general sense. To claim "'tis imposture all" (6) is to reject the good with the bad, the sensible with the foolish. The end of the first stanza has the tone of personal disappointment, if not of self-hate: "lovers dreame a rich and long delight, / But get a winter-seeming summers night" (11–12). Expressing skepticism about finding "happinesse" in love, either through fashionable amorousness or marriage, the poem seems more than a mere literary experiment in desentimentalization. It seems to speak for a shared discontent.

"Farewell to Love"[29] is in the same mode. A. J. Smith has brilliantly analyzed this poem in terms of the literary tradition of the renunciation lyric and of Donne's mind and temperament. He sees it as evidence of Donne's dismissal of the Neoplatonic theory of love in favor of a more tough-minded, pragmatic, sexually realistic point of view.[30] Rhetorically assuming an all-male audience, this lyric appeals to coterie attitudes and a common fund of experiences in the worlds of City and Court. The "wee" (21) of the lyric is a community of sophisticated males familiar with contemporary modes of amorous verse and wooing proper to both courtly and noncourtly circumstances. The poem is addressed to an audience that has, like the speaker, pursued "love" (2) both as a social fashion and as a means to sexual satisfaction. It criticizes equally both libertine and Petrarchan/Neoplatonic amorousness as it applies the idea of the *remedia amoris* to all kinds of love, not simply to the Ovidian variety. But it specifically locates sexual experience in a courtly environment, as the last stanza makes clear:

>   Since so, my minde
> Shall not desire what no man else can finde,
> I'll no more dote and runne
> To pursue things which had indammag'd[31] me.
> And when I come where moving beauties be,
> As men doe when the summers Sunne
>   Growes great,
> Though I admire their greatnesse, shun their heat;
> Each place can afford shadowes. If all faile,
> 'Tis but applying worme-seed to the Taile.
>   (31–40)

In this section, the word "greatnesse," like the earlier terms "reverence" (3) and "admire" (15), suggest the politely complimentary situation of the kind of amorousness suitable to fashionable courtly society. Donne, I think, knew that his reader would identify the place "where moving beauties be" as what he calls elsewhere the "Torrid Zone at Court" ("Obsequies to the Lord Harrington," 124). He demystifies courtly Petrarchan and Neoplatonic amorousness by pointing out that it has no proper object: it is a fabrication of men's "desires" (9), not the acknowledgment of perceived worth. Furthermore, as the second stanza of the poem suggests, its teleology is sexual—a fact courtly writers like Gascoigne, Oxford, and Ralegh occasionally acknowledged. The fashionable courtly lover, then, is depicted as pursuing the same self-destructive sexual ends as the libertine. In this lyric the familiar Donnean fantasy that love hurts or kills does not simply take the form of post-coital sadness ("A kinde of sorrowing dulnesse to the minde" [20] or the loss of a day of one's life for every orgasm [24–25]); it involves a larger fear and disappointment. As Smith has put it, Donne's sweeping "dismissal of love" in "Farewell to Love" signals his "coming to recognize the point of repeated disillusionments, seeing the true state of things and then exercising the limited freedom we can have by deliberately standing aside, in full awareness of what that, too, entails."[32]

In both palinodes there is a sense of self-revulsion, a jaded rejection of familiar social and literary rituals in which Donne himself presumably engaged. But the context of the statements these lyrics make is as much social and personal as intellectual and literary. One finds in the verse and prose letters of the late nineties an extended exploration of disillusionment, set against the background of Donne's growing courtly involvement, both before and after his employment by Egerton. The epistle he probably wrote in 1597[33] to Rowland Woodward, for example, seemingly in response to his friend's request for copies of his poems, expresses an attitude toward his literary productions similar to that expressed toward love in the palinodes.

In this piece, Donne specifically disparaged poetic composition as he developed the classical epistolary theme of the value of spiritual self-cultivation. He explained that he was writing no verse at the time and regretted both having wasted his energy in such activity and having shown his work to others:

> Like one who'in her third widdowhood doth professe
> Her selfe a Nunne, ty'd to retirednesse,
> So'affects my muse now, a chaste fallownesse;
>
> Since shee to few, yet to too many'hath showne
> How love-song weeds, and Satyrique thornes are growne
> Where seeds of better Arts, were early sown.
>
> Though to use, and love Poëtrie, to mee,
> Betroth'd to no'one Art, be no'adulterie;
> Omissions of good, ill, as ill deeds bee.
>
> For though to us it seeme,'and be light and thinne,
> Yet in those faithfull scales, where God throwes in
> Mens workes, vanity weighs as much as sinne.
>
> (1–12)

At a time of uncertainty about his future, Donne looked back on the previous few years he spent as an Inns-of-Court gallant who occasionally wrote poetry as a period of a sinful waste of his talents.[34] The negative attitude toward poetry as a lesser craft ("Art") compared to more worthy endeavors is of a piece with comments he makes elsewhere about verse-making,[35] but it is deliberately exaggerated in an epistle whose basic terms are those of Senecan Stoicism and its moral application to his and his friend's social experiences. Although Donne probably had no intention at the time of ceasing to write either satiric or amorous verse, he did engage in the sort of self-examination cultivated in the humanist epistle, even as he moved toward greater political involvement in the pursuit of preferment and career. Especially in the verse letters to such friends as Christopher Brooke, Henry Wotton, and Rowland Woodward, he shared with coterie readers some of the conflicted feelings with which he acted on his ambitions in a world whose realities he and his audience clearly perceived.

"The Storme" and "The Calme," the two epistles to Christopher Brooke written on the occasion of the Islands voyage[36] are especially powerful poems of self-examination and self-criticism. In the first, "The Storme," Donne reflects on his entry into the public world through his military service. He treats his friend and former chambermate from Lincoln's Inn as an alter ego in these poems, blurring the line between meditative self-address and the interpersonal communication—a fruitful and characteristic technique for Donne:

> Thou which art I ('tis nothing to be soe)
> Thou which art still thy selfe, by these [lines] shalt know
> Part of our passage . . .
> (1–3)

he begins, assuming a responsive reader able to infer much from little in understanding the implications of what he has written. Donne later revealed his attraction to the familiar epistle as the most intimate form of written communication. And in the case of some of his verse and prose letters he was not simply reciting a commonplace idea: he meant it.

The moral, philosophical, and religious reflections in "The Storme," and in the succeeding epistle as well, do not simply have the force of general observations on life; they suggest, in context, a particular set of attitudes toward social and political involvement. The storm that Donne metaphorizes has some of the moral and theological dimensions of Shakespeare's tempest (underscored in both cases by biblical imagery),[37] but it also suggests the perilousness of the political winds of Fortune that could alternately favor or destroy ambitious men. Discovering the hazards of fruitless military adventure, the speaker of this poem finds pursuit of honor and fortune deeply disillusioning, morally wrong, ultimately self-destructive. Although he does not wish his longed-for friend to share his misery in person—"So violent, yet long these furies bee, / That though thine absence sterve me,'I wish not thee" (73–74)—he does want to communicate the moral and emotional meaning of his experience. Whatever idealism or romantic expectations Donne still had when he joined the Islands Expedition, he was forced to acknowledge, from experience, that "Fates, or Fortunes drifts none can soothsay, / Honour and misery have one face and way" (11–12). Disillusioned by his adventures, he tried to save his idealism by relocating it in the friendship he and his addressee shared.[38]

In "The Calme" Donne again wrote to a man who shared with him both the serious and the recreational life of the Inns-of-Court gentleman—including the activity of "Mistressing" ("To Mr. Tilman after he had taken orders," 30). What he says about the tattered tackling of the becalmed ship suggests that it is a symbol not only of the superficial luxury of the world but also of the state of the ruined gallant: ". . . All our beauty, and our trimme, decayes, / Like courts removing, or like ended playes" (13–14).[39] He makes a point similar to the one made by Sir Arthur Gorges, who described the effects of the earlier storm on the dandified gentlemen-volunteers, recounting the way harsh experience at sea could dispel their romantic illusions: "This violent and dangerous tempest had so cooled and battered the courages of a great many or our young Gentlemen (who seeing that the boysterous winds and mercilesse Seas, had neither affinitie with London delicacie, nor Court bravery) as that discharging their high Plumes, and imbroydered Cassockes, they secretly retired themselves home, forgetting either to bid their friends farewell, or to take leave of their Generall."[40]

Donne, who might have had earlier military experience, was undaunted by hardship, but he acknowledged in this poem that he had poor reasons for becoming a gentleman-volunteer, confessing "I lose my end" (42). Helpless, unable to control his experiences, miserable both physically and emotionally on the becalmed ship, Donne was pessimistic about his military adventure and about his usefulness in the world of action: "wee are for nothing fit" (53). Although the Cadiz raid had been a limited success, the Islands Expedition was a fiasco, his own and his fellow mariners' dreams of wealth and glory dashed. The real benefit he derived from this military experience was the friend-

THE WRITING OF THE EMPLOYED COURTIER

As Bald points out, Sir Thomas Egerton the elder was, like Donne, a Lincoln's Inn man with a recusant background. He was also one of the Earl of Essex's most important clients, a trusted government minister in whose service a young and talented man like Donne might have expected to prosper.[41] In the four-year period Donne functioned as one of Egerton's secretaries, he earned the Lord Keeper's respect and, if we can believe Walton,[42] his friendship. He was involved in transacting business at Court and in Parliament—obviously progressing well in a career in which he could have obtained eventually a prestigious government appointment. Donne's employment affected the matter and manner of his fifth (and last) satire; it is obviously not, like the previous four satires, the work of a political outsider. Although he still criticized contemporary social ills, naming particularly the abuses of the legal system Elizabeth had charged Egerton to investigate and reform,[43] Donne here addressed both Queen and minister in a way that carefully advertised his own position in the political hierarchy:

> Greatest and fairest Empresse, know you this?
> Alas, no more then Thames calme head doth know
> Whose meades her armes drowne, or whose corne o'rflow:
> You Sir, whose righteousnes she loves, whom I
> By having leave to serve, am most richly
> For service paid, authoriz'd, now beginne
> To know and weed out this enormous sinne.
> (28–34)

The "sinne" Donne discusses is the abusive legal-fee charging of court officers, but the kind of relationship he describes between officers and suitors applied to political transactions in general. The subject of "Officers rage, and Suiters misery" (8) is one that he could handle with more equanimity than was possible in the fourth satire, where he uncomfortably identified with the sorry lot of courtly petitioners. But, even here, there is a disturbance caused by Donne's sense of his own vulnerability.

Although the section addressing the Queen and her minister proclaims Donne to be part of the Establishment, there is a curious use of pronouns in this satire that reveals his inability to separate himself (and his readers) from the vexed condition of suitorship. In the metaphoric definitions of the officer-suitor relationship, Donne switches from the third to the second person:

> . . . man is a world; in which, Officers
> Are the vast ravishing seas; and Suiters,
> Springs; now full, now shallow, now drye; which, to
> That which drownes them, run: These selfe reasons do
> Prove the world a man, in which, officers
> Are the devouring stomacke, and Suiters
> Th'excrements, which they voyd. All men are dust;
> How much worse are Suiters, who to mens lust
> Are made preyes? O worse then dust, or wormes meat,
> For they do'eate you now, whose selves wormes shall eate.
> They are the mills which grinde you, yet you are
> The winde which drives them; and a wastfull warre
> Is fought against you, and you fight it; they
> Adulterate lawe, and you prepare their way
> Like wittals; th'issue your owne ruine is.
>   (13–27)

The "you" of this passage are "Suiters,"[44] but they are speaker's audience and the poet's readers as well. The word carries the sense of "one," which would include the speaker himself. In the light of this, the address to Elizabeth and Egerton that follows this passage seems like a way of establishing the speaker's (and author's) own position of authority and security, a gesture, on Donne's part, of separating himself from the abject misery of both courtly and judicial suitorship.

Although the "you" of line 40 refers to the "gamsters" being apostrophized, the singular pronoual forms of "thou" and "thee" of a succeeding passage seem to be directed at the reader (as well as functioning, perhaps, partly, as self-address):

> If Law be in the Judges heart, and hee
> Have no heart to resist letter, or fee,
> Where wilt thou'appeale? Powre of the Courts below
> Flow from the first maine head, and these can throw
> Thee, if they sucke thee in, to misery,
> To fetters, halters; But if th'injury
> Steele thee to dare complaine, Alas, thou go'st
> Against the stream, when upwards: when thou'art most
> Heavy'and most faint; and in these labours they,
> 'Gainst whom thou should'st complaine, will in the way
> Become great seas, o'r which, when thou shalt bee

> Forc'd to make golden bridges, thou shalt see
> That all thy gold was drown'd in them before;
> All things follow their like, only who have may'have more.
> (43–56)

Donne wrote this poem, like the other satires, to the audience of friends he felt most comfortable addressing in the 1590s, men he knew from the Inns of Court and from his succeeding social experience. Identified with this group in intellectual, social, and career interests, he could, as in the above passage, address them familiarly in the second person, or, as he does in some of the lines that follow this passage, switch to the first-person-plural form that includes them both:

> . . . When supplications
> We send to God, to Dominations,
> Power, Cherubins, and all heavens Courts, if wee
> Should pay fees as here, daily bread would be
> Scarse to Kings; so 'tis.
> (59–63)

Donne writes as a peer-group representative, one who, moreover, has found the sort of position of service he and his fellows sought. Yet in discussing the officer-suitor relationship as that of oppressor and oppressed, it is clear with which party he and his audience identified. Despite the attempt at a somewhat more magisterial tone than can be found in *Satires* 1, 2, and 4, Donne's conflicts and ambivalences about the Court and the Establishment come through strongly in this poem.

As I. A. Shapiro has argued in a recent essay, Donne probably composed "A Funeral Elegy" on the occasion of the death in the Irish wars of his friend Sir Thomas Egerton, Jr.[45] A member of the Lord Keeper's household, Donne wrote as one whose social position and whose friendship with the deceased young man entitled him to carry the fallen soldier's sword in the funeral procession. Donne referred to York House ("this house" [1]) as one who lived there on terms of social familiarity, but, of course, the very composition of the poem was an obvious act of clientage on his part—as were the later commemorative poems for Elizabeth Drury and Lord Harington. Donne owed his secretaryship to the young Egerton as he did his continued employment and prospects of advancement to the bereaved father. In such circumstances, the primary readership of the poem was probably Sir Thomas Egerton, Sr.,[46] and the other inhabitants of York House, in addition to those friends with whom the poet and the younger Egerton had been associated. In this situation of emotional agitation, Donne, as a securely employed young courtier, could use economically and politically significant terms like "heire" (2), "rise" (12), "Venturers" (15), and "Venture their states" (16) with a kind of calm missing in the more-importunate earlier and later verse. In the elegy, Donne wrote as one who was enjoying some of the benefits of official patronage.

Nevertheless, the prose and verse letters written about this time, especially those to Henry Wotton, contain a surprisingly strong strain of anticourtly and antiestablishment feeling. Composed in the context of a long-standing friendship as well as in their mutual connection with, and attraction to, the Earl of Essex, these epistles use the language of Christian Stoicism [47] to deal with contemporary politics and the experiences of friends with common ambitions. The first of the pieces, "Sir, more then kisses, letters mingle Soules," was probably written between Donne's return from the Islands voyage and the beginning of his employment with Egerton. In many ways, it sets out most of the themes developed in the succeeding Wotton epistles: the perils of ambition, the corruption of the Court, the disillusionments of political involvement, the value of stoical adherence to virtue, and the value of friendship. Grierson argued that this verse letter was part of a literary debate or exchange among Essex clients—Bacon, Wotton, and Donne—but it is probably more likely that Donne and Wotton wrote an epistolary exchange on the occasion of their agreement to develop the ancient topic handled in one of the four stanzas of Bacon's "The world's a bubble":[48]

> . . . since with sorrow here we live oppressed,
>   What life is best?
> Courts are but only superficial schools
>   To dandle fools:
> The rural parts are turned into a den
>   Of savage men:
> And where's a city from all vice so free,
> But may be termed the worst of all the three.[49]
>   (9–16)

In his lyrical exercise in pessimism, the desperately ambitious Bacon rehearsed old opinions that might lead to stoic apathy or to an attitude of Christian *contemptus mundi*, the stances of those sick in fortune. His rejection of the Court was patently disingenuous: one has only to read the mass of letters he composed in the 1590s asking for courtly advancement to have a clear record of his ambitious strivings in this period. In the context of Donne's and his friends' energetic pursuit of political preferment, stoical and Christian celebrations of virtue in the medium of the humanist verse epistle, then, seem to have been a form of moral atonement or an intellectual idyll through which they could affirm certain values that might have been compromised by their actual behavior.

Poetic discussion of the merits and demerits of life in the Court, City, and Country was, thus, more than mere literary imitation or the recitation of intellectual commonplaces; it was, in its immediate context, the expression of individual responses to Elizabethan sociocultural codes. Donne and Wotton composed their poems from the point of view of educated, cultivated, ambitious courtly aspirants, as men who regarded the Country as a desert or region of exile, the City as a place for meaner pleasures and crass business dealings, and the Court, however dangerous or corrupt, as the social and political center of attraction. Both men were impatient and frustrated in their search for preferment. Wotton was following an Earl whose political fortunes were clearly declining; Donne, who was disillusioned by his adventures as a gentleman-volunteer, had yet to assume the position as Egerton's secretary. In particular, the pose of stoical fortitude that Wotton strikes in his epistle suits the situation of the disappointed political aspirant.

Wotton's epistle defines intellectual self-possession and stoic apathy as the true source of happiness: "It is the mind that make the mans estate / For ever happy or unfortunate" (5-6). Whether one is in the Country or the Court, it is one's moral and intellectual disposition that counts:

> ... the mind of passions must be free
>   Of him that would to happiness aspire;
> Whether in Princes Pallaces he bee,
>   Or whether to his cottage he retire;
> For our desires that on extreames are bent
> Are frends to care and traitors to content.
>   (7-12)

Celebrating friendship and virtue, Wotton concluded his poem by modestly asserting that he was not presuming to advise his addressee (who supposedly did not need to learn from him), but rather that he was using the occasion of writing to another to recall certain truths to himself: "For men doe often learne when they do teach" (30).[50]

Donne's poem, which appears to reply to Wotton's in its last stanza, is a much more elaborate analysis of the Country, Court, and City in the context of the vicissitudes of ambition. The epistle opens with an appeal to friendship as the emotional and moral sustenance of men of the world like Wotton and himself: "Sir, more then kisses, letters

The Writing of the Employed Courtier 121

mingle Soules: / For, thus friends absent speake" (1–2). In one of his prose letters of the period (probably also to Wotton) he called letters "frendships sacraments" (Simpson, *Prose*, p. 311), the medium for what he elsewhere termed the "religion of friendship" (Simpson, *Prose*, p. 316).

From the point of view of moral idealism, Donne treats City, Court, and Country all as dangerous environments:

> Life is a voyage, and in our lifes wayes
> Countries, Courts, Towns are Rockes, or Remoraes;
> They breake or stop all ships. . . .
> (7–9)

One can be "Parch'd in the Court, and in the country frozen" (15), but the City is no better. He defines all three places as unfavorable, suggesting, however, that the Court is the least boring:

> Cities are Sepulchres; they who dwell there
> Are carcases, as if no such there were.
> And Courts are Theatres, where some men play
> Princes, some slaves, all to one end, and of one clay.
> The Country is a desert, where no good,
> Gain'd (as habits, not borne,) is understood.
> There men become beasts, and prone to more evils;
> In cities blockes, and in a lewd court, devills.
> (21–28)

Donne takes a moral tack in dealing with the Court in this section, but what really seems to have bothered him the most were the power relationships in which he was felt he would be in a disadvantageous position.

In naming "pride, lust, and covetize" (31) as endemic to City, Court, and Country, Donne identified motives for which he later excoriated himself in both the *Essays in Divinity* and the *Sermons*. Here he suggests that the man involved in the world lies to himself and to others if he claims that he can participate in an evil environment but remain innocent:

> Let no man say there, Virtues flintie wall
> Shall locke vice in mee,'I'll do none, but know all.
> Men are spunges, which to poure out, receive,
> Who know false play, rather then lose, deceive.
> (35–38)

This reasoning exposes the rationalization Donne himself offered for his own courtiership in a later prose letter to Wotton: "I am no Courtier for wthout having liued there desirously I cannot haue sin'd enough to haue deserv'd that reprobate name: I may sometymes go thither & bee no courtier as well as they may sometymes go to chapell & yet are no christians" (Simpson, *Prose*, p. 310). In the verse letter Donne was more skeptical about his or anyone's ability to remain untainted by courtly vices, conscious of the process by which "white integritie" (42) could be lost as a "Utopian youth" became an "old Italian" (46).

In this poem the moral solution to the dangers facing the man involved in the political world is a radical one, stoical withdrawal: ". . . in thy selfe dwell. . . . Bee thine owne Palace, or the world's thy Gaole" (47, 52). Recognizing the conventionality of periodic retreats from Court to Country undertaken for a variety of motives, Donne advises his correspondent to avoid simply playing the courtly game of alternating involvement and withdrawal:

> . . . To make
> Court hot ambitions wholesome, do not take
> A dramme of Countries dulnesse; do not adde
> Correctives, but as chymiques, purge the bad.
> (59–62)

This is the kind of social and moral retreat recommended in the first four satires.

In the context of Donne's and Wotton's common desire for secular advancement, however, a poem like "Sir, more then kisses" would have been read with an awareness that its stoical advice was disingenuous. Its real purpose, I believe, was to express intellectual and emotional reservations about pursuing one's ambitions, not to indicate any serious intention of retreating from the world of action into that of contemplation. Both Donne and Wotton were energetically ambitious young men eager for preferment and its rewards, interested in the skills by which one could succeed at Court. Although Donne professed a devotion to the life of contemplation implied by his motto, "Per Rachel ho servito e non per Lea," his actions, at least from the late 1590s through 1614, indicated that he was only content when he was politically active.[51]

In another verse letter, "Here's no more newes," written while Wotton was still away from London and from the gossip of Court and City, Donne expressed the same moral reservations about worldly involvement found in "Sir, more then kisses," but the difference is that he wrote as a man with courtly employment, not as a disgruntled aspirant.[52] The date given for the poem in the Westmoreland and Drummond manuscripts is 20 July 1598,[53] some three weeks after the famous incident at Court in which Elizabeth boxed the Earl of Essex's ears for his public display of insolence toward her. Since Wotton was still secretary to Essex (who was in exile from the Court from July to September) and since both he and Donne shared a keen interest in the fortunes of the Earl, the anticourtly sentiments of the verse letter are not simply general attitudes of moral disapproval, but the shared feelings of two men of the same faction and background. Donne's stance of skepticism, distanced criticism, and cynicism suited the situation of clients whose great patron had begun his disastrous decline.[54]

Unlike the fifth satire, which expresses trust in benevolent authorities within the Establishment, this verse letter harbors no illusions about the Court and its inhabitants. Donne explains to his rusticating friend, "I haunt Court, or Towne" (6), but the subscription of the final line of the poem seems to apologize for his presence in a degenerate environment: "*At Court*; though *From Court*, were the better stile" (27). Again, he assumed that political involvement could either corrupt or harm good men:

> If they stand arm'd with seely honesty,
> With wishing prayers, and neat integritie,
> Like Indians 'gainst Spanish hosts they bee.
> (13–15)

The honest, but sophisticated man of the world knows how to approach courtly business with skepticism and to view it scornfully as an absurd spectacle:

> Suspitious boldnesse to this place belongs,
> And to'have as many eares as all have tongues;
> Tender to know, rough to acknowledge wrongs.
>
> Beleeve mee Sir, in my youths giddiest dayes,
> When to be like the Court, was a playes praise,
> Playes were not so like Courts, as Courts'are like playes.
> (16–21)

Although Donne was engaged in the daily business of one of Elizabeth's chief ministers and came to know the workings of the Court much more closely than before, this did not prevent him from communicating feelings of aversion, disappointment, and disillusionment.

These were the attitudes of many of Essex's civilian and military clients, even of those who were fortunate enough to find courtly employment. Francis Bacon, for example, was dissatisfied with his position as one of the Queen's solicitors and, with the Earl's help, frantically strove to get the job of Attorney General, the post that Sir Edward Coke obtained. There were clear limits to Essex's ability to secure important places in Elizabeth's government for his followers,[35] because the Queen, who ruled by balancing factions against one another, did not want to find herself surrounded by too many of Essex's clients. The ears-boxing incident, in fact, was precipitated by the Earl's failure, after Lord Burghley's death, to obtain for himself the Mastership of the Court of Wards, a position of great economic and political power. Jealously guarding his prerogatives, Essex was forced, when the generalship of the expeditionary force to Ireland was being discussed in the Privy Council, to request the post for himself—against the express advice of Bacon, who knew that Elizabeth feared most a man who could command a military force capable of overthrowing her.[56]

Like many of Donne's other friends, Wotton followed Essex to Ireland on the campaign that the Earl bungled badly. One verse epistle, "H. W. in Hiber. Bellegranti," survives from this period—a time defined by Essex's glorious departure from London in March to his unauthorized return in September, when he burst into Elizabeth's bedchamber.[57] The poem is a teasing reminder to Wotton to keep up their correspondence as the vehicle of their friendship. In asking for the kind of plain, honest letters friends wrote to one another, it is interesting that Donne mentioned both the "labor'd letters" (17) composed in the complimentary mode and the politically dangerous epistles that "feare / Dishonest carriage" (19).[58] He probably knew, in the case of the latter sort, that Elizabeth, who expressly forbade Essex to return to England without her permission, feared his military power, and had many spies and informants watching his and his followers' actions, including their correspondence. Thus Donne acknowledged the danger Wotton faced if he put in writing anything that could have been interpreted as politically threatening. In one of his prose letters to Donne, Wotton, in fact, alluded to the antagonism of the anti-Essex faction at Court (primarily that of Cecil) and their wish to denigrate anything accomplished on the Irish expedition:

Whatsoever we have done, or mean to do, we know what will become of it, when it comes amongst our worst enemies, which are interpreters. I would there were more O'Neales and Macguiers and O'Donnells and Macmahons, and fewer of them. It is true that this kingdom hath ill affections and ill corruptions; but they where you are have a stronger disease, you diminish all that is here done; and yet you doubt (if you were nearly examined) the greatness of it; so as you believe what is contrary to as much as you fear. These be the wise rules of policy, and of Courts, which are upon earth the vainest places. I will say no more, and yet peradventure I have said a great deal unto you.[59]

The "great deal" that Wotton said was as much a product of the content of his letter as the implications his knowing correspondent would tease out of it, the situation of verse epistles as well. Things were going poorly for Essex and his followers not only on the battlefield (largely through his own fault) but also back in London at the center of power. Thus, when Donne said, in a prose letter to Wotton, that he sent "the loue & seruices of one who had rather bee honest then fortunate" (Simpson, *Prose*, p. 307) he alluded to the poor political position of a typical member of the Essex faction and to the sense of moral superiority that supposedly compensated for political disadvantages.

After Essex's return and his being remanded to the official custody of Egerton, Donne had the opportunity to watch the Earl's behavior at York House as well as to notice the doings in the Court from which the Earl was barred.[60] The kind of disillusionment that courses through much of Donne's moral and satiric poetry of the 1590s found a certain focus in the plight of the Earl and of his devoted followers. And so, in one of his contemporary letters to Wotton, Donne referred to "these tymes wch are ariued to y^t height of illness y^t no man dares accuse them bycause every one contributes much himself to y^t accesse." Using the typical complaint of the courtly loser, Donne said "envy . . . is now growne a pfect vice, for heretofore it was but oposed to good fortune & so men might be thought to rich now it is oposd to vertue & a man may be to good" (Simpson, *Prose*, p. 311)—a highly partisan attitude, especially if used as an explanation of Essex's political troubles. Again, Wotton was in the country when Donne wrote him, probably having retreated there after the Queen's forceful response to the Earl's unauthorized and dangerous return from Ireland.[61] Donne wished his friend back in London where he could "a little trip though not fall nor stumble att ambition or other distractions. least I seing an honest man happy should begin for y^r sake to loue the world again wch I would be loath to do" (Simpson, *Prose*, p. 312). Other letters from 1600 deal with the Court as the center of "envie & detractions of ielousy" (Simpson, *Prose*, p. 308). The connection between Donne's hostility to the Court and his sympathy for the fallen Essex is explicit in another letter to Wotton in which he explained his necessary presence at Court:

I am there now where because I must do some evill I envy y^r being in ye country not that it is a vice will make any great shew here for they liue at a far greter rate & expence of wickednes. but because I will not be vtterly out of fashion & vnsociable. I gleane such vices as the greater men (whose barnes are full) scatter yet I learne that ye learnedst in vice suffer some misery for when they haue reapd flattery or any other fault long there comes some other new vice in request wherein they are vnpracticed. only ye women are free from this charg for they are sure they cannot bee worse nor more throwne downe then they haue beene: they haue pchance heard that god will hasten his iudgment for ye righteous sake. & they affect not that hast & therfore seeke to lengthen out ye world by their wickednes. The Court is not great but full if iollyty & revells & playes and as merry as if it were not sick. her m^{tie} is well disposed & very gratious in publique to my Lo: Mountioy my lo: of Essex and his trayne are no more mist here then the Aungells wch were cast down from heaven nor (for anything I see) likeyer to retourne. he withers still in his sicknes & plods on to his end in the same place where y^o left vs. the worst accidents of his sicknes are y^t he conspires wth it & y^t it is not here beleeved. that wch was sayd of Cato y^t his age vnderstood him not I feare may be averted of y^r lo: that he vnderstood not his age: for it is a naturall weakes of inno-cency. That such men want lockes for themselues & keyes for others. (Simp-son, *Prose*, p. 310)

Essex's sickness reached its worst point in late November and early December 1599.[62] Donne's letter probably belongs to the Christmas season during which there would have been plays and revels at Court. In order to express his moral aversion to courtly degeneracy in the context of a devotion to the Earl he and his correspondent shared, Donne contrasted the depressed, outcast Essex, who was languishing at York House, with the merriment of the Court functioning without his presence. Although his partisanship is clear, he does admit, at the end of this letter, that Essex's temperament caused many problems.

In an interesting letter mentioning some of the reading he was doing, Donne reacts to Dante in terms of his present political percep-tions by taking issue with that author's treatment of Pope Celestine's withdrawal from public life: "Even when I begun to write these [lines] I flung away Dant the Italian a man pert enough to bee beloved & to much to bee beeleeued: it angred me that Celestine a pope far frō the manners of other popes y^t he left even there a seat should by ye court of Dants witt bee attached & by him throwne into his purgatory. . . . if he will needs punish retyrednes thus what hell can his witt devise for ambitiō? if white integrity merit this what shall Male or Malū wch Seneca condems most, deserve?" At least from the point of view of the Senecan ideals of the prose and verse epistles, private contempla-tion was preferable to ambitious activity, withdrawal to the Country better than immersion in the Court. Donne, however, acknowledged the problematic character of his moral stance. He made the truth he was articulating both complex and provisional: "Hatton being told after a decree made y^t his p^{r}decessors was of another opinion he answered hee had his genius & I had myne: So say I of authors that they thinke & I thinke both reasonably yet posibly both erroniously; that is manly: for I am so far from pswading yea conselling ẙ to beleeue others ẙᵗ I care not ẙᵗ ẙᵒ beleeue mee when I say ẙᵗ others are not to bee beleeued" (Simpson, *Prose*, p. 313). In the context of Donne's and Wotton's active pursuit of advancement, the anticourtly sentiments and the condemnation of ambition were more rhetorical than moral gestures.

In Sir Henry Wotton, Donne had a friend he regarded as his ideal coterie reader and apparently sent him, as he did Sir Henry Goodyer, much of his verse and prose. In a letter in which he enclosed some of his prose paradoxes, in response to Wotton's request, Donne indicated how he wanted them read, denigrated them along with his other pieces as light recreations, but insisted that no further transcripts be made—partly because of the "feare" and "shame" associated with them:

Only in obedience I send you some of my paradoxes: I love you and myself and them too well to send them willingly for they carry with them a confession of their lightnes, and your trouble and my shame. But indeed they were made rather to deceave tyme than her daughter truth: although they have beene written in an age when any thing is strong enough to overthrow her. If they make you to find better reasons against them they do their office: for they are but swaggerers: quiet enough if you resist them. If perchaunce they be pretyly guilt, that is their best for they are not hatcht: they are rather alarums to truth to arme her than enemies: and they have only this advantadg to scape from being caled ill things that they are nothings. Therefore take heed of allowing any ot them least you make another. Yet Sir though I know their low price, except I receive by your next letter an assurance upon the religion of your friendship that no coppy shalbee taken for any respect of these or any other my compositions sent to you, I shall sinn against my conscience if I send you any more. I speake that in playnes which becomes (methinks) our honestyes; and therfore call not this a distrustfull but a free spirit: I meane to acquaint you with all myne: and to my satyrs there belongs some feare and to some elegies, and these perhaps, shame. Against both which affections although I be tough enough, yet I have a ridling disposition to bee ashamed of feare and afrayd of shame. Therefore I am desirous to hyde them with out any over reconing of them or their maker. But they are not worth thus much words in theyre disprayse. (*Selected Prose*, p. 111)[63]

One gets the impression from this letter that, as Bald has suggested, Donne regarded literary recreations as the kind of activity that could embarrass a serious-minded and ambitious government servant—an attitude that Lord Burghley had certainly held.[64] The *Elegies*, *Satires*, and *Paradoxes* belonged, to Donne's way of thinking, to the youthfully impudent atmosphere he had known at the Inns of Court and, by extension, to the private communications between close friends: to have allowed them to reach a wider public would have been to risk personal embarrassment and misinterpretation, dangers highlighted by the 1599 bishops' order banning satires, epigrams, and obscene and politically dangerous literature.[65]

While in Egerton's employ, Donne nonetheless, as in the case of the prose paradoxes,[66] continued to compose some satiric and witty pieces. Perhaps the strangest of these, and the fitting conclusion to a discussion of Donne's political feelings toward the end of Elizabeth's reign, is the satirical, paradoxical, mock-heroic or antiepical *Metempsychosis*, a poem that, despite its ironic presentation as a public literary document, was a coterie work directed to a politically and intellectually sympathetic audience. It takes on particular significance if read against the background of the political disenchantment of the late 1590s Donne expressed in his verse and prose correspondence with Wotton.[67]

In a wryly ironic preface, dated 16 August 1601, several months after Essex's revolt, trial, and execution, Donne indicated the kind of readership he expected for his highly parodic and, therefore, strongly metapoetic poem. It was, first of all, one that could appreciate his satiric point of view and the risks it involved: "I censure much and taxe; And this liberty costs mee more then others, by how much my owne things are worse then others. Yet I would not be so rebellious against my self, as not to doe it, since I love it; nor so unjust to others, as to do it *sine talione*" (pp. 25–26). As in the *Satires*, he wrote for fellow "alienated intellectuals." Having evidently immersed himself in some of the abstruser philosophical and theological musings of ancient and Renaissance Pythagorean, Gnostic, and cabalistic writers,[68] he addressed himself to men receptive to an intellectual travesty of such ideas, assuming at least a limited familiarity with the material he exploited: "All which I will bid you remember, (for I would have no such Readers as I can teach) is, that the Pithagorian doctrine doth not onely carry one soule from man to man, nor man to beast, but indifferently to plants also . . ." (p. 26). Such a readership would not have been bothered by the incompatibility of epic and satiric genres, which are conflated in the piece, but, being used to the flexible form of Ovidian narrative handled with parodic virtuosity by such writers as Chapman, Marston, and Beaumont, they would have appreciated the poem as a metapoetic discourse on its own ironically presented materials.[69] The metacommunicative framing of such a work was implicit in its coterie circumstances.

The immediate political context was crucial to an understanding of the poem. Critics from the time of Herbert Grierson have recognized some connection between this "bitter and sardonic" (Grierson, 2: xvii) work and the fall of the Earl of Essex.[70] In tracing the progress of that soul that transmigrated through "all her passages from her first making, when she was that apple which Eve eate, to this time when shee is hee, whose life you shall finde in the end of this booke" (p. 26), Donne knew that his sophisticated readers were able to identify the contemporary target of his satiric attack. As van Wyk Smith has convincingly shown,[71] this was Robert Cecil, the most powerful political figure in late Elizabethan England, a man hated by his enemies for his rapacity, his craftiness, his success, *and* his undoubted competence, as well as for his supposed part in engineering the political decline and fall of the Earl of Essex. The general comments on the degeneracy of man—presented as an ironic critique of optimistic Renaissance humanism—had their root in specific circumstances. Like Robert Sidney's agent Rowland Whyte, who responded to Essex's fate by remarking, "This is the greatest downfall I have seen in my daies, which makes me see the vanity of the world,"[72] Donne globalized his feelings and those of his audience in a work that, in effect, was both "revenge and obsequies" (365) for the Earl.

Donne no doubt expected his readers to recognize that his "darke heavy Poem" (55) was a political satire or libel written from the point of view of a disillusioned Essex partisan. They would have been able to perceive, for example, that the sections on the whale and elephant alluded to the betrayal and defeat of the Earl at the hands of his friends and enemies.[73] The wolf and his offspring would have been seen as fairly obvious references to the greed and power of the late Lord Burghley and of his son Robert Cecil,[74] the latter being the last (male) host of the transmigrating soul, the force who supposedly controlled the aging Queen Elizabeth:

> . . . this great soule which here amongst us now
> Doth dwell, and moves that hand, and tongue, and brow,
> Which, as the Moone the sea, moves us. . . .
> (61–63)

But the topicality of the satire is finally less important than the articulation of a general vocabulary of disappointment to which Donne and his readers could relate their own failed aspirations, whatever their retrospective feelings about the deceased Essex. As in his earlier coterie writing, Donne used intellectual exclusiveness and convoluted wit as the means of fostering group solidarity with a class of sophisticated readers who, like him, were frustrated by their lack of success in the public world. He expressed a kind of personal discontent in *Metempsychosis* to which they could relate sympathetically on the basis of their similar experiences. As in the case of the earlier satires, the thematic center of the work is not the bad moral condition of the world or of the Court, but the shared political dissatisfaction of poet and audience.

As Donne approached the age of thirty, he examined his own "progress" in the world. Comically addressing "Great Destiny" (31), he worried about what the future held for him and hoped, if his was not to be a long life, that he would make a quick end:

> To my sixe lustres almost now outwore,
> Except thy booke owe mee so many more,
> Except my legend be free from the letts
> Of steepe ambition, sleepie povertie,
> Spirit-quenching sickness, dull captivitie,
> Distracting business, and from beauties nets,
> And all that calls from this, and t'other whets,
> O let me not launch out, but let mee save
> Th'expense of braine and spirit; that my grave
>   His right and due, a whole unwasted man may have.
>   (41–50)

In a sense he says his struggles and troubles weren't worth it unless he could look forward to a long, ultimately prosperous life. Donne seemed to regard his position as Egerton's secretary as one of little profit and satisfaction: "Distracting business" and "beauties nets" allude to some of the serious and recreational activities in which he engaged as a courtly servant, but he regarded his "steepe ambition" as unfulfilled. Although he says of both the poem he was writing and the life he was living, "I launch at paradise, and saile toward home" (57), the disillusioned idealism expressed in *Metempsychosis* was related to his desire to succeed in the political world.

There are some specific features of the narrative that underscore the personal resentment behind the political satire. As in the fifth satire, the author's feelings about political exploitation break through the general treatment of the topic. For example, the treatment of the powerful patron in the allegory of the whale is dealt with partly from the point of view of the importunate clients:

> He hunts not fish, but as an officer
> Stayes in his court, as his owne net, and there
> All suitors of all sorts themselves enthrall;

> So on his backe lyes this whale wantoning,
> And in his gulfe-like throat, sucks every thing
> That passeth neare. Fish chaseth fish, and all,
> Flyer and follower, in this whirlpoole fall;
> O might not states of more equality
> Consist? and is it of necessity
>   That thousand guiltlesse smals, to make one great, must die?
>   (321–30)

Earlier in the poem Donne's simile describing a fish carried off into the air by a bird expresses similar resentment about the relationship of great patrons and their vulnerable dependents: "Exalted she'is, but to th'exalters good, / As are by great ones, men which lowly stood" (278–79). In both cases, Donne seems to have examined retrospectively the kind of relationship he, Wotton, and a number of other friends had with Essex. Although he allegorized the destruction of Essex at the hands of his enemies, the "envy" (396) that caused the disaster is a feeling the speaker of the poem expresses to some degree. It certainly is a constant theme in Donne's work dealing with the great and the powerful in his society.

The frenetic wit of *Metempsychosis*, which, as W. Milgate says, partly "lies in . . . twisting and colouring of the material to bring out its sinister, or ironic, or grotesque facets, and to suggest the gulf between human pretensions and practice,"[75] reveals the emotional vexation Donne must have felt at the time he wrote it. Donne expressed his cynicism and disillusionment in a work that suggests its satiric exposure of degeneracy is a potentially endless process. The allegory is less a logically developed ironic progress of evil than a repetitive preoccupation with a current set of political events and circumstances centering on the fall of Essex and the power of the Cecils: the poem breaks down rather than ends, concluding with the narrator's self-reflexive turning to his authorial role and to the reader's responses to the first fifty-one stanzas:

> Who ere thou beest that read'st this sullen Writ,
> Which just so much courts thee, as thou dost it,
> Let me arrest thy thoughts; wonder with mee,
> Why plowing, building, ruling and the rest,
> Or most of those arts, whence our lives are blest,
> By cursed *Cains* race invented be,
> And blest *Seth* vext us with Astronomie.
> Ther's nothing simply good, nor ill alone,
> Of every quality comparison,
>   The onely measure is, and judge, opinion.
>   (511–20)

132 Young Man of Fashion and Courtly Servant

Having brought his account of the transmigration of the evil soul to Themech, the sister-wife of Cain, that biblical inventor of "plowing, building, ruling and the rest" (514), Donne reflected on the irony of finding the origin of "those arts, whence our lives are blest" (515), and thus the symbol of the active life, in the first murderer, the man who is the prototype not only of th hated Cecil, but of those who, like the author and his audience, entered the world of action to pursue their careers. The antitype of Cain, Seth is the symbol of contemplation and of the intellectual and spiritual self-cultivation[76] that the poet took seriously in his Senecan epistles but here embedded in a hopelessly problematic relativism. It is no wonder that readers have detected an element of self-destructiveness in such a work.

Donne portrayed politics as sexual in his satiric poetry and sex as political in his libertine and amorous verse. In *Metempsychosis*, sexual aggression is a metaphor for political power in the rape of the sheepdog by the wolf and the forceful attempt on Siphatecia by the ape. The "ridling lust" (437) Donne anatomized in these allegories is the greed for power, money, and prestige that motivated so many ambitious men of the Court. In this context, the satirization of Petrarchan and Neoplatonic love conventions in the account of the "toyful Ape" (451) as the "first true lover" (460) unmasks the self-serving motives behind the fashionable amorous language and behavior of the Elizabethan Court. In Donne's narrative, the association of courtly amorousness with animal behavior includes, by way of suggesting the connection of love and ambition, an attack on Neoplatonic loving, the same conjunction of the bestial and angelic found in "Loves Alchymie":

> He was the first that more desir'd to have
> One then another; first that ere did crave
> Love by mute signes, and had no power to speake;
> First that could make love faces, or could doe
> The valters sombersalts, or us'd to wooe
> With hoiting gambolls, his owne bones to breake
> To make his mistresse merry; or to wreake
> Her angers on himselfe. Sinnes against kinde
> They easily doe, that can let feed their minde
>   With outward beauty; beauty they in boyes and beasts do find.
>
> By this misled, too low things men have prov'd,
> And too high; beasts and angels have been lov'd.
> This Ape, though else through-vaine, in this was wise,
> He reach'd at things too high, but open way
> There was, and he knew not she would say nay;
> His toyes prevaile not, likelier meanes he tries,

> He gazeth on her face with teare-shot eyes,
> And up lifts subtly with his russet pawe
> Her kidskinne apron without feare or awe
>   Of nature; nature hath no gaole, though shee have law.
>
> First shee was silly'and knew not what he ment:
> That vertue, by his touches, chaft and spent,
> Succeeds an itchie warmth, that melts her quite;
> She knew not first, now cares not what he doth,
> And willing halfe and more, more then halfe loth,
> She neither puls nor pushes, but outright
> Now cries, and now repents. . . .
>   (461–87)

Courtly athletic performances, Petrarchan gesturing, Neoplatonic worship of beauty, and a crude sexual approach are confused in this account of the actions of the "first true lover." Donne satirized courtly-love rituals as he exposed the sexual substratum of Petrarchan and Neoplatonic amorousness.

Given the association in Elizabethan England between love language and the pursuit of ambition, the satire in this section has a political dimension. Both the lover and the ambitious "reach'd at things too high" in Donne's time and, thus, affected gesturing in love and Machiavellian scheming for political advantage are juxtaposed in this satiric poem. The sordid portrayal of love and sex sprang from a moral and emotional aversion to involvement in the public world. Conversely, when Donne experienced mutual love and celebrated it in some of his best lyrics, he defined it as a private world apart from the corrupt and corrupting sphere of social and political activities, a distinction he maintained (fictionally) only with great effort, especially after his marriage ruined his career.

THE POETRY OF COURTSHIP

Information about Donne's relationship with Ann More before their marriage in December 1601 is scant. She was the third of five daughters of a prosperous and prominent country squire, Sir George More, and had come to live at York House at the age of fourteen to be raised by her aunt Lady Egerton in one of those exchanges of young men and women that characterized the upper classes in the English Renaissance.[77] Donne fell in love with her some time before she returned to her father's house after Lady Egerton's death (January 1600).[78] She was some twelve years younger than he, an underage seventeen at the time of their marriage and certainly something less than a mature woman when they first made one another's acquaintance. Nevertheless, their intimacy and love had ripened sufficiently for some kind of solemn commitment to have been exchanged before she went back to Loseley. In the fascinating letter Donne wrote his father-in-law in February 1602 breaking the news of their marriage, he explained the wedding as a deliberate, not an impulsive, act (although he later called it "that intemperate and hastie act of mine"):[79] "So long since as her being at York House this had foundacion, and so much then of promise and contract built upon yt, as withowt violence to conscience might not be shaken" (*Selected Prose*, p. 113). Though nothing is specifically said about a contract *per verba de praesenti*,[80] or mutual agreement to marry that would have, in Elizabethan times, carried much of the force of a marriage contract, Donne's words indicate a determination of purpose in the face of parental disapproval that led the couple to the last-resort expedient of elopement: ". . . I knew (yet I know not why) that I stood not right in your opinion. I knew that to have given any intimacion of yt had been to impossibilitate the whole matter" (*Selected Prose*, p. 113). Walton claimed that Sir George More "had some intimation" of Donne's relationship with his daughter and that "friends of both parties used much diligence, and many arguments, to kill or cool their affections to each other."[81] Whatever the particular circumstances, Donne knew that he was breaking certain social rules and the law in marrying his young bride.

Donne and Ann More probably were seriously involved by late 1599 or early 1600 at the latest. Their relationship grew in the cosmopolitan and courtly setting in which the poet found himself during his employment with Egerton. On terms of familiarity with a group of young men and women at York House[82] that included, first, both Ann and the Egerton sons and then, after the Lord Keeper's remarriage in October 1600, the dowager Countess of Derby's daughters, Donne functioned, in effect, at a social level above his own. Of course, for him, as for other former Inns-of-Court men, finding a wife who could improve one's status and wealth was an understandable, and recognizably common, desire, one aspect of the ambitions of young educated men of the time. As Shakespeare's *The Merchant of Venice* attests, in the Elizabethan grammar of cultural fantasies love and wealth were desired complements rather than opposites. To suggest that Donne might have regarded Ann More as the symbol of desired social and economic success is not to deny that he loved her.

The economic realities of Donne's position in the late 1590s were all too apparent to him. He had burned through his modest inheritance—according to Walton, through the excesses of "youth, and travel, and needless bounty"[83]—and was hardly growing rich on his secretary's salary. Bald points out that, compared to the men who wed More's other daughters—Nicholas Throckmorton, Sir Thomas Grymes, and Sir John Oglander, "country gentlemen of wealth and assured position"[84]—Donne was an inappropriate match for Ann More. Donne himself acknowledged as much when he apologized to his father-in-law for his socioeconomic status and promised to succeed through hard work: "I knew my present estate lesse than fitt for her . . . [but] my endevors and industrie, if it please yow to prosper them, may soone make me somewhat worthyer of her" (*Selected Prose*, p. 113). Clearly Donne's relationship with Ann was bound up with the economic and social realities of marriage arrangements in Elizabethan society and, as he painfully learned, with the related transactions of patronage and preferment. He was ambitious for a beneficial marriage as well as for a profitable career.

Donne's lyrics of mutual love were the product of inextricably linked literary, personal, and socioeconomic contexts. Others have noted that Donne was somewhat unusual in dramatizing amorous reciprocity in his verse, for love poetry since the troubadours and Petrarch had thrived in situations of rejection and frustration, most men believing, with Andreas Capellanus, that marriage put an end to the love poets expressed.[85] Donne knew he was going against the current of literary and cultural tradition (as did Spenser in the *Amoretti*) in defining "Correspondencie" ("Loves Deitie," 12) as love's essence. In a sermon he later preached before Queen Anne, Donne said:

> . . . all that belongs to love . . . is to desire, and to enjoy; for to desire without fruition, is a rage, and to enjoy without desire is a stupidity: In the first alone we think of nothing, but that which we then would have; and in the second alone, we are not for that, when we have it; in the first, we are without it; in the second, we are as good as if we were without it, for we have no pleasure in it; nothing then can give us satisfaction, but where those two concurr, *amare* and *frui*, to love and to enjoy. (*Sermons*, 1:237)

The sexual teleology of love he defined in his early verse is transformed into the full erotic/spiritual mutuality ideally present in a marital relationship.

A tough-minded Francis Bacon wrote in his 1612 essay "Of Love," ". . . loue is euer rewarded either with the reciproque, or with an inward and secret contempt" (*Works*, 6:558). He articulated a general moral and social principle whose implications, certainly for him, extended beyond the sphere of private amorousness. The "reciproque" here and in Donne's poems, as assuredly as the Petrarchan sufferings of courtly poets, was a social, economic, and political phenomenon. In the context of the strict rules for marriage arrangements in Elizabethan England, mutual love was a cultural fantasy that expressed the wish to escape the social and economic laws that governed the choice of marriage partners and that operated as well in other, less private, circumstances. In the *Gesta Grayorum*, the "Prince of Purpoole" decrees that "No knight . . shall procure any letters from His Highness to any Widow or Maid, for his enablement and commendation, to be advanced to Marriage; but all Prerogative, Wooing set apart, shall for ever cease, as to any of these Knights, and shall be left to the Common laws of the Land, declared by the Statute, *Quia Electiones liberae esse debent*."[86] The law that demanded that both partners enter into marriage of their own free will was thus interpreted broadly, in this witty fiction, as an ideal of amorous freedom and the free choice of spouses by those who would marry. Open competition was also imagined for social, economic, and political transactions in general—a message particularly congenial to the young Inns-of-Court wits who participated in these revels. Ambitious men, like amorous suitors, or ambitious men in the guise of amorous suitorship, supposedly wished to succeed through their own merits and virtue rather than through social coercion. From the time of the early Tudor interlude *Fulgens and Lucres* through Sidney's *Astrophil and Stella* and Shakespeare's romantic comedies, this issue had broad implications. Marriage for love was an ideal or model that corresponded to advancement by merit and abilities rather than by birth or influence. But since the patronage and power of individual important families were bound up with the economic, social, and political functioning of the Establishment, at least among the upper classes, arranged marriages remained the norm and in neither courtship nor preferment did merit ensure success.

As Lawrence Stone has observed, "Bacon was right when he said that 'the stage is more beholding to love than the life of man.' It was part of a fantasy world, rather than a reality, for all but a handful of idle young courtiers and attendants in noble households."[87] Literature aside, romantic love was generally recognized as an impractical basis for action in Elizabethan England, a mental aberration that was a totally inadequate motive for contracting a marriage. The literary depiction of a love match, then, compensated imaginatively for the way things were. Just as Donne, in his epistolary verse and prose, used a relationship of friendship and of intellectual and spiritual seriousness as a refuge from the corrupt social system, so in his love lyrics he treated mutuality of affection as the space within which he could find an analogous private world of value and satisfaction apart from the public world of selfish competition, but he found the one world constantly intruding upon the other.

The emotional and the social circumstances of the lyrics Donne wrote in the context of his relationship with Ann More differ considerably for the periods before and after their marriage and warrant separate examination of these two groups of poems. The problem is that we cannot determine with any certainty which works belong to each of these categories. We have Walton's unreliable testimony that "A Valediction: forbidding Mourning" was written for Ann when the poet was about to leave with Sir Robert Drury for the Continent in 1611,[88] and, although he was probably wrong about identifying the occasion, he was right to associate this lyric with Donne's marriage. Given its political and autobiographical references, it is practically inconceivable to assign "The Canonization" to any time before 1603. But there is little external or internal evidence of any specificity to help us date lyrics or point to their original social matrices. J. B. Leishman's list of some twenty poems that "Donne addressed to the woman he married or wrote concerning their relationship"[89] is certainly too long, for it includes both some obviously early pieces and some poems of compliment that belong to other circumstances. Helen Gardner's categorization of the lyrics of mutual love has less to do with biographical and social contexts than with Donne's putative intellectual interests.[90] Most critics sidestep the problem by maintaining a convenient separation of life and art and denying the close relationship of Donne's poems and his personal experiences.

In the case of coterie writing like Donne's, however, there are signs that the poet wished his readers, both Ann and the friends to whom he showed such work, to respond to these lyrics in specific personal and social contexts. One of the most important indications of this is his deliberate punning on his wife's maiden name. Harry Morris[91] has discussed this practice as a far-reaching one in Donne's verse—almost an obsessive act on the poet's part related to his love, his guilt, and (finally) the deep fears associated with his marriage. But, at least initially, Donne's purpose was a more casually witty one. The technique allows us, with some confidence, to identify lyrics like "The Broken Heart," "Loves Growth," "Loves Infiniteness," and "A Valediction: of my Name in the Window" along with "The Canonization," "A Valediction: of Weeping," and "The Dissolution" as poems concerned with his relationship with Ann More written both before and after their marriage.

In the humorously affectionate "The Broken Heart," the speaker describes his sudden falling in love with a comically literal-minded version of the Petrarchan loss-of-the-heart motif. He denies that his heart took flight to his beloved because, he reasons, if it had, it "would have taught thy heart to show / *More* pitty unto mee" (22–23, italics mine), self-consciously punning on Ann's last name. In the final, epigrammatic lines of the piece the pun looks quite explicit: "My ragges of heart can like, wish, and adore, / But after one such love, can love no *more*" (31–32, italics mine). In "Loves Infiniteness," which reviews the history of a relationship of mutual love, the speaker states:

> All my treasure, which should purchase thee,
>   Sighs, teares, and oathes, and letters I have spent,
> Yet no *more* can be due to mee,
>   Then at the bargaine made was ment.
>   (5–8, italics mine)

One is tempted to associate this poem and these lines in particular with the time following Ann's return to her father and the young lovers' exchange of promises to one another. "A Valediction: of my Name in the Window," seems not only to refer specifically to the beloved's name in saying of the reflection of the mistress in the window "'Tis *more*, that it shewes thee to thee" (9, italics mine) but also to acknowledge a shared "love and griefe" (37) manifested in a woman who is "*more* loving" and "*more* sad" (40, italics mine). "Loves Growth" mentions a love that "cures all sorrow / With *more*" (7–8, italics mine) in the context of celebrating the lastingness of a relationship. The tears in "A Valediction: of Weeping" are "emblemes of *more*" (7, italics mine) and an alternate reading of one line in "The Canonization" has the speaker denying that his loving could "Adde one *more* to the plaguie Bill" (15, italics mine). The pun in the final word of "The Dissolution" may be either conscious or unconscious. The further away from the marriage date, the stronger Donne's ambivalent feelings about his spouse seem to have grown. For example, what Morris calls the "terrifying pun" of "A Hymn to God the Father," "A Hymne to Christ, at the Authors last going into Germany," and the sonnet on his wife's death reveals deeply disturbing fear and guilt on the author's part. Donne may have unconsciously punned on his Ann's maiden name in one of his marriage sermons when he said a wife "must *helpe*; and then she must be *no more*, she must *not Governe*" (*Sermons*, 2:337) and, again, "she was made for, *Adjutorium*, a helper. . . . But she must be no more" (*Sermons*, 2:346). Both late in his marriage and after Ann's death, Donne found it hard to speak positively about the sustaining love of husband and wife: this particular sermon is a chilly performance.

In many of the lyrics, the pun on the name More looks like a gesture of affectionate wittiness for Ann's benefit; in other cases, it seems to refer *to* her. This, of course, raises the tricky question of audience for the poems of mutual love.

What I would suggest is that, in the case of many of these poems, Ann was the intended primary audience and the lyrics were, therefore, one means of polite, but finally serious, social intercourse between lovers. In such pieces Donne extended his manner of plain-speaking honesty and affectionate intimacy from the all-male circumstances of much of his earlier verse to the context of an actual love relationship. From this point of view, the gestures of anticonventionality are his way of authenticating the poems as emotional vehicles—a device Sidney ostentatiously used in *Astrophil and Stella*. But the rhetorical and literary self-consciousness of such a gesture in Donne, as in Sidney, implies an intertextually competent readership in addition to the putative addressee or primary reader, a (male) coterie readership aware of both the literary and social circumstances of the verse. This is certainly true by the time Donne wrote "The Canonization" and "The Sunne Rising," works that seem more concerned with the judgment of peers than with the responses of a beloved, but it is also implicitly a factor in the more private pieces like the valedictions and the early amorous compliments. I believe Donne never lost touch with his male coterie readership, even when he wrote lyrics for the woman he loved. It makes sense, therefore, to regard the poems of mutual love either as double-audience performances (for Ann and male friends) or as exclusively male-audience work—the latter certainly the situation of "The Extasie" and "The Dissolution."

The group of lyrics I would associate with Donne's relationship with Ann More before their marriage includes "Loves Exchange," "The Broken Heart," "The Anniversarie," "The Good-morrow," "Loves Growth," "Loves Infiniteness," "A Lecture upon the Shadow," and "A Valediction: of my Name in the Window."[92] These poems deal with the discovery of love, the celebration of its growth and durability, and the internal and external dangers and problems that the lovers face together. All these pieces communicate an intimacy and mutuality that are expressed vividly in the dramatic speaker's emotional sensitivity to his beloved. No matter how self-consciously witty or literarily complex, these pieces locate their rhetorical and dramatic action in the context of strong amorous feeling.

"Loves Exchange" is a wittily affectionate lyric about falling in love for the first time. It is presented as the worldly sophisticated man's surprising discovery of the value and pain of an experience he had previously resisted. Whether or not Donne consciously or unconsciously punned on the name More in the sixth line ("Onely I have nothing which gave more"), the political and legal allusions of the second stanza suggest that the work was composed during the Egerton years, during which time he fell in love with the woman he married. As in a number of his contemporary prose and verse letters, Donne poses as someone familiar with the ways of the Court—a place associated specifically with "th'art of Riming" (4), by implication the kind of Petrarchan amatory verse he plays with in this comically hyperbolic lyric.[93] Enacting the role of the rebel to love who falls in love against his better knowledge—perceiving it as a "weaknesse" (15), a blindness, and something childish—Donne keeps a critical distance on the conventions he exploits, humorously viewing both his own behavior and the literary conventions used to express it. The fifth stanza, for example, treats the bright beauty of the Petrarchan beloved in a mischievously literal way. The last stanza comically literalizes the "paine" (20) and suffering of the lover in terms of torture on the rack and the practice of doing autopsies on executed criminals.

The legal and political allusions of the second stanza, however, mark the poem not only as one written with a male readership in mind (whether or not the lyric was given to the woman it fictionalizes), but also as a piece composed after the discussions in the Parliament of 1597–98:

> I aske not dispensation now
> To falsifie a teare, or sigh, or vow,
> I do not sue from thee to draw
> A *non obstante* on natures law,
>   These are prerogatives, they inhere
>   In thee and thine; none should forsweare
> Except that hee *Loves* minion were.
>   (8–14)

As Gardner has noted, the issue of "*non-obstante* clauses in letters-patent granting privileges, monopolies, and licenses [that] protected the holders against being sued in the courts of Common Law" was much debated in the last two Elizabethan Parliaments. "The question was a burning one in the Parliament of 1597–98 and the struggle against patents and monopolies came to a climax in the Parliament of 1601 in which Donne sat."[94] While in the employ of the man who was the chief legal officer of the Crown, Donne would have been quite familiar with the context within which the relationship of prerogative and common law, or of the Crown and Parliament, was defined by such an issue. In any event, the Parliamentary discussions of late 1597 are a *terminus a quo* for the lyric's composition. Since the Parliament of

1601 met in the autumn in which Donne married, it is unlikely the poem was composed at the latter time.[95] It reads, in any event, like a lyric fictionalizing the early stage of a serious relationship, a piece of antisentimental sentimentality, the self-mocking performance of an intellectually sophisticated and independent man meant to serve as affectionate compliment for the beautiful woman who has put him in his happily embarrassed position.

"The Broken Heart" and "The Anniversarie" both mark the completion of the first year of mutual commitment in love. The first of the two pieces is a good example of the way Donne addresses himself, rhetorically and psychologically (if not actually), to a double audience—beloved and male peers. "The Broken Heart" opens with a characteristically bold statement that proves to be misleading in both its tone and content: "He is starke mad, who ever sayes / That he hath been in love an hour" (1-2). Like similar remarks in the verse and prose paradoxes, this one seems to embody an antisentimental attitude toward love to be shared with a primarily male audience fond of such aggressive wit. Although the direction of the verse argument changes, the first two stanzas of the poem seem to assume this peer group of males, a communal "us" (14) for whom the lover speaks. They can understand love metaphorically not only as a sickness but as "the plague" (6) and appreciate the comic description of the power of love contained in the following lines:

> . . . us Love draws,
> He swallows us, and never chawes:
> By him, as by chain-shot, whole rankes doe dye,
> He is the tyran Pike, our hearts the Frye.
>   (13-16)

The method of the first half of the poem resembles that of many of the earlier lyrics written for a readership used to playfully iconoclastic gestures.

The third and fourth stanzas, however, reveal that the whole piece is a dramatic performance for the benefit of a mistress. This section begins:

> If'twere not so, what did become
> Of my heart, when I first saw thee?
> I brought a heart into the roome,
> But from the roome, I carried none with mee. . . .
>   (17-20)

The speaker portrays the act of falling in love as a comic, but nonetheless factual, event. In this half of the poem, which contains the pointed puns on Ann's maiden name, the antisentimentality and comic Petrarchan literalism imply an emotional referent. The manner accordingly changes from that of the tough-minded critic of conventional amorous foolishness to that of the gently ironic lover communicating his affection. Despite the complaint about the insufficiency of the beloved's "pitty" (23)—probably a teasing reference to her sexual modesty—the effect of the humorously precious variation of the broken-heart motif is to emphasize the power of a love relationship that has lasted a full "yeare" (6) and is superior to any other the lover can experience.

Like "The Broken Heart," "The Anniversarie" celebrates the completion of a year of mutual loving, but in a way that pointedly relates the sphere the lovers inhabit to the large world of social and political activity:

> All Kings, and all their favorites,
> All glory'of honors, beauties, wits,
> The Sun it selfe, which makes times, as they passe,
> Is elder by a yeare, now, then it was
> When thou and I first one another saw. . . .
>   (1–5)

J. B. Leishman suggests that this poem does not mean that the lovers had known one another only a year but that "Donne first 'saw' Ann More (in the sense in which Romeo first 'saw' Juliet)"[96] when he fell in love with her. "The Anniversarie" tries to cope with the possible destructive effect of time on a love that ideally "hath no decay" (7), but it seems concerned as much with what is going on outside the sphere of the lovers' relationship as with that which takes place in it. The conceit of love's kingdom that Donne introduces in the second stanza when the speaker tells his beloved that they "Prince enough in one another bee" (14) facetiously establishes the sphere of love as a realm superior to the ordinary social world, a favorite formulation in the poems of mutual love. Within their relationship, the lovers supposedly can find freedom and autonomy denied in the larger society: "Here upon earth, we'are Kings, and none but wee / Can be such Kings, nor of such subjects bee" (23–24). But the metaphor that leads to the observation that the lovers have only to worry about their fidelity to one another since "none can doe / Treason to us, except one of us two" (25–26) is really the speaker's way of persuading his beloved not to be bothered by the outside threats to the relationship: "True and false feares let us refraine" (27). The lover argues that their love is timeless and indestructible (stanza 1), that its spiritual power can overcome death (stanza 2), and that the only danger to it lies within the lovers themselves (stanza 3), but his statements are really only an indirect means of conveying an emotional message of loving reassurance, a romantic gesture made within the context of a shared awareness of the (unspecified) difficult circumstances in which the couple find themselves. This would have been an appropriate kind of lyric for Donne to have written to Ann before their marriage when they both knew the risks, the opposition, and the dangers they faced in becoming seriously involved with one another.[97]

"The Good-morrow," a much-studied lyric, is perhaps the most famous example of Donne's depiction of the microcosm of love. Clay Hunt, who associates this piece with the poet's relationship with the woman he married, states that "Donne's real concern is to analyze and articulate a personal experience in his fully developed personal style."[98] It makes more sense, however, to examine it in the context of the premarital lyrics concerned with the question of love's lastingness rather than in that of the postmarital poems that claim the world is well lost for love. In "The Good-morrow" the speaker's hyperboles assure the beloved that his previous amorous relationships meant little (stanza 1), that the little world of love is space enough for them to find satisfaction (stanza 2), and that their love will endure (stanza 3). By implication, such poetic statements are defenses against the fears that this love is only the latest of many amorous entanglements, that it is a feeble attempt to escape social and economic realities, and that it might not last. While not insensitive to the beloved's fears and misgivings, this lyric, like "The Anniversarie," tries to communicate, with humorous self-irony, a confidence about their relationship. The durability of their love finally rests on the balance of their reciprocity: "If our two loves be one, or, thou and I / Love so alike, that none doe slacken, none can die" (20–21).

"The Good-morrow" takes the awakening of mutual spiritual love as its thematic starting point, wittily manipulating Petrarchan and Neoplatonic commonplaces to dramatize a personal relationship. "Loves Growth" celebrates a developing human relationship that has both physical and spiritual dimensions. The audience of this lyric, like that of "The Good-morrow," probably included Donne's male friends as well as Ann More, since the context in which the love is set is that of the Renaissance *trattati d'amore*[99] and the various traditions of amorous verse with which they, rather than she, would have been familiar. Donne assumed a readership familiar with Neoplatonic philosophizing and versifying when he wrote:

>Love's not so pure, and abstract, as they use
>To say, which have no Mistresse but their Muse,

> But as all else, being elemented too,
> Love sometimes would contemplate, sometimes do.
> (11–14)

The puns in the first stanza on Ann's last name (6, 8) seem to be witty allusions to his beloved for the benefit of a knowing and sympathetic audience familiar with his personal circumstances.

In the second stanza, however, the rhetorical shift to the second-person form of address suggests not only that this half of the poem but the whole piece is a gesture of loving compliment. The first ten lines of this part of the lyric have a tone that is gentler and more affectionate than that of the rest of the work:

> And yet not greater, but more eminent,
>   Love by the spring is growne;
>   As in the firmament,
> Starres by the Sunne are not inlarg'd, but showne.
> Gentle love deeds, as blossomes on a bough,
> From loves awaken'd root do bud out now.
> If, as in water stir'd more circles bee
>   Produc'd by one, love such additions take,
>   Those like to many spheares, but one heaven make,
> For, they are all concentrique unto thee. . . .
> (15–24)

In a poem whose first stanza mocks the folly of "abstract" spiritual loving in order to emphasize that mutual love is "mixt of all stuffes, paining soule, or sense" (9), Donne turns the admission of mutability and "impurity" in love into a celebration of the way an affection centered on the beloved can grow in time.

The final four lines of the poem, however, are humorously antisentimental. Donne turns to a facetious economic metaphor to define love's growth in yet another way:

> And though each spring doe adde to love new heate,
> As princes doe in times of action get
> New taxes, and remit them not in peace,
> No winter shall abate the springs encrease.
> (25–28)

Financial metaphors are a constant in Donne's, as in Shakespeare's, love poetry, signaling the extraromantic awareness of the economic world in which amorous relationships were inevitably involved.[100]

"Loves Infiniteness," a poem related thematically to the preoccupations of the other premarital poems of mutual love, deals with the topics of commitment and growth in love within such a pronouncedly economic framework. Although this lyric undoubtedly affirms the amorous relationship as genuine, the language of the poem suggests paradoxically that love is not simply an environment opposed morally to the system of bargaining, buying, selling, getting, and spending, but also that it is part of it. Donne rings variations in this poem on the word "All" (one of his favorite terms),[101] beginning the piece with the false premise that love is quantifiable:

> If yet I have not all thy love,
>   Deare, I shall never have it all;
> I cannot breath one other sigh, to move,
>   Nor can intreat one other teare to fall.
> All my treasure, which should purchase thee,
>   Sighs, teares, and oathes, and letters I have spent,
> Yet no more can be due to mee,
>   Then at the bargaine made was ment.
> If then thy gift of love were partiall,
> That some to mee, some should to others fall,
>   Deare, I shall never have thee All.
>   (1–11)

Donne comically fuses the mercenary language of libertine Ovidianism with the terminology of Petrarchan wooing, but subordinates both to the personal context of a relationship of commitment. Using "treasure" to "purchase" a woman belongs, alternately, to the situations of rakish whoremongering and courtly economic opportunism, but the pun on Ann's name (17) points to a "bargaine" that is presented as an emotional and moral commitment far more important than either the polite rituals of courtship or the economic considerations surrounding love relationships.

The complaint in the first stanza that the mistress either gave a partial commitment and/or apportioned some of her love to the speaker's rivals introduces an (ultimately false) issue that might have been quite relevant to the socioeconomic circumstances of Donne's relationship with Ann More. The second stanza explicitly deals with rivalry in love as a kind of competitive bidding, but the counters in such a game are identified as Petrarchan "sighs," "oathes," and "letters" rather than, as in the actual world of marriage arrangements, wealth and social status. In any event, competitive wooing reflects the character of the economic system:

> Or if then thou gav'st mee all,
>   All was but All, which thou hadst then,
> But if in thy heart, since, there be or shall,
>   New love created bee, by other men,

> Which have their stocks intire, and can in teares,
>   In sighs, in oathes, and letters outbid mee,
> This new love may beget new feares,
>   For, this love was not vowed by thee.
> And yet it was, thy gift being generall,
> The ground, thy heart is mine, what ever shall
>   Grow there, deare, I should have it all.
>   (12–22)

In amorous poetry love rivals are figuratively economic rivals; in society they were actually so. As in "The Anniversarie," the speaker pretends that the real danger to love comes from the "treason" of which the lovers themselves may be guilty, not from relevant external factors. The lover's claims of jealousy and possessiveness are facetious ones, the means of treating once again the topic of love's growth.

> Yet I would not have all yet,
>   Hee that hath all can have no more,
> And since my love doth every day admit
>   New growth, thou shouldst have new rewards in store;
> Thou canst not every day give me thy heart,
>   If thou canst give it, then thou never gav'st it:
> Loves riddles are, that though thy heart depart,
>   It stayes at home, and thou with losing savs't it:
> But wee will have a way more liberall,
> Then changing hearts, to joyne them, so wee shall
>   Be one, and one anothers All.
>   (23–33)

As the pun in the second line of this stanza suggests, this lyric was probably written for the woman Donne married. The comic economics of the poem is extended in this section into an argument for sexual union, a persuasion grounded in the morality of reciprocity through which the beloved can respond to the lover's "New growth" of love with "new rewards." Instead of requesting payment in kind, an increase in affection on her part, the lover mischievously suggests she must give him something else, since she has already granted her heart. In focusing in a teasing manner on the sexual union that would express their mutual commitment, the speaker discards both the Petrarchan framework of sighs and tears and the potentially troubling economic framework of the first two stanzas, as he uses the occasion to celebrate the fact that they are "one, and one anothers All." The chronology that this lyric implies—the ongoing history of mutual lovers who have given their hearts to one another, are worried about circumstances hostile to their love, but can look forward to a deepening of commitment—may be a fictional one, but it probably was well suited to the situation of Donne's relationship with Ann More in the stage following their formal pledge of mutual fidelity.[102]

"A Lecture upon the Shadow" explicitly relates the question of love's growth and development to the deceptions the lovers have used to maintain their relationship safe from outside interference. Secrecy is, of course, a basic feature of the love treated in the courtly lyric, but here the treatment of the theme has the marks of something quite personal and specific, the cooperative strategy of two lovers who knew, as Donne and Ann More probably did, that the discovery of their love by others could be disastrous to them:

> . . . whilst our infant loves did grow,
> Disguises did, and shadowes, flow
> From us, and our care . . .
> (9–11)

The couple were secretive and deceitful to protect themselves. But, the speaker suggests, the fear of observation by others may actually be a sign of weakness or guilt, a flaw in the relationship itself and, from this point of view, it could be said: "That love hath not attain'd the high'st degree, / Which is still diligent lest others see" (12–13). The desire to reveal what was kept hidden, quite apparent in such later poems as "The Sunne Rising," "The Canonization," and "The Extasie," is a wish to be free of the fears associated with defensive secrecy and to enjoy moral and social autonomy—a fantasy that could not easily be realized, as Donne learned when he announced his marriage to his father-in-law several weeks after the fact.

The "Lecture . . . in loves philosophy" (2) in this poem is less an abstract discussion of ideal love or a serious recommendation that the couple reveal their love to the world than, as the second stanza indicates, an invitation to affirm their commitment to one another. As in some of the other lyrics of amorous mutuality, Donne transformed a problem having to do with the social circumstances of a love relationship into the more manageable one having to do with the personal attitudes of the lovers. The speaker of this lyric thus pretends that if he and his beloved maintain their full reciprocity of commitment and refrain from deceiving one another, their problems will be solved. Instead of being concerned with the outside world's discovery of and potential opposition to their love, they should be wary lest the deceptions they used "to blinde / Others" (16–17) enter their mutual relations.

This poem is less buoyantly optimistic than the other lyrics concerned with love's development. Whereas poems like "Love's Growth" and "The Anniversarie" celebrate the possibility of a constantly improving relationship, "A Lecture upon the Shadow" depicts full, honest mutuality as a point of perfection from which the lovers can only "faint, and westwardly decline" (19). The final epigrammatic couplet suggests improvement and growth before the achievement of true reciprocity, but destruction the moment it begins to deteriorate: "Love is a growing, or full constant light; / And his first minute, after noone, is night" (25–26). As Louis Martz has remarked: "There is no comfort in this poem, only the presentation of a precarious dilemma. Love's philosophy, it seems, begins with the recognition of the shadow of decay."[103] Donne, apparently, could not postulate a love removed from the world of time any more than he could forget that it was involved in a larger set of social relationships. The only consolation that is offered in this lyric—which is less a philosophical discussion of a *quaestio amoris* than an emotional persuasion of the beloved—is that the lovers have something valuable in their relationship that is worth their utmost efforts to preserve.

In the course of Donne's relationship with Ann More before their marriage, actual separation probably provided a clear focus for some of the feelings associated with the difficult circumstances in which their love existed. Ann's return to her father after Lady Egerton's death might have been a fitting occasion for a poem dealing with the situation of parting in relation to the lovers' fears about their future, just as Donne's 1605 departure from his wife probably generated other valedictions. One work I would suggest belongs to the premarital period is "A Valediction: of my Name in the Window," a lyric whose content marks it as a courtship poem.

"A Valediction: of my Name in the Window" is the longest of the valedictory lyrics. The process of poetic amplification which it follows through the first ten of its eleven stanzas is an imaginative tour de force that has to be halted abruptly rather than concluded, as the poet gives every indication that he can continue indefinitely composing variations on his central conceit.[104] One finds in this poem the signs of Donne's attraction to the dramatic world of the Ovidian elegy manifested in so much of the early love poetry. In stanzas 8 through 10 the woman resembles the venal mistress of Ovid and Propertius, someone who might be attracted to a wealthier suitor and be approached by this *dives amator* by means of a predictably corruptible maidservant. Although the comparison is facetious, it would have been a suitable one to have made in the courtship period, but utterly inappropriate in a postmarriage poem.

Like the other valedictions Donne wrote over a period of years, this lyric handles certain expected themes. It begins, for example, by raising the issue of constancy and fidelity:

> My name engrav'd herein,
>   Doth contribute my firmnesse to this glasse,
> Which, ever since that charme, hath beene
> As hard, as that which grav'd it, was;
> Thine eyes will give it price enough, to mock
> The diamonds of either rock.
>   (1–6)

The title of the poem in one of the manuscripts emphasizes the contrast set out in this stanza, "The Diamond and Glass":[105] the one is a symbol of purity, durability, and constancy, and the other of fragility and inconstancy. The lover, who assumes *his* "firmnesse" can never be doubted, hopes that the act that symbolizes it, the scratching of his name on glass with a diamond ring, can magically transform a potentially fickle mistress. Although he compliments his beloved by conventionally praising the brightness of her eyes, in the rest of the piece he calls her constancy into question, if only jestingly. By focusing on the possibility of her "treason" (55), he takes his fidelity for granted and thus gives one of the assurances expected of the departing lover.

The speaker also makes the conventional pledge of a safe return. When he assures his beloved that, just as no "showers and tempests" (15) can wash his name off the window, "So shall all times finde me the same" (16), he means not only that he will be faithful but also that he will survive whatever dangers and troubles he might face in absence. Stanzas 4 and 5 suggest the ideas of death and dying in their metaphors: the lover calls his name in the window a "deaths head" (21) and a "ruinous Anatomie" (24), regarding it as a bare skeleton and, since both it and his (Aristotelian tripartite) soul are with her, his flesh will return to "recompact" (32) him, as assuredly as body and spirit will be reunited at the end of the world. As in the later "A Valediction: forbidding Mourning," Donne bases the promise of return on the doctrine of the resurrection of the body, but he is less serious about the metaphor here, wishing to portray death in a humorous way that can allow him to cope with the woman's fears through affectionate teasing.

The wit of this poem is quite complex, at times recondite—a feature that suggests the awareness of a coterie audience. Donne, for example, alludes not only to astral influences but also to what Frances Yates has called the "occultized art of memory."[106] He refers to the Renaissance practice of memory notation which, as Eric Jacobsen notes, "was pursued by means of maps, diagrams, and sentences written on walls and windows":[107] the scratched name of the lover is supposed to enter the mistress's mind to trigger the memory of him, serving a purpose analogous to that of the picture in the elegy "His Picture." The "learning" (20) of the explanations offered in this poem might be "hard and deep" (19), the kind of witty conceitedness Donne designed for his male coterie readers, but there is an underlying emotional line of development that is, finally, more important. As in the other poems of mutual love, we must attend to the quality of the relationship being portrayed and to the affectionate intimacy being dramatized.

There are signs that the "firme substantiall love" (62) that is the subject of "A Valediction: of my Name in the Window" is as much a fact as a literary fiction. Donne plays with Ann's last name quite self-consciously in this lyric, and in a way that suggests that she was the primary audience of the piece. The reflection of the fictional beloved in the glass of the window is punningly that of the poet's actual beloved: "'Tis *more* that it shewes thee to thee" (9, italics mine), he says. The emotional state of the woman who is "*more* loving" and "*more* sad" (40, italics mine) is related to the kind of shared situation of "love and griefe" (38) the couple might have faced when they were separated by Ann's recall to Loseley. Although the speaker of the poem says he is worried about the rivalry of suitors whose "wit or land" (45) might be better than his, the pretense converts the potential coerciveness of a matchmaking father into the more manageable matter of the woman's own attitude—which is only teasingly put in doubt. In the actual circumstances of their relationship, Donne was probably acutely aware that Sir George More's plans for his daughter, if implemented, would have meant an end to their relationship. The emotional message of this lyric is one of confident reaffirmation of love and a reassurance that all will be well—even in the face of adverse conditions more serious than mere separation. The wit, the conceits, the reasoning, next to the affective content of the poem, are only "idle talke" (65) finally, ways of communicating a love that is inexpressible, but understood.[108]

In general, the early poems of mutual love subordinate their wit and imaginative manipulation of traditional intellectual and poetic materials to the drama of feeling centered in a love relationship whose growth has led to a shared commitment in the face of difficult social circumstances. They dramatize the lover's concern for and sensitivity to his beloved's emotional state even as they look beyond their probable primary audience to a coterie readership that could appreciate their skill, inventiveness, and force. Romantic without being soft-headed, these lyrics combine affectionate intimacy with an awareness of the larger social world of which the lovers were a part. Obliquely witty, but at the same time personal, they are the kind of intellectually and emotionally complex verse we associate with Donne at his best.

3
Donne as Social Exile and Jacobean Courtier

Donne married Ann More sometime in December 1601 while she was in town with her father, who was a member of the Parliament in which the poet also served. His marriage cost Donne his secretaryship and, as he learned slowly, spoiled all his chances for future secular advancement. Although he managed to move from relative poverty and social exile back into the prestigious social circles of City and Court, he was a painfully disappointed man in the period from 1602 to his ordination 1615. His desperate desire for preferment and a successful career moved him to seek advancement through the mediation of friends, patrons, and patronesses, but his efforts were constantly thwarted and his serious ambitions unfulfilled. The love poetry, the religious and encomiastic verse, and the other wittily recreative verse and prose Donne wrote at this time all reflect his sociopolitical situation. They express personal aspirations and disappointments in socioculturally encoded literary modes, genres, and conventions. Since much of what could have been understood or inferred by his coterie readers is lost when the works are examined apart from their historical setting, it is important to define the particular biographical and social contexts in which they were composed and read.

THE LOVE LYRICS OF THE MARRIED MAN

Donne was living as a gentleman of fashion when he wrote Sir George More from his "lodgings by the Savoy" (*Selected Prose*, p. 114)[1] in early February 1602 to announce his marriage to Ann six weeks earlier. He used as his messenger the ("Wizard") Earl of Northumberland, a man whose connection with him is unclear.[2] The document itself, which Donne signed with a kind of elegant flourish missing from the hum-

The Love Lyrics of the Married Man 153

bler letters that followed,[3] is a remarkably arrogant piece of writing. Conscious of the social rules he broke in marrying an underage bride without her father's permission, Donne nonetheless tried to justify his behavior even as he apologized for it, requesting the assistance of the very man he had injured. He acknowledged his own unworthiness as a husband for More's daughter, but defended the decision to marry for which, he claimed, they were both responsible (". . . we adventured equally. . . ."). He was careful to state that no one who had "dependence or relation" to More took part in the clandestine wedding ceremony: ". . . in all the passage of it did I forbear to use any suche person, who by furtheringe of yt might violate any trust or duty towards yow." At the same time he emphasized the couple's determination in the face of known parental disapproval as he assured his father-in-law both of his affection for Ann and of his resolution to provide well for her. He was conscious of the fact that his wife was back at her father's house and, therefore, a convenient target of his wrath: ". . . I humbly beg of you that she may not to her danger feele the terror of your sodaine anger." But he foolishly adopted a patronizing manner that must have infuriated the man he was trying to calm: "I know this letter shall find yow full of passion; but I know no passion can alter your reason and wisdome, to which I adventure to commend these particulars; that yt is irremediably donne; that if yow incense my Lord yow destroy her and me; that yt is easye to give us happiness, and that my endevors and industrie, if it please yow to prosper them, may soone make me somewhat worthyer of her" (*Selected Prose*, p. 113). Humble submission would have been more politic in these circumstances, and the tone of this letter certainly did not help to prevent the worst effects of Sir George More's punitive anger.

Instead of forgiving Donne and his daughter and assisting them financially and socially, the irascible More tried unsuccessfully to get the marriage annulled and asked that his son-in-law be dismissed from Sir Thomas Egerton's service.[4] Donne's worst fears were realized when the Lord Keeper acceded to Sir George More's request, dismissing his young secretary, as Walton claims, with great reluctance: ". . . the Lord Chancellor said, 'He parted with a friend, and such a Secretary as was fitter to serve a king than a subject'." Walton's statement that Donne thereafter wrote his wife a letter subscribed "John Donne, Anne Donne, Un-done"[5] may be accurate, for the Middle Temple diarist John Manningham used the same pun to refer to the poet's bad fortune: "Dunne is Undonne; he was lately secretary to the L[ord] Keeper, and cast of because he would match him selfe to a gentlewoman against his Lordes pleasure."[6] The example of the young man who spoiled his own chances of success by marrying imprudently for love or passion was an Elizabethan moral commonplace. One of the soundest, and most conventional, pieces of advice Lord Burghley offered to his son concerned the wise selection of a mate: "When it shall please God to bring thee to man's estate, use great providence and circumspection in the choice of thy wife, for from thence may spring all thy future good or ill; and it is an action like a strategem in war where man can err but once."[7] When Donne later referred to his stolen marriage as "my disorderlie proceedings . . . in my nonage" and "that intemperate hastie act of mine,"[8] he spoke within such a framework.

The effect of Donne's elopement on his career was devastating. In the letter he wrote to his employer asking to be restored to his position, he both reviewed his past progress and defined the hopelessness of his condition cut off from Egerton's political patronage:

> How soone my history is dispatched! I was carefully and honestly bred; enjoyd an indifferent fortune; I had (and I had understandinge enough to valew yt) the sweetnes and security of a freedome and independency; without making owt to my hopes any place of profitt. I had a desire to be your Lordships servant, by the favor of which your good sonn's love to me obtein'd. I was 4 years your Lordships secretary, not dishonest nor gredy. . . . To seek preferment here with any but your Lordship were a madness. Every great man to whom I shall address any such suite, wyll silently dispute the case, and say, would my Lord Keeper so disgraciously have imprisond him, and flung him away, if he had not donne some other fault, of which we hear not. So that to the burden of my true weaknesses, I shall have this addicion of a very prejudiciall suspicion, that I ame worse than I hope your Lordship dothe think me, or would that the world should thinke. I have therefore no way before me; but must turn back to your Lordship, who knowes that redemtion was no less worke than creation. . . . I know myne own necessity, owt of which I humbly beg that your Lordship wyll so much entender your hart towards me, as to give me leave to come into your presence. Affliction, misery, and destruction are not there; and every wher els where I ame, they are. (*Selected Prose,* pp. 119–20)

Donne put himself at the mercy of the Lord Keeper, but to no avail. Even when his mollified father-in-law pleaded on his behalf, Egerton refused to reverse his decision, explaining to More, in the language of patron-client relationships, that "it was inconsistent with his place and credit, to discharge and readmit servants at the request of passionate petitioners."[9] Donne's career was in shambles and he had no immediate hope for the future. He had flouted the rules that bound marriage arrangements to his society's patronage transactions and thereby displaced himself.

About a year later, at the beginning of the reign of James I, when there were unprecedented opportunities for advancement at Court, Donne was living in virtual social exile in the country, forced to accept for himself and his growing family the charity of his friend, Sir Francis Wooley, in whose house at Pyrford they resided. Without either income or immediate prospects, he enviously watched his close friends take advantage of the change of government and of the King's neurotic generosity: Sir John Egerton, Sir Edward Herbert, Sir Thomas Roe, Sir Richard Baker, and Sir Walter Chute got places of varying importance; his closest friend Sir Henry Goodyer became a Gentleman of the Privy Chamber; Sir Henry Wotton was appointed ambassador to Venice. When Wotton was about to travel abroad to assume his prestigious position, Donne composed a propempticon[10] or bon voyage poem in the form of a verse letter ("To Sir Henry Wotton, at his going Ambassador to Venice"). Although he followed classical precedent in affirming their friendship and offering general moral advice on the occasion of parting, he could not resist comparing his friend's honorable employment and good fortune with his own sorry condition, ironically treating Wotton's responsibilities as more distastefully burdensome than his own social isolation:

> . . . 'tis an easier load (though both oppresse)
>   To want, then governe greatnesse, for wee are
> In that, our owne and onely businesse,
>   In this, wee must for others vices care;
>
> 'Tis therefore well your spirits now are plac'd
>   In their last Furnace, in activity;
> Which fits them (Schooles and Courts and Warres o'rpast)
>   To touch and test in any best degree.
>
> For mee, (if there be such a thing as I)
>   Fortune (if there be such a thing as shee)
> Spies that I beare so well her tyranny,
>   That she thinks nothing else so fit for mee. . . .
>   (25–36)

As in the earlier verse letters, Donne maintained a kind of moral and intellectual disengagement from the various social environments in which he and his addressee had been involved ("Schools and Courts and Warres") as well as the one Wotton was entering. He used a religious idiom to portray his own rustication as a contemplative removal from the world of "activity," an ironic stance that dignified his ruined state and thinly disguised both his envy of his friend's success and his own desperate desire for advancement.[11]

In some of the love lyrics written early in his marriage, Donne used ironic means to demonstrate the superiority of private life to public involvement. The wit of "The Sunne Rising" rests on the pretense that the lovers in their private world are morally superior to the ambitious scramblers of the public world. The line "Goe tell Court-huntsmen, that the King will ride" particularly alludes to the game of seeking royal patronage as it was conducted in a Court that was on the move every time James could flee London to indulge his strange passion for hunting.[12] Since the Court was, in effect, the place where the monarch was, many men tried to accompany the King, whose regular retainers included Donne's close friend Sir Henry Goodyer, who also would have been the most likely primary audience for such a poem as this one. The first four lines of the third stanza use comic hyperbole both to disguise and reveal the sense of exclusion and loss Goodyer and Donne's other friends knew he felt at the beginning of the Jacobean era. The poet could wittily claim about himself and his beloved

> She is all States, and all Princes, I,
> Nothing else is.
> Princes doe but play us; compar'd to this,
> All honor's mimique; All wealth alchimie.
> (21-24)

But Donne's friends were aware that he longed for the kind of social and political involvement that could bring "wealth" and "honor." His wittiness signaled his frustrated needs.

The displaced anger of this comically antiauthoritarian lyric expressed a real frustration. In its hyperbolic wit, the insistent repetition of the word "all" (9, 20, 21, 24) is related to the feeling of being "nothing" that Donne mentioned in other poems and letters. The reversal of voice implied in the active imperative mode of this piece is an imaginative compensation for passive helplessness. Donne responded to narcissistic injury[13] by fantasizing omnipotence: he fictionally converted a social impotence into an assertion of personal power and, as elsewhere in his poetry, sexual potency indicates socioeconomic powerlessness.

This lyric comically distorts the circumstances of Donne's relationship with Ann More, her father, and figures of authority. The voyeur in the primal-scene fantasy underlying the poem's situation is not the excluded child, to whom Donne punningly refers in the expression "unruly Sunne" (1), but instead a father figure connected with both social disapproval and personal guilt.[14] Covert or furtive erotic activity evokes the presence of an observer—a character who reappears, in a different guise, in "The Extasie" and in some other poems—but the retribution feared by the Oedipally guilty son is wished upon the father-figure in this poem, whose "eyes" (like those of Oedipus) might be blinded in an act of symbolic castration. "The Sunne Rising" is a jauntily comic piece, but the psychological vexations and social desperation implicit in it disturb its witty surface.

The same combination of features can be seen in "The Canonization," an ironic love lyric almost certainly composed fairly early in his married life and addressed to an audience that would have read it in relation to its author's own social circumstances. This work is usually viewed as a witty and eloquent expression of the theme that the world is well lost for love. A. J. Smith remarks: "If that splendid poem conveys anything beyond its lamenting outcry it is that love is a kind of religion, but a religion which ruins its devotees in terms of worldly success to *make* them in another and better sense."[15] Earl Miner mentions this lyric as the most explicit example of Donne's "insistence that his poems turn their backs upon the world."[16] In his classic essay, Cleanth Brooks interprets it in terms of the paradox in which "the poet daringly treats profane love as if it were divine love"[17] and many other critics emphasize the serious moral and philosophical implications of the poem's religious metaphors. Despite the features that make it "satiric comedy," N. J. C. Andreasen claims, for example, "In *The Canonization*, the real ideal [of love] is Christian sainthood."[18] In its original context, however, "The Canonization" communicated a very different message. Donne's readers knew that he was expressing his personal longing for the public world he pretended to scorn in this lyric and they would have read the poem as a more ironic, hence more aesthetically complex, work than the one formalist critics and scholars utilizing literary and intellectual history have interpreted.

In "The Canonization" Donne inventively mixed a number of literary and sociocultural codes in a fictionally autobiographical, ironic discourse on his own situation as an ambitious, placeless, newly married man. In the gesture of maintaining a holy retreat from the world of social and political competition,[19] Donne was using a common courtly literary signal for frustrated ambition. In this respect, some of the conceits in this love lyric resemble material found in the earlier satires and verse letters as well as in the later religious and philosophical poetry. In addition, Donne comically literalized and parodically mystified a Petrarchan idiom with a deliberate indecorum, attributing to a private, socially stigmatized marital relationship the literary vocabulary associated both with the tradition of the academic Petrarch and with the manner of polite courtly verse. Finally, both kinds of material are counterbalanced by the erotic realism of the poem's Ovidian-Propertian opening.

The point of Donne's manipulation of multiple literary codes was not the mere demonstration of artistic complexity or skill; "The Canonization" served interrelated emotional and social functions. It was a witty recreation intended to make his painful and dejected state more tolerable as well as a means of maintaining his habitual social intercourse with friends who were actively involved in the social and political world of London and the Court. In ironically denying his own needs and ambitions, he gained a kind of emotional control over them as he compensated for his socially inferior position by exercising intellectual and rhetorical mastery over his coterie readers. The disingenuous and witty denial of his ambition and the playfully aggressive relationship to his audience were closely related. From its angrily defensive opening through its subtle modulations of tone to its elated conclusion, "The Canonization" is a masterful lyric whose internal rhetoric reflects both the private emotional conflicts of the poet and his imaginatively adversarial relationship with his coterie readers.

> For Godsake hold your tongue, and let me love,
>   Or chide my palsie, or my gout,
> My five gray haires, or ruin'd fortune flout,
> With wealth your state, your minde with Arts improve,
>   Take you a course, get you a place,
>   Observe his honour, or his grace,
> And the Kings reall, or his stamped face
>   Contemplate; what you will, approve,
>   So you will let me love.
>
> Alas, alas, who's injur'd by my love?
>   What merchants ships have my sighs drown'd?
> Who saies my teares have overflow'd his ground?
> When did my colds a forward spring remove?
>   When the heats which my veines fill
>   Add one more[20] to the plaguie Bill?
> Soldiers find warres, and Lawyers finde out still
>   Litigious men, which quarrels move,
>   Though she and I do love.
>
> Call us what you will, wee'are made such by love;
>   Call her one, mee another flye,
> We'are Tapers too, and at our owne cost die,
> And wee in us find the'Eagle and the Dove;
>   The Phoenix ridle hath more wit
>   By us, we two being one, are it,

> So, to one neutrall thing both sexes fit.
>   Wee dye and rise the same, and prove
>   Mysterious by this love.
>
> Wee can dye by it, if not live by love,
>   And if unfit for tombes or hearse
> Our legend bee, it will be fit for verse;
> And if no peece of Chronicle wee prove,
>   We'll build in sonnets pretty roomes;
>   As well a well wrought urne becomes
> The greatest ashes, as halfe-acre tombes,
>   And by these hymnes, all shall approve
>   Us *Canoniz'd* for Love.
>
> And thus invoke us; You whom reverend love
>   Made one anothers hermitage;
> You, to whom love was peace, that now is rage;
> Who did the whole worlds soule extract, and drove
>   Into the glasses of your eyes,
>   So made such mirrors, and such spies,
> That they did all to you epitomize,
>   Countries, Townes, Courts: Beg from above
>   A patterne of your love!

The lyric begins with an angry response to an imaginary interlocutor, presumably a friend who, in the speaker's best interests, has been advising him to relinquish a self-destructive love relationship in order to pursue a course of worldly self-improvement, to turn from private erotic satisfaction to place-seeking and career pursuits. The materially ruined and morally debased lover defensively reacts with what looks like disarmingly honest self-accusation, in effect joining his antagonist's attack, but at the same time skillfully satirizing the world from which he is excluded. He then moves, by means of subtle rhetorical strategies, to a position in which he can morally and intellectually patronize both his adversary-friend and others as well. The work seems to move toward a witty self-vindication: what begins as disgrace ends as self-congratulation as Donne converts a poem of blame into one of praise.

The use of the *adversarius* figure is a crucial reference point for the poem's rhetorical development and for the poet's witty relationship with his readers. The imaginary interlocutor whom the speaker answers has an interesting history in the traditions of love poetry on which Donne self-consciously draws. The first line of the lyric is like the opening of the fifth poem of Propertius' first book of elegies, where a lover objects to a friend's urging him to abandon his mistress:

"Invide, tu tandem voces compesce molestas/et sine cursu, quo summus, ire pares'" ("My envious friend, now restrain your violent appeals and let us go hand in hand along the path we now tread").[21] Such an antagonist is close to the one in "The Canonization." Donne's adversary-figure, however, is also affiliated with the "losengier" of troubadour and courtly verse who spreads slanders and calumnies about lovers.[22] But since the critic in this poem is also portrayed as a friend, he is closer to the Propertian model and more nearly resembles the kind of personally sympathetic and morally concerned character the lover of Sidney's *Astrophil and Stella* addresses in Sonnets 14, 21, and 69 of that sequence, someone who objects to amorous entanglement because it is immoral, imprudent, and ultimately harmful to his friend. For Sidney, such a figure probably embodied not only his own self-consciousness but also the presence of a coterie reader like Fulke Greville.[23] Similarly, Donne employed this kind of character as a way of expressing self-doubts and of addressing himself wittily to a male audience whose values he recognized and was more inclined to share than oppose.[24]

With its pointed allusion to the poet's "ruin'd fortune" (3) and his distance from the society's political center, "The Canonization" is self-consciously autobiographical. In both the poem and his life, Donne was particularly aware of the possibilities and means of advancement at the beginning of James's reign that he was unable to exploit. The message that the critic-friend seems to have been giving in the fictional world of the lyric is similar to one sent by one of Donne's own correspondents in 1604:

Your friends are sorry, that you make your self so great a stranger; but you best know your own occasions. Howbeit, if you have any designe towards the Court, it were good you did prevent the losse of any more time. For Experience and Reasons are at odds in this, that the places of Attendance, such as may deserve you, grow dailie dearer, and so are like to do. Notwithstanding that, the King's hand is neither so full, nor so open, as it hath been. You have not a poor friend, that would be gladder of your good fortunes; and out of that conscience, I challenge my self this liberty.[25]

Undoubtedly Donne's friends wanted to see him reinvolve himself in the world from which he had removed himself after his loss of employment, especially given the exciting atmosphere of opportunity in the early Jacobean period.

The strategy of seeking preferment that the speaker of this poem suggests the antagonist is following is one that Donne's friends were certainly pursuing[26] and that he felt he could not, perhaps because of his poverty and family obligations, the freshness of his public disgrace, the damaging effect of having been dismissed by Egerton, or the depression from which he suffered. It is interesting that Donne later used the word "course" (5) in a letter to Sir Henry Goodyer before his departure of France in 1611 to refer, not scornfully, to the active pursuit of ambitions: "It is ill to look back, or give over in a course, but worse never to set out" (*Letters*, p. 94). Although Donne took as his personal motto a line from Petrarch referring to the superiority of the contemplative over the active life—"Per Rachel ho servito e non per Lea"[27]—he actually behaved as though his motto were that of Sir Robert Sidney, "Inveniam viam aut faciam" ("I'll find a way [course] or make one").[28] Despite his customary aversion to deferential suitorship—the words and actions of the man ready to "Observe his honour, or his grace"—he assumed the manner himself when he was ready to seek patronage and advancement again. He was certainly under no illusion that love was sufficient for him, any more than were stoical withdrawal or intellectual and religious contemplation.

The speaker of the poem uses a patently disingenuous rhetoric to disarm criticism, then to reduce all those beyond the private world of the couple to the position of reverential respect. Admitting that his love may be imprudent, wasteful, immoral, self-destructively lustful, the speaker uses a defensive strategy in the first two stanzas and the beginning of the third—one that has its roots in the impudently antisocial stance of the youthful Ovidian libertine whose only moral response to the society that criticizes his behavior is to charge that the supposedly normative public world is itself deeply flawed.[29] Donne, of course, satirically suggests that the world outside the space of a mutual love relationship is one of grasping ambition and fawning flattery, greed, bellicosity, and crazy litigiousness (stanzas 1 and 2). In this context the allusion to the current plague[30] calls forth the usual moral framework in which this phenomenon was interpreted—that of God's punishing man for his sins and enormities.[31] Next to the explicitly antisocial actions of ambitious, avaricious, combative men, the supposedly self-destructive behavior of lovers looks less socially harmful.

The combination of indirect satire and passive aggression is abandoned in the course of the third stanza, which ends with a total redefinition of the love union, of the speaker-listener interaction, and of the poet-reader relationship. This central section of the poem has presented the most interesting interpretive challenge. Those who have written about "The Canonization" have usually focused on the metaphors of this stanza as the key to Donne's definition of the mystery of mutual love that is celebrated in the poem. Despite the difficulties of doing so, critics have attempted to fix the meanings of the perplexing symbols and conceits as one means of articulating the total lyric statement of the work. Donald Guss, for example, acknowledges that "the stanza is full of obscure emblems," but emphasizes their "Petrarchan parallels" and Neoplatonic symbolism as ways of determining meaning:

> The Petrarchan analogues . . . show Donne's stanza to rest on the contrast between moth in flame, and phoenix: a contrast traditionally employed to argue that love is life-giving, not destructive. They thereby indicate a probability that lines 2–3 are both about the moth in the flame: and so they are. For what Donne says is that his opponent may call the lovers moths burning in tapers, but, since each is the taper in which the other burns, it is not his opponent who will have to pay the candle. . . . Line 4 continues the defense begun in line 3, declaring that from their point of view the lovers are not moths at all, but eagle and dove: from at least the time of the "Song of Solomon," the dove is a symbol of a beloved lady; and the eagle is a stock Petrarchan symbol of the high-minded lover whose eyes are eternally fixed on his beloved lady. . . . The stanza concludes with the assertion that the silly riddle of the phoenix makes sense when it is interpreted as referring to the lovers: for the phoenix is unique, sexless, and self-resurrecting, and so are the lovers. Thus, Donne denies that the lovers are moths to assert that they are the phoenix. . . .
> The heart of the stanza is the assertion that the lovers are like the phoenix through their union (l. 6); their sexual neutrality (l. 7); and their resurrection (l. 8). Each of these similarities assumes a Neoplatonic theory.[32]

The problem with this interpretation is that it assumes that the poem's readers would have understood the metaphors of this stanza and the general import of the lyric only in terms of Renaissance Petrarchism and Neoplatonism. But neither the conceits nor the lyric's meanings were univocal, as the variety of modern historical interpretations suggests.

In this stanza, the possibilities of meaning are multiple. The "flye" (20), for example, may mean either housefly or butterfly (or moth). As the former, it was, as A. B. Chambers has explained, a figure of unrestrained and self-destructive sexual activity or a symbol of "impudence." It was also sometimes considered a bisexual creature, a detail that would have connected it with the subsequent hermaphrodite image. In addition it was believed to be capable of dying a fiery death and being resurrected, resembling, therefore, the phoenix referred to later in the stanza.[33] Considered in combination with the taper image that follows, it is the moth flying toward the flame of a candle, a figure of lustful self-destruction. As Francis Meres put it, "the Flie that playeth in the fire is singed in the flames: so he that dallieth with women is drawn to his woe."[34] But the same figure could symbolize the pursuit of the light of truth[35] or the Petrarchan lover's devotion to the spiritual ideal symbolized by his mistress's radiant beauty. The eagle and dove may be "emblems of strength and gentleness,"[36] symbols of masculinity and femininity (the one Jove's bird, the other Venus'),[37] of "action and passion,"[38] or of the "marriage of Voluptuousness and Sorrow."[39] By itself, the eagle symbolized resurrection ("Thy youth is renewed like the eagle" [*Psalms*, 103.5]), "virtue tired by wandering,"[40] sainthood or the Trinity,[41] and the dove the Holy Spirit[42] or, as Guss notes, "anything from Christian resurrection to marital fidelity, or from contemplation to an alchemical reaction."[43] The phoenix was a symbol of resurrection, of constancy, and of marriage.[44] It was associated with the celebration of famous deceased heroes like Sidney and Essex[45] and it appeared prominently in the woodcut and poem prefaced to the Giolito editions of Petrarch, where it was a figure for the exemplary relationship of Petrarch and Laura, who had become saints of love in death.[46] The "neutral thing" to which "both sexes fit" (25) is probably the hermaphrodite, a symbol of marriage as well as of Neoplatonic soul-union.[47] Religious, Neoplatonic, alchemical, as well as Petrarchan and other literary sources are possible aids to interpretation, but it would seem that for the coterie reader these metaphors, finally, would have been multivalent, ambiguous, and fundamentally *resistant* to interpretation.

I conclude this not only because the obvious possibilities for meaning are many or because, at normal reading speed, this stanza would probably have perplexed even the most adept member of Donne's coterie audience, but also because Donne had every reason to use such a strategy in this ironic and rhetorically adroit poem in order to give the speaker a moral and intellectual advantage over the antagonist and, thus, to grant himself a playful control over his readers. The very ambiguity of the images permits the transition from the denigration of love to its idealization, from insult to praise.[48] Whereas the first three lines of the stanza have the feel of continuing the self-disparagement of the previous stanzas, the fourth line ("And wee in us find the'Eagle and the Dove") is uncertain in tone, potentially either complimentary or depreciatory. So too the notion of "dying" in this stanza, whose bawdy meaning Guss is at pains to deny in order to define the love relationship as asexual, must ambiguously refer both to the lovers' physical relationship and to their mysterious spiritual joining. The effect of the whole stanza, particularly of the mystifying explanation offered in the last six lines, is to put the listener at the mercy of the speaker and to assert the intellectual authority of the ironic poet. Just as the dramatic antagonist in the lyric loses the power to criticize or threaten the speaker or the love relationship, so too the reader is aesthetically assaulted with what must have been originally, as it is still today, a bewildering set of conceits.

The third stanza finally establishes a mode of hyperbolic self-praise that is extended through the rest of the poem. Donne utilizes encomiastic techniques with deliberate comic impropriety: one can detect some of the customary features of complimentary verse to which Barbara Lewalski has called our attention, including "praise of the subject as an exemplar of virtues" or "as an 'image' or 'pattern' of virtue in the Neoplatonic sense" or "as regenerate soul, saint, heir to the Scripture promises."[49] Donne's speaker, with witty exaggeration, idealizes himself and his beloved as models of sanctified, virtuous loving who embody the divine "pattern"[50] or ideal to be imitated by lesser mortals. The religious amatory conceits are highlighted as the socially disgraced lovers are now celebrated as saints. They thus resemble, as Horst Meller has shown, the exemplary Laura and Petrarch depicted in the Giolito woodcut who are pictured on a "well wrought urn" (33) that contains their "sacre cineri," the reliques of a couple "Canoniz'd for Love" (36) and joined with one another after death.[51]

The Giolito image and accompanying poem contain many of the elements found in "The Canonization"—the phoenix, the well-wrought urn, the ashes of sainted lovers, the idea of resurrection. But, while relevant, the contexts of literary and intellectual history to which these features belong are not the primary ones in Donne's poem.[52] Irony, not moral or aesthetic idealization, was Donne's purpose. In the immediate coterie context, the Petrarchan framework had social and political implications connected with the situation set forth in the first stanza of the piece, which suggests, by opposing them, that love and ambition are connected. Like the gesture of stoical withdrawal or the language of Christian *contemptus mundi*, here the Petrarchan/Christian renunciation of baser love for the sake of higher spiritual experience elevates human motives above the level of either socioeconomic or erotic covetousness. In terms of the basic dialectic of this poem, those for whom love is "rage" (39)[53] correspond to the careerist of stanza 1 and the selfish worldly men of the second stanza: structurally the loving couple are opposed to both. But the speaker returns, in the last stanza of the lyric, to an awareness of the bonds between the lovers and the outside world. "Countries, Townes, Courts" (44), the three environments with which socially and politically active men were concerned (as in the verse letter to Wotton discussed earlier) represent a public world that, as in "The Sunne Rising," insistently intrudes on the private retreat both of lovers and of the disgraced ambitious man. The mention of the larger environment that surrounds the loving couple contaminates the context of religious, amorous, and aesthetic idealization with a pointed reference to the society in which the poet's career has been "ruin'd" (3). The speaker finally claims that he and his beloved can "the whole worlds soule extract" (40)—that is, possess in essence everything valuable outside of their relationship—and that they can "epitomize/Countries, Townes, Courts" (43–44), but these exaggerations reveal the breakdown of the strategy of idealizing rather than the transcendence of the context in which the conflicts between love and ambition are painfully experienced. Despite what the speaker of "The Anniversarie" says, the lovers cannot be "Prince enough in one another" any more than can the bedroom in "The Sunne Rising" serve as their whole world. Comically ironic, albeit eloquent, hyperbole could not dispel the social and emotional problems to which Donne self-consciously alluded in "The Canonization." Though this poem is a rhetorical tour de force that contains an attractive fantasy of love's triumph over social disadvantages, Donne knew and was aware his coterie readers knew that neither poetry nor wit could solve the serious difficulties he faced in his painful social exile.

As a response to the kind of message Donne received from his friends who urged him to return to London to try to repair his "ruin'd fortune," "The Canonization" is, in a sense, no answer or a refusal to answer. It is what Donne called, a few years later in his continuing state of frustration, one of the "squibs" (*Letters*, p. 71) kindled in his melancholy, a gesture of wit that psychologically relieved his pain. It proved that he could keep his humor and intellectual agility in the face of personal disaster, but intense wittiness signals, as it does in some speeches in Shakespeare's *Hamlet*, that things are at the emotional breaking point. Donne underscored this message in this ironic lyric, conscious that he was writing for a coterie audience sensitive to his social and political desperation.[54] Comic irony is an instrument for avoiding their patronizing pity and for reversing the positions of moral superior and inferior apparent in the letter urging his return to London. Emphasizing the metacommunicative level of discourse, that is the "relationship aspect" of communication between writer and reader, Donne asserted, within the play frame of the poetic fiction, an intellectual and rhetorical mastery that, if only momentarily, could psychologically counteract the helplessness of his actual social condition. As another ritual in his "religion of friendship," "The Canonization" was one means of maintaining contact with his male coterie.

Donne's life at Pyrford, however, was not one of absolute social isolation. After all, James on his first progress spent his first night there on 10 August 1603 and then two more at nearby Loseley with Sir George More. Bald claims that on this occasion, "Donne must have had the opportunity of being presented to the King . . . and of renewing many old friendships among those who followed the court" (*Life*, p. 141). "Friends came to visit him as well as the Wooleys," Bald surmises (*Life*, p. 143), and Donne probably visited London to bid farewell to his friend Sir Henry Wotton, who left to assume his duties as ambassador to Venice in 1604. But Donne seems not to have resumed his active pursuit of secular advancement until he decided, in 1605, to travel abroad with another friend, Sir Walter Chute. Donne probably intended his journey to serve as a way of reentering the public world, the only environment in which he could hope to improve his fortunes.[55] If the journey took place some time after Donne secured a license to travel on 16 February 1605 and ended by April 1606, Donne was absent about a year from his wife and family, whom he had left at his sister-in-law's house.[56] The separation would have been an emotionally charged event, especially since Ann was pregnant at the time with their third child.

Other politically ambitious husbands in similar situations reconciled themselves to such absences from their spouses, sometimes responding to their wives' protests at parting by claiming the necessity of heeding the call to public duty while professing continuing marital affection and fidelity. When Sir Robert Sidney, for example, was leaving for the Low Countries in 1593 to perform those services for which he hoped to be rewarded with substantial advancement at Court, he wrote, in an affectionate parting letter to his wife:

There is no desire in me so deer as the love I bear you and our children. But this jorney is absolutly forsd upon me without my seeking and so far now I ame imbarked into yt as I cannot pluck out my neck without both toutch of my reputation and danger to loose all hope of reward for the services I have already done. You are maried, my deer Barbara, to a husband that is now drawn so into the world and the actions of yt as there is no way to retire myself without trying fortune further. . . . And I do not dout but this imploiment will bring me some good requital, or if yt do not, it must and shalbe the last ever I wil undertake.[57]

Practically speaking, this politically competitive brother of Sir Philip Sidney (whose place of military service in the Low Countries he inherited) had to separate himself from his wife and the famous Penshurst estate that Ben Jonson later celebrated as a pleasant refuge from a troubled world. Had he chosen to stay at home or close to home, he could not have succeeded in public life, as he did in the Jacobean era when he finally was named the second Earl of Leicester in 1618. His behavior in the last part of Elizabeth's reign and in the early part of James's indicates clearly that his own ambition, rather than simple patriotic duty, took him away from his family. During those long periods he not only received newsy letters from his agent at Court, Rowland Whyte, but also wrote some of the most atypically affectionate conjugal love letters that have survived from this epistolarily formal period.[58]

Occasionally, husbands dealt with the situation of separation from their wives in a poetical idiom. Sir John Harington, for example, wrote two epigrams to his wife on the subject of his protracted absences from her while he was at Court. One wittily portrayed her critical mother as the emotional troublemaker even as it assured her that their love was continual, that absence was able to "whett it" (*Epigrams*, 369.17) further, and that their communication was still possible through "thoughts" (10), "letters" (11), and verse. The other poem is more emotionally realistic and bluntly antisentimental, revealing the actual aversion to remaining at home disguised by the conventional affectionate rationalizations in which Harington and others engaged:

> *To his wife in excuse of his Absence*
>
> Mall, in mine absence this ys still your song:
> "Com home, sweet heart, yow stay from home too long."
> That thow lov'st home, my love, I like yt well,
> Wives should be like thy Tortas in the shell.
> I love to seeke, to see, to learn, know, be knownc;
> Men nothing know, know nothing but their owne.
> "Yea, but," yow say to me, "home homely is,
> And comly thervnto." And what of this?
> Among wise men, they demed are but momes,
> That allwayes ar abiding in their homes.
>   To have no home, perhapps it is a curse;
>   To be a prisoner at home 'tis worse.
>   (*Letters and Epigrams*, p. 304)

Harington, of course, was not unusual in regarding confinement to a domestic environment as imprisonment. His statement to his wife that, in their culture, men and women are expected to have different proper spheres of activity was a normal one in a time before the affective bonding of companionate marriage became the social norm.[59] One can obviously detect that husbands nevertheless experienced emotional conflicts between love and ambition, between marital affection and duty on the one hand, and the attraction to a life of competitive public activity on the other.

168   Social Exile and Jacobean Courtier

Donne responded to the situation of parting from Ann in 1605 by composing several poems, insistently locating conventional valedictory themes in autobiographical actuality. He knew that he had foolishly thrown away a career to marry her and that he wanted to take leave of her to resume the aggressive pursuit of his career goals. Since, however, the impending period of travel with his friend constituted his first prolonged separation from Ann, the parting was undoubtedly an especially difficult one for both husband and wife. What heightened the sense of stress for Donne was probably more than the usual tension between love and ambition; it was some very strong ambivalent feelings for the woman he married. Although Donne nowhere allowed himself to state bluntly, as Walton later did, that his marriage was "the remarkable error of his life,"[60] he was all too conscious of its disastrous effect on his promising career in government service: referring to his elopement and wedding, he wrote in 1612, "I dyed ten years ago" (*Letters*, p. 122).

Consistently he thought of his wife as much in terms of duty and guilt as in terms of love and affection, at times regarding her and his children as encumbrances, the "hostages to fortune"[61] Bacon named from the point of view of the determined careerist. Apparently not a man capable of settling comfortably into the roles of husband and father, Donne obviously enjoyed his separations from his wife and family. In a 1613 letter, written when Ann, who had recently given birth to their son Nicholas, was away in the country visiting friends, he made a revealing remark: "I have . . . two of the best happinesses which could befall me, upon me; which are, to be a widower and my wife alive" (*Letters*, p. 179). In the light of the hostile fantasy underlying this statement, Donne's expressed fear in a 1612 letter from France that he had suffered the "losse of a wife" (*Letters*, p. 74) looks like an unconscious wish.[62]

Set against the background of his ambivalent feelings, the valedictions Donne wrote after his marriage poetically idealize an emotionally vexed love relationship, rationalizing both the need and the motives for parting, propitiating the fictive mistress (and the real addressee) for the act of leaving her. The lover-speaker of these poems answers fears, gives assurances, and attempts to communicate through poetic indirections the sense that his love is strong and nothing is or will go wrong—all in the context of the poet's own inner conflicts, many of whose elements are projected on the figure of the woman being left behind. Though chronology is impossible to prove, "A Valediction: of the Booke," "A Valediction: of Weeping," and "A Valediction: forbidding Mourning" better fit Donne's 1605 than his 1611 departure from his wife, since the earlier parting after four years of shared poverty and social exile would have been the emotionally more volatile occasion, one to which the poet might have found it more appropriate to respond by composing several lyrics. One can find in each of these valedictions more or less plausible allusions to Donne's marital situation within which the lovers' parting had poignant meaning.

"A Valediction: of the Booke," "A Valediction: of Weeping," and "A Valediction: forbidding Mourning," like some of the other poems of mutual love, might have been shown to some of the poet's friends, for the witty conceits and other self-conscious aesthetic complexities of the verse certainly suggest these lyrics were quite suitable for this purpose. But the poems' emotional strategies imply a set of personal circumstances in which Donne engaged in a characteristic form of self-persuasion that demanded an intimate audience of a particular kind, his wife. In one sense, she functioned as a typical sympathetic coterie reader; in another, she was, of course, quite different, for her personal response to the rhetoric was bound to have had immediate implications in the context of their marriage. As I suggested earlier, something of the same circumstances probably existed before, for the elegy "His Picture" and perhaps for some of the other valedictory lyrics, but much more was obviously at stake in the mature valedictions. These poems mark a shift from one stage to another in the Donnes' marital relationship, after which the poet ceased writing verse for his wife.

J. B. Leishman has made the interesting suggestion that "A Valediction: of the Booke" actually "accompanied a manuscript volume of love poems . . . which . . . can hardly have been other than those of the *Songs and Sonets* . . . which had been inspired by [Donne's] wife."[63] Whether or not this was really the case, the poem does call attention to the history of a mutual love relationship as it attempts to come to terms with the occasion of parting that seems to threaten it.[64] In this lyric, Donne projects those forces that are antagonistic to love onto people and circumstances in the outside world, treating separation itself as the enemy and naming an impersonal "destiny" (2), not his wish to pursue personal ambitions, as the reason for his leaving. In earlier love poems, he had found it useful to employ antagonist figures—such as spies and rivals, irate or suspicious parents, jealous husbands, blabbermouths and slanderers, even faithless mistresses—as part of the dialectical means for working out emotional conflicts within a particular love relationship. In "A Valediction: of the Booke" such a strategy freed him to give expression to the feelings of anger, annoyance, and frustration connected with his marriage. Starting from the position of shared suffering, the lover-speaker of this poem aggressively goes on the attack for six of the poem's seven stanzas, on his own and on his beloved's behalf, taking as his target a public world that has supposedly mistreated them.

Once the forces inimical to love have been located outside of the love relationship, "A Valediction: of the Booke" can convert the emotionally resolute couple from victims to aggressors. The speaker's satiric assault on the larger world functions as an oblique proof to his beloved of the capacity he and she have to persevere through their mutual commitment. With insistent irony and humor, the first six stanzas distance and control the feelings implicit in the situation, offering, at the same time, the kind of affectionate assurances and consolations Donne could express with dramatic force. Like "The Canonization," the poem concludes with the establishment of emotional equilibrium in the final stanza. All the "idle talke" ("A Valediction: of my Name in the Window," 65) is intended to have a salutary effect, as Donne fictionally transforms his own ambivalent feelings for his wife in a work he presents as an aesthetic solution to some of the problems of parting.

The poem begins with the speaker's boasting of four feats he and his mistress will perform:

> I'll tell thee now (deare Love) what thou shalt doe
>   To anger destiny, as she doth us,
> How I shall stay, though she esloyne me thus,
> And how posterity shall know it too;
>   How thine may out-endure
>   Sybills glory, and obscure
>   Her who from *Pindar* could allure
> And her, through whose helpe *Lucan* is not lame,
> And her, whose booke (they say) *Homer* did finde, and name.
>   (1–9)

Through maniacal exaggeration, which Johan Huizinga claims is a basic feature of the lyric imagination,[65] Donne defines in this and the succeeding five stanzas a love that is so rare, so mysterious, so grand, that all other serious human endeavors are absurd by comparison. What the lover says, through his pedantic mask,[66] is that he will show his mistress how to change from victim to aggressor, how he can remain with her through his forced absence, how he will record their experience for posterity (the same concern for an audience outside the relationship expressed in "The Canonization"), and, finally, how she will enjoy a fame superior to that of the great women of the past. The first two boasts, which are closer to the emotional actualities of the situation of parting, announce the basic rationale for the poem and assert the conventional valedictory paradox of presence in absence. The third and fourth indulge in that mode of imaginative hyperbole through which Donne handled psychological conflict through fictional indirection and, beyond this, engaged the attention of an implied, if not actual, audience other than the immediate addressee. This lyric follows the same method as a poem like "The Extasie," which similarly publicizes a love relationship for those outside the couple's world, who supposedly study, admire, and are edified by the lovers' example.

Beneath its learned foolishness, "A Valediction: of the Booke" contains a serious definition of love. The speaker, in the context of the history of a relationship recorded in "letters, which have past twixt thee and mee" (11), reminds his beloved that their love is profound, precious, and lasting (stanza 3), both physical and spiritual (stanza 4), true devotion (stanza 5), and ultimately indefinable (stanza 6). In "The Canonization" the lover contrasts the world he and his mistress share with the self-serving and absurdly busy one of courtiers, soldiers, lawyers, landowners, and merchants. In mocking alchemists, chroniclers, clerics, divines, Platonizing love philosophers, lawyers, and statesmen, the speaker of "A Valediction: of the Booke" assures his beloved that, in leaving her for their world, he does so with an emotional aversion to it and with a continuing emotional commitment to her in absence. Both the rhetorical hyperboles and the biographical evidence, however, suggest that this is a rationalization of motives that ran, at least partly, in the opposite direction, from the private world of love to the public world of sociopolitical involvement toward which Donne moved in 1605. In referring in the penultimate stanza of the poem to the book recording the history of their love as one worth the study of divines, lawyers, and statesmen, Donne's conversion of political codes into amorous ones suggests that the translation could also work the other way. It was, after all, the "occupation" (47) of "Statesmen" (46) for which he longed.

To a degree, this poem, like Donne's other exercises in this form, was a fictional counterpoise to a disturbing actuality. Certainly a male coterie readership represented by a friend like Sir Henry Goodyer would have read it this way, however Donne's wife would have responded to it. The final stanza, whose purpose seems to be to assure the fictional mistress that the lover will be constant in his commitment through the period of absence, contains a conceit that seems, like the cleverness of the preceding stanzas, more suitable for a literarily sophisticated audience outside the lovers' microcosm (and outside the marital relationship of poet and spouse):

> Thus vent thy thoughts; abroad I'll studie thee,
>   As he removes farre off, that great heights takes;
>   How great love is, presence best tryall makes,
>   But absence tryes how long this love will bee;
>   To take a latitude
>   Sun, or starres, are fitliest view'd
>   At their brightest, but to conclude
>   Of longitudes, what other way have wee,
>   But to marke when, and where the darke eclipses bee?
>
> (55–63)

Lovers can measure the greatness of their love when they are together and its lastingness when they are apart. Through this complex metaphor the speaker consoles his beloved that their separation will strengthen their relationship, implying also that, like an eclipse, the period of absence will be temporary. Donne repeats an intellectual truism of the valedictory situation that can be traced back to Andreas Capellanus, who recommends that a couple experience absence from one another in order to intensify their love.[67] The intention of the astronomical figure in this stanza, like that of the imaginative hyperboles and comic distractions of the poem as a whole, seems to be one of affectionate reassurance, but the ingenuity and the emotional message do not quite seem to coincide, suggesting that Donne could not simply write a love poem for his wife without introducing the rhetorical coordinates of the coterie literature designed for sophisticated male readers. The poetic pyrotechnics of this lyric compete with, rather than simply serve, its dramatic and emotional design, reproducing in the possible conflict of audiences the kind of tension between love and ambition Donne felt and expressed so well in his other poetry.

By contrast, a poem like "A Valediction: of Weeping" probably accommodated itself more gracefully to a double audience of spouse and friends. Its emotional message, at least, is expressed more successfully, its psychological and dramatic elements more carefully attuned to the personal situation of Donne and his wife. The high comedy of this lyric's opening stanza both inventively reformulates the conventions of the valedictory form and, like the opening stanza of "The Canonization," locates the emotional dynamics of the poem in shared experience:

> Let me powre forth
> My teares before thy face, whil'st I stay here,
> For thy face coines them, and thy stampe they beare,
> And by this Mintage they are something worth,
> For thus they bee
> Pregnant of thee;
> Fruits of much griefe they are, emblemes of more,
> When a teare falls, that thou falls which it bore,
> So thou and I are nothing then, when on a divers shore.
>
> (1-9)

The four years of genuine hardship and desperation Donne and his wife had experienced together may be the referent of the "much griefe" to which this stanza alludes. The speaker's comic identification with the emotionally distraught woman he is leaving temporarily reverses the usual valedictory polarities of emotionally distraught woman and rationalizing man.[68] But it also allowed Donne to allude specifically to his wife's pregnancy. The lover's tears are "emblemes of more" not only in the primary sense of the seventh line, but also because they bear the reflected image of a woman whose maiden name was More.[69]

Given the personal allusions of the first stanza, the poem seems to have a strong emotional center for its wit. Analytically extending the mode of sympathetic response away from the dramatic confrontation of a sorrowing, protesting woman and a determined, rationalizing man, the rest of the poem never loses touch with the emotional purpose of affectionate consolation, despite its deeper ambivalences. In his most skillful fashion Donne uses intellectual complexity to create one of his most successful dramatic lyrics of mutual love.

Despite its cool rationality, which contrasts sharply with the emotional intensity of the first stanza, the second stanza of this poem actually develops its feelings of affection and concern:

> On a round ball
> A workeman that hath copies by, can lay
> An Europe, Afrique, and an Asia,
> And quickly make that, which was nothing, *All*,
> So doth each teare,
> Which thee doth weare,
> A globe, yea world by that impression grow,
> Till thy teares mixt with mine doe overflow
> This world, by waters sent from thee, my heaven dissolved so.
>
> (10-18)

Offering both indirect compliment and a more precise definition of the dramatic situation, the speaker tells his beloved, in effect, that she is his world, if not his "heaven." We learn also that she is crying as they embrace and that their tears mix. Reversing the movement from all to nothing associated with the contrast between union and separation, the lover suggests through this stanza's central metaphor that annihilation can be succeeded by recreation, departure by return.

Here, and in the first stanza, Donne symbolized what he elsewhere defined as a married couple's "unseparable union" ("Epithalamion, or Marriage Song on the Lady Elizabeth, and Count Palatine being married on St. Valentine's Day," 46) by the joining of the mistress's image and the lover's tears. By suggesting through the conceit of the drowning of these images in the mistress's own tear-deluge that the real threat to the lovers' world lies not in separation but in the possibility of the wrong response to departure, the speaker in the poem cleverly redefines the basic situation. He intimates that he and his beloved do not really have to worry about any real damage to their love from the experience of living apart but rather that they only have to be concerned that they handle the parting properly, an occasion he instructs her how to master.

The speaker suggests that he and his beloved have the power to renew rather than destroy their love by ceasing the emotional protest against separation. Having reached this realization first, he encourages his mistress to follow his example:

> O more than Moone,
> Draw not up seas to drowne me in thy spheare,
> Weepe me not dead, in thine armes, but forbeare
> To teach the sea, what it may doe too soone;
>   Let not the winde,
>   Example find,
> To doe me more harme, then it purposeth;
> Since thou and I sigh one anothers breath,
> Who e'r sighes most, is cruellest, and hasts the others death.
>   (19–27)

It is comically ironic for the character who begins the poem in an emotional outburst to preach emotional restraint, but, in this lyric of sympathetic responses, the humor is deliberate: just as he imitated her tearful protests, so she should assume his more rational control. The fantasized alternative is that nature will realize the woman's fears by assailing the journeying lover with tempests and rough seas—a familiar danger alluded to in valedictory poetry. At a deep level, the beloved who is portrayed as a victim up to the end of the second stanza of the poem becomes figuratively the aggressor whose ostensible fears imperfectly disguise the wish to retaliate for being abandoned.

In this poem, as elsewhere, Donne deflects the intellectual attention, but not necessarily the emotional focus, away from a charged dramatic center to a conceit or argument whose formal execution serves as a model for the resolution of a conflict of feelings. This kind of poetic departure-and-return movement constitutes the linguistic and metaphoric counterpoint to the lyric's affective message. The final conceit of "A Valediction: of Weeping" joines the discursive and emotional lines of the work in the kind of closure Donne habitually sought. The image of the lovers' souls in their breaths is not only a version of the conventional soul-kiss that is a familiar figure in Renaissance poems of parting but also a reappearance of the Donnean conceit of interinanimation that can be found in such poems as "The Expiration" and "The Extasie," a metaphor for mutual commitment in love. Such an image has a more obviously direct emotional message than the more casually playful conceits of the preceding sections of the poem as it brings the imaginative displacements of the piece back to the immediate dramatic situation. The expiration of breath of the two lovers in the sorrowful sighs of parting becomes the symbol of their intimate oneness.[70]

"A Valediction: forbidding Mourning" begins with another form of expiration, the last breath of a dying man:

> As virtuous men passe mildly'away,
>   And whisper to their soules, to goe,
> Whilst some of their sad friends doe say,
>   The breath goes now, and some say, no:
>
> So let us melt, and make no noise.
>   No teare-floods, nor sigh-tempests move,
> 'Twere prophanation of our joyes
>   To tell the layetie our love.
>   (1–8)

Equating separation with death and leaving with dying,[71] Donne's poem opens with a conceit that is the central one of the Sidney valediction he may have begun imitating,[72] but it is used only in the first two stanzas to introduce a subject implicit in "A Valediction: of Weeping," the proper way of parting. There are, the poem argues, good and bad ways of separating, just as there are good and bad ways of meeting death. The speaker draws the analogy to the traditional art of "holy dying" in order to encourage his beloved to accept separation gracefully without making an emotional protest. He fuses this suggestion with the plea not to profane by a public display of grief a relationship whose sacredness is wittily implicit in the metaphor. Donne

176 *Social Exile and Jacobean Courtier*

uses a comically hyperbolic strategy both to acknowledge the feelings of the woman and to distance them so that they can be controlled.

The poem's first two stanzas define a love that is rare, holy, and assured, but the conceit introduces at the start the troubling fear that death will make the lovers' separation permanent, an anxiety that is a common valedictory theme. Other poems of parting, such as "Song: Sweetest love, I do not goe" and "The Expiration," joke about the notion of separation as death or about the danger that the lover will die in absence, but this poem seems less concerned with denying either that parting is a kind of death or that the lover(s) might die. From the start, this valediction suggests that the couple should accept not merely separation but physical dissolution as well. At least they should be able to forsake physical presence and satisfy themselves with a spiritual joining. What is being offered is something more than the traditional valedictory consolation that lovers who are apart physically can remain together spiritually—although the poem does say this as well:

> Dull sublunary lovers love
> (Whose soule is sense) cannot admit
> Absence, because it doth remove
> Those things which elemented it.
>
> But we by'a love, so much refin'd,
> That our selves know not what it is,
> Inter-assured of the mind,
> Care lesse, eyes, lips, and hands to misse.
>
> Our two soules therefore, which are one,
> Though I must goe, endure not yet
> A breach, but an expansion,
> Like gold to ayery thinnesse beate.
>   (13–24)

The contrast between the couple and more ordinary "sublunary lovers," which Donne handles more playfully in "The Canonization," here seems more serious, part of an effort to place a particular relationship in a theological-astronomical setting, a context in which, as John Freccero has shown, the parting and reuniting of a couple who are husband and wife are related to the mystery of death and resurrection as well as to the symbolic movements of a Platonic-Christian cosmos.[73] In this framework, the spiritual relationship of lovers has its teleology not in the return following separation but in the resurrection following death.

As the most religious of the valedictions, "A Valediction: forbidding Mourning" touches the boundary between Donne's secular and sacred verse. Donne spiritualizes married love here as he does in no other poem, with the possible exception of "A Nocturnall upon S. Lucies Day." He confronts the mortality of the lovers and of the very world in which they exist as he does in none of the other valedictions, not only depicting a return following a separation, but also foreseeing the dissolution of their relationship and their spiritual rebirth in their Creator. He seems to have been trying to transform one of the central facts of his existence, his marriage, from the disaster Walton said (and Donne knew) it was, into an occasion for spiritual awareness and growth. The man who wrote after his wife's death that "Here the admyring her my mind did whett/To seeke thee God" ("Since she whome I lovd, hath payd her last debt," 5–6) looks in this valediction beyond the temporary separations and reunions of lovers to other more important separations and reunions—of soul and body, of man and his Creator. The famous compass image then, which is a symbol of the constancy that guarantees the lover's return to his beloved, as Freccero's analysis suggests, affirms the priority of the speaker's relationship to God over that to his beloved.

"A Valediction: forbidding Mourning" ends with an affirmation of the lovers' bond and an assurance that reunion will follow separation. As in the other poems of this kind, a lover distracts his beloved from the immediate pain of separation in order to help her (and himself) gain emotional equilibrium. But there is a sense in which this lyric never really returns from its intellectual peregrinations to the vivid immediacy of human feeling.[4] The metaphoric complexities of this piece, whose intellectual and literary roots Freccero has uncovered, alter the emphasis from the usual one of the valedictory lyric: instead of offering a definition of love intended to quiet a woman's immediate fears through implicit or explicit promises of constancy and safe return, this poem moves away from "sublunary" concerns with conceits that reorient the attention toward the God that Dante and the mature Petrarch put at the center of love's universe. It is inevitable here, as in the 1617 sonnet Donne wrote after Ann's death, that the human relationship of the lovers be diminished in importance even as it is philosophically and religiously expanded. Of all the valedictions, this one comes the closest to transforming love into an idea—one that is eloquently expressed and adorned, but a suprapersonal reality nonetheless.

This suited the poet's, more than his spouse's needs. Donne wished, in 1605, to escape the confinement of domestic duties to reengage the social world in which he hoped to find other kinds of fulfillment. He had ulterior motives, therefore, for using ingenious metaphors for stretching out his marital ties in time and space. The religious or theological definition of marriage in "A Valediction: forbidding Mourning" facilitated disengagement as well as departure. Donne allowed neither his amorous nor his spiritual commitment to stand in the way of his active ambition, nor would he again, despite his intermittent expressions of guilt about his wife. It could be argued that "A Valediction: forbidding Mourning" and the other mature valedictions bring Donne's poetry of mutual love to an end. They signal the shift away from the poetry of amorous intimacy Donne composed from the time he wrote elegies like "The Perfume" and "On his Mistress" to that of lyrics like "A Lecture upon the Shadow," "The Anniversarie," and "The Sunne Rising." These separation poems express affection in the context of a (rationalized) act of disengagement for which Donne made emotional reparation. Their witty ingenuity, manifested, for example, in the conceits of "A Valediction: forbidding Mourning," suggests that Donne was less comfortable in addressing his own wife than his intellectually elite male audience, a coterie readership with whom he established closer social contact shortly after his return from his travels.

DONNE'S WRITING AND THE JACOBEAN ENVIRONMENT

Soon after his return from the Continent, Donne, who had moved his family to Mitcham, took lodgings for himself in the Strand (in Walton's words) "near to Whitehall, whither his friends and occasions drew him very often, and where he was as often visited by many of the nobility and others . . . who used him in their counsels of greatest consideration, and with some rewards for his better subsistence."[75] He thus reentered the social world from which he had been somewhat distanced by his loss of employment, resuming contact with the Court and with those satellite-courtly environments he knew. As Bald notes, the house in which Donne lived "apparently had a number of lodgers, one of whom was George Garrard" (*Life*, p. 159), who became one of the poet's closest friends and, apparently, one of the favored coterie readers of his verse.[76] Before considering the poetry Donne wrote in the period between his reimmersion in London life and his ordination in 1615, it is important to discuss the social and political environment in which he found himself and to which he responded in his letters, other prose works, and verse. The urban and courtly worlds from which he was exiled by his marriage and its consequences were Elizabethan; the City and Court with which he reestablished contact were Jacobean. There was significant differences, despite the many obvious similarities, between the two.

Donne reentered a politically and socially changed world after his Continental travels. In place of a parsimonious, authoritative queen who cautiously ruled by balancing factions against one another and by calculated procrastination and compromise, there was a foreign (Scottish) monarch on the throne, a man who had an aversion to handling the business of government for any length of time, and who delegated authority to his chief minister, Sir Robert Cecil, while he spent as many weeks as possible each year away from London at his hunting lodges.[77] Although James mystified his royal authority and defined it publicly in ideologically absolute terms, he wavered and vacillated when faced with opposition, thus exacerbating the power struggles between Crown and Parliament and between rival familial and factional groups. Thinking of himself as a theologically moderate man with a deep interest in religion, James was both constantly troubled by Puritans and, particularly after the Gunpowder Plot, involved in conflict and controversy with international Catholic forces. Wishing to rule as a peacemaker-king, his accommodations to Spain infuriated most of his subjects and he finally involved England in European religious warfare.[78] His lavishing of favors on his Scottish followers caused such widespread resentment that by 1607 he felt it necessary to explain apologetically to the Parliament that his "Liberalitie" toward his countrymen was much reduced after an initial spree of gift-giving: . . . "my first three yeeres were to me as a Christmas, I could not then be miserable."[79] Presiding over a wastefully extravagant Court, and responsible also for providing for the maintenance of separate establishments for his Queen and Prince Henry, James's economic imprudence led him to some undignified bargaining with Parliament for subsidies, to the unpopular exercise of royal prerogative in imposing taxes without Parliamentary approval, and to the sale of old titles and the creation of new ones. Bisexual in practice, but homosexual by preference, he selected as favorites handsome young courtiers like Robert Ker and George Villiers, men whose political and moral limitations did not prevent him from raising them to the peerage and giving them great power. Fearful of crowds and, therefore, unable to engage as fully as his predecessor in the ceremonial strengthening of political ties between monarch and populace such as occurred during royal progresses, desperate for consensus and the affectionate agreement of his subjects, James was hypersensitive to political opposition, but at the same time unskillful at the (sometimes quite harsh) means Elizabeth had used to control it. Although, partly due to the King's too-free hand, there were many more possibilities for courtly advancement and reward than in the last Elizabethan years, even many of those who participated in the game of political competition harbored a critical, if not cynical, attitude toward the Court and the monarch at its center.

One measure of difference between the Jacobean and the Elizabethan socioliterary climates is the record of books dedicated to the monarch. In Franklin Williams's list[80] for the last three years of Elizabeth's reign and the first three of James's, one can detect some marked changes. Not only was there a tremendous increase in such dedications with the accession of the King (a not-unexpected phenomenon), a rate that did not drop off to the level of the Elizabethan period even after the first few years, but also the number of religious and controversial works so dedicated grew dramatically. For 1603, twelve of the thirty-five items fall into this category; for 1604, nineteen out of thirty-three; and for 1605, thirteen out of twenty-seven. By contrast, of the six works dedicated to Elizabeth in 1600 only one is religious; in 1601, one of five; and in 1602, one of four. Even more remarkable is the drop-off in literary and historical volumes dedicated to the monarch. In the 1600–1602 period we find dedicated to the Queen such works as translations of Tasso, Plutarch, and Livy, one of William Camden's historical books, Sir William Segar's *Honor, Military and Civil*, Daniel's *Works*, and *Palestina*, Robert Chambers's romance based on the Gospels. By contrast, in the first three years of James's rule, literary works dedicated to the King constitute a very small portion of the total: these include Sir William Alexander's tragedy *Darius*, John Davies of Hereford's *Microcosmos*, Hugh Holland's *Pancharis*, *The poetical essayes of A. Craig Scotobritane*, a religious poem by Nicholas Breton, and Sylvester's tradition of DuBartas. Historical works virtually disappear. The rest include political pieces on James's proposed union of England and Scotland, some moral and philosophical treatises (including a translation of Plutarch's *Moralia* and Bacon's *Advancement of Learning*) and a fair number of panegyrical and congratulatory pieces.

If one looks ahead to the years 1608–10, one can detect a continued high percentage of religious and controversial works—occasioned not only by the King's general interest in religion, but also by the interconnected religious and political consequences of the (1605) Gunpowder Plot, the international controversy over the Oath of Allegiance, and the continuing pressure from Puritans. The political topic of Union, at issue in the parliament of 1604–10, probably lay behind a work dedicated to James on the Scottish constitution and laws and perhaps also Morgan Colman's printing of genealogies of King James and Queen Anne from the time of the Conquest. But when John Donne, for example, published *Pseudo-Martyr* in 1610, his was one of eight religious or polemical works out of the ten books dedicated to James that year.

The literary genres and modes in favor in the Jacobean period that constituted the literary system of the period were markedly different from those prominent in the Elizabethan era. For example, as the preceding account suggests, religious and philosophical works took on greater importance as amorous, romantic, and historical writing diminished. Love poetry, prose romance, romantic comedy, and historical drama lost positions of prominence as sacred verse, and devotional, controversial, and philosophical writing flourished in the changed sociocultural circumstances.[81]

The shift from Elizabethan to Jacobean had some obvious effects on Donne's writings. Certainly the polemical works he penned for publication—*Pseudo-Martyr* and *Ignatius His Conclave*—were the product of changed political circumstances. But, I suggest, so too were the religious poems—works that I would relate as much to their social environment as to Donne's own intellectual or spiritual history. As I have argued elsewhere, the marked decline in love poetry and the increase in religious verse that took place with the accession of a new monarch was a general feature of the movement from the Elizabethan to the Jacobean period[82] and Donne was, at least partly, responding to these altered circumstances in composing sacred poems. Similarly, in his encomiastic verse epistles as well as in his *Anniversaries*, he adopted an ideologically encoded philosophical and religious language that was characteristically Jacobean—found, for example, in the masques performed for James and his Court. The witty coterie pieces in verse and prose—works like the *Problems*, *Biathanatos*, and the competition or literary-exchange poetry—were also markedly Jacobean literary exercises: one has only to note the contemporary vogue of the essay, the character, and of other forms of witty literature[83] to perceive how well these sophisticated iconoclastic pieces were attuned to their specific sociocultural milieu. Of course, Donne's basic preoccupations and style did not significantly change, despite his altered personal circumstances.

It makes sense to discuss as a unit the years between Donne's return from traveling with Chute (1606) and his ordination (1615). What Bald says of Donne's activities in 1606–1611 applies to this whole time span:

His life seems more complex during these years than at any other period. . . . Donne was in London as often as with his wife and family at Mitcham; he followed the Court and cultivated patrons and patronesses; he devoted laborious hours of study and research to problems of divinity and canon law; and while he addressed poems to great ladies and theological pamphlets to the King, he also cultivated a certain Bohemianism in his leisure hours and liked to relax in the company of wits and writers. His friends and acquaintances were to be found in every rank of society, and he moved from one group to another with surprising ease. The very lack of regular employment and of a sense of definite direction contributes to the sense of complexity in Donne's life at this period, though doubtless no one regretted it more than he or wished more fervently that his varied endeavours could be reduced and dominated by singleness of purpose. (*Life*, p. 155)

At this time, Donne wrote a number of more or less literarily self-conscious works in poetry and prose for different coterie audiences. He composed individual secular poems for friends like Sir Henry Goodyer and Sir Edward Herbert, for patronesses like Lucy, Countess of Bedford, and for members of social circles like those associated with the Countess and with the Mermaid and Mitre Tavern groups. He wrote *Holy Sonnets* and other religious verse, sending the *La Corona* sequence to his friend Magdalen Herbert and some other religious pieces to the new Earl of Dorset (a potential patron) as well as to friends such as Goodyer. He wrote the philosophical-satiric-religious *Anniversaries* for his patron Sir Robert Drury, making the act of praise public by having the poems printed. He wrote familiar letters, especially to Goodyer, as well as recreatively witty problems, essays, characters, the monstrously long paradox *Biathanatos*, and the privately meditative *Essays in Divinity*, all for limited readerships. But, having helped Dean Morton in composing religious polemic,[84] he also entered into the public arena of theological and political controversy by publishing *Pseudo-Martyr* and *Ignatius His Conclave*, obviously hoping to win royal favor through such service.

Donne was simply neither the social and intellectual rebel nor the flattering importunate courtier: he contradictorily assumed both roles and his complex behavior changed according to circumstances. To characterize him accurately, one need not accept either the hagiographical pattern laid down by Walton and followed, with variations, by a number of critics since, or the model of Donne as the intellectual skeptic-hero who refused to compromise himself for crass worldly ends. The fact is that he was both jauntily, if not self-destructively, *subversive of* as well as contritely *deferential toward* the Establishment. Donne had conflicting attitudes, especially in this period of uncertain employment. He regretted his hasty marriage and its disastrous consequences for his career, but felt the need to express domestic love and care as well as to make some reparation to his wife for the unprosperous life into which he had led her.[85] He both blamed himself for his lack of advancement and criticized the corruption and injustice of the system. He energetically pursued opportunity and involved himself in both the serious and the recreational activities of various social circles, but he had also an inclination to depressive withdrawal and solitude. He combined manic activity with (sometimes suicidal) loneliness. At the very time he associated himself with witty, sometimes oppositionist Parliamentarians and frustrated courtiers like Richard Martin and William Hakewill, he approached for patronage such powerful men of the Court as the Earl of Somerset and Lord Hay.

DONNE'S POLITICS AND HIS EARLY JACOBEAN PROSE

Donne's public and private stances in his life and art were markedly different. Publicly, he tried to present himself as a learned, rational, responsible, and properly deferential aspirant to government service—one who could accept and defend the Jacobean political ideology and government. Privately, he remained the skeptical, iconoclastic, socially rebellious individual who wished to exercise his personal autonomy, sometimes by satirizing and criticizing his social superiors and the established order. One has only to contrast the private and public prose of the 1606–15 period to note the contradictory impulses. For example, the skeptical attitudes, satiric force, and personal resentment that come through in the *Problems*, many of the letters, *Biathanatos*, the characters, "The Essay of Valour,"[86] and *The Courtier's Library* contrast sharply with the public defense of the official political mythology in *Pseudo-Martyr* and *Ignatius His Conclave*. To understand the social and political contexts and significance of both kinds of work, we need to recognize how they incorporated (at least) two different Jacobean styles of expression, culture-specific idioms utilized in contemporary social and political transactions—one reflecting the mystification of royal authority and the established hierarchical order, the other expressing political opposition, disappointment, and alienation. The latter style, especially suited to private coterie communication, was characterized by critical and satiric rigor, plainspoken directness, and versatile wit.

In the *Problems*, for example, Donne cultivated a witty, rhetorically aggressive, sometimes bluntly direct manner that has its roots in some of the Inns-of-Court literature of the 1590s, but that reappears, in somewhat changed socioliterary circumstances, in the prose and verse of the first half of the Jacobean era. It was the preferred intellectual and stylistic idiom of much private correspondence as well as of such social groups as the Mitre and Mermaid Tavern circles to which Donne belonged,[87] as well as of other often courtly situations of recreative communication like that of the "News" game played in the Cecilia Bulstrode circle.[88] But, in the context of contemporary political realities (such as the Crown-Parliament conflicts), the wittily critical rhetoric and convoluted paradoxical or ironic reasoning that characterizes some of the poems and prose pieces written by Donne and his peers had a political dimension that would not have been missed. After all, the Mitre and Mermaid groups, for example, included some prominent oppositionist M.P.s from the 1604–10 and 1614 Parliaments as well as a number of discontented courtier-aspirants: what they played at in their ephemeral literary pieces they worked at in their public business—the exercise of intellectual and political freedom.[89]

The related issues of free speech and of individual intellectual, moral, and political freedom were live ones both inside and outside of the Parliament and Court. Both at work and at play, a man like Richard Martin, who was a prominent oppositionist leader in Commons,[90] exercised liberties of thought and language that represented a heightening of political consciousness and conflicts. Even when abused, as they were by the waggish John Hoskins in the 1614 "Addled" Parliament,[91] such freedoms were at issue in Crown-Commons conflicts in this interesting pre–Civil War period. Wallace Notestein points out that James was temperamentally more strongly averse to opposition than was Queen Elizabeth, but, especially since he lacked the kind of controlling presence of key Privy Council members sitting in the House of Commons (officials on whom Elizabeth depended), he was forced to tolerate a more vociferous Lower House.[92] Faced with a more intellectually and professionally capable Commons that included a large number of active common lawyers,[93] James repeatedly complained not only about their reluctance to grant him subsidies and to approve his plan for the Union of England and Scotland but also about their aggressive criticisms and grievances. Constantly confronted with complaints of Puritans, country gentlemen, and London lawyers about the abuses in the systems of purveyance, of wardship, of trade, and of ecclesiastical preferment, he wished the English House of Commons to behave more like the Scottish Parliament with which he was more comfortable. Referring to an M.P. whose anti-

Scots remarks landed him in the Tower, James said in a 1607 speech: "I know there are many *Piggots* amongst [the Scottish Parliament members], I meane a number of seditious and discontented particular persons, as must be in all Common-wealths, that where they dare, may peradventure talke lewdly enough." Pointing to the differences between the two Parliaments, he continued, "there they must not speake without the Chauncellors leaue, and if any man doe propound or vtter any seditious or vncomely speeches, he is straight interrupted and silenced by the Chauncellors authoritie: whereas here, the libertie for any man to speake what hee list, and as long as he list, was the onely cause he was not interrupted" (*Political Works*, 1:301). Like a number of others who were angry about and envious of the rewards showered on James's Scottish followers, Piggot had attacked the Scots—in the context of a discussion of the Union of Kingdoms that was so strongly desired by the King. But his speaking was only an extreme case of a general liberty exercised by the Commons in its regular business. Threatened by loose speech, James had said in his 1605 address to Parliament: "Men should bee ashamed to make shew of the quickness of their wits here, either in taunting, scoffing, or detracting the Prince or State in any point, or yet in breaking iests vpon their fellowes, for which the Ordinaries or Ale-houses are fitter places, then this Honourable and high Court of Parliament" (*Political Works*, 1:289).

To some degree, James was probably right to look on much of what transpired in the House of Commons as a waste of time in inefficient and self-indulgent speechmaking. But it is also curious that in his 1607 address he should have portrayed his own intentions and sometimes mystifying language as plain in contrast to the overingenious language and convoluted reasoning of Parliamentary discourse. He objected to the members' "delicate speeches" and "long precogitate Orations," claiming "I am onely to deliuer now vnto you matter without curious forme, substance without ceremonie, trewth in all sinceritie." "Studied Orations and much eloquence vpon little matter," he lectured the M.P.s, "is fit for the Vniversities, where not the Subiect which is spoke of, but the triall of his wit that speaketh, is most commendable: but on the contrary, in all great Councels of Parliaments, fewest wordes with most matter in all doeth become best, where the dispatch of the great errands in hand, and not the praise of the person is most to bee looked vnto . . ." (Political Works, 1: 290).[94] Commons members delved into the issue of the Union and its implications for the English Constitution, for international commerce, and for the system of common law (through which many members had their professional livelihood), but James thought of their actions as unnecessary "searching out as it were the very bowels of Curiositie" (*Political Works*, 1:291). The King was clearly bothered that discussions on this and other issues spilled over into the larger society: he told the Parliament in his surprisingly accommodating 1610 speech that he was disturbed that the political matters were treated "not onely in talke amongst you in the Parliament, but even in many other peoples mouthes, as well within, as without Parliament . . ." (*Political Works*, 1:306). In an inchoate constitutional struggle between royal prerogative and Parliamentary powers, M.P.s used (selective) antiquarian research, critical reasoning, and rhetorical skill to defend their rights and further their (often private) interests.[95]

Donne's political attitudes make sense in a Jacobean context but they are also, at best, the product of his temperament, his interests, and his desperate wish for employment. He seems to have been obsessed with the realities of patronage and preferment—alternately satirizing and idealizing the Court and those wellborn or powerful individuals from whom benefits could be obtained. In the decade before his ordination Donne continually pursued secular advancement: we know that he specifically tried to use the assistance of friends and benefactors to obtain a position in Queen Anne's household, a bureaucratic post in Ireland, a secretarial appointment in the Virginia Company, the clerkship of the Council, and the ambassadorship to Venice. Through Sir Edward Phelips, Master of the Rolls and former Speaker of the House of Commons (and a supporter of the Crown), he finally got a seat in the 1614 Parliament. Donne approached individuals like Sir James Hay and Sir Robert Ker (cousin of the Earl of Somerset) for assistance in obtaining a position of responsibility in the government, but at the same time associated himself socially with those who valued acts of critical and skeptical independence and who could appreciate witty, iconoclastic assaults on the Establishment. Sir Henry Goodyer, for example, whose position as one of the Gentlemen of the Privy Chamber marked him as a recipient of James's favor, could serve as the audience for some of Donne's most forthright satiric pieces: in both letters and the prose *Problems* (often sent along with them) Donne expressed critical attitudes and personal resentments, portraying in a wittily, but bitterly, negative manner the system that excluded him.

In his *Problems*, Donne was preoccupied with the Court, with advancement, with good fortune and bad. His position as a frustrated aspirant resentful of the success of supposedly lesser men freed him to satirize once more the political establishment he hoped to join. Referring clearly to the situation of early Jacobean England, he referred scornfully to "newe men Ennobled from Grasiers" (*Problem* 12 ["*Why is there more variety of greene, then any other colour?"*]), those who won royal patronage as politicians in an "age wherein all men . . . hunt" (p. 40): even though Goodyer himself was one of these "Court huntsmen," Donne expressed envy for men whose "hawkings" (*Letters*, p. 88) brought them better fortune than he could enjoy. *Problem 9* (*"Why have Bastards best Fortune?"*) tries to equate being fortunate with being wicked, being preferred with being foolish, as "the Divell and Princes" are named as "the two greatest powers in the world" (p. 32)—a conjunction Donne later suggested in *Ignatius His Conclave*. In this anticourtly piece, Donne's anger at the (perceived) unfairness of the system of advancement and his resentment about his own poor fortunes come through strongly. He defines being a fool as "one of [the] cheefest helpes to preferment" (p. 32) and says that (metaphoric as well as actual) bastards "abound most at Court, which is the forge where fortunes are made, or at least the shopp where they are sold" (p. 33). His envious resentment of the success of others appears also in *Problem 14* (*"Why are new Officers least oppressing?"*) where his consciousness of the courtly environment of "competitions and oppositions" (p. 42) is very strong. *Problem 4* refers to the corrupt economic system of bribery in which "Love, Honour, Justice" (p. 26) are bought. *Problem 1* (*"Why are Courtiers sooner Atheists than men of other Conditions?"*) indicates Donne had no illusions about the morals of the powerful: for he suggests that "a familiarity with greatnesse, and dayly Acquayntance and conversation with it, breede[s] a contempt of all greatnesse" (p. 23).[96] Neither nature, nor a just social order, but "feare, makes the degrees of Servants Lords and Kings" (p. 23), he quips. Sir John Roe similarly observed in his 1604 epistle to Ben Jonson, "God threatens Kings, Kings Lords, as Lords doe us" (Grierson, 1:414). Donne seems to have regarded the patronage system as both corrupt and monstrously unfair. In *Problem 3* (*"Why doe Greate Men choose of all dependants to preferre theyr Bawds?"*) his bitterness about his dismissal from Egerton's service still seems to have been quite strong several years after the fact: he sarcastically states that "Lords fling off none but such as they may destroy by it" (p. 25).

Whereas in the later opportunistic public prose of *Pseudo-Martyr* Donne defended James's wish to keep the *arcana imperii*, or mysteries of royal power, free from critical scrutiny,[97] in *Problem 16* (*"Why are Statesmen most Incredible?"*) he explicitly connected the term with the king's homosexuality. In this satiric piece, Donne names as an example of *arcana imperii* the identities of those "by whome the Prince provokes his lust, and by whome hee vents it" (p. 45), alluding, I believe, to James's erotic involvement with his male favorites,[98] associating it satirically with the political vocabulary of absolutist mystification.[99]

Although, in a sermon preached at Whitehall in 1617, Donne used the analogy of the royal court as heaven (". . . as Princes are Gods, so their well-govern'd Courts, are Copies, and representations of Heaven" [*Sermons* 1:223]), his attitude toward King and Court in the early Jacobean coterie prose was quite otherwise. In "*The Description of a Scot at first sight*," he mocked James's outlandish dress, portraying him as a kind of provincial bungler, scornfully referring to his function as a "knightwright" selling the title as "100, 150 and 200[lb] price" (p. 59), alluding to the creation of over 900 knights at the start of the Jacobean era. Considering the trouble M.P.s got into when they indulged in anti-Scots remarks, this private jeu d'esprit was a dangerous indulgence of political wit. So too was "*An Essaie of Valour*," a humorous discourse on masculine aggressiveness. In this occasional piece, Donne criticized contemporary wooing codes along with the styles of behavior prescribed for men and women in an "Age of Witt" (p. 64), in which the older gender differentiations were being reformulated. Like the authors of *Haec Vir* and *Hic Mulier* or the Jonson of *Epicoene*, Donne objected to the violations of sex roles represented by "neat youths" and "Woamen in Menns *Apparrell*"—in actuality opposing the realignment of sex-specific behavior associated with the Jacobean Court and Court-centered society, in which a pacifist bisexual King and women of fashion who lived apart from their husbands exercising "hermaphroditical authority"[100] both regarded aggressive masculinity as a socially undesirable quality. As a former soldier, Donne addressed himself to sympathetic social equals who could be critical of the new norms, attacking prescribed deferential behavior (in either amorous or political activity) as unmanly and ineffectual.

Donne's *Catalogus Librorum Aulicorum*, a Rabelaisian mock-catalog of books, contains pointed political satire. In this work, obviously designed for a male coterie readership, Donne included a number of specifically political examples of wit, among them the hostile reference to Bacon as a betrayer of Essex and a scornful reference to the democratic sympathies of James's famous tutor George Buchanan.[101] Both items, however, could have been read by Donne's audience in the context of the contemporary contest between Parliamentary powers and royal prerogative. Since Cecil and other members of the Privy Council were in the House of Lords, Bacon was virtually alone in Commons as an official spokesman of royal policies—and he created no small hostility for himself in this role.[102] Item 30 of the catalog refers to a special apartment in Hell in which "Kings are tortured by a recollection of the past" (p. 51): James's ambivalent feelings about his mother, Mary, Queen of Scots, and his remembrance of his early personal vulnerability in Scotland were never far from his consciousness.[103] Item 24, "Edward Hoby's Afternoon Belchings; or, A Treatise of Univocals, as of the King's Prerogative, and Imaginary Monsters, such as the King's Evil and the French Disease" (pp. 50–51), is a particularly pointed satiric assault on James. As Evelyn Simpson notes, Sir Edward Hoby was a recipient of James's favors and Donne's "univocals" is applied "derisively to the King's prerogative and to the chimera, both of which might be regarded as particularly ambiguous and doubtful subjects" (pp. 70–71). Item 34, "Tarlton, *On the Privileges of Parliament*" (p. 53) suggests that, in *Realpolitik* terms, Parliamentary powers and privileges were a joke.

Such witty prose pieces as the *Problems, Characters*, "An Essay of Valour," and the *Catalogus* can easily be recognized as literary recreations suitable for private circulation—perhaps having been designed for the men with whom Donne associated in the Mitre and Mermaid Tavern clubs and in the Sir Thomas Overbury circle.[104] Although the 300-page *Biathanatos* is a piece of witty paradoxical reasoning, it would have been inappropriate for such casual circumstances. Donne nevertheless regarded this treatise on suicide as a work for coterie circulation, not for print, sending it, as the Preface indicates, to some scholars at Oxford and Cambridge and probably also to some friends in London. We know from one of his letters that he gave it to Goodyer[105] and so it was not only scholars who were meant to puzzle over this work's complexities.

From the Preface on, it is clear that Donne expected this extended paradox to be read by a select audience capable of enjoying its false analogies, logically fallacious arguments, wittily false definitions, outrageous or absurd examples, *and*, less obviously, its politically subversive elements. Whatever its function in his own psychic life, perhaps as a bizarre suicide note designed to purge suicidal urges,[106] *Biathanatos* was a work of satiric intellectuality composed for an audience aware, among other things, of the political implications of some of the issues it discusses. Donne used its convoluted reasoning and problematic conclusions for witty assault on contemporary political, as well as traditional moral and religious, dogmas.[107]

Biathanatos constitutes a critical discourse on the political milieu in which the unemployed Donne and his readers lived. For example, in the light of the issue of Union, which involved the problem of uniting a country whose legal system was that of civil law with one that relied mainly on common law, Donne's association of the civil law of which James was so fond with Catholicism is a subversive one. In one of a number of statements defending the autonomy of individual conscience, Donne says: ". . . this obligation which our conscience casts upon us is of stronger hold and of straiter band than the precept of any superior, whether law or person, and is so much *iuris naturalis* as it cannot be infringed nor altered *beneficio divinae indulgentiae* . . ." (p. 137). Instead of depicting nature as the source of royal authority, he made it the basis of the moral and political autonomy of the individual. On the other hand, Donne questioned the mystification of royal power that was at the heart of the Jacobean ideology by suggesting that definitions of what is natural are cultural: for instance, he facetiously selected the example of St. Paul's condemnation of long hair "for delicacy and effeminateness" (p. 59) and noted that Calvin pointed out that this judgment was based on the Greek custom of wearing short hair, not on the inherent law of nature.

Elsewhere Donne defended relativism in morals in a way that could easily have been extended into political circumstances: "No law is so primary and simple, but it foreimagines a reason upon which it was founded; and scarce any reason is so constant, but that circumstances alter it, in which case a private man is emperor of himself" (p. 61).[108] In a section that seems to associate Papal pretensions with James's, right after stating ironically that "prerogative is incomprehensible, and overflows and transcends all law," he also asserts that "what law soever is cast upon the conscience or liberty of man, of which the reason is mutable, is naturally conditioned with this: that it binds so long as the reason lives" (p. 63). In a skeptical, ironical essay like *Biathanatos*, James's political ideology does not bear up well under such oblique critical scrutiny. Drawing an analogy between the authority of reason and the authority of a king, Donne suggested that just as logical fallacies corrupt reason and produce bad conclusions (a process demonstrated extensively in this work), so too bastardy sullies a royal bloodline and causes diminished authority in a monarchy:[109] given James's mystification of blood and Nature, this is a particularly subversive suggestion.

James's willful blindness to subtly satirical attacks on himself made it relatively safe for Donne also to build certain subversive material into his published prose works, *Pseudo-Martyr* and, particularly, *Ignatius His Conclave*.[110] Although the two books took a public stand in defense of the official political ideology and attacked those who undermined the loyalty of English Catholics and, thus, threatened the security of the State, they contain some elements that reflect a more critical stance toward official beliefs. In a letter to Goodyer about

Pseudo-Martyr Donne revealed deep qualms about the argument he set forth in the work:

In the main point in question [the requiring of all Englishmen, including Catholics, to take the Oath of Allegiance], I think truly there is a perplexity (as far as I see yet), and both sides may be in justice and innocence; and the wounds which they inflict upon the adverse part are all *se defendendo*: for, clearly, our State cannot be safe without the Oath; since they profess that clergymen, though traitors, are no subjects, and that all the rest may be none to-morrow. And, as clearly, the supremacy which the Roman Church pretend were diminished, if it were limited; and will as ill abide that, or disputation, as the prerogative of temporal kings, who being the only judges of their prerogative, why may not Roman bishops (so enlightened as they are presumed by them) be good witnesses of their own supremacy, which is now so much impugned? (Gosse, I, 221–22)

Donne openly states the problem inherent in the controversy over the Oath of Allegiance, that both sides were right from their own points of view (and so it was really political expediency and self-interest, not clear moral law, that stood behind James's position). In the letter to Goodyer there is a troubling association of sacrosanct royal prerogative, which was not to be questioned too closely (as Parliamentarians tried to do), and the mystified authority of the Papacy and the Catholic Church that had been broadly extended into secular, political spheres. The attack on the overblown claims to authority of the Catholic Church that takes place throughout the work, then, can be read as an exercise in political criticism applicable as well to the ideology of royal absolutism. Although Donne defends kingly authority in *Pseudo-Martyr* as derived from a divine source and from the "Law of Nature," he carefully identifies the latter with "rectified reason" (p. 168), a faculty whose proper exercise, he consistently believed, fallen men were incapable of sustaining. Furthermore, given what he did to problematize the definition of "Nature" in *Biathanatos*, he certainly knew that he was being self-consciously disingenuous in many of the arguments he offered in *Pseudo-Martyr*.

The political criticism and subversiveness of the satiric *Ignatius His Conclave* are more pronounced. Presented as a comically hyperbolic attack on Jesuits and corrupt foreigners, this work (like some of the dramas of the period) satirized the corrupt workings of contemporary Jacobean politics under the guise of directing its aim elsewhere. For example, the portrayal of Machiavelli clearly suggests the practices of the Jacobean court. Donne possibly mocked Bacon in this character—who in the fiction "had thrust himselfe into the office of *kings Atturney*" (p. 25)—but, in the rivalry of Machiavelli and Ignatius for Lucifer's favor, he portrayed Court rivalries and machinations in a topically allusive way. The Ignatius that Machiavelli deceitfully addresses as "*Arch-chancellor* of this *Court*" and commends for "stupendous wisedome, and the government of this state" (p. 25) looks suspiciously like the (by-now-declining) Earl of Salisbury, in whose hands James had left so much government business. Donne seems clearly to allude to the James-Cecil relationship in the Lucifer-Ignatius one when he has the narrator comment: ". . .*Lucifer* . . . seemed to have admitted *Ignatius*, as his *Lieutenant*, or *Legat a latere*, and trusted him with an absolute power of doing what hee would, yet he quickly spied his owne errour, and danger thereby. He began to remember . . . that kings do forfeit their dignity, if they give themselves to other matters, and leave the government of the State to their officers" (pp. 69, 71). But whether or not the satire was personal (as in *Metempsychosis*), Donne was expressing his contempt in *Ignatius His Conclave* for the vicious power plays of major Court officers. This is clear in the narrator's comments on the behavior of both Machiavelli and Ignatius:

So I saw *Machiavel* often put forward, and often thrust back, and at last vanish. And looking earnestly upon *Lucifers* countenance, I perceived him to bee affected towards *Ignatius*, as *Princes*, who though they envy and grudge, that their great Officers should have such immoderate meanes to get wealth; yet they dare not complaine of it, least thereby they should make them odious and contemptible to the people: so that *Lucifer* now suffered a new *Hell*: that is, the danger of a *Popular Devill*, vaine-glorious, and inclined to innovations there. (p. 65)

At a time in which the Earl of Somerset was growing in power and Salisbury diminishing (partly because of his inability to control Parliament,[111] partly because James no longer wanted his politically realistic advice), Donne and his contemporaries witnessed the completion of the shift from a government that rewarded bureaucratic expertise to one that relied more on the uncertain whims of royal favor and processes of economic rapine. With the death of Salisbury in 1612 the Court lost its most capable administrator.

In his coterie prose and in his two published polemical works, Donne, therefore, called attention to the contemporary political milieu in which he wrote and lived. For deeply personal expressions of his own thoughts and feelings as an ambitious man frustrated in his search for advancement, one must look to some of the letters he wrote in the dozen or so years before his ordination. In these, the most private of his prose works, he used the form of the Renaissance familiar epistle to compose literarily and personally self-conscious discourses in the context of confessional intimacy, especially when writing (often weekly) to his close friend Sir Henry Goodyer. Fond of such authors as Aretino and Montaigne, he used the letter as a genre of writing that overlapped with the essay, the personal meditation, the lecture or sermon, the paradox, the problem, and the character. Sometimes he enclosed some of his other prose and poetry in his correspondence, clearly setting coterie works in the context of private communication. As he maintained intellectual and emotional contact with friends like Goodyer, George Garrard, and Sir Thomas Roe, he used the epistolary medium to work out ideas, to instruct, to preach, to exercise wit as well as to affirm his (shaky) social identity.[112]

Compared to the missives exchanged by John Chamberlain and Dudley Carleton, which are full of reports, gossip, names, and dates, Donne's letters are peculiarly contentless, hardly the typical courtier's epistles. In them, as in most of his other writing, Donne emphasized the bond between writer and reader, placing a higher value on this relationship as his prime subject matter than on any specific information or news to be transmitted. He is at his most interesting in his correspondence when he conveys the least information, when he pretends to be avoiding the role of news-presenter. The letters are, in fact, the most explicitly metacommunicative of Donne's coterie works and, as such, they clarify the metacommunicative features of his other writings. He constantly comments upon the context and conditions of the communicative relationship of writer and addressee, reflecting also on the medium of letter writing itself. Composing his own personal version of the humanist epistle, Donne used letters for "meditations" (*Letters*, pp. 61, 73, 78), for instruction, for "evaporations" of his "wit" (*Letters*, p. 36), for presenting objects of intellectual "curiosity" (*Letters*, p. 118), as well as for saying "nothing" (*Letters*, p. 121)—the last being his term for the peculiarly un-newsy discourse he shared with friends.

In a piece written to Sir Henry Goodyer in 1607, Donne particularly reflects on the nature of his correspondence with his friend and the medium he was using:

In the History or style of friendship, which is best written both in deeds and words, a Letter which is of a mixed nature, and hath something of both, is a mixed Parenthesis: It may be left out, yet it contributes, though not to the being, yet to the verdure, and freshnesse thereof. Letters have truly the same office as oaths. As these amongst light and empty men, are but fillings, and pauses, and interjections; but with weightier, they are sad attestations: So are Letters to some complement, and obligation to others. For mine, as I never authorized my servant to lie in my behalfe, (for it were officious in him, it might be worse in me) so I allow my Letters much lesse that civil dishonesty, both because they go from me more considerately, and because they are permanent; for in them I may speak to you in your chamber a year hence before I know not whom, and not hear myself. They shall therefore ever keep the sincerity and intemeratenesse of the fountain, whence they are derived. And as wheresoever these leaves fall, the root is in my heart, so shall they, as that sucks good affections towards you there, have ever true impressions thereof. Thus much information is in very leaves, that they can tell what the tree is, and these can tell you I am a friend, and an honest man. Of what generall use, the fruit should speake, and I have none: and of what particular profit to you, your application and experimenting should tell you, and you can make none of such a nothing; yet ever of barren Sycamores, such as I, there were use, if either any light flashings, or scorching vehemencies, or sudden showres made you need so shadowy an example or remembrancer. But (Sir) your fortune and minde do you this happy injury, that they make all kinde of fruits uselesse unto you; Therefore I have placed my love wisely where I need communicate nothing. All this, though perchance you read it not till Michaelmas, was told you at *Micham*, 14. *August*. 1607. (*Letters*, pp. 114–16)

This style of writing assumes the context of shared attitudes and feelings much as do a number of the coterie poems.

Friendship, the context of so much of Donne's literary work, becomes in the letters a topic of explicit concern. Donne portrayed it as a refuge from social and political frustrations, as he took advantage of the goodwill of his addressee(s) to express some of his conflicted thoughts and feelings. Disappointed continually by "great persons" (*Letters*, p. 27), by "friendship" (*Letters*, p. 65) in the sense of beneficent patronage, Donne turned to affectionate communing with peers as a "second religion" (*Letters*, p. 85). The very medium of correspondence was, for Donne, that of true friendship: "I nurse . . . friendship by Letters" (*Letters*, p. 68), he wrote, elsewhere claiming such writing to be "a sacrifice, which though friends need not, friendship doth" (*Letters*, p. 116).

The letters from Donne in the years 1604–14, especially those addressed to Goodyer, are an extraordinary record of the poet's psychological vicissitudes in a very painful and difficult stage of his life. They contain many of the themes represented in the other prose and poetical writing from this period. In this correspondence, certain personally charged interests recur with great frequency, not only Donne's continued concern with matters of religion and theology, but also his intense preoccupation with worldly success and failure. Donne depended on Goodyer for both sympathetic understanding and practical assistance to help him win his way back into government service: ". . . my fortune doth bring all my debts into one hand," he wrote in

1608, "for I owe you what ever Court friends do for me, yea, whatsoever I do for my self, because you almost importune me, to awake and stare the Court in the face" (*Letters*, p. 146). Donne's friend was, no doubt, a good source of fresh information about opportunities and a means of introduction to men and women of the Court like Lady Bedford, Lord Hay, and Sir Robert Ker. But Donne also knew his friend could sympathize with the pain caused by the frustration of his ambitions and with the pain of being a sociopolitical nonentity. In writing Goodyer in 1608, Donne referred to himself several times as "nothing" (*Letters*, p. 117), elaborating upon the idea in an emotionally distraught (if not downright suicidal) letter:

... I would fain do something, but that I cannot tell what, is no wonder. For to chuse, is to do: but to be no part of any body, is to be nothing. At most, the greatest persons, are but great wens, and excrescences; men of wit and delightfull conversation, but as moales for ornament, except they be so incorporated into the body of the world, that they contribute something to the sustentation of the whole. This I made account that I begun early, when I understood the study of our laws: but was diverted by the worst voluptuousnes, which is an Hydroptique immoderate desire of humane learning and languages: beautifull ornaments to great fortunes; but mine needed an occupation, and a course which I thought I entered well into, when I submitted my self to such a service, as I thought might imployed [sic] those poor advantages, which I had. And there I stumbled too, yet I would try again: for to this hour I am nothing, or so little, that I am scarce subject and argument good enough for one of mine own letters: yet I fear, that doth not ever proceed from a good root, that I am so well content to be lesse, that is dead. (*Letters*, pp. 50–52)

Donne's history from his early Inns-of-Court period through his service to Egerton to the present time of unemployment and the depression it occasioned are all reviewed in this self-harrowing letter. It is particularly noteworthy that here Donne clearly identifies "wit" and learned sociability as useless in terms of winning a fulfilling place of active service in the public world.

THE VERSE OF POETIC EXCHANGE: DONNE AND SIR EDWARD HERBERT

On at least one occasion Donne turned to the verse letter to communicate with Goodyer, continuing a practice that he began in his early Inns-of-Court days. In "Who makes the Past"[113] Donne gave advice to his amiable friend, whose addiction to hawking and whose leisurely life at Court were symptomatic of a prodigal and self-indulgent ease from which the poet claimed it was good to take leave. He urged Goodyer to make travel the opportunity for personal growth and spiritual toughening. As in the prose correspondence, Donne thus placed the man on whom he depended for help at Court in the position of the intellectual and moral inferior in need of his counsel. Given scope to play the patronizing moralist-adviser—a function proper to the author of a humanist verse letter—Donne felt the need also to mock his serious purpose, admitting toward the end of the piece that his platitudes might not have been the valuable parting-gift he has suggested, since "Fables, or fruit-trenchers teach as much" (44). As in the prose letters, the center of the coterie communication was not the moral and religious advice, but the personal friendship that impelled the poet to write something suitable to his addressee that reflected their relationship and its context of mutual understanding.[114]

In this younger man, Donne probably found an intellectually kindred spirit. One of Donne's other close friends in this period was Sir Edward Herbert, someone especially fit to appreciate the more convoluted turns of his poetical wit.[115] After all, Herbert himself had a mind attracted to philosophical and theological speculation[116] and composed poems that, in some ways, exceed even Donne's own in intellectual abstruseness. Both men were part of the same social circles of City and Court and on terms of social intimacy because of Donne's friendship with the members of the Magdalen Herbert household.[117] Donne admitted Herbert to his select coterie readership and even engaged with him in some forms of literary competition and exchange, as he did earlier with a man like Sir Henry Wotton. He not only wrote his Prince Henry elegy, as Jonson reported, to "match Sir Ed: Herbert in obscurenesse"[118] but also he used a 1610 verse letter as an occasion to answer portions of Herbert's satire "The State Progress of Ill," and joined him in writing elegies for Cecilia Bulstrode.[119] Like such other contemporaries as Sir Benjamin Rudyerd and the Earl of Pembroke (whose poems were published by Donne's son in 1660, long after their original dates of composition),[120] Donne and Herbert seem to have exchanged lyrics as well: of the *Songs and Sonnets*, "The Extasie," "The Primrose," and such other pieces as "The Undertaking" and "Negative Love" were probably connected with this private literary relationship.[121]

The most argumentatively complex of Donne's lyrics, "The Extasie," appears to have been written in a situation of literary competition: this poem and Herbert's "Ode upon a Question Moved," a piece whose title points to the social game of composing verse on set themes, creatively rehandle the matter of the eighth song of Sidney's *Astrophil and Stella*.[122] Both works describe an experience of amorous ecstasy, but Herbert's lyric, unlike Donne's, takes its Platonism seriously, climaxing with a soulful exchange of looks in which the "ravished spirits" (140) of the lovers communicate with one another. Herbert was attracted to the kind of love in which someone could "grow a pure intelligence" ("Platonick Love," 12) and, like an angel, "on contemplation feed" (20). Ezra Pound's epithet for Donne's poem, "Platonism believed"[123] really belongs to the "Ode upon a Question Moved," for Herbert, like the authors who contributed to *Loves Martyr*, celebrated the virtues of a purely spiritual love. Donne, however, characteristically attacked such a desexualization of love, using an argument replete with logical equivocations and contradictory metaphoric suggestions to reject, in turn, not only simple sensuous eroticism but also what he called elsewhere "abstract spiritual love" ("A Valediction: of the Booke," 30). In "The Extasie," Donne wittily played with the terms and assumptions of Renaissance love philosophy and the poetry of that tradition as he undermined the Platonic foundation of the amorous ecstasy, proving that the very experience the poem dramatically presents is, by the work's own logic, impossible. Into the intellectual wreckage of its argument Donne insinuated his usual definition of love as a fused physical/spiritual reality whose pattern is best expressed in a situation of reciprocity, particularly that of conjugal relationship.

The poem's discursive reasoning wittily undoes itself as the reader is finally left in a perplexity in which he is at the mercy of a rhetorically and intellectually superior author. In its internal rhetorical situation, "The Extasie" assumes the presence of a fictive listener who must be disabused of illusions and convinced of certain truths about love. He receives the account of the (supposed) ecstatic experience and the sketchy history of the love relationship. Although the "we's" and "our's" of the first fifteen lines create the impression that a man is speaking to the woman he loves about some past experience they shared, the pronoun "her" in line 16 makes it clear that this other party is being addressed, someone whose intellectual and emotional distance on the world of the lovers mirrors the reader's aesthetic perspective. This fictive auditor stands structurally in the same position in relation to the lovers as the hypothetical witness the poem twice invokes (in stanzas 6 and 7 as well in the final four lines). Like the fictive listener and the observer-figure (a device of Mannerist self-consciousness),[124] the reader is moved back and forth between the poles of sympathy and judgment, at first drawn into a scene of amorous intimacy, then reminded of his outsider status as the poet tells him, in effect, that he is aware of his aesthetic responses.

As in the case of "The Canonization," where Donne obviously played with the connection between the *adversarius* and the coterie reader, the poet engaged in a kind of wittily dialectical relationship with his primary audience. Given the arguments presented in the lyric, the reader (like the fictive listener and the hypothetical witness of the ecstasy), is assumed to hold a Neoplatonic point of view like Sir Edward Herbert's, to regard natural sexual urges as "lustful and corrupt desires" ("Ode," 67) and a marital relationship, therefore, as a lower form of love. He must, like Ficino, make a distinction between intellectual and bestial love, the first involving spiritual propagation alone, the second springing from a desire for merely physical procreation. To such a person, marriage would have seemed the pedestrianization, if not the utter destruction, of a love that should, ideally, move contantly away from the world of the flesh until it is consumed in "heavenly fires" ("Ode," 66) and enjoys the experience of spiritual ecstasy. Whether or not the coterie reader of "The Extasie" seriously adhered to such a love philosophy, the poem assumes that he at least was attracted to it, if only as a part of a fashionable literary vocabulary. Such a reader, who, by definition, is an antagonist to the lovers of the poem, must be defeated philosophically and emotionally; and this is exactly what the poem accomplishes as it puts him on the psychological defensive, only to welcome him finally, like the *adversarius* of "The Canonization," as a convert to the speaker's point of view.

Donne located the poem's thematic material in an autobiographical context of which he expected his primary reader to be aware. He cleverly demonstrated that he still could perform the role of a love poet in his domestic state—paradoxically defending conjugality as the highest love relationship in a poem whose terminology is drawn from a tradition antipathetic to married love as well as to any other kind of fully heterosexual union.[125] As in "The Canonization," Donne used the situation of coterie communication to enact in a social framework some personal psychological conflicts, utilizing an intimate relationship with a known reader as an opportunity to engage in a form of self-persuasion, sublimating a personal conflict of love and guilt concerning his marriage into a lively author-reader dialectic. After his return to London, Donne tried to keep up an active and satisfying social life, in the face of social and political frustrations and an attendant psychological depression. In this context, "The Extasie" was possibly one of the "squibs" he "kindled in [his] melancholy" as he used poetry as one means of maintaining contact with friends and associates, or, in Walton's terms, a "paradox" in which he justified his marriage in the face of the world's "severe censures."[126] Its poetic intellectuality belongs as much to an autobiographically allusive private game of coterie communication as to the philosophical and literary traditions of which Donne expected his reader to be aware.

A similar set of circumstances surrounded the composition and transmission of a lyric like "The Primrose."[127] Helen Gardner suggests that this poem (connected in one manuscript with Montgomery Castle) was "an admirable cooling-card to such high-flown poems of Herbert's as the three called 'Platonick love'"[128]—therefore an answer poem that, like "The Extasie," was part of a literary competition between Donne and his poetic disciple. Gardner dates this lyric after 1610, agreeing with Coffin that its use of the term "Galaxie" (6) suggests it was written after the appearance of Galileo's *Siderius Nuntius*.[129] Whether or not this is so, the poem clearly belongs to the ongoing personal-literary relationship between Donne and Herbert that ran from about 1607 at least through the time of the rival elegies on Prince Henry. "The Primrose" deals with a major issue that figures in "The Extasie," similarly arguing against the Platonic view of love as exclusively spiritual. In "The Primrose," Donne portrays woman as neither angelic nor bestial, treating love as a spiritual/physical union—such as takes place in marriage, an institution symbolized by the number five on which the lyric concentrates.[130] The woman who is a "true Love" (8) is the mean between two "monsters" (18) or unnatural creatures: the first one a merely sexual being, less than woman, the second one "above/All thought of sexe" (15–16) like the angelic mistress of the kind of Platonic and encomiastic verse Herbert himself composed. The wit of this poem lies in reminding Herbert, with whose own Platonic love lyrics Donne probably argued, that sex is an integral part of love in both life and literature. To conclude in a comically pointed way, he converts arithmetic to bawdry in the last lines: since for women to "take halfe us men" (27) will not "serve their turne" (28), "women may take us all" (30) in the sense of phallic penetration rather than in the abstract meaning of the poem's numerological wittiness.

In the Group I manuscripts of Donne's verse, "The Undertaking" (in untitled form) follows "The Extasie";[131] in Group II manuscripts it is called "Platonique Love," a title that suggests some connection with Sir Edward Herbert's own similar titled lyrics. Given this evidence, and the poem's thematic content, it makes sense to examine it along with the other pieces Donne wrote in the context of his friendship with Magdalen Herbert's eldest son. Herbert's attraction to Neoplatonic amorousness apparently did not prevent him from enjoying courtly flirtations and sexual adventures on his travels—"follies which I afterward repented,"[132] as he states in his *Autobiography*. As was probably the case with "The Extasie," Donne evidently felt he could poetically tease his younger contemporary, mocking his romanticism and idealism, the quaintly chivalric stance that led Herbert to risk a duel with a French courtier over the stealing of an eleven-year-old girl's ribbon.[133]

"The Undertaking" is an exercise in sophisticated comic hyperbole. it metapoetically comments on some of the conditions for Platonic and complimentary amorousness, wittily denying its own act of utterance at the same time as it engages in the high-definition rhetoric of boasting. The supposed discovery of "loveliness within" (13), the Neoplatonic vision of "Vertue'attir'd in woman" (18), and the refined transcending of "the Hee and Shee" (20) in love are set in hypothetical circumstances that make these possibilities quite problematic, if not utterly ridiculous.[134] Doing something "braver" (1, 25) than the deeds of "all the *Worthies*" (2, 26) is, by the poem's logic, as likely an occurence as attaining the goals of Neoplatonic loving. Beyond this, keeping such (an impossible) love "hid" (4, 28) from "prophane men" (22) whose natural impulse would be to "deride" (24) it, is rendered impossible by the poem's own act of publicizing.

"Negative Love" is a witty definition poem aimed at a literarily and philosophically sophisticated reader who, like Sir Edward Herbert, was attracted to polite modes of amorousness and to such intellectual speculations as the possibility of true self-knowledge. Its speaker, like that of "The Undertaking," engages in comical boasting as he (metapoetically) analyzes love and amorous success specifically in terms of the poetical idioms that can express them. In this aggressively paradoxical lyric, which converts losing into winning by abusing language and logic, Donne argues that literary language based on the theological *via negativa* better renders the experience of loving than do the terms of Petrarchan or Neoplatonic amorousness. He facetiously asserts that "negative love" is far superior to the refined loving of those who "prey" on the elements of physical beauty ("an eye, cheeke, lip" [2]) or those who "soare no higher/Then vertue or the minde to 'admire'" (3–4). Assuming a reader habituated to these conventional vocabularies (as Herbert himself was), Donne not only portrays nescience as a finer intellectual mode for understanding love, but also uses the philosophical-theological possibilities of negativity to deal with the issue of success in a wider sense than that of private amorousness. In both the personal letters and religious lyrics from the same period, the same witty language is used to express Donne's frustrations in his pursuit of a career and his sense of social placelessness. The last line of the poem—"Though I speed not, I cannot misse" (18)—implies a context of success and failure beyond the literary one of amorous lyricism or the personal one of a love relationship. As in "The Canonization," "The Sunne Rising," and "The Extasie," the public standards of achievement and status intrude on the world of private desire. Though the rhetorical and intellectual aggressiveness of the piece signals the social vulnerability of the author, the poem is the kind of witty "nothing"[135] or trifle Donne used to maintain the social intercourse that sustained him in his desperate moments.

Donne never forgot that a friend like Herbert, an active Parliamentarian, was an ambitious young man whose public involvement represented a goal for which he himself strove. This is clear in the verse letter Donne sent his friend in 1610 which selectively responds to Herbert's "The State Progress of Ill."[136] Herbert's poem, composed while he was traveling in France in 1608, maintains a generally critical attitude toward the Jacobean political establishment, expressing sentiments that would have been read as topically relevant and not merely as abstractly moral, given the author's involvement in the House of Commons and the life of the Court.

In "The State Progress of Ill," Herbert ironically suggests that countries need hereditary monarchies much as mankind needs original sin (in order to be saved). He portrays "Nobility" (82) with the downright antiaristocratic hostility of the lower-born gentleman suffering what Sir Fulke Greville called the "oppressions of the grandees";[137] he views flattering Churchmen ("sugred Divines" [103]) who preached patient political subservience to the multitudes as supporters of a corrupt status quo; and he idealistically asserts the rights of "freeborn man . . . at first indu'd/With equal power over all" (119–21)—all sentiments not unusual in the House of Commons in which he had been serving.

When Donne came to write a verse epistle to Herbert when the latter was fighting with English forces supporting William of Orange at the siege of Juliers in 1610, he made his poem into something of an answer to his friend's satire, developing some of its conceits and ideas. At the same time he took the opportunity to communicate personally with a man whose activity contrasted painfully with his own directionless inactivity. The poem itself is an example of Donne's conceited wittiness at its most complex, its ethical, religious, and philosophical content resembling that of *The First Anniversarie* and some of the more intensely intellectual verse letters. Although Donne portrayed his fanciful meditations as virtually useless compared to Herbert's engagement in a life of (military) action he seems to have envied, he implicitly paid his friend the compliment of addressing to him some of his most intellectually sophisticated verse.[138] Herbert was one of Donne's identifiable coterie readers; his life and writings shed light on both his own and on Donne's political and intellectual interests.

DONNE, LADY BEDFORD, AND THE POETRY OF COMPLIMENT

In the eight or so years before his ordination, Donne composed a large proportion of his verse in the context of relationships with actual or sought-after patrons and patronesses. One can distinguish these readers as a type of coterie audience different from the male acquaintances for whom Donne wrote most of his earlier and much of his contemporary work. Particularly in the case of the encomiastic verse epistles, the social superiority of his addresses affected the conventions, content, and rhetorical techniques Donne employed. His ambivalent feelings about the decorum of complimentary poetry were rooted in his conflicting personal and social needs and subverted the polite ritual of such verse in both conscious and unconscious ways.

Donne wrote the largest number of his patronage poems for Lucy, Countess of Bedford.[139] About the end of 1607, he made the acquaintance of this powerful favorite of Queen Anne through the help of his friend Goodyer, who was her client. In need of social access to a courtly world in which he sought new employment, Donne looked to Lady Bedford for social and political, rather than for simply monetary, assistance, hoping to use her offices as a courtly mediator or broker to win preferment.[140] He assumed the role of a courtly literary suitor, offering her complimentary letters[141] and poems—the latter consisting of both verse epistles and lyrics. But he did not wish to be treated as her artistic client, a role professional poets like Jonson and Daniel readily accepted in order to benefit from her economic favors.[142] Donne instead enjoyed a certain measure of social familiarity with the Countess, who agreed in 1608 to serve as godmother to his daughter Lucy.[143] He told Goodyer that he wished to be regarded as a man pursuing "a graver course, than of a Poet" (*Selected Prose*, p. 148), and consequently in his encomiastic verse to Lady Bedford, he felt the need of adopting a rhetorical stance that could simultaneously signal deference and personal independence. He praised his patroness for her "eloquence of beauty," calling her "learned" (*Letters*, p. 68),[144] making her into a symbol of a transcendent Virtue he reverenced in "lownes of devotion." But he also attempted to assert, in some of his usual ways, his own poetic, intellectual, and moral authority, the result being a sometimes awkward, sometimes inventive combination of flattery and condescension. Often Donne broke away from the rehearsal of complimentary commonplaces to indulge in ingenious philosophical-satiric lucubrations that could establish his authorial authority, but the decorum of this particular socioliterary situation, for the most part, prevented him from composing the energetically and wittily intellectual verse found in the best passages of the epistles to male addressees.

In becoming a client of Lady Bedford, Donne was introduced into the courtly social circle surrounding her. This consisted not only of such women as Lady Markham, Cecilia Bulstrode, and Jane Meautis, but also of such men as his friends George Garrard and Sir Thomas Roe, in addition to Goodyer and others.[145] Donne took other steps at this time to become an active courtier once again—such as approaching Sir Robert Ker (the cousin of James's favorite of the same name), but his membership in the Bedford circle certainly put him in the midst of Jacobean high society, an environment about which, of course, Donne himself had few illusions. Despite what he said in his idealizing encomia of Lady Bedford, he knew that the social sphere in which she functioned was something less than a heaven on earth.

A woman of beauty and charm, some nine years younger than Donne himself, Lady Bedford was at the brilliant center of the social world of the Jacobean Court. She performed in a number of masques including Daniel's *Vision of the Twelve Goddesses* (1604), and Jonson's *The Masque of Blackness* (1605), *The Masque of Beauty* (1608), *The Masque of Queenes* (1609), and *Hymenaei* (1609). After the bizarre *Masque of Blackness*, in which the Queen and her ladies appeared in blackface, Lady Anne Clifford wrote: ". . . all the Ladies about the Court had gotten such ill names that it was grown a scandalous place, and the Queen herself was much fallen from her former greatness and reputation she had in the world."[146] Dudley Carleton wrote to a friend about the women's costumes in this masque: "Their Apparll was rich, but too light and Curtizan-like for such great ones."[147] Evidently Court men and women behaved barbarously after the performance, the contrast with the masque's idealization of the Court becoming all too apparent.

Lawrence Stone observes in his study of the aristocracy of the English Renaissance that "the sexual license at the Jacobean Court . . . may have rivalled or excelled the more notorious conditions at the Court of Charles II."[148] In one of his epigrams, the experienced courtier Sir John Harington (a cousin of Lady Bedford) wrote his rusticating wife comparing the moral qualities of women of the Country, City, and Court. The last group he described satirically as "statly Heroyns [of] noble mynde" (*Letters and Epigrams*, p. 291) unwilling to be confined to more limited private or civil spheres:

> These entertayne great princes; these have lerned
>   The tongues, toyes, tricks, of Room, of Spain, of Fraunce;
>   These can Currentos and Lavoltas dance,
> And though they foot yt false tis nere discerned,
> The vertues of these dames are so transcendent.
>   Themselvs ar learnd, and their Heroyk sperit
>   Can make disgrace an honor, sinn a merit.
> All penns, all praysers ar on them dependent.
>   (*Letters and Epigrams*, pp. 292–93)

The last line particularly measures the ironic distance between courtly compliment and the actual moral state of the women being praised. The Earl of Worcester in a letter to the Earl of Shrewsbury from the early Jacobean period referred to the powerful women of the Court, in whose number Lady Bedford would have been numbered, as viciously competitive: "The plotting and malice amongst them is such, that I think envy hath tied an invisible snake about most of their necks to sting one another to death."[149] As Margaret Maurer has pointed out in her fine article on the effect of the real presence of Lady Bedford on Donne's verse epistles, the Countess was a pragmatic courtly manipulator whose offices as a mediator someone like Donne would have found attractive and whose less-than-saintly character he exaggeratedly praised in order to enter and remain in her good graces. Years later, he preached a sermon in which he expounded upon the text "*Surely men of high degree are a lie*," reflecting upon his own flattery not only of powerful men of the Court but also of women like Lady Bedford: ". . . when men of high degree doe not performe the duties of their places, then they are a lie of their own making; And when I overmagnifie them in their place, flatter them, humor them, ascribe more to them, expect more from them, rely more upon them, then I should, then they are a lie of my making" (*Sermons*, 6:306–7). Revealingly, the issues of flattery and lying recur in the encomiastic verse. Donne himself made a number of critical remarks on the Court in the letters and prose contemporary with his complimentary poetry, but Ben Jonson seems to have satirized Lady Bedford's circle most strongly in two of his works, "An Epigram on the Court Pucell" and *Epicoene*.

    In the poem, which its author claimed was stolen from his pocket by some prankster and shown to the satirized Cecilia Bulstrode,[150] this friend of Lady Bedford's, who was also a lady-in-waiting to the Queen, is criticized for her loose sexual morals; she is accused, for example, of using piety to disguise amorous assignations with supposed "Sermoneeres" (39). She is characterized as a vain court lady surrounding herself with admirers: "What though her Chamber be the very pit/ Where fight the prime Cocks of the Game, for wit?" (3–4). Both conversation and literary jeux d'esprit were appropriate in such a setting, and Jonson makes it clear that Cecilia Bulstrode herself insisted on composing verse and in participating in the literary games played by the members of her social circle:

> What though with Tribade lust she force a Muse,
>   And in an Epicaene fury can write newes
> Equall with that, which for the best newes goes
>   As aerie light, and as like wit as those?
> What though she talke, and cannot once with them,
>   Make State, Religion, Bawdrie, all a theame.
>
> (7–12)

Jonson expressed social antagonism toward the gentlemen of the Bedford-Bulstrode circle who did not make their living by their pens. In claiming "I never stood for any place" (23)—he contrasted his intellectual and literary ambitions with their courtly ones. Because he was not fully accepted into their group he himself could not participate in the "news" game to which he scornfully referred.

But Donne and his friends could. As James Savage has shown, they composed pieces according to a formula that prescribed a set structure and a thematic consideration of "State, Religion, Bawdrie."[151] Donne's contribution to the game was his "Newes from the very Country." In it, he posed as someone expert in the inner workings of the Court and involved in some of its sophisticated recreations. Writing from the vantage point of his rustic setting at Mitcham, he referred to the politically symbolic hunting of James and his retainers: "Statesmen hunt their fortunes, and are often at default: Favourites course her[e] and are ever in view" (p. 68).[152] "Court motions are up and downe," he quipped, conscious of the hierarchy of power and favor. Referring generally to courtly society, he asserted "every great vice is a Pike in a pond that deuoures vertues and lesse vices" (p. 67). He joked about the "pox" in terms of courtly licentiousness as well as about political and personal "secrets" and "trechery" (p. 68). In his epigram Jonson not only satirized Cecilia Bulstrode for indulging in the language of "bawdry" (26) that was part of the "news" game but also for taking part in what he conceived of as an essentially male sport (an act that supposedly compromised her femininity). In his portrayal of the "collegiate ladies" in his comedy *Epicoene*, it appears that Jonson extended such criticism to all courtly women. Truewit's description of the group makes it look suspiciously like the Bedford-Bulstrode circle: "A new foundation . . . here i' the towne, of ladies, that call themselves the Collegiates, an order betweene courtiers, and country madames, that liue from their husbands; and giue entertainement to all the *Wits* and *Braueries* o' the time, as they call 'hem, crie downe or vp what they like, or dislike in a braine, or a fashion, with most masculine, or rather *hermaphroditicall* authoritie and euery day, gaine to their colledge some new probationer" (I.i.73–81). When asked who is the "President" (I.i.82) of this group, Truewit replies "The graue, and youthfull matron, the lady Havghty" (I.i.83–84). This may be a specific reference to Lady Bedford, who did live apart from her estate-bound spouse, who had been exiled to the country after being freed from imprisonment for his involvement in the Essex conspiracy. But this satire does not depend on a particular identification. Jonson satirized a way of life followed by women who, as either patronesses or as influential courtiers, exercised the literary and social authority to which he objected—even as he, like Donne, submitted himself to it.[153]

As his epigram accompanying their transmission indicates, Jonson was the one who obtained for Lady Bedford, at her request, copies of Donne's *Satires*. Herbert Grierson (2:cxxvii) postulates that the Countess kept a commonplace book in which she transcribed poems that interested her and, if this were so, as is likely, she followed the usual practice of those involved in the system of manuscript circulation of verse. In addition to the poems and letters Donne wrote especially for her, she was probably meant to have read some of the letters to Goodyer in which she is mentioned favorably,[154] and she might have seen other compositions of Donne's, such as some of the religious verse. Conversely, some of the work written for her probably was shown to other coterie readers, especially to Goodyer, who served as an intermediary who passed particular pieces to her. In such a situation, Donne would have been aware of other possible responses to his verse epistles and lyrics to Lady Bedford than those of the Countess herself. With or without this larger audience, the poems have interesting complexities and tensions built into them whose nuances can be highlighted by attending to the social context of the verse and not simply to the private relationship of poet and patroness.

So long as their meanings have been taken as straightforward, if politely exaggerated, the encomiastic poetical epistles Donne wrote to

Lady Bedford and others have interested very few critics. Placed in the tradition of verse letters and read in terms of the conventions of compliment, these pieces have either been overvalued on shaky aesthetic grounds or set aside, for the most part, as Donne's markedly lesser achievements, tainted in some way by flattery and the crass motive of seeking patronage. It appears that Donne's adoption of the traditional vocabulary of praise in his complimentary poetry and letters proclaims his respect for his patroness(es) and his acceptance of the hierarchical status quo. Accordingly, he used a language that was part of a ritual transaction whose formality the participants maintained and whose stylized hyperboles, euphemisms, and abstractions they understood in relation to an immediate social context. But Donne used several means to subvert the mode in which he was writing and to render the very act of poetic praise deeply problematic. First, he drove the polite hyperboles of encomiastic verse to outrageous extremes, calling attention to the social and moral bases of the currency he was inflating. Second, he allowed hard-edged detail, critical commentary, and strained intellectual complexities to intrude into this verse—often as the means of assaulting the corrupt world with which an idealized individual was contrasted—thus destabilizing the context within which the encomiastic act was set. Third, as David Aers and Gunther Kress have demonstrated in their groundbreaking article, Donne built into his complimentary epistles creatively conflicting attitudes toward the self and the social establishment that made the poems, in the biographical and social contexts in which they were composed and read, more lively and subversive texts than modern readers have been willing to acknowledge: Donne contradictorily defined the self as both autonomous and socially dependent as he depicted the object of praise contradictorily as inherently good and as valuable only because of contingent social circumstances.[155] Fourth, and finally, in these works Donne characteristically called such attention to himself as a thinking subject and laid out arguments of such metaphoric and intellectual complexity that he seems to have been competing with, rather than self-effacingly paying tribute to, his addressee, forcing his primary audience to submit to his intellectual and literary authority. He might have partly been complimenting his patroness-reader's intelligence in assuming that she could follow ingenious poetical arguments with an appreciation of his creative use of the encomiastic mode, but, in effect, he was also undermining the very medium in which he was working. The playfully adversarial relationship he liked to establish with his readers resurfaces in the complimentary poems as an expression, I believe, of the strong resentment he harbored about the role as a deferential suitor he assumed in such verse. His motives were mixed and so were his poetic strategies.

Donne began writing complimentary poetry to Lady Bedford before he was formally introduced to her and ended the practice with a curiously incomplete verse letter reflecting the strains in their relationship. Although he approached her hoping for political not artistic patronage, when he wrote his last poem for her, the "Obsequies to the Lord Harrington, brother to the Countesse of Bedford," he made a rather bald appeal for money to help him settle his debts before ordination. Donne's social, political, and economic needs were at the heart of his relationship with the Countess; and so too were the ambivalent feelings generated by his uncomfortably subservient position.

Donne's first verse letter to the Countess probably had the purpose of introducing himself to her and requesting her patronage. "Reason is our Soules left hand" is a witty complimentary act of a man aware of Lady Bedford's power to assist him socially, politically, and economically. When Donne states in this epistle that her "election glorifies" (10) those "friends" (10) she has chosen, what is said is not confined to the abstract terms of the theological metaphor the poem unfolds, but is significant also in the courtly social context in which she and the ambitious courtiers who were her suitors functioned. Donne praised the Countess for her "birth and beauty" (24) as well as for her "learning and religion,/And vertue" (25-26). He identified her, in her socially preeminent position, with a "divinity" (2) he approached through "far faith" (4) rather than through "Reason" (1)— that is, from a social distance. In the last part of the poem, however, Donne changed the terms of his governing metaphor to redefine Lady Bedford as "Gods masterpeece" (33) and "His Factor for our loves" (34). The choice of the term "Factor" is an interesting one, given Lady Bedford's actions as a courtly manipulator.[156] In this case, and throughout the poem, Donne's religious language has social and political significance. After all, the political and the theological were mixed in the Jacobean ideology (as James's speeches testify) so that, in Maurer's words, "Donne's style mirrors a political-religious order"[157] in which he hoped to win preferment through the help of prominent courtly figures like the Countess.

There are some elements in the poem, however, that wrinkle its polite surface, features that proclaim their author as a strong-minded and critically independent man unwilling simply to efface himself in the act of flattery. Having said that "Reason is our Soules left hand" (1), inferior as a means of approaching the divinized patroness, he argues its usefulness as a way to "understand" (8) their relationship. Although he suggests his own critical awareness in admitting that "a squint lefthandednesse" (5) could be "ungracious" (6)—that is, that a rational, analytic approach to a patronage relationship might produce insights of a less-than-complimentary kind—he employs his rational faculties in the rest of the poem, exercising the intellectual authority on which his encomiastic definitions and his poetical argument are based. He was not content simply to rehearse graciously the topoi of praise; he insisted on putting the personal stamp of his wit on them. For example, in reformulating the commonplace notion of the *donna angelicata*, he calls the Countess "The first good Angell, since the worlds frame stood,/That ever did in womans shape appeare" (31–32), simultaneously elevating in esteem the woman he praised and teasingly suggesting an underlying set of antifeminist assumptions on his part—a combination that appears as well in other complimentary verse.[158] In the light of the militant Protestantism of the Bedfords, Donne's mischievous use of a "Catholique" (16) / "Heretique" (17) contrast was wittily inappropriate. Finally, in stating that the Countess's "learning and religion,/And vertue" (25–26) were the "ingredients" (26) of "A methridate" (27) needed to protect her against "what can be done or said" (28), that is, the evil practices and malicious gossip of the Court, he raised the uncomfortable question (that reappears throughout the complimentary epistles) of how Lady Bedford, so much at the center of the serious and frivolous courtly dealings, could be regarded as morally untainted. Donne had to resort to intellectual and metaphoric ingenuity to avoid expressing his belief in the intrinsic moral corruption of the Court and of all its inhabitants—an attitude expressed earlier in his *Satires* as well as in his verse and prose epistles to male friends. His moral awareness, like his emotional ambivalence about adopting the role of the deferential suitor, unsettles the polite ritual of his complimentary verse, creating in it interesting tensions. Donne's problem was to maintain a decorous client-patroness relationship in the midst of such disturbances.

Once Donne achieved a degree of social familiarity with Lady Bedford, he operated poetically on the assumption that she was able to appreciate his mischievously witty playing with the conventions of praise: what was, for him, partly a manifestation of his discomfort with suitorship, was probably meant to be enjoyed by her as a compliment to her intelligence and sophistication. In "You have refin'd me," for example, a poem that indicates Donne enjoyed the Countess's hospitality at Twickenham,[159] Donne metapoetically comments, in a stanza following two others of pronouncedly hyperbolic praise, that "these [exaggerations] . . . Tast of Poëtique rage, or flattery" (61, 63). The last stanza of the epistle refers to what has taken place in the first ten as "busie praise" (67) as it compliments the patroness for her own beauty and for that of her (leased) estate. Since these qualities are appreciated better by the senses than by the intellect, Donne comically inverts the usual hierarchy of the faculties found in Neoplatonic complimentary poetry, as he completes what looks like a poetic thank-you note of appreciation for a visit to his patroness's home:

> The story'of beauty,'in Twicknam is, and you.
> Who hath seen one, would both; As, who had bin
> In Paradise, would seeke the Cherubin.
>
> (70-72)

In dealing somewhat with a Country-Court contrast in this verse letter, Donne once again pointedly separated Lady Bedford from the moral corruption of the Court, "which is not vertues clime" (7), depicting himself, in relation to her, as one who could "usher [her] vertue" (12): as a client he offered his poetical services to call attention to her worth. In the metaphor that explains their relationship in different terms, he is like the scholarly annotator of "darke texts" (11), one skilled at interpreting the rare character of her virtue.[160] Either way, he facetiously argued that *she needed him*. He, on the other hand, professed that he accepted his role as one of her "new creatures" (22) or (client) "sacrificers" (28). In identifying his stanzas as "*Petitions*, and not *Hymns*" (33) he alluded to the quid pro quo of the patronage transaction in which compliments were exchanged for benefits—though, of course, he pretended only to be asking for permission to praise the Countess's beauty in the last part of the epistle.

After the first two stanzas of the poem, Donne moves away from a poetic discourse on Lady Bedford's virtue to a praise of her physical beauty. Although Donne treats her physical features nonsensuously in the calculatedly hyperbolic metaphors of the verse, he refers to the "eyes, hands, bosome" (46) she enjoyed displaying in those masques in which she, Queen Anne, and other ladies of the Court (sometimes scandalously) engaged. Donne, I think, knew that, depending on one's purposes, one could regard Lady Bedford's beauty satirically as a sign of personal vanity and self-indulgence or complimentarily as the symbol of inner worth. In elevating sense over intellect as a means of appreciating the Countess as an object of praise, Donne concludes "You have refin'd me" with an inverted Platonism. Instead of ascending the ladder of being from a perception of particular beauty to a vision of the transcendent forms of the beautiful and good, Donne descends from the ideal to the actual: the beautiful Countess in the pleasant setting of her Twickenham estate provides the "senses" (68) with all the material needed for true praise. Petrarchan amatory conventions (in addition to Platonic topoi of praise) underlie this poem's encomiastic techniques.

An epistle coauthored with his friend Goodyer points to the place of polite Petrarchanism in the social transactions of the Bedford circle. "A Letter written by Sir. H. G. and J. D. *alternis vicibus,*" is an "interlinearie poeme"[161] in which Donne and Goodyer, in alternate stanzas, professed their decorous love for two women of station, one of whom was probably Lady Bedford, and the other, no doubt, a member of her social circle such as Lady Markham or Cecilia Bulstrode. Composed during Donne's visit to Goodyer's Polesworth estate, the poem presents greetings to two women who are portrayed as Petrarchan mistresses whose bright radiance awakened in the poets "buds of love" (9). Part of an ongoing social relationship, the poem was one of those "devotions" (10) in which, Donne and Goodyer professed, "Wee . . . seale the bands/By which w'enthrall our selves to your Commaunds" (11–12). Treating the women as morally pure recipients of praise, the poet-friends depicted their own love as "free from impure thoughts" (15). Sexuality was not allowed to intrude on the decorous Petrarchanism proper to the patronage relationship.

When Donne composed lyrics, rather than epistles, of compliment, however, he used sexuality to disturb the ritual of Petrarchan and Platonic politeness, moving daringly to the brink of an explicit offensiveness that would have violated the social contract of patronage.

Donne, I believe, composed for Lady Bedford lyrics like "Twicknam Garden," "Aire and Angels," "The Funerall," and "The Feaver," demonstrating, by his very choice of genre, that he enjoyed a social familiarity with her that was denied to such artistic clients of hers as Michael Drayton, Samuel Daniel, and Ben Jonson. He was privileged to participate with her in the socially prestigious activity of exchanging verse—not only on the occasion of writing poems about the death of Cecilia Bulstrode,[162] but also in more playful circumstances. One of the letters Donne wrote to the Countess mentions that she not only accepted the tribute offering of Donne's own compositions, but also allowed him to see some of hers:

Happiest and worthiest Lady,
I do not remember that ever I have seen a petition in verse, I would not therefore be singular, nor adde these to your other papers. I have yet adventured so near as to make a petition for verse, it is for those your Ladiship did me the honour to see in *Twicknam* garden, except you repent your making; and having mended your judgement by thinking worse, that is, better, be-

cause juster, of their subject. They must needs be an excellent exercise of your wit, which speake so well of so ill: I humbly beg them of your Ladiship, with two such promises, as to any other of your compositions were threatenings: that I will not shew them, and that I will not beleeve them; and nothing should be so used that comes from your brain and breast. If I should confesse a fault in boldnesse of asking them, or make a fault by doing it in a longer Letter, your Ladiship might use your style and old fashion of the Court towards me, and pay me with a Pardon. Here therefore I humbly kisse your Ladiships fair learned hands, and wish you good wishes and speedy grants.

Your Ladiships servant
J. DONNE (*Selected Prose*, p. 135)

In the framework of the hierarchical poet-patroness relationship, Donne and Lady Bedford were engaged in the courtly private circulation of verse, much as the Earl of Oxford and Ann Vavasour or Queen Elizabeth and Sir Walter Ralegh were.[163] What they wrote probably included love lyrics in the mode of a socially decorous Petrarchanism. The reference to the Countess's poems as products of her "breast" as well as of her "brain" and Donne's promise that he "will not beleeve them" strongly suggest this. Part of Lady Bedford's practice of using the "style and old fashion of the Court" probably took the form of her joining the poet in penning works in the language of courtly amorousness. Since such private work was shown perhaps only to an audience of patroness and close friends, it is essential to read it in the proper context. This involves understanding the ways the separate genres of verse epistle and courtly lyric assume different kinds of social transactions.

Donne's courtly lyrics of compliment display the same resistance to dependency he expressed in the verse letters as well as a characteristic approach to the subject of love, even in such a fictionalized and conventionalized form as this kind of poetry represents. Donne's first verse epistle to the Countess of Huntington ("That unripe side of earth") offers some useful points of reference. With its strange combination of intellectual speculation and poetic double-talk, conventional compliment and comic impropriety, disarming directness and confessional arrogance, this epistle highlights some of the conflicts and characteristics that appear in the lyrical poetry of compliment. It is apparent from the epistle that Donne had trouble defining the kind of love proper to complimentary poetry. Aware of the conventional vocabularies of adoration and idealization, he rejected both Petrarchan and Neoplatonic stances. He told the addressee, an old friend from York House:

> Yet neither will I vexe your eyes to see
> A sighing Ode, nor cross-arm'd Elegie.
> I come not to call pitty from your heart,
> Like some white-liver'd dotard that would part
> Else from his slipperie soule with a faint groane,
> And faithfully, (without you smil'd) were gone.
> I cannot feele the tempest of a frowne,
> I may be rais'd by love, but not throwne down.
> Though I can pittie those sigh twice a day,
> I hate that thing whispers it selfe away.
> (21–30)

Teasing a seventeen-year-old Countess with whom he had been on socially familiar terms,[164] Donne explicitly resisted the expected languages of amorous compliment that he had himself utilized in an earlier poem like "O let me not serve so." Conscious of the high absurdity of the abject lover who addressed a remote, scornful mistress, he asserted his rationality and autonomy, aphoristically satirizing conventional love behavior as he assumed love to be an appetitive, emotional, and spiritual experience of mutuality:

> It is not love that sueth, or doth contend;
> Love either conquers, or but meets a friend.
> . . . .
> A weather-beaten Lover but once knowne,
> Is sport for every girle to practise on.
> Who strives, through womans scornes, women to know,
> Is lost, and seekes his shadow to outgoe. . . .
> (57–58, 63–66)

He demanded reciprocity in love, impatient with any other kind of relationship:

> Let others sigh, and grieve; one cunning sleight
> Shall freeze my love to Christall in a night.
> . . . .
> The honesties of love with ease I doe,
> But am no porter for a tedious woo.
> (69–70, 75–76)

The final suggestion of a sexual teleology for love concludes a witty, rhetorically familiar introduction to the part of the epistle that recites some of the conventional topoi of praise for the young noblewoman, in effect subverting the gesture before it is performed. Donne expressed a conflict he felt between his working definition of human love and its portrayal in encomiastic verse. He refused to disengage spirit from flesh even in complimentary poetry, unable to accept the Neoplatonic or Petrarchan underpinning of such verse. He could here (as elsewhere) denigrate a love that "onely tempts mans appetite" (128), but, since he believed physicality to be essential to human love, he could not be comfortable with a more sublimated form of affection.[165]

This is an important issue in the complimentary love lyrics. Since appetite figures, to some degree, in these poems, we find a lively tension between natural urges and the proper social decorum of the situation, which demanded a desexing of the man-woman relationship. Thematically this conflict enabled Donne to express in the lyric form his resistance to dependency. His aesthetic iconoclasm, as usual, signals his response to a social reality.

In "That unripe side of earth" Donne mocked the situation of a refined Petrarchan lover who "to trees/Doth talke" (31–32) to express a flattering affection for a scornful (i.e., socially superior) woman. But this is the Petrarchan situation used in the complimentary lyric to Lady Bedford, "Twicknam Garden," a poem that speaks a recognizably Petrarchan literary language as it comically imitates Petrarch's "Zefiro torna," a sonnet about an unrequited lover in a Springtime garden.[166] It is probably an overstatement to call "Twicknam Garden," as Andreasen does, a "terrifyingly bitter poem,"[167] but it is important to acknowledge the friction between its conventions and its emotional content. Although one critic calls it fruitless, if not foolish, to speculate about the connections between this lyric and the Donne–Lady Bedford relationship,[168] it is crucial, I believe, to read it historically as a private poem addressed specifically to the Countess as its primary audience and expressing Donne's response to the very context of its composition.[169]

As is the case with most of Donne's lyric poetry, "Twicknam Garden" depends for its success on its clever manipulation of only partly defined terms and a half-disguised pattern of argument. Donne's speaker assumes a conventional stance and the poem, at least initially, contains enough familiar signals so that the reader would have recognized only gradually the degree to which the work is innovatively iconoclastic. But there is, nonetheless, a noticeable clash in the very first stanza between the blurred generality of the Petrarchan setting and the sharp specificity of the supportive metaphors:

> Blasted with sighs, and surrounded with teares,
> Hither I come to seeke the spring,
> And at mine eyes, and at mine eares,

> Receive such balmes, as else cure every thing;
>   But O, selfe traytor, I do bring
> The spider love, which transubstantiates all,
>   And can convert Manna to gall,
>   And that this place may thoroughly be thought
> True Paradise, I have the serpent brought.
>
> (1–9)

The first four lines, with their image of the sighing, crying lover are relatively untroubled, but the rest of the stanza presents, with imaginative vigor, particular conceits that seem as much to call attention to themselves as to describe the conventionalized setting. These metaphors break the Petrarchan mood of reverent devotion and place the speaker's poetically expository powers (and Donne's artistic self-consciousness) at the center of attention.

Although the "spider love" and "serpent" seem to refer to the Petrarchan lover's typical conflict of conscience and desire, the force of the figures seems greater than their application requires. There is a tone of urgency implicit here, an insistence on self-examination that disturbs the usual placid fictionality of this kind of lyric. Donne creates the sense that he is seriously exploring personal emotions, despite the conventionality of their expression. The exclamation "O, selfe traytor" in the middle of the stanza, like similar rhetorical gestures in the rest of Donne's poetry, raises the emotional level beyond that required by the poem's basic situation. But, at this point, there is no sure referent for the unspecified feelings, only the general Petrarchan conflict between love and rejection, desire and moral restriction.

The second stanza more deliberately highlights the clash between the poem's Petrarchan situation and the speaker's subversive feelings:

> 'Twere wholsomer for mee, that winter did
>   Benight the glory of this place,
>   And that a grave frost did forbid
> These trees to laugh, and mocke mee to my face;
>   But that I may not this disgrace
> Indure, nor leave this garden, Love let mee
>   Some senslesse peece of this place bee;
> Make me a mandrake, so I may groane[170] here,
> Or a stone fountain weeping out my yeare.
>
> (10–18)

In order to be in Twickenam Garden and not experience emotional conflict, these lines state, the lover would have to become "senslesse," an interesting word in these circumstances. It means, first, that he would have to be without his sense faculties, for with them he is a man whose love involves physical desire, not simply spiritual longing. Second, the word means "unconscious," for only in such a state would he be freed from the conflict within. Both these meanings assume that a human being is a creature of flesh and bone whose body is essential to the experience of loving. And only unconsciousness—not Petrarchan or Neoplatonic good behavior—can free the lover from the demands of the physical. Third, the word can mean "stupid" or "foolish." Donne implies not only that man's sensitive soul demands from love some kind of physical satisfaction but also that one would have to be subhuman—a mandrake or a fountain, plant or animal—not to experience this as a source of conflict. This poet's usual assumption that love without sense is impossible resurfaces here to call into question the complimentary lover's refined feelings. This Donald Guss seems to notice when he remarks that the images of this lyric offer simultaneously "polite compliment and common-sense critique of Neoplatonic love."[171]

Donne undoubtedly knew quite well, both in this poem and in his social behavior when he was a guest at Lady Bedford's estate, that he was supposed to be properly senseless in his affection for the Countess. Whereas, in "Zefiro torna," Petrarch does not question the demand for spiritualized, virtuous love, protesting only against the pain it causes him, in "Twicknam Garden" Donne seems uncomfortable with the code that demands only sublimated affection. The image of the groaning mandrake, given the traditional associations of this plant,[172] suggests the presence of strong sexual feeling that might disrupt the artfully mannered mode of this kind of poetry, if not the polite relationship to which the lyric refers, for the sexual disruption is a metaphor for a social critique. Thus the love lyric in its way reasserts the criticism implicit in the verse letters.

> Hither with christall vyals, lovers come,
>   And take my teares, which are loves wine,
> And try your mistresse Teares as home,
> For all are false, that tast not just like mine. . . .
>   (19–22)

But, instead of following the figure through to the kind of poetically hyperbolic conclusion found in "The Canonization," Donne breaks the structuring artifice of his conceit to finish the lyric with lines containing both criticism and oblique compliment:

> Alas, hearts do not in eyes shine,
> Nor can you more judge womans thoughts by teares,
>   Then by her shadow, what she weares.

> O perverse sexe, where none is true but shee,
> Who's therefore true, because her truth kills mee.
>
> (23–27)

The antifeminism of the early libertine lyrics seems, for a moment, to reappear incongrously in a complimentary setting: even if they are virtuous at heart, the lines suggest, women are deceivers.

The end of the lyric, which seems to have left a number of critics dissatisfied, defines the Petrarchan mistress's scorn as an adherence to virtue. In the social setting of Donne's relationship to Lady Bedford, it praises a noblewoman for her marital fidelity. As in the poem addressed to Magdalen Herbert, "Mad paper stay," Donne uses the vocabulary of courtly Petrarchanism to celebrate a woman above his station for her virtue, specifically for her constancy in love. In its private context, the compliment would have been understood by the primary audience through the polite fiction of courtly love. But, despite what the words of the poem say, it is possible to detect in the last two lines a reassertion of the same tension that runs throughout the lyric between the poet's subversive feelings and the socially sanctioned role he is performing. The rejected Petrarchan lover Donne uses as a persona in this poem has a comically appropriate reason for calling a virtuous woman "perverse" and claiming that her "truth" has a sadistic purpose, but the jarring note of conflict between the tone and meaning of the lines signals Donne's discomfort with the basic socioliterary circumstances of the work.

Temperamentally aggressive, Donne found it difficult to accept the necessary self-effacement required by the patronage relationship with the Countess and by the conventions of complimentary verse that expressed it ritually. He found himself in a social and literary transaction with a woman who could treat poets as pets and the whole code of courtly behavior as a way of indulging her vanity, if not actually as a method for engaging in amorous adventure.[173] In a less direct way than in the epistle to the Countess of Huntington, Donne rebelled against the situation in which he found himself at the same time as he followed its rules closely enough to be an active participant. In "Twicknam Garden," he destabilized the decorum of the poet-patroness relationship through his use of a sexuality that is more disturbingly specific than Petrarch's generalized desire. It is a comically disruptive element, like the groaning mandrake, but one that expresses the poet's characteristic social iconoclasm. Donne was not so foolish as to spoil a sustaining patronage relationship, like a spider turning food to poison; he might have felt and expressed the kind of envy for which the serpent in the poem was a conventional symbol, but he settled instead for writing a self-consciously innovative lyric—which is, in a sense, a poem about writing complimentary verse—embedding his criticism in an imaginatively charged display of wit. J. B. Leishman was right about the tone and intent of "Twicknam Garden" when he perceptively remarked: ". . . one cannot but feel that its real subject is that mood of dejection and emptiness and unrelatedness which we find expressed in some of Donne's letters to his friend Sir Henry Goodyer."[174] At the time he wrote the piece Donne was impatiently ambitious, depressed about his immediate situation in life, and only halfheartedly committed to the kind of polite social rituals in which he was engaged with Lady Bedford. These truths of experience were bound to make themselves felt in his verse.

The evidence for the connection of other lyrics with the Donne–Lady Bedford relationship may be more tenuous, but it makes sense to interpret "The Funerall," "Aire and Angels," and "The Feaver" in the same social context as that of "Twicknam Garden." "The Funerall" is a polite gesture in the tradition of witty Petrarchanism[175] embodying a complex set of conflicting attitudes related to its coterie circumstances and to Donne's resistance to the codes and rules of complimentary poetry. The wit of the poem rests in the successive redefinitions of its central figure, the hair-bracelet that the mistress gave as a gift to her devoted lover. "What ere shee meant by'it" (17), it is regarded first as being able, when the martyred lover is dead, to serve as his "outward Soule" (5), holding his body together and preserving it from dissolution. It cannot be his own soul, "which then to heaven being gone" (6) cannot serve this function, so the bracelet will be its "Viceroy" (6). Since, as the second stanza states, the soul which is implicit in the hair-bracelet is the mistress's, she, in a variation of the exchange-of-hearts conceit, can be said to control the lover. Through lines 1 to 13 and half of line 14, the attitude toward the mistress is complex, but assuredly complimentary: she is the Petrarchan lady from whom a symbolic gift is precious and who can be praised for her intelligence ("better braine" [13]).

What follows is a reformulation of the situation, however, as the subservience of the lover is portrayed negatively:

> . . . Except she meant that I
>   By this should know my pain,
> As prisoners then are manacled, when they'are condemn'd to die.
> (14–16)

The gift-giving is thus reinterpreted as an act of aggression rather than as a favor on the mistress's part. In the last stanza the hair-bracelet is regarded as a "relique" by virtue of its association with the martyrdom of the lover. But Donne does not leave the conceit in this form. Instead, he finally has the suffering lover define it in terms of his wish to retaliate:

> As 'twas humility
> To'afford to it all that a Soule can doe,
>   So, 'tis some bravery,
> That since you would have[176] none of mee, I bury some of you.
> (21–24)

The complimentary context of most of the poem assumes a humble stance on the part of a lover willing to accept a position of subservience to his elevated mistress, but these final lines reverse the situation. In doing so they define the hair-bracelet yet another way. Synecdochically, it is a symbol of the woman herself, a magical object by which she can be attacked. One of the most important features in the poem is the rhetorical shift in the final line. The poem reads like a lover's address to a general audience of (male) peers, hypothetically to a someone who can find his love-slain body to prepare for burial. From this vantage point the mistress is referred to in the third person (see 14, 17). The last line, however, reveals that the speaker has been addressing his mistress all through the poem and that his language and conceits have been for her benefit. With a witty comic hostility, the rejection that made the speaker into love's martyr is identified here as a *sexual* refusal. In the light of this, the hair-bracelet becomes a symbol of the woman's sexuality. Without being bawdily explicit, Donne thus breaks the decorum sustained by the lyric's Petrarchan language and conventions. The change from "humility" (21) to "bravery" (23) in the conclusion constitutes Donne's critique of the very conditions of the poem's composition.

It is useful to read a lyric like "Aire and Angels" against the background of the encomiastic topoi of the verse epistles.[177] Like "Reason is our Soules left hand," this poem uses, as a complimentary hyperbole, the idea of loving a woman one has not met. It employs the formulae of praise with comic self-consciousness—simultaneously validating and mocking the terms of complimentary amorousness. For instance, in his own conceitful version of the notions of Platonic transcendence and of the *donna angelicata*, Donne calls the spiritually exalted mistress "some lovely glorious nothing" (6), a phrase whose last word wittily deflates the polite language of praise. Donne uses the term "love" in this poem in two contradictory ways: he treats it as the "child" of the "soule" (7), the product of the intellect and will, and as a supernatural entity that can be incarnated mysteriously in matter. This set of alternatives bears directly on the dynamics of the encomiastic relationship: regarded as a personal act, love of an idealized lady is a matter of subjective perception and deliberate choice; seen as a transcendent reality embodied in the love object, it is something that demands the lover's proper (and deferential) acknowledgment. The complimentary fiction typically rests on the latter formulation, since that makes the subject inherently worthy of praise. But Donne's somewhat distorted syntax cannot disguise the fact that he really preferred the former alternative. He undermines the Neoplatonic convention of the beloved's beauty as the manifestation of the ideal:

> . . . what thou wert, and who,
> I bid Love aske, and now
> That it assume thy body, I allow,
> And fixe it selfe in thy lip, eye, and brow.
> (10–14)

The displaced governing subject and verb in the second part of this compound sentence ("I allow") indicates not that the incarnation of love in the mistress's beauty is something that has taken place by some mysterious process, but rather that it was the lover's decision to view things this way. By making conventional metaphors into hypotheses, Donne asserted a personal poetic control that could somewhat compensate for his inferior position as a client complimenting a patroness.

The start of the second stanza emphasizes this active stance of the poet-lover's:

> Whilst thus to ballast love, I thought,
> And so more steddily to have gone,
> With wares which would sinke admiration,
> I saw, I had loves pinnace overfraught. . . .
> (15–18)

As the lover exercises considerable freedom in praising his beloved, the encomiastic poet assumed a confident assertiveness in relation to the woman he complimented. Although the maritime commercial metaphor certainly does not strike a politely reverential note, the speaker reasserts his encomiastic purpose by explaining why the beauty of the mistress is too much for his "admiration" (17): "Ev'ry thy haire for love to worke upon/Is much too much" (19–20).

Like so many other Donne lyrics, this poem moves dialectically through two possibilities toward a synthesizing solution to a problem—here that of finding the right focus for praise. If love can "inhere" (22) "nor in nothing, nor in things/Extreme, and scatt'ring bright" (21–22)—that is, if the lover finds it impossible to praise either the invisible spirit or the all-too-beautiful body of the mistress—then the only imagined compromise is to concentrate on the manifestation of love in a rarefied substance midway between spirit and matter such as "aire" (24). But, in ringing new variations on the relationship of the soul and body in love, Donne changed the context of his argument at the end of the poem from that of the search for the right means to compliment to beloved to that of a comparison of the relative purity (and value) of men's and women's love:

> Then, as an Angell, face, and wings
> Of aire, not pure as it, yet pure doth weare,
> So, thy love may be my loves spheare;
> Just such disparitie
> As is twixt Aire and Angells puritie,
> 'Twixt womens love, and men will ever bee.
> (23–28)

Donne structurally repeats the same point in these lines: as a purer angel puts on a less-pure apparel to manifest itself, so too the speaker's love finds a less pure medium in which to move. Or, more directly, there is the same difference in spiritual purity between women's and men's love as there is between air and angels. As the lines return to the Platonic valuation of male love as superior to female love (and homosexual affection to heterosexual intercourse), they engage in some witty antifeminist teasing, demand the reciprocity that enables love to exist, and daringly, but entertainingly, threaten the decorum of the complimentary situation. In the final formulation, Donne portrays men as active and women as passive in love.[178] Together with the assertions of choice and control earlier in the lyric, this conclusion reveals Donne's resistance to the kind of humble passivity implicit in the Neoplatonic and Petrarchan stances of complimentary devotion that express the client's acceptance of his dependency in the patronage relationship.

Like so many of Donne's other lyrics, "Aire and Angels" plays a metapoetic game with its reader. It assumes and makes use of the expectation of encomiastic conventions, the reader's recognition of the complimentary purpose of Neoplatonic and Petrarchan formulations. But it first questions the appropriateness of these terms, rejecting, in turn, the praise of spiritual loveliness and the praise of physical beauty. The speaker says, in effect, that he cannot express his love either way as Donne indicates that he cannot (will not) travel either poetic route.

Like Ben Jonson in the epigram to Lady Bedford beginning "This morning, timely rapt with holy fire," Donne wrote a poem that self-consciously considers the terms of praise available to an encomiastic poet; but unlike Jonson, who politely suggested that complimentary topoi fell short of the inexpressible reality of the Countess, Donne abruptly changed the whole direction of his lyric at the end, leaving behind the search for the right means of compliment and, like the Duke in Shakespeare's *Twelfth Night*,[179] producing an unflattering comparison of male and female love. The teasing antifeminism of the conclusion of this lyric—one more example of Donne's strategy of literary surprise—would have to have been communicable to a sophisticated reader like Lady Bedford, but the underlying resentment it implied would have remained hidden, perhaps perceivable only by the poet and by his friends, some of whom were members of the Lady Bedford circle.

Composed possibly on the occasion of Cecilia Bulstrode's 1609 illness or that of Lady Bedford in 1612, "A Feaver" seems to have been written as a complimentary lyric. It portrays the addressee as one whom the poet can "celebrate" (3) and ultilizes for this purpose some encomiastic conceits found also in the *Anniversaries*, "A Nocturnall upon S. Lucies Day," and the prose letters to women of station[180]—for example, the metaphor that "The whole world vapors with [the] breath" (8) of the dying beloved, becoming a "carkasse" (10) when she, its "soule" (9), is gone. But the poem, characteristically, also subverts its ostensible purpose. It is a tonally flat, passionlessly logical performance that reveals that Donne was more interested in asserting his poetic and personal authority than in graciously abasing himself for the sake of polite compliment.

The most appropriate socioliterary context for a work such as this was that of a double audience of (socially superior) mistress and (socially equal) friends, a situation that may account for the lyric's rhetorical shifts from second-person address to the woman being complimented (stanzas 1 to 3) to third-person reference to her (stanzas 4 and 5) back again to direct address to her (stanzas 6 and 7). The intellectual allusiveness of the fourth and fifth stanzas, like other such manifestations in Donne's lyrics, implies an audience of male peers—one presumably capable of reading the poem metapoetically as well as poetically as an innovative adaptation of conventional Petrarchan complimentary situation. Once the lyric's intellectual and intertextual self-consciousness has been underscored, and hence its metapoetic features emphasized, the ending can be perceived as the wittily equivocal statement that it is.

Donald Guss, in commenting on Donne's poem as a rehandling of a Petrarchan model that had its own peculiar literary history down through the sixteenth century, remarks that "A Feaver" "expresses an adoration so extreme as to deny its own occasion, the lady's illness."[181] What is really implied by such an observation is Donne's strong resistance to the very act in which he engaged, that is, his habitual ambivalence about poetic compliment. The end of the lyric is revealing. Having asserted, in the penultimate stanza, that the feaver could not harm the "unchangeable" (24) "beauty" (23) of the beloved—a denial of one of the obvious effects of such diseases as smallpox—the poet relocates the illness in the mind of the amorously burning lover. But this restatement of a familiar love symptom was hardly innocent, for it allowed Donne to make explicit an egotism that runs through the work and undoes its complimentary gestures. The last two lines of the poem, which imply a familiar conceit of interinanimation, may not say anything remarkable, but they sound crudely, selfishly assertive, concluding the piece on a note that is anything but deferentially polite: ". . . I had rather owner bee/Of thee one houre, than all else ever" (27–28). Apart from the suggestion of *sexual* possession implicit in the phrase "one houre," these lines emphasize the stance of authoritative assertiveness that runs throughout the poem. The attitude of deferential humility steadily weakens after the first two stanzas and the last lines of the poem thus culminate a process that has been taking place all along rather than simply surprising the reader with a new tone or attitude.

Whatever their particular occasions in the social circumstances of the Lady Bedford circle, Donne's Jacobean complimentary lyrics, then, like his contemporary verse epistles, express Donne's ambivalence about his clientage. The signs are apparent that, while he might have found Lady Bedford's elite social world congenial enough for him in 1608 and 1609, he continued to feel ill at ease with his participation in it. In poems like the 1609 verse letter "You that are she" and the elegies for Cecilia Bulstrode and Lady Markham (for the last of which the epistle probably served, in Milgate's words, as a kind of "covering letter"),[182] Donne seemed to have been most uncomfortable complimenting the noblewomen with whom he and some of his friends were associated. Like that of the emotionally cool funeral elegies, the wit of the verse letter seems quite forced. Whatever actually occurred to change their relationship in its various stages, something seems to have happened to disillusion Donne with or distance him from the Countess of Bedford.[183]

There are signs of this in the epistle "T'have written then"—a poem whose rhetorical-syntactic development manifests a degree of strain and antagonism. This is a very strange verse epistle. It begins as a witty excuse for not responding to a letter of the Countess's, alluding to the danger of committing the client's cardinal sin, "thanklessenesse" (4). Donne abased himself as one of the "nothings" (7) of the public world, someone painfully conscious of not having the "Profit, ease, fitnesse, plenty" (23) of more fortunate, if corrupt, courtiers. He once again defined his relationship to Lady Bedford through which he was sanctioned to write complimentary verse:

> . . . whether my hymns you admit or chuse,
> In me you'have hallowed a Pagan Muse,
> And denizened a stranger, who mistaught
> By blamers of the times they mard, hath sought
> Vertues in corners,[184] which now bravely doe
> Shine in the worlds best part, or all It; You.
>
> (15–20)

He hyperbolically praised the Countess's virtue, which "ransomes one sex, and one Court preserves" (26), morally segregating her from the notorious corruption of the world in which she functioned. But at the very point one would expect him to develop the praise of his patroness's "worth" (27, 30), he leaves off abruptly, beginning instead a crazily agitated discourse on "others ills" (32), a satiric meditation on human degeneracy, a topic he handles more skillfully and at greater length in *The First Anniversarie*.[185]

This change, however, is only one of several in this poem of marked discontinuities. As in earlier works written for male readers, Donne seems to assert his poetic and intellectual authority or control as he continually alters the development of his poetic argument, repeatedly surprising his reader-addressee. The major changes follow lines 30 and 71: the first ostentatiously alters a poem of praise into a satiric meditation on the world's corruption; the second signals an end that is actually delayed until further complications have been introduced. Both points are marked by the conjunction "but," which also notes countermovements at lines 7, 81, and 87. In the next to last of these cases, Donne pretends to be breaking away from the abstract complexities of his discourse to make a simple statement—"But these are riddles, some aspersion/Of vice becomes well some complexion" (81–82)—but he only continues the same kind of convoluted argument in the succeeding lines. Here, however, he offers a patently misleading argument that "Vertue hath some perversenesse" (73), suggesting for a moment that he wants to defend Lady Bedford's behavior as a worldy-wise sophisticate not averse to devious courtly manipulation. He states that "ignorance of vice, makes vertue less" (79), and seems to have been looking for a way to accommodate the idealized Countess who was the object of encomiastic literary treatment with the actual woman who handled herself adroitly at Court: "Even in you, vertues best paradise,/Vertue hath some, but wise degrees of vice" (75–76). Yet, after explaining how, in a political context, one can beneficially "purge vice with vice" (83) and thus "tame ill" (85), he reversed himself in asserting that Lady Bedford was actually quite free of moral taint, advising her to remain virtuous:

> . . . in your Commonwealth, or world in you,
> Vice hath no office, nor good worke to doe.
> Take then no vitious purge, but be content
> With cordiall vertue, your knowne nourishment.
> (87–90)

It is as though Donne deliberately resisted coming to the logical conclusion of his poetical discourse, forcing a conventional complimentary statement into a structure in which it really does not fit.

The final couplet—unusually for a complimentary epistle—is in the imperative mode, which underscores the authority the poet has been exercising throughout the work through his complex moral and intellectual analyses as well as through his rhetorical and argumentative strategies. Donne ends the piece with advice disguised as compliment, but the issue raised in the last part of the poem remains a troubling one—that of the supposedly virtuous patroness's participation in a corrupt world in which one (inevitably) resorted to questionable means to achieve one's ends. What comes through here is Donne's consciousness of Lady Bedford's actual courtly dealing, an awareness that upsets the encomiastic formulations of the verse. The sudden departure from the consideration of the Countess's virtue in line 31 looks like the result of the poet's realistic awareness not only of the degenerate world in which she functioned, but of her moral involvement in its inner workings. Thus the earlier hyperbolic assertion that Lady Bedford's virtue "ransomes one sex, and one Court preserves" (26) implies not only Donne's latent antifeminism but also his clear knowledge of his patroness's courtly maneuverings—from which he desperately wished to profit.

In "This twilight of two yeares," an epistle sent at New Year, a conventional occasion for tribute-paying to social superiors, Donne plays an interesting game with pronominal forms in order to assert personal authority (in spite of his stance of humility). The first two stanzas are dominated by first-person pronouns, eight of them compared to only one second-person pronoun at the very end of the tenth line. In stanzas 3 through 7, there is a kind of balance between first- and second-person forms (eight to six) as Donne concentrates on his role as the poet eternizing a woman in "recompence" (11) for her benefaction. But in these stanzas, he metapoetically defines the character of poetical compliment and indicates the difficulty he has in executing his high purpose: he does not really engage in direct praise. Instead, having reached an impasse, he switches from compliment to advice-giving, a function he does not openly undertake (since that would have been presumptuous): he pretends to "turn to God" (33) as the source of instruction for his noble patroness and, through this fiction, he authoritatively instructs Lady Bedford in the last six stanzas of the poem. In this section fifteen third-person forms (referring to God) are balanced against nineteen second-person ones,[186] but delivering the messages of "God," the speaker is condescending to the addressee, thus reversing the positions of inferior and superior in the encomiastic situation.

Wesley Milgate may be right when he claims that Donne felt confident enough about his relationship with the Countess "to offer some advice . . . with implied gentle criticism of her indulgence in Court frivolities,"[187] a fair inference from the final section of this verse epistle, but what is significant here is Donne's strong assertion of poetic, moral, and social authority. In a sense he treated Lady Bedford in this poem in much the same way he did Sir Henry Goodyer in the cajoling propempticon occasioned by that friend's departure for the Continent. Donne presumed to tell Lady Bedford to behave carefully at Court, to make the best use of her personal and social resources (her *"beauty, learning, favour, blood"* [37]). He, not "God," presumed to instruct her that the Court was a complex environment in which morally "Indifferent" (43) realities outnumbered simple "good and bad" (41) ones. While he pointedly offered a justification of "vain disport" (44)—an obvious allusion to her participation in masques and other Jacobean courtly ceremonials—he made it clear that he regarded this activity as allowable only so long as it was "On this side sinne" (45), a distinction that could easily be debated, depending on the scope of one's moral tolerance. Donne suggested that the Countess needed as a counter-balance to the life of sophisticated pleasure certain "houres/Which pleasure, and delight may not ingresse" (46–47), presumably times of devotion and withdrawal from the business and recreations of the

Court, a moral retreat he portrayed in earlier verse letters to male friends as a rejection of that immoral environment.

What follows this advice is a grammatically difficult statement:

> And though what none else lost, be truliest yours,
> Hee [God] will make you, what you did not, possesse,
> By using others, not vice, but weakenesse.
> (48–50)

Milgate paraphrases this to mean "God will give you ways to exercise and increase your virtue, even beyond what you now possess, in your dealings with the weaknesses of others."[188] But these lines also suggest a kind of acquisitiveness that is less innocent, an exploitation of others habitual at Court, where maneuvering for advantage often took ruthless forms. Both this stanza and the following two imply that the Court was a dangerous place in which it was easy to be compromised morally, where there were liars and "spies" (54) and where, to protect her "fame" (57)—the object of defamatory gossip—Lady Bedford had to exercise "a discreet warinesse" (57). Donne advised emotional restraint in such a social world, the use of the ability to "represse/*Joy,* when your state swells, *sadnesse* when 'tis lesse" (59–60), for envy and scorn threatened, alternately, those who prospered and those who did not.

Couched in the language of religious and moral counsel, this whole six-stanza section of the epistle makes the same association of courtly success and spiritual health one finds in the prose letters, some other verse epistles, and the two *Anniversaries.* Margaret Maurer observes that "Donne's style" in his encomiastic verse letters to Lady Bedford "embodies the dynamic of the royal prerogative." It demonstrates "his capacity to function in the sphere he seeks to enter," illustrating a "command of the idiom of the court."[189] But, as is obvious in Donne's religious prose from the same period, this politically religious language offered him the opportunity to question and criticize the official ideology that sanctioned its use. As Maurer notes, Donne used wittily blasphemous religious terminology in "grossly hyperbolical" complimentary poems whose "conspicuous impropriety"[190] was deliberate, thus making his act of praise the ironic gesture of a man composing encomiastic verse with ambivalent feelings and only under duress.

"Honour is so sublime perfection" is the epistle Maurer discusses at greatest length in her consideration of the effect of "the Real Presence of Lucy Russell, Countess of Bedford" on Donne's complimentary epistles. She is right in naming "the relative merits of . . . 'discretion' and 'religion'"[191] as the major theme of this verse letter, a topic that brought under scrutiny the Countess's own courtly behavior—the contrived balance of "*Beeing* and *seeming*" (32) that Donne excused in his own courtiership. But I would argue that this poem is an even more subversive work than Maurer suggests.

Encomiastic epistles, like prayers, are phatic utterances,[192] ways of keeping open a channel of communication and thus maintaining favorable circumstances for continued transactions between speaker and addressee. In his complimentary verse letters, however, Donne's repeated metapoetic digressions had the contradictory effect of both confirming the patronage relationship in which he was involved and undermining it. By scrutinizing the conditions and conventions of praise, Donne wittily resisted performing the encomiastic act directly. "Honour is so sublime perfection" asserts, as Maurer notes, that the patroness needed the praise of a social inferior like her poet-client in order to possess the "honour" that her culture valued so highly, but, in analyzing the poet-patroness relationship in this way, Donne subversively relocated the source of both "honour" and power in society's inferiors rather than in its superiors. The observation by Aers and Kress that Donne deliberately relativized value is exactly to the point.[193] The act of honoring is what bestows the quality of honor on eminent persons and, this poem argues, "from low persons" (like the unprosperous Donne) "doth all honour flow" (7). In the political order, "Kings, whom they would have honour'd, to us show,/And but *direct* our honour, not *bestow*" (9). Respect, "reverence," "honour," are all within the power of individuals to grant to those they deem worthy. At a time in which royal favor and preferment as well as the awarding of "titles of honour" were notoriously erratic—usually much more the result of royal economic needs than of individual merit or abilities—such a theory as the one Donne espoused in this epistle was a mischievously iconoclastic one, suggesting as it did both the capriciousness of royal or aristocratic favor and the peculiar political dependency of superiors on inferiors.

There is a facetiously false humility on the speaker's part in this verse letter—a pretense that he is a lowly nothing—metaphorically "despis'd dung" (12), but at the same time someone who was essential as a means of validating Lady Bedford's honorable status. After the first third of the epistle, which is preoccupied with the relationship of inferior and superior in both society at large and in the social circumstances of the poem itself, Donne turns to the business of imaginatively defining the Countess's beauty, her virtuous worldly wisdom, and her religion. After pretending her (cosmeticized) body transparently revealed her soul (25-33), he tries to reconcile her artful pragmatism with her stance of religious integrity, claiming that both "discretion" (37) and "religion" (40) were necessary in such a public figure—the one to govern means (or "wayes" [51]), the other "ends" (51). The final characterization of Lady Bedford as both "great and innocent" (54) may have suited the hyperbolically complimentary context, but it hardly squared with the behavior of the actual courtly woman through whose social, political, and economic dealings Donne hoped to be advanced.

The mock-epitaphic verse letter sometimes entitled "Epitaph on Himself: *To the Countesse of Bedford*" followed by a longer poetic unit headed "*Omnibus*" may have been, as Milgate suggests, a valedictory poem written on the occasion of Donne's leaving for France with Sir Robert Drury.[194] In this case, the speaker's pose as a dying man resembles that of "A Valediction: forbidding Mourning." In making his patroness's "Cabinet" his "tombe" (1) and sending the verse epistle as a kind of epitaph for himself, he might have been making witty excuses for a decision that was the product of his concern for his "Fortune" (7). The poetic lecture he delivers on the soul and the body— with his characteristic metaphoric fascination with the idea of the buried corpse—might really have been intended to disguise the fact that, in journeying with Drury, Donne was giving up hope that the Countess could be an avenue to courtly advancement and was looking elsewhere for patronage. The poem both bade farewell and attempted to maintain a relationship that clearly was weakening.

The epistle "To the Countesse of Bedford *Begun in France but never perfected*" suggests, in both its forced ingenuity and lack of completion, that something essential in Donne's relationship with Lady Bedford was irrecoverably gone. Donne depicted his state in absence as that of one "*dead*, and buried" (1), extending, it would seem, the metaphoric language of the "Epitaph on Himself." He expressed a client's "thankfullnesse" for "favours" (5), but admitted, in the face of his embarrassment following the reaction to the printing of his *Anniversaries*, that he had turned to other expressions of his encomiastic art:

> . . . I confesse I have to others lent
> Your stock, and over prodigally spent
> Your treasure. . . .
> (11-13)

And yet he could not work through this confession, indulging in complex explanations and rationalizations as the poem seems to break down under the weight of his forced excuses: whatever genuine regrets Donne had about the printing of the *Anniversaries*, he probably did not want to apologize for the decision to seek others' patronage. In a prose letter Donne told George Garrard that if any lady took offense at the treatment of Elizabeth Drury (in the *Anniversaries*), she ought to "make her self fit for all those praises in the book, and they shall be hers" (*Letters*, p. 239). This sarcastic statement is an apposite commentary not only on Donne's bitter feelings of disappointment in his relationship with Lady Bedford (which brought him virtually none of the benefits he sought)[195] but also on all the idealizing hyperboles of the verse letters to her. He knew that a fifteen-year-old girl he never met was a better recipient of exaggerated praise than was a vain and conniving court lady like the Countess. The corollary to Donne's statement in the Garrard letter was that a perceptive and knowledgeable reader (other than Lady Bedford) could detect in the basically unmerited praise given her an element of criticism, if not of satire. When Donne remarked in his *Essays in Divinity* that "overpraysing is a kind of libelling" (p. 34)[196] he may have been referring confessionally to his own as well as to others' practice.

The other encomiastic epistles to (actual or potential) patronesses utilize the same inflated rhetorical currency found in the Lady Bedford poems. In particular, the verse letters to Lady Carey and Mrs. Essex Rich[197] and to the Countess of Salisbury repeat, in an even less convincing form, the familiar formulae of praise. The former poem was written to women Donne had not yet met: thus, as in the case of the first Lady Bedford epistle, he said he approached them "by faith alone" (12). Donne combined instruction and hyperbolic praise in his characteristic way, ending his piece with a gesture of witty self-consciousness about the conventions he employed:

> May therefore this be'enough to testifie
> My true devotion, free from flattery;
> He that beleeves him selfe, doth never lie.
> (61–63)

The explicit reference to lying, in this context, compromises the ostensible purpose of such a poem, enacting Donne's (later stated) belief that a great person can be a lie of one's own making.

The epistle to the Countess of Salisbury is one of the last encomiastic poems Donne composed in his search for patronage. As he had done in approaching Lady Bedford through a friend, Donne used George Garrard as an intermediary through whom he could forward this encomiastic piece to the Countess.[198] This noblewoman was the sister of the infamous Frances Howard and therefore the sister-in-law of the man through whom Donne hoped to obtain preferment in the last years before his ordination, the Earl of Somerset (Robert Ker). The verse letter itself is a particularly unimaginative pastiche of elements found in the other encomiastic epistles and in the *Anniversaries*. But the exasperation that seems to come through in this poem is probably a product of Donne's (by now) repeated frustrations in his search for advancement. For example, the world is portrayed as a place emptied of "Integritie, friendship, and confidence,/(Ciments of greatnes)" (13–14). He bitterly states that "Court, Citie, Church, are all shops of small-wares" (16). In context, the act of priase is compromised by the emotional ambivalence Donne typically brought to such verse. Under the pretext of explaining how he came to place the Countess of Salisbury at the center of the moral universe of complimentary verse (having spent so much energy earlier praising others), Donne allowed some of his antihierarchical attitudes to be expressed, even as he spoke the euphemistic language of patron-client economics:

> . . . I adore
> The same things now, which I ador'd before,
> The subject chang'd, and measure; the same thing
> In a low constable, and in the King
> I reverence; His power to worke on mee:
> So did I humbly reverence each degree
> Of faire, great, good; but more, now I am come
> From having found their *walkes*, to find their *home*.
> (57–64)

In the language of formulaic praise, the "power" Donne reverences is moral: in reality, it was (and Donne knew that it was) social, economic, and political. Neither here nor elsewhere in his verse letters to patronesses could Donne escape this awareness. Only, perhaps, in the special case of the *Anniversaries* and in the two epistles to his friend the Countess of Huntington,[199] with whom he was on more informal terms of social familiarity, could Donne move some distance from the emotionally vexing power relationships of the encomiastic situation.

With the exception of some of the lyrics, Donne's relationship with the Countess of Bedford or with his other noble patronesses did not produce the best literary results. The situation of patronage and the decorum of the complimentary situation imposed constraints that caused conflicts in him that undermined his encomiastic purpose.[200] He needed more social freedom and greater confidence in the goodwill as well as in the intellectual and literary competence of his coterie reader in order to write his best poetry. He seemed to have found this in the circumstances in which he composed his two *Anniversaries*, poems whose distance from their object of praise afforded Donne the opportunity for his most leisurely poetic ruminations. Because these poems were only loosely tied to the context of compliment, they broke free of its restrictions to become, at once, more private and more public poems.

"A NOCTURNALL" AND THE ANNIVERSARIES

Donne probably composed "A Nocturnall upon S. Lucies Day" about the same time as the *Anniversaries*. Frank Kermode calls this lyric "Donne's finest poem."[201] It is also a work that is most difficult to relate to any clear social context. It appears in very few manuscripts, which suggests it was deliberately kept quite private by the poet, accessible only, perhaps, to his closest friends. Because it is a lament for a deceased beloved and seems to register an extraordinary degree of personal anguish, many critics have associated "A Nocturnall" with the death of Donne's wife in 1617. Helen Gardner, in fact, has recently decided to support this dating, finding it congruent with the manuscript evidence that indicates the absence of this lyric and of "The Dissolution" from the Group I manuscripts deriving supposedly from Donne's 1614 effort to collect his verse.[202]

Few critics, however, would claim a late date for "The Dissolution"—even though its thematics and those of "A Nocturnall" are similar (the lament for the deceased beloved, the emphasis on amorous mutuality, the yearning for spiritual exaltation). Whether or not we accept Jay Levine's ingenious argument that Donne was cleverly fusing the erotic and funereal forms of the elegy through a systematic semantic duplicity,[203] it is evident that "The Dissolution," like many of Donne's secular poems of love, is a self-consciously witty performance utilizing Petrarchan conventions and sophistical reasoning. Despite the possible pun on Donne's wife's maiden name in the last word of the piece (if not also in line 18), it would be difficult to associate the poem with the behavior of the clergyman Donne on the occasion of his spouse's death: references to "fire of Passion, sighes of ayre,/Water of teares, and earthly sad despaire" (9-10) would have been singularly inappropriate for use by a poet committed in his late verse to devotional idioms and to the stance of the serious man of religion. It is also highly unlikely that Donne, in 1617, would (fictionally or otherwise) have addressed other "lovers" (10, 38) in "A Nocturnall" as one of their company. In abandoning his Muse in the "Obsequies to the Lord Harrington, brother to the Countesse of Bedford" he not only gave up the practice of writing complimentary verse for noble patronesses, but also, I believe, dissociated himself from the various other kinds of role-playing in which he indulged in the *Songs and Sonnets*, including the marital poems of mutual love. In the context of the quite small, and markedly occasional body of verse composed after his ordination, both "The Dissolution" and "A Nocturnall upon S. Lucies Day" would have been anomalies.

But if we reject a late date for a poem like "A Nocturnall," what circumstances of composition can we postulate for it? At least for an indication of the genesis of the work, we can return to Herbert Grierson's association of the lyric with Donne's relationship to the Countess of Bedford. After noting the possible allusion in the title to the Christian name of Donne's patroness, Grierson asked:

> Is it possible that [the work] was written when Lady Bedford was ill in December, 1612? "My Lady Bedford last night about one of the clock was suddenly, and has continued ever since, speechless, and is past all hopes though yet alive," writes the Earl of Dorset on November 23, 1612. It is probable that on December 13 she was still in a critical condition, supposing the illness to have been that common complaint of an age of bad drains, namely typhoid fever, and Donne may have written in anticipation of her death. But the suggestion is hazardous. The third verse speaks a stronger language than that of Petrarchan adoration. Still it is difficult for us to estimate aright all that was allowed to a 'servant' under the accepted convention. It is noteworthy that the poem is not included in any known MS collection made before 1630. The Countess died in 1627. (Grierson, 2:10)

Both Grierson's general point, that the poem was composed in an encomiastic/elegiac context, and his troubling doubt, that the sentiments expressed transcend this situation, need to be taken seriously. One possible answer to the difficulty Grierson found with his own theory is that Donne began to write one kind of poem and ended up composing another, as an encomiastic piece became a quite private psychological and religious act of meditative self-scrutiny.

Like "The Canonization," "A Nocturnall" finally has a devotional orientation,[204] but its idioms are more like those of the encomiastic poems than those of the later religious verse. Applied both to the figure of the deceased beloved and to the psychological state of the distraught lover, the poem's stark and extreme formulations push the language of the complimentary poetry in the direction of the vivid hyperboles of the *Anniversaries*, the works this lyric most closely resembles stylistically and thematically.

The poem depicts a beloved who was the spiritually animating center of the lover's existence, a figure whose loss devastated him and made the world a dead place, but whose heavenly exaltation points the way to this spiritual regeneration. Like the transcendent female of the *Anniversaries*, she cannot be identified either with Lady Bedford or with Donne's wife, for the poem's hyperboles grant her an extraordinary ideality. Conversely, however, the language used to depict her represents a fusion of complimentary idioms with the terms found in Donne's poetry of mutual love. The jargon of spiritual alchemy[205] found in the complimentary epistles is set alongside formulations found in verse of amorous reciprocity—for example, in the following lines:

> . . . I am every dead thing,
> In whom love wrought new Alchimie.
> For his art did expresse
> A quintessence even from nothingnesse,
> From dull privations, and leane emptinesse:
> He ruin'd mee, and I am re-begot
> Of absence, darknesse, death; things which are not.
>
> All others, from all things, draw all that's good,
> Life, soule, forme, spirit, whence they beeing have;
> I, by love's limbecke, am the grave
> Of all, that's nothing. Oft a flood
> Have wee two wept, and so
> Drownd the whole world, us two; oft did we grow
> To be two Chaosses, when we did show
> Care to ought else; and often absences
> Withdrew our soules, and made us carcasses.
>
> But I am by her death, (which word wrongs her)
> Of the first nothing, the Elixir grown. . . .
>   (12–19)

This passage converts the complimentary alchemical metaphors and the affectionate protestations of the speaker of the poetry of mutual love to new purposes, as Donne seems to turn away from the context of any specific human relationship to depict a solitary anguish and yearning.

Through a language of all-or-nothing extremity, Donne communicates in the first half of the poem a message found elsewhere in the preordination verse and prose: "[love] ruin'd mee" (17). In his fine sociolinguistic analysis of the lyric, Gunther Kress connects the "nothing" (22) with which the speaker associates himself with the emptiness Donne felt in the years leading up to his decision to take orders, the depression and frustration manifested in a letter to Goodyer complaining about being "no part of any body" in his continued lack of an "occupation" (*Letters*, p. 51).[206] Dealing with the lyric in terms of Halliday's concept of "anti-language," Kress notices the way it undertakes a "semantic reclassification" of its terms as it transforms processes into states, emphasizing negation, inanimacy, and the diminishment of human agency. This "act of creating an anti-language is an act of self-alienation from [the] community"[207] normally constituted by the language the poem redefines. In this respect the ambivalent relationship to the social establishment Donne expressed in the encomiastic epistles appears in a new guise in this poem. The language of "A Nocturnall upon S. Lucies Day" is a private one, but not simply in the sense that it expresses the poet's deepest feelings about love, loss, and spiritual yearning. The privacy toward which Kress's argument points rests in the radical reformulation of language and meaning Donne undertook, the context of an act of idealization that was as much a critique of the public order as a manifestation of personal desire—the same strategy used in the paradoxically public/private *Anniversaries*.

Within a period of a few months in 1611, Donne wrote the *Anniversaries*, two ambitious long poems to commemorate the death of the daughter of Sir Robert Drury, a man whose patronage the poet sought and accepted.[208] Having approached this wealthy Jacobean courtier through Joseph Hall and having tested the waters with a shorter funeral elegy,[209] Donne undertook the composition of the longer works in the context of the assured patronage of the man with whom he left England for an extended period of Continental residence and travel. The *Anniversaries*, which share many of the literary strategies of the encomiastic verse letters, should also be read as patronage verse reflecting Donne's continuing desire for advancement and his ambivalent attitude toward the world in which he hoped to prosper. Whatever their function in expressing his intellectual and spiritual preoccupations, these poems are also a self-conscious commentary on his social and political situation.

Scholars interested in the various intellectual and literary materials that went into the making of Donne's *Anniversaries* have for the most part lost sight of the fact that the hyperboles of these mixed-genre works[210] exceed even the broad limits of encomiastic convention, as the responses to the poems from Donne's time to the present indicate. Ben Jonson's quip—"if it had been written of ye Virgin Marie it had been something"[211]—points to the obvious disproportion between the acts of praise and the supposed referent, Elizabeth Drury, a gap modern critics have tried to bridge by looking for a subject more deserving of such treatment than the deceased fifteen-year-old who served as the pretext for composition.[212] But such redefinitions of the encomiastic object of the *Anniversaries* imply a context for the poems that is that of the study (or of the chapel) rather than of the social world in which Donne functioned.[213] Critics have largely ignored or taken for granted the patronage context in which the *Anniversaries* were composed. They have assumed that the larger framework of Donne's continuing desire for secular success and security was relevant (if at all) in only an incidental way to the content and method of these works.

The *Anniversaries* are about loss and the need for recovery: the modes Donne chose to render these themes are those of (satiric) scorn and (spiritual) idealization, stances suitable to one responding strongly to narcissistic injury.[214] One of the fantasies Donne elaborates in *The First Anniversarie* is that something has happened that has made the world a lifeless place, an event portrayed as the death of the "shee" celebrated in the poems, a being related to, but clearly something greater than Drury's deceased daughter. Donne defended himself against misinterpretation by claiming that he portrayed "the Idea of a Woman and not as she was,"[215] but this statement does less to explain the poems than to call attention to the motives behind the extreme acts of idealization. I suggest that the poems were not only, as all critics agree, the "Occasion"[216] for Donne to engage in intense meditation and speculation, but also the means to express feelings associated with his personal disappointments arising from his experiences in the decade preceding their publication.

The First Anniversarie does, in an elaborate way, what "A Nocturnall upon S. Lucies Day" accomplishes more economically: it portrays the world as dead because of the experience of loss and idealizes a female figure as the way of escaping an emotionally intolerable situation. Both *Anniversaries* enact a rejection *of* the world, but these poems resulted from Donne's feeling that he had been rejected *by* the world. As the refuge for the man whose ambitions were frustrated or who had fallen from prosperity, this *contemptus mundi* attitude implies more than a general philosophical or religious context. From the time of Henry VIII and that of the midcentury authors represented in the miscellany *The Paradise of Dainty Devises*[217] up through the later Elizabethan period, writers conventionally used philosophical and religious stances to cope with political and social defeat. When a courtier or ambitious gentleman fared badly, he could always claim stoically

"My mind to me a kingdom is"[218] or make a show of stepping outside the arena of social and political competition: "Like to a hermit poor in place obscure/I mean to spend my dayes of endless doubt."[219] Morally critical or Christian *contemptus mundi* attitudes toward the world and its selfish practices were probably more a question of emotional necessity than of keen ethical and religious sensibilities. Fulke Greville, at a low point of his own courtly career, wrote his idealizing biography of Sir Philip Sidney, adopting a satiric *contemptus mundi* point of view as one suitable to his sociopolitical desperation. Like Donne, whose *Anniversaries* were written at about the same time, Greville complained about the degeneration of the system of patronage, convinced that his own merit was unrewarded. Ronald Rebholz remarks in his biography of Greville that "the idea of the temporal degeneration of human stature helped Greville explain, in a way that would save self-respect, his failure to acquire office in James's reign: men of the 'modern discipline' could not recognize and reward the true worth of one bred in the previous age."[220]

In his *Second Anniversarie* Donne defined the transcendent "shee" he was praising as "such a Chaine, as Fate emploies/To bring mankind, all Fortunes it enjoies" (143–44). He came close to making explicit the connection between his object of praise and his own ambitions for a success he feared was unavailable to him. Conversely, in depicting woman as harmful to man—"sent/For mans reliefe, [but] cause of his languishment" (*First Anniv.*, 101–2)—he was probably saying (unconsciously, or at least indirectly) what Bacon was bolder to state outright, that wives harmed their husbands' careers. He habitually avoided making this charge directly, preferring instead to accuse himself (in his marriage, if not in his life generally), of being self-destructive, a tendency he attributes, in *The First Anniversarie*, to mankind generally:

> We seeme ambitious, Gods whole worke t'undoe;
> Of nothing he made us, and we strive too,
> To bring our selves to nothing backe. . . .
> (155–57)

But the truth of the remark "We kill our selves, to propagate our kinde" (*First Anniv.*, 110) lies as much in the context of the careerist hampered by "hostages to fortune," as in that of the (hardly serious) belief that orgasms shortened one's life span.

Beneath the surface preoccupations with the decay of the world and the need for spiritual transcendence in the *Anniversaries*, Donne argues (from personal experience) that the world is an unfair place. In

The First Anniversarie he elaborates the idea that those parts of "the world's beauty" (254) having to do with "colour, and proportion" (250) are decayed, indulging in intellectually and emotionally trivial complaints about astronomical irregularities and supposed deformities in the shape of the earth. But he smuggles a personally more pertinent issue into this comically hyperbolic context with the following comment:

> . . . But yet confesse, in this
> The worlds proportion disfigur'd is,
> That those two legges whereon it doth relie,
> Reward and punishment are bent awrie.
> (301–4)

The gesture of rejecting the world that concludes this and the other discrete sections of this poem looks like a reaction to a morally monstrous environment in which, of course, the politically dissatisfied Donne (and his patron Drury) felt treated unfairly. When Donne wrote late in the poem that "some people haue/Some stay, no more then Kings should giue, to craue" (421–22), he evoked a situation of disappointed ambition both he and his patron shared.[221] Despite the assertion in *The Second Anniversarie* that spiritual "Honour" (401) was far superior to the worldly favor of "Princes" (408), Donne continued to long for the latter.

The First Anniversarie states that the world is corrupt because it has lost its spiritually and morally animating center (symbolized by the transcendent "shee"). But Donne subverts this argument by presenting a comically inadequate series of subarguments. In the course of the exposition he exclaims "How witty's ruine!" (99) and it seems he was more interested in playing comic variations on his major theme than in offering a philosophically and religiously serious analysis. The major reason for this subversion is that the "ruine" Donne was really interested in dealing with poetically was his own, not the world's, a disaster that had more to do with his personal ill fortune than with the corruption of the physical world and of mankind. There is a subtext in the five-part exposition in this poem that can be detected once one notices he basic pattern Donne follows. In each of the sections Donne offers patently inadequate or facetious arguments to support the overt thesis that the world is a corrupt place. He repeatedly postpones serious moral discussion to the end of each part—presenting it almost as an afterthought, and, significantly, in a personal context.

The pattern is set in the first argumentative unit of the poem, which develops the thesis that "There is no health" (91). Here, and in the following parts of the work, one would expect the tone and content to be earnestly moral and religious, but instead Donne is comically eccentric. He offers six pieces of evidence, only the last of which really matters, to support the claim that mankind lives in a diseased world. In the first subsection he specifies what he means by the statement "We are born ruinous" (95), not, as expected, by mentioning original sin and its disastrous consequences, but by complaining facetiously that babies are born head first, "An ominous precipitation" (98). The second subsection substitutes comic antifeminism for genuine evidence, punningly equating postcoital fatigue with that explanation of the Fall that makes Eve the cause of Adam's sin: ". . . woman, sent/for mans reliefe [is] cause of his languishment" (101–2). The third piece of evidence rests on the flimsy folk belief that every orgasm costs a day of one's life: "We kill our selues, to propagate our kind" (110). The fourth and fifth points are that proof for man's degeneration can be found in the supposed shrinking of his life span and of his physical stature. Again the details are comic. The speaker asks "who liues to age,/Fit to be made *Methusalem* his page" (127–28) and fantasizes that man in primitive times was a giant:

>. . . one would haue laid
>A wager that an Elephant, or Whale
>That met him, would not hastily assaile
>A thing so equall to him. . . .
>(139–41)

When Donne finally gets close to the moral center of the topic of this part of the poem and considers how "our mindes are cramp't" (152) as fallen men, he cannot resist puns and other comic elements as he points to the self-destructiveness of mankind, jokingly referring to "new diseases" (159) (like syphilis) and the dangerous "new phisicke" (160) practiced by Paracelsan doctors. Naming man (punningly) "this worlds Vice-Emperor" (161) hardly constitutes a serious moral indictment. But from the point of view of Donne's own past and in particular his personal preoccupation with suicidal impulses—here generalized as the common human urge "To bring our selues to nothing backe" (157)—there is a hint that the "ruine" with which he is concerned in this, and in the other parts of the poem, is *his own*.

This is confirmed by the other sections of his argument, which similarly suggest the personal dimension of the poem's subject, most clearly in their last parts. In the second section, which elaborates the statement that "the worlds whole frame [is]/Quite out of ioynt" (191–92), again the focus should be moral and religious, but it is not initially. Donne presents the Fall as a funny accident—"The world did in his Cradle take a fall" (196)—and then leaps to the supposed disruption caused by the new astronomy in a much-quoted passage that has been taken out of context as a sign of the poet's serious preoccupation with contemporary intellectual issues. The comic treatment of the topic is, however, quite obvious:

> . . . new Philosophy cals all in doubt,
> The Element of fire is quite put out;
> The Sunne is lost, and th'earth, and no mans wit
> Can well direct him, where to looke for it.
> (205–8)

This is hardly a serious complaint about moral and spiritual dislocation since Donne did not invest the old astronomy with the kind of comforting certainty Galileo's persecutors did. The section does end with potentially more serious matters, however, as Donne alludes to social and political disorder:

> 'Tis all in pieces, all cohaerence gone;
> All just supply, and all Relation:
> Prince, Subject, Father, Sonne, are things forgot,
> For every man alone thinkes he hath got
> To be a Phoenix, and that there can bee
> None of that kinde, of which he is, but hee.
> (213–18)

While the satiric force of this passage is aimed outward at those narcissistic individuals who basically cared little about the proper forms of authority in the society, the subversiveness and egotism about which Donne complained was also his own.

The third and fourth sections of the argument are concerned with the thesis that "the worlds beauty is decay'd, or gone,/Beauty, that's colour, and proportion" (249–50). Donne deals with that aspect of beauty that is "proportion," but, again, not initially in moral or religious terms. The first evidence of the disproportion of the world he presents is a set of observations associated with the new astronomy, which has discovered "New starres" (260) and the irregularity of celestial orbits: "none ends where he begunne" (276), including the sun. Next he considers the unevenness of the Earth, whose ideal spherical shape is supposedly deformed by mountains and seas: "solidnes, and roundnes have no place" (299). Celestial and terrestrial disproportions, no matter what their symbolic potential and no matter what their place in the theological arguments associated with the Goodman-Hakewell controversy,[222] are not presented as truly serious evidence. Only as an afterthought does Donne turn to more morally, socially, and personally important matters when he notes that the "worlds proportion" has been "disfigured" (302) because ". . . those two legges whereon it doth relie,/Reward and punishment are bent awrie" (303–4). Especially in light of the conclusion of this section, which argues for the rejection of the world because "here is nothing to enamor thee" (328), it would seem that the contexts of the remark on "reward and punishment" are social and political, the implications simultaneously general and personal. After all, it was traditional for unrewarded and politically persecuted individuals to strike just such an attitude of contempt of the world.

For the most part, the short treatment of the way "colour" has decayed is even more frivolous than the discussion of "proportion." Donne generally contrasts the imagined beauty of God's fresh Creation, represented most clearly in the "Rainbow" (352) that is a sign of His covenant with man,[223] with the supposed deterioration of color in the contemporary world:

> . . . color is decayd: summers robe growes
> Duskie, and like an oft dyed garment showes.
> Our blushing redde, which us'd in cheekes to spred,
> Is inward sunke, and onely'our souls are redde.
> (355–58)

The real direction of the comparison is toward the metaphoric use of color of the last line of this passage. Donne here, as elsewhere, refers to the color associated with guilt and shame, a blushing red he appropriates for himself and connects elsewhere with his sins and follies."[224]

In the fifth, and final, section of the argument Donne treats the topic of "*the want of correspondencie of heaven and earth*" (marginal note after line 374). But, again, instead of dealing immediately with the conflicting values of the two orders, he first concentrates on morally irrelevant or trivial matters, complaining about adverse climactic and meteorological conditions and then bemoaning the loss of magical and primitive medical arts. When, however, he turns to yet another analysis of the value and power of the "shee," he introduces a political perspective that is much more to the point. The beneficial influence of the "shee" is diminished, he argues, "by Receivers impotencies" (416) in what Donne calls "our age [of] Iron" (426) so that, instead of ideal kingdoms, one finds only a sorry state of affairs in which only

> . . . some Princes have some temperance;
> Some Counsaylors some purpose to advance
> The common profite; and some people have
> Some stay, no more then Kings should give, to crave. . . .
> (419–22)

The general import of these lines would have been evident to contemporary readers, but since Sir Robert Drury, like his poet-client Donne, had "craved" royal patronage and had been repeatedly frustrated in his efforts, he might have responded particularly to the political dimension of this passage and of the whole poem.

The general argument of *The First Anniversarie* concludes with the rationalizing rejection of worldliness that is a conventional gesture of men disappointed in their all-too-worldly ambitions:

> . . . no thing
> Is worth our travaile, griefe, or perishing,
> But those rich joyes, which did possesse her hart,
> Of which shee's now partaker, and a part.
> (431–34)

In this poem idealization and scorn are the means of dealing with thwarted ambition. In the formulaic ending of the work, Donne publicly assumes a role that is out of keeping with his usual coterie stance, that of the poet-prophet mediating between the earthly and the heavenly, a strange function for the writer of such an eccentric long poem whose coarse, prosaic[225] features and comical and satirical deformities do not fit thematically or tonally with the pious matter and high style of the final lines.

"A Funeral Elegy" found between the *Anniversaries* in the 1612 edition was apparently written before the longer poems. As a work whose initial circulation was probably in manuscript, it is another example of Donne's private patronage poetry, like his verse epistles to Lady Bedford and the elegies written for Cecilia Bulstrode and Lady Markham, "ragges of paper" (11) marked by the pen rather than the press. When, in the poem, Donne describes the various components of the contemporary social order, he includes "Princes," "Counsailors" (22), "Lawyers" and "Divines" (23), "the Rich" and "the Poore" (24), as well as "Officers" and "Marchants" (25), characterizing the "shee" that is the object of praise as the animating spirit whose loss leaves the world a "decrepit" (30) place. The basic argument of *The First Anniversarie* is thus adumbrated in this earlier work that, placed after it in the printed edition, serves well to recapitulate the longer poem's argument.[226] In optimistically concluding that the virtuous, who imitate the example of the deceased, might "accomplish that which should have been her fate" (100), Donne assumes that the world is not so wretched an environment as to prevent "vertuous deeds" (103) from flourishing. This message, and the formulaic ending—in which it is claimed "the good play her, on earth" (106)—look forward to the content of *The Second Anniversarie*, and thus the elegy serves as an appropriate transition between the two longer poems.

The Second Anniversarie initially extends the metaphoric language of *The First Anniversarie* in depicting a world that is mere "fragmentary rubbidge" (82). This work, whose generic elements are a different mixture from those of "The Anatomy of the World,"[227] is more explicitly a self-persuasion that uses its religious and philosophical materials to argue that the world is a worthless place one should reject for a heaven of whose accidental and essential joys the "shee" partakes. Whatever his other purposes, Donne certainly makes a gesture whose significance was quite conventional, a rejection of the world (by which he felt rejected)—an act he only seriously performed many years later, if at all.

The "shee" of the poem again serves as a point of reference for social and political as well as for religious and devotional ideas. For example, at one point the "shee" is presented metaphorically as the ideal state:

> Shee, who beeing to herselfe a state, enjoyd
> All royalties which any state emploid,
> For shee made wars, and triumph'd; reson still
> Did not o'erthrow, but rectifie her will:
> And shee made peace, for no peace is like this,
> That beauty'and chastity together kisse:
> Shee did high justice; for shee crucified
> Every first motion of rebellious pride:
> And shee gave pardons, and was liberall,
> For onely'her selfe except, shee pardond all:
> Shee coynd, in this, that her impressions gave
> To all our actions all the worth they have:
> Shee gave protections; the thoughts of her brest
> Satans rude Officers could nere arrest.
> As these prerogatives being met in one,
> Made her a soveraigne state, religion
> Made her a Church; and these two made her all.
>   (359–75)

Warmaking, peacemaking, justice and liberal mercy, and the granting of legal immunity are all defined as "prerogatives" of monarchy whose ideal exercise Donne imagines in a context that invited unfavorable comparisons to the actual state of affairs in England. The first item in his list, for example, was triumphal warmaking, an activity the pacifist James desperately tried to avoid.

The ideal state of affairs contrasted sharply, for Donne, with the way things were. In other passages, he suggested some of the things that were wrong in Jacobean England, his satiric energies fueled by his resentment and disappointment. When he imagines a dead body being eaten by worms, he draws the analogy with the destruction of the kings by parasitic clients (117-18), indirectly repeating a charge often leveled at James, especially by some of the more outspoken Parliamentarians, among whom were numbered some of Donne's friends. When Donne imagines the kind of "conversation" (324) one might enjoy in heaven, he contrasts it with the fawning of ecclesiastical clients over "Great men" (329) and with the poisonous speech of courtly "Libellers" (333), glancing scornfully at two types of vicious men who enjoyed the patronage he lacked. As noted earlier, he elsewhere repeats sentiments expressed in a verse epistle to Lady Bedford, defining "honor" in an ideologically subversive way:

> . . . all honors from inferiors flow,
> (For they doe give it; Princes doe but show
> Whom they would have so honord). . . .
> (407-9)

Finally, in a passage that sounds strong notes of resentment and disappointment, he belittles those given titles of honor:

> If thy Prince will his subjects to call thee
> My Lord, and this doe swell thee, thou art than,
> By being greater, growne to be lesse Man.
> (474-76)

Both the idealism of the spiritual aspiration and the scorn implicit in such depictions of worldly transactions have their roots in Donne's ambitions and their frustration in the years preceding the composition of both anniversary poems.

The *Anniversaries* had *both* a coterie readership and a public audience reached through the medium of print. As patronage works that succeeded in winning Donne some limited economic benefits, they were addressed to Sir Robert Drury and were shared with a (former) Drury client, Joseph Hall, who obligingly wrote commendatory poems to introduce each of the two *Anniversaries* in their published form. Beyond this fairly restricted readership, the poems reached, in either manuscript or printed form, Donne's circle of friends and acquaintances, men like Garrard and Goodyer, with whom the poet communicated by letter while he was on the Continent.[228] In the last part of *The Second Anniversarie*, Donne alluded specifically to his particular situation in Catholic France: "Here in a place, where mis-devotion frames/ A thousand praiers to saints" (511-12). The technique of autobiographical self-reference customary in his manuscript-circulated coterie verse was, strictly speaking, quite out of place in a printed work. But then so too were the witty idiosyncracies of style and content that especially baffled a general readership unused to Donne's poetry and its peculiar communicative matrix.[229] Donne resisted making the necessary adjustments demanded by the more public circumstances of print and suffered the consequent misinterpretations and unsympathetic criticism.

As Barbara Lewalski indicates, the immediate literary impact of the *Anniversaries* is to be found in the elegies written to mourn the death of Prince Henry.[230] Significantly, these were works of coterie literary competition set in a framework in which the death of a princely patron constituted, for the elegist-clients, an actual, not merely (as in the *Anniversaries*) a metaphoric, indication of social and political loss. Donne may have provided some of those witty young men of Prince Henry's court with an intellectually complex literary model, but the social and political coordinates of their verse had been long established.

THE RELIGIOUS VERSE AND PROSE
OF THE SECULAR MAN

Donne's religious poems, particularly those pieces he composed in the decade preceding his ordination, were fundamentally coterie literature. He gave sacred verse to such friends as Sir Henry Goodyer, George Garrard,[231] and Magdalen Herbert. The appearance of religious poems in Rowland Woodward's manuscript collection suggests that such work went through processes of transmission similar to those of the *Elegies* and *Satires*. Donne even expected this poetry to help him win patronage: he sent six "Holy Sonnets" to the new (and notoriously extravagant) Earl of Dorset along with a brazenly flattering introductory sonnet.[232] The poems no doubt express Donne's private psychological, religious, and moral struggles, but they were also, to a great extent, witty performances designed for an appreciative readership. Donne wrote in "A Litanie," "When wee are mov'd to seeme religious/Only to vent wit, Lord deliver us" (188–89), suggesting his awareness of some of the less-edifying motives that led him to compose religious verse. The divine poems of the preordination period certainly represent a mixture of secular and religious intentions; after all, when he composed them he was vigorously pursuing worldly advancement by all available means.

The context of the religious verse was not only that of Donne's personal desires and private relationships with friends, patrons, and patronesses; it was also the more general one of Jacobean culture. Under the new monarch religious literature took on greater importance than it had in the Elizabethan era for a number of reasons including the King's own interests as well as the increasingly heated national and international polemical atmosphere. In *both* Tudor and early Stuart times religious poetry served as a way for courtier-careerists to express slight or serious political disappointment: Wyatt's penitential psalms and many subsequent religious lyrics expressing a contempt for worldly involvement and success were composed as responses to setbacks to or failures of secular ambitions.[233] The Psalm translations done by Sir Philip Sidney with his sister, poems admired by Donne for their artistry,[234] were probably read along with Sidney's other work in the context of the myth of his glorious political failure. Such cultural encoding of sacred poetry carried over into the Jacobean era, as the example of Donne himself testifies. But from the start of James's reign, religious verse also assumed a higher place in the hierarchy of genres within the literary system as other genres, such as the love poetry that flourished in Elizabethan times, declined drastically in importance. For a politically sensitive courtier like Fulke Greville, who wrote poetry during both reigns, the change was dramatic: his Elizabethan love lyrics suddenly gave way at the start of the Jacobean period to religious poems reflecting both his political poor fortune during the first half of James's reign and the new changes in the literary system.[235] Donne, too, responded to the changed sociocultural conditions in turning to the composition of religious verse, just as he did in writing controversial prose.[236] The very act of composing sacred verse in the reign of a monarch who had himself written religious poetry and especially favored pious and polemical writing was a political gesture.[237] By authorizing the composition of religious works, King James created a situation in which religious poetry could, paradoxically, both continue to signal the frustration of ambition (with a consequent sense of alienation from the world of power and wealth) and express active suitorship in an officially sanctioned literary vocabulary. It didn't take a conversion experience to move a politically active Jacobean courtier-poet to compose religious literature. Even in private circulation, such work was responsive to the changed sociocultural environment.

In *La Corona* (and in his other religious verse) Donne accepted the poet's role. He refers to his Muse (*LC* 1.6 and 7.13) in a serious way, whereas, for the most part, he earlier used the term quite negatively or ironically. To a significant degree, this acceptance of *poetic* authority was possible because King James himself had written sacred poetry and, therefore, sanctioned such activity as proper for the politically active man. While, in an Elizabethan situation, religious verse was the recourse of courtly losers and an indirect form of social protest by recusant authors (like Constable and Southwell),[238] in Jacobean England, despite retaining its effectiveness as the expression of sociopolitical frustration, it was more assuredly establishment literature. No better testimony to this fact can be found than the dedicatory poem presented as the fourth of Jonson's *Epigrams*:

> How, best of Kings, do'st thou a scepter beare!
> How, best of Poets, do'st thou laurell weare!
> But two things, rare, the Fates had in their store,
> And gave thee both, to shew they could no more.
> For such a *Poet*, while thy dayes were greene,
> Thou wert, as chiefe of them are said t'have beene.
> And such a Prince thou art, wee daily see,
> As chiefe of those still promise they will bee.
> Whom should my *Muse* then flie to, but the best
> Of Kings for grace; of *Poets* for my test?

In composing encomiastic verse, Donne exercised himself in a mode sactioned for patron(ess)-client relationships. In penning religious verse, he officially (if not actually) followed the example of the King himself. He felt no need, therefore, in *La Corona*, to apologize for playing the poet.

Donne's personal feelings connected with his search for employment and advancement in the early Jacobean period intruded into his religious verse. Court politics and personal ambition account for some of the language and metaphors Donne utilized for both the conscious and the unconscious connections he made between the religious and the political. In the sonnet to Magdalen Herbert sent along with the *La Corona* sequence, for example, Donne chose the politically encoded term "advance" (3) to apply to Mary Magdalen's salvation. Although in *La Corona* and the other religious poems he portrayed private spiritual struggle as separate from the secular environment in which men pursued worldly success[239] (just as he earlier set the private sphere of mutual lovers apart from the larger public world), the two orders overlapped for him. The grief and despair with which Donne's early religious poems are preoccupied (particularly the *Holy Sonnets*) seem to have been rooted, as the letters to Goodyer indicate, in *both* personal piety and secular needs.[240] And so, when Donne confessed that "vehement griefe has beene/Th'effect and cause, the punishment and sinne" (1635 HS 3.13–14),[241] he expressed himself in an idiom he used elsewhere to discuss his economic and political misfortunes. In mentioning that "Kings pardon . . . punishment" (HS 7.10), Donne may have been expressing his wish that James would forgive him his past indiscretions and accept him into royal service. Conversely, courtiership, like amatory courtship, provided Donne with a scheme for his relationship with God:

> I durst not view heaven yesterday; and to day
> In prayers, and flattering speeches I court God.
> To morrow'I quake with true feare of his rod.
> (W-HS 3.9–11)

While Donne seems to have made divine favor the object of his suits and to have thought of the raising of his Muse by the Holy Spirit (LC 7) as a much greater benefit than courtly advancement, his political consciousness betrayed itself. Through contrasts as well as analogies between the monarchical and the divine, the courtly and the heavenly, Donne reinforced the connection between the political and the religious in his sacred poetry. Even when he depicted "tyrannies" (HS 4.6) and "kings" (HS 6.9) as evil and destructive, he signaled, by the use of such terms, his insistent awareness of the political order.

Written probably in late 1608[242] at a time Donne was sick in body, mind, and fortune, "A Litanie" is a good example of this politically encoded religious verse. Lewalski claims that this poem, and the later "A Hymn to God the Father," "transpose public forms into private devotions," exemplifying the Protestant practice of applying religious truths to the self.[243] While this is certainly true, it is also the case that Donne used the poem to comment, for a knowledgeable audience, on his sociopolitical condition as well as on his private spiritual state. It functioned, in many respects, as social verse. Donne, we know, sent a copy of the poem to his friend Goodyer, with the explanation that, though it was an exercise in a form originally designed for "publike service in . . . Churches," it was aimed primarily at a restricted readership, "for lesser Chapels, which are my friends" (Letters, p.33). He offered the work "for a testimony of that duty which I owe to your love, and to my self, who am bound to cherish it by my best offices" (Letters, p. 33–34): it was, therefore, like the prose letters, part of an ongoing self-revelatory private communication with a receptive audience. Donne relied on his coterie reader's ability to understand "A Litanie" in the context of its author's personal situation. The "ruinous" (4) state and susceptibility to "dejection" (5) Donne mentions, then, were not simply the adverse conditions of the representative Christian's tormented soul; they were the particular contemporary circumstances about which Donne constantly complained at this low point in both his private and public life.

Donne admitted in this poem, as he did four years later in the *Essays in Divinity*, that he had "wasted" himself "with youths fires, of pride and lust" (22); he saw in his restless thirst for knowledge and in his indulgence in versifying culpable "excesse/In seeking secrets, or Poetiquenesse" (71–72). He prayed to be delivered

> From being anxious, or secure,
> Dead clods of sadnesse, or light squibs of mirth,
> From thinking, that great courts immure
> All, or no happinesse. . . .
> (127–30)

He thus characterized his own behavior and interests as those of a witty, depressed, ambitious but frustrated careerist seeking preferment at the Jacobean court. He even admitted that his "Pietie" might have been "intermitting" and "aguish" (209), more the product of sickness and poor fortune than of a steady religious commitment. So, too, he retrospectively considered his own attraction to "learning" (235), "beauty" (237), and "wit" (239) as sinful, dangerous, and debilitating.

In referring, in stanza 26, to his being criticized and slandered by others, he alluded to the burden of the bad reputation he bore, which apparently still kept him from being entrusted with a position of responsibility in the government. Ostensibly addressing God, Donne seems to have had King James in mind as well:

> That living law, the Magistrate,
> Which to give us, and make us physicke, doth
> Our vices often aggravate,
> That Preachers taxing sinne, before her growth,
> That Satan, and invenom'd men
> Which well, if we starve, dine,
> When they doe most accuse us, may see then
> Us, to amendment, heare them; thee decline;
> That we may open our eares, Lord lock thine.
> (226–34)

Donne autobiographically claimed that political authority (Egerton?) and envious competitors magnified the seriousness of his sins and errors, stating that public disapproval beneficially led to "amendment." This is his contention in those letters he wrote to people in power in which he distinguished his mature self from his indiscreet younger (but not much younger) one.[244] In praying that "Lord lock" his ears to the voices of his critics and slanderers, however, Donne probably hoped that the human monarch, James, would admit him into service despite his past mistakes.

Throughout "A Litanie" Donne conflates spiritual and secular monarchical authority, God and King—something he does also in his controversial prose. This strategy reinforced the Jacobean ideology of divinely sanctioned kingship. In the poem the language of courtly relationships describes spiritual affiliations: men are "in Wardship to [God's] Angels" (47), and heaven has "faire Palaces" (48). Donne's defense of wealth in stanza 18 looks suspiciously like an apology for the extravagance of James's court:

> . . . through thy poore birth, where first thou
> Glorifiedst Povertie,
> And yet soone after riches didst allow,
> By'accepting Kings gifts in th'Epiphanie,
> Deliver, and make us, to both waies free.
> (158–62)

Donne conspicuously omitted the biblical commonplace of the rich man and the eye of a needle, as he took pains to suggest that the wealthy had as easy moral access to heaven as the poor. Stanza 25 asserts that some "bold wits jest at Kings excesse" (223), but Donne suggested, in defending James, that mocking the monarch was only one step away from mocking God, "majestie divine" (224). It suited his purpose, as the last term indicates, to mix royalty and divinity, as Jonson did in his masques. For, whatever his spiritual needs, as an importunate courtly suitor Donne wanted James's favor to make him prosper.

"A Litanie" is a text parallel to many of the contemporary letters to Goodyer. The religious and the political, the private and the public are merged in both kinds of writing. Both literary genres assume the existence of sympathetic and knowledgeable readers able to understand the nuances of Donne's writing. In asking for the acceptance of his prayer-poem by God, Donne in effect once again called for the competent receptivity of his coterie audience (even as he fantasized a similar benevolence on the part of the King). Such well-wishing was for Donne a precondition for the very act of communication: "Heare us, for till thou heare us, Lord/We know not what to say" (203–4). The relationship portrayed between the speaker and God in the poem thus reflects the desired poet-reader transaction.

In the 1590s, when the fashion was at its height, Donne avoided composing an amorous sonnet sequence, probably largely because such an activity bespoke professional authorship and/or the search for artistic patronage.[245] He did use the sonnet form for epistolary exchange, but he cast his love lyrics in other shapes that were, at once, more formally complex and more affectedly casual. In Jacobean England, nevertheless, Donne felt free to turn to the sonnet for sacred verse—partly because the King wrote some holy sonnets himself, and partly because the religious sonnet was not stigmatized, as was the love sonnet, by being associated with importunate suitorship.

Like Donne's other coterie writings, the *Holy Sonnets* are witty performances that exploited a knowledgeable audience's awareness of their author's personal situation and history. Just as Donne expressed religious ideas in his letters to Goodyer specifically in relation to his immediate social circumstances, in his *Holy Sonnets* and other religious verse he presented the themes of despair and hope, spiritual pride and humility, sin and redemption in ways that signaled specific personal, social, and political coordinates for these typical preoccupations of a devout Christian. He self-consciously referred to his past life (and verse)—for example, in mentioning his erotic "idolatrie," his "mistresses" (*HS* 9.9–10), and his "humorous" "prophane love" (*W-HS* 3.5–6). He also allowed his current secular concerns with ambition and preferment to intrude upon—or rather to be translated into the language of—his sacred verse. It took a conversion to Roman Catholicism to make Henry Constable into a religious sonneteer, but no such dramatic change in Donne accounts for his divine poems. He might have been deeply bothered about his apostasy, as John Carey has argued,[246] and he might have expressed abiding interests in religion and in the welfare of his soul, but, at least when he wrote his early Jacobean religious poems, Donne was no saint and his energies and desires were directed toward worldly success. As late as 1614, Lady Bedford, who obviously thought she knew the kind of man he was, was astonished that someone with Donne's unedifying personal history had decided to enter the ministry.[247]

By Donne's own standards, the religious sonnets and other preordination sacred verse were contaminated by self-interest. In a letter to Goodyer in which he discussed prayer, he named thanksgiving and praise, rather than petition, as the properly selfless purpose of true devotion:

... I had rather [devotion] were bestowed upon thanksgiving then petition, upon praise then prayer; not that God is indeared by that, or wearied by this; all is one in the receiver, but not in the sender: and thanks doth both offices; for, nothing doth so innocently provoke new graces, as gratitude. I would also rather make short prayers then extend them, though God can neither be surprised, nor beseiged: for, long prayers have more of the man, as ambition of eloquence, and a complacencie in the work, and more of the Devil by often distractions . . . . (*Letters*, pp. 111–12)

Insofar as they request or demand divine help or become self-aggrandizing performances, the religious poems veer away from this devotional ideal.

Whatever the circumstances of their original composition (perhaps as an exercise in private devotion), the coterie transmission of the *La Corona*[248] sonnets to Magdalen Herbert exemplifies the social uses of religious verse. There survives a prose letter accompanying the poems from Donne to Mrs. Herbert, whose acquaintance he had made and whose patronage he was securing in the years 1607–9:

Madam,
    Your Favours to me are every where; I use them, and have them. I enjoy them at *London*, and leave them there; and yet, find them at *Micham*: Such Riddles as these become things unexpressible; and, such is your goodness. I was almost sorry to find your Servant here this day, because I was loth to have any witness of my not coming home last Night, and indeed of my coming this Morning: But, my not coming was excusable, because earnest business detain'd me; and my coming this day, is by the example of your St. *Mary Magdalen*, who rose early upon *Sunday*, to seek that which she lov'd most, and so did I. And, from her and my self, I return such thanks as are due to one to whom we owe all the good opinion, that they whom we need most, have of us—by this Messenger, and on this good day, I commit the inclosed *Holy Hymnes* and *Sonnets* (which for the matter, not the workmanship, have yet escap'd the fire) to your judgment, and to your protection too, if you think them worthy of it; and I have appointed this inclosed *Sonnet* to usher them to your happy hand.
                    Your unworthiest Servant,
                    unless your accepting him
                    have mended him.
                JO. DONNE (*Selected Prose*, pp. 124–25)

He used the formally deferential language of client-patroness relations in this piece, addressing himself to a woman he knew took devotional practices quite seriously and who might, thus, welcome a set of religious poems.[249] Taking the verse into her "protection" involved strengthening her social bond with the poet. In the case of a patroness and friend like Mrs. Herbert, religious language could serve as a medium of social intimacy. In the dedicatory poem prefixed to the *La Corona* sequence Donne relates "Mrs. Magdalen Herbert" to "St. Mary Magdalen" as a way of complimenting the addressee for her piety even he chose her as a proper recipient for what he had written, work he supposedly refrained from burning only because of its edifying "content." After playing with the Mrs. Herbert–Mary Magdalen association, Donne asked this coterie reader to "Harbour" the "*Hymns*" he sent her.

The language of *La Corona* is that of the religious transvaluation of the secular. The personal depression Donne experienced at the time—largely because of his lack of an "occupation"—appears in the poems as a "low devout melancholie" (*LC* 1.2). The secular rewards symbolized by the various crowns such as the laurel wreath (of poets and military victors) are subordinated to the "crowne of Glory" (*LC* 1.8) won by a Christ who wore a "thorny crowne" (*LC* 1.7). In the religious context of Scriptural meditation on Christ's life, Herod, a model of bad kingship, is "jealous" (*LC* 3.8) of the virtuous Christ, a reversal of a frustrated political inferior's resentment of the great. So too, in the poems, evil "ambitious" (*LC* 5.3) men express "envie" (*LC* 5.2) of a suffering Christ with whom the poems' speaker identifies, another inversion of Donne's own social and political situation. The "sparks of wit" (*LC* 4.3) Donne praises in the fourth sonnet of the sequence are the wisdom of Christ, not the skeptical, riddling, or paradoxical utterances of a man whose poetry proclaimed an ambivalence toward the Establishment. In *La Corona*, salvation and glorification replace advancement and preferment as the objects of desire. Generally, then, the conversion of secular into religious values represents an attempt to reaffirm self-worth and regain a measure of control in the most unfavorable of social circumstances.

In the *Holy Sonnets* Donne relocated in a religious framework the conflict between autonomy and dependence he expressed in his encomiastic verse. These emotionally charged and intellectually tortuous poems enact personally and socially the contradictory attitudes of assertion and submission that were intrinsic to Donne's temperament, but that were heightened by the desperateness of his ambition in the early Jacobean period.[250] The social and political dimensions of this basic conflict were highlighted by a number of related features of the sonnets: the portrayal of male authority, the rhetorical elaboration of the struggle of spiritual pride and humility, the subversive indecorum of particular works, and the general transformation of a (religiously expressed) passive aggression into an aesthetically sadomasochistic relationship with his readers.

One way the religious verse noticeably differs from the earlier secular poetry is in its changed attitude toward male authority. Whereas fathers and other authority figures are portrayed negatively, often derisively, in Donne's erotic and satiric verse (the major exception being *Satire* 3), in the divine poems the basic attitude is changed. In the fourth "penitential" sonnet, Donne imagines the father who died in his early childhood benevolently looking down from heaven on his spiritual triumphs:

> If faithfull soules be alike glorifi'd
>   As Angels, then my fathers soule doth see,
>   And adds this even to full felicitie,
> That valiantly I hels wide mouth o'rstride. . . .
>   (1635-HS 4.1–4)

Such a figure functions psychologically as what Roy Schafer has called the "loving and beloved superego,"[251] sanctioning behavior that satisfies the individual's ideals. More typically in the *Holy Sonnets*, Donne depicts a paternal diety with whom he wishes to come to terms and whose love he wishes to enjoy. He expresses some angry, resentful, and rebellious feelings, but he capitulates before a God who seems, in some ways, to have been for him a lost father found.[252]

The sudden serious interest in fathers and the depiction of paternal deity reveal Donne's preoccupation with powerful authority and his relationship to it. John Carey has observed that Donne's primary emphasis in his later *Sermons* is upon God's power, rather than His love: "It is Power that does all" (*Sermons*, 8:128).[253] So, too, in the *Holy Sonnets*, the Donne who felt neglected and abused by secular authorities, including the King, portrayed a paradoxically hurtful and helpful God whose power he both resisted and felt drawn to. Not only is the angry, judgmental Old Testament God whose "sterne wrath . . . threatens" (*HS* 5.8) present in his poems, a deity whose violent punishment the speaker masochistically calls upon in "Batter my heart," but also Christ himself, usually portrayed as loving and merciful, is seen (in *HS* 9) as gruesomely fightening, his redemptive act primarily one of power: "Christs blood" has "might" (*HS* 2.13). The Beatific Vision does not evoke a sense of radiant love and comfort, but rather an image of "that face,/Whose feare already shakes my every joynt" (*HS* 3.7–8). In the Incarnation, a powerful God became "weake enough to suffer woe" (*HS* 7.14), but "weaknesse" (*HS* 8.7) is associated with God's creatures generally. The language of courtly suitorship is drawn into the *Holy Sonnets* to define the Christian's relationship to a strong kingly God, which suggests that behind Donne's theological preoccupation with strength and weakness lay his experiences in the secular world. *Holy Sonnet* 11, for example, imagines "God the Spirit, by Angels waited on/In heaven" (2–3) in the way King James was attended at Court. This poem presents the fantasy of being made "by adoption/Coheire to'his glory" (7–8) and *Holy Sonnet* 12 deals with getting part of a "double interest" in his "kingdome" (1–2) in language that suggests the economic benefits of royal patronage. When Donne in a later sermon reflected on the idea of enjoying the "friendship" of a "King" (*Sermons* 1:210–14), he elaborately developed just such analogies. In the light of this material, the statement "Thou lov'st mankind well, yet wilt not chuse me" (*HS* 1.13) sounds like a translation of a neglected client's complaint from a political into a religious context.

The conflict between assertion and submission is enacted in the *Holy Sonnets* in the thematic and rhetorical interplay of spiritual pride and humility. This familiar devotional material (portrayed, as Herbert later handled it, as the individual Christian's resistance, then capitulation, to God's grace and love) is developed throughout the series of poems—at least through the first twelve that have been considered as a structured sequence.[254] *Holy Sonnet* 1, for example, seems more concerned with blaming God than with loving Him, with complaining about ill treatment rather than with humble petitioning for grace. When the speaker cries out "Why doth the devill then usurpe in mee?/Why doth he steale, nay ravish that's thy right?" (9–10), he does so petulantly, accusingly, as though it were God's fault that he is plunged in sin. He seems to deliver God a moral ultimatum: "Except thou rise and for thine owne worke fight,/Oh I shall soone despaire" (11–12). The speaker arrogantly puts all the responsibility on God, having, in the first part of the poem, set out in lawyerlike terms the contractual relationship of creature and Creator, sinner and Redeemer. The problem of spiritual attitude in this poem is one that must be solved in the succeeding sonnets. A number of the other lyrics do dramatize the speaker's coming to terms with it by adopting the piously affectionate humility that is a precondition to receiving divine grace. *Holy Sonnet* 4, for example, self-consciously pulls back in the sestet from the tone and tenor of the octave, in which the speaker, in effect, has usurped God's role as the initiator of the Apocalypse:

> At the round earths imagin'd corners, blow
>   Your trumpets, Angells, and arise, arise
> From death, you numberlesse infinities
> Of soules, and to your scattred bodies goe,
> All whom the flood did, and fire shall o'erthrow,
> All whom warre, dearth, age, agues, tyrannies,
> Despaire, law, chance, hath slaine, and you whose eyes,
> Shall behold God, and never tast deaths woe.
> But let them sleepe, Lord, and mee mourne a space,

> For, if above all these, my sinnes abound,
> 'Tis late to aske abundance of thy grace,
> When wee are there; here on this lowly ground,
> Teach mee how to repent; for that's as good
> As if thou'hadst seal'd my pardon, with thy blood.

This poem's sharply contrasting attitudes of prideful assertion and humble submission are made into a structural balance. Analogously, *Holy Sonnet 5* is divided into an accusatory disputatious octave and a self-consciously meek sestet. But the scheme of spiritual pride overthrown and replaced by proper religious humility does not adequately account for what Donne is doing with the interplay of assertion and submission in these poems. There is something intractably boastful and self-advertising about the works that remains despite the gestures of self-effacement. Repeatedly, especially in poems like "Oh my blacke Soule" (*HS* 2), "This is my play's last scene" (*HS* 3), and "Spit in my face yee Jewes" (*HS* 7), Donne pridefully *over*dramatizes the self. As Lewalski and others have noticed, Donne legitimately employed the Protestant devotional technique of "application to the self" in both his poems and sermons,[255] but this does not explain the impression of boastfulness some sonnets create. Whereas a religious poet like George Herbert repeatedly expressed embarrassment over just such a tendency in himself, Donne seems to have reveled in it.

Meditative practice might have sanctioned vivid imagery and emotional heightening in devotional acts of the imagination, but the octave of a poem like *Holy Sonnet 2* has an aura of self-consciously witty melodrama about it:

> Oh my blacke Soule! now thou art summoned
>   By sicknesse, deaths herald, and champion;
> Thou'art like a pilgrim, which abroad hath done
> Treason, and durst not turne to whence hee's fled,
> Or like a thiefe, which till deaths doome be read,
> Wisheth himselfe delivered from prison;
> But damn'd and hal'd to execution,
> Wisheth that still he might be' imprisoned. . . .
>   (1–8)

Similarly, the chain of epithets in the first quatrain of *Holy Sonnet 3* is less functional than wittily overdramatic:

> This is my playes last scene, here heavens appoint
>   My pilgrimages last mile; and my race
> Idly, yet quickly runne, hath this last pace,
> My spans last inch, my minutes last point. . . .
>   (1–4)

The Religious Verse and Prose 257

The poetic act of intensification is as much one of self-reflexive performing as of emotional scene-setting.

Holy Sonnet 6 may rest on sound theological grounds and on the conventional devotional sharing in Christ's victory over death through the redemption, but Donne seems to have formulated religious truth in this poem in a particularly self-aggrandizing manner; joyful confidence in the power of the redemption and arrogant boasting are hard to disentangle. Likewise, in *Holy Sonnet 7*, Donne creates the impression—at least in the octave—that the speaker is engaging as much in an act of shockingly witty self-assertion as in a gesture of repentance:

> Spit in my face yee Jewes, and pierce my side,
>   Buffet, and scoffe, scourge, and crucifie mee,
> For I have sinn'd, and sinn'd, and onely hee,
> Who could do no iniquitie, hath dyed:
> But by my death can not be satisfied
> My sinnes, which passe the Jewes impiety:
> They kill'd once an inglorious man, but I
> Crucifie him daily, being now glorified.
>   (1-8)

The last phrase of this passage contains a (perhaps unconscious) grammatical ambiguity. Is the subject of "glorified" Christ or the self-assertive speaker? Lewalski's remark that "the speaker seeks to arrogate to himself all the elements of Christ's passion"[256] points to the problem of tone in this poem. The self in performance and the self in humble devotion seem here, and throughout the *Holy Sonnets*, to be intractably, if creatively, at odds. In the religious lyrics Donne's fascination with the experiencing self produces a form of that self-conscious poetic performing in which he habitually engaged before his coterie readers.

Donne's presentation of the self's conflicts between assertion and submission included the acts of witty indecorum to which he called attention in the *Holy Sonnets*. In the performative context of the poems, Donne used shocking indecorum as a metacommunicative device to signal the emotional ambivalences at the heart of his religious verse, thus extending into a new genre a technique he had employed in his prose paradoxes, his amorous verse, and his complimentary poetry. Just as in his encomiastic epistles and lyrics Donne used calculated violations of decorum to express conflicts related to the situation of patronage, so too, in the divine poems, he seems to have restated the problem, but in a new thematic context. William Kerrigan has discussed some of those shocking elements of the religious verse that cannot be explained by references to the intellectual-historical or literary-historical precedents—such features as the sexualization of the speaker's relationship to God. Kerrigan is right to notice that such indecorum is a means of simultaneously assaulting the self and the reader in an attempt to express spiritual and psychological conflicts in a forceful manner.[257] But there are further (social) implications to the technique having to do both with Donne's relationship with his coterie audience and with his attitudes toward the political establishment.

Because the precedents for sonnet sequences were basically amorous ones and because Donne's own lyrics had been love poems, he turned to the language of love and to familiar erotic conventions to express religious desire in his *Holy Sonnets*, enlivening and testing the rhetoric of prayer and meditation as he alluded to his own past amorous experiences. In one of his sermons, Donne later spoke of Solomon in an autobiographical way:

. . . *Salomon*, whose disposition was amorous, and excessive in the love of women, when he turn'd to God, he departed not utterly from his old phrase and language, but having put a new, and a spiritual tincture, and form and habit into all his thoughts, and words, he conveyes all his loving approaches and applications to God, and all Gods gracious answers to his amorous soul, into songs, and Epithalamions, and meditations upon contracts, and marriages between God and his Church, and between God and his soul . . . (*Sermons* 1:237).

Donne's eroticized spirituality manifests itself in *Holy Sonnet 9* ("What if this present were the worlds last night?") where he explicitly connects his amorous wooing with his religious suitorship in addressing the figure of the crucified Christ:

> . . . as in my idolatrie
> I said to all my profane mistresses,
> Beauty, of pitty, foulnesse onely is
> A signe of rigour: so I say to thee,
> To wicked spirits are horrid shapes assign'd,
> This beauteous forme assures a pitious minde.
>   (9–14)

Such analogizing between the erotic and the spiritual—present in another form in the secular verse—has been explained in terms of the conversion experience Donne was supposed to have undergone (an Augustinian transformation of the unholy amorist into the holy Christian). There are, of course, biblical and other precedents for erotic spirituality, such as the one Donne cites in the sermon passage. And it is certainly possible to associate Donne's practice with that of other

Mannerist and Baroque artists. This last context has been used to account for the strategy of shock and excess adopted by Donne in the erotic metaphors and other techniques of the *Holy Sonnets*.[258] And yet such erotic material is basically indecorous and Donne presumably knew what he was doing with it. In the lines just quoted, for example, Donne does not simply connect the general terms of Petrarchan amorousness with his spiritual solicitation of Christ. Since the "pitty" sought from "mistresses" in his secular lyrics (if not in his life) was specifically sexual yielding, the opposite of "rigour," the analogy between the erotic and the religious seems to have been shocking by design.

A similar indecorum is to be found in the erotic spirituality of *Holy Sonnet* 10 ("Batter my heart")—a poem whose cry for "Divorce" (11) may, incidentally, express Donne's deep misgivings about his marriage. Kerrigan discusses this poem in terms of the tradition of "accommodation" and of Donne's imaginative testing of the limits of theological anthropomorphism.[259] But the holy rape the speaker of this sonnet invites—"I/Except you'enthrall mee, never shall be free,/ Nor ever chast, except you ravish mee" (12–14)—reveals more than the intensity of spiritual yearning. Through its rhetorical aggressiveness, it also calls attention to the *sadistic* undercurrent in the poet-reader relationship expressed through the *masochistic* formulations of the verse. The indecorous sexualization of the individual's relationship to God is only one way in which the rhetorical sadomasochism of the *Holy Sonnets* operates, the extreme communicative circumstances in which Donne again enacts his conflict of assertion and submission in the poems.

Of all the *Holy Sonnets*, "Batter my heart" best illustrates some of the aspects of the change in sociopolitical codes from the Elizabethan to the Jacobean periods. The sexualization of the speaker's relationship to God at the end of the sonnet is shocking partly because it has the shape of a passive homosexual fantasy. Assuming a homologous relationship among the religious, political, and sexual orders, Donne made the connection, in *Pseudo-Martyr*, between sodomy and preferment; here he homoerotically sexualized salvation. The cultural logic underlying both associations was not simply that of devotional topoi or of polemical scurrility; it was, in Jacobean England, in the reformulation of the heterosexual metaphor of Petrarchan amorousness into a (more or less sublimated) homosexual one suited both to male-male patron-client transactions generally (as in Shakespeare's *Sonnets*) and to Jacobean courtier-King relationships specifically. Being loved in the spiritual homoerotic context of "Batter my heart" corresponded to being favored in the political order. In the early Jacobean period, then, Donne's metaphoric capitulation to a divine lover took a peculiarly Jacobean form.

The rhetoric of the religious poems, particularly these *Holy Sonnets*, operates in interesting ways. Donne utilizes the "symbolic I"[260] of Protestant meditation and preaching as a way of forging a bond with an audience by means of which personal religious experience and insight, communal piety and general truths, can be joined. In contrast to most of his earlier verse, in which the reader was often overtly treated as an antagonist, the divine poems emphasize the collective "we" and the representativeness of the speaker to affirm an emotional-intellectual bond between speaker and listener, poet and reader.[261] There are, however, also opposite gestures of aggression toward the listener and the reader by means of which the poet, as in the complimentary verse, asserted his intellectual and literary authority in the very midst of his expressions of personal vulnerability and need. The strong language, the violent and shocking metaphors, the poems' sudden changes of thought and turns of development characteristically proclaim Donne's individuality and aesthetic superiority in ways that seem to undercut the stance of humble piety and communal spokesmanship.

In style and manner, then, Donne expressed his basic conflict between assertion and submission, alternately sharing deep spiritual experience with his readers and assaulting them aesthetically by various means. One final remark needs to be made about the rhetoric of the *Holy Sonnets* and of the religious poetry in general. Since this verse only really acknowledges one hierarchical relationship—that between man and God—and posits a communal equality of all Christians, it offered Donne the opportunity to treat any reader—friends like Sir Henry Goodyer and George Garrard, as well as Mrs. Herbert and the Earl of Dorset—with the kind of familiarity impossible in complimentary poetry, where the social distinctions were emphasized. Just as, in his controversial prose Donne assumed the kind of authority that allowed him (as he put it in one of his *Problems*) to satisfy "an *Ambition* . . . to speak *playnly* and *fellowly* of Lords and Kings" (p. 28), so too in the sacred poems he exercised the kind of religious authority he enjoyed in his later preaching, acting as a master of a discourse within which individuals from all social strata were theologically leveled. The only deference he needed to express was toward God. Hence, in such verse he could imaginatively escape the social conditions that generated conflicts between assertion and submission in the first place.

As Gardner, Martz, Lewalski, and others have noted, the *Holy Sonnets* are private meditations utilizing a variety of conventional devotional techniques.[262] The sonnets no doubt satisfied some of Donne's personal emotional and intellectual needs at the time he composed them, offering within a religious sphere ways of dealing with anxieties and struggles that were less manageable in his actual social life. But, in both their thematic design and in their coterie "publication," these poems were attuned to the religious and political realities of Jacobean England. Whatever personal spiritual conflicts Donne experienced in the eight or so years preceding his ordination, he expressed them in relation to his career ambitions in the Jacobean environment. Although I am suspicious of any scheme that has Donne moving gradually toward a serious religious commitment (since, for example, as late as 1614 he was still vigorously pursuing secular preferment), his experience as a religious apologist,[263] his continued failure to find political advancement in the Court of a King ready only to grant him ecclesiastical preferment, and his private study and agonized meditation all certainly led him to the inevitable acceptance of a religious vocation.

Donne obviously thought deeply about the decision to take orders, even though he resisted making it for a considerable time. Falling sometime between the time of composition of the early religious verse and the *Anniversaries* and that of the poetically valedictory "Obsequies to the Lord Harrington" and his ordination, that strange prose work later published as his *Essays in Divinity* records some of Donne's vexed thinking about the possibility of an ecclesiastical career. Usually viewed as a devotional exercise written with no particular audience in mind,[264] this work can, like the earlier *Holy Sonnets* and the subsequent (?) "Goodfriday, 1613. Riding Westward," fruitfully be read not only as private religious acts of meditation and prayer but also as coterie literature laden with both specific and general sociopolitical significance. Like his other coterie prose writing, the *Essays in Divinity* can help us to read Donne's contemporary poetical texts with a better sense of their contextual implications.

The *Essays in Divinity* is a mixed-genre work: a piece of mock- or comical-scholarship, parodying the methods of scriptural exegesis and mystical writing, a religiopolitical commentary in which Donne took advantage of his position as an amateur theologian and political outsider to comment on both the secular and religious spheres of activity, an exercise in private meditation and devotion experimenting with the rhetorics of prayer and preaching. Donne engages in both straightforward and paradoxical arguments, simultaneously valorizing the rational faculties as the means to truth and driving them into nonsensical helplessness. He treats learning, particularly theological tradition, as both magisterially authoritative and intellectually absurd. By mixing trivial and serious matters, important with insignificant authors, he disorients the reader, creating a vexing perplexity from which state, he suggests, only the intuitions of faith can rescue both the writer and the reader from a condition of intellectual and emotional impasse. In its rhetorical strategies, erratic thematics, and intellectual mischievousness, this work extends the manner and some of the matter of coterie prose pieces like *Biathanatos* and the *Paradoxes and Problems*—if not also of the polemical *Pseudo-Martyr* and *Ignatius His Conclave*. But, especially in its prayer sections, Donne engaged in a kind of writing that characterizes his mature religious poetry and prose, a form of devotional rhetoric that attempts to transcend intellectual perplexity by means of both plain and metaphoric perception grounded in faith and the material of Revelation.

In their intellectual convolution, Donne's *Essays in Divinity* signals a crisis of motive, belief, and commitment. It devastates its own intellectual materials and, in the process, also assaults the forms of order and value that are sanctioned in the public world. Donne's comments about secular authority, worldly success, and the pretensions of earthly monarchs (like Milton's in *Paradise Lost*) bespeak a bitter personal disillusionment, if not a pained cynicism—here the kind of rhetorical violence found in *Biathanatos* is aimed more frequently outward at nameless, faceless objects than it is at the masochistic self. *Essays in Divinity* is a text whose powerfully satiric force has not been properly acknowledged—partly because in it, as in the *Anniversaries*, satire and earnest idealization are combined in a way that directs attention toward positive intellectual, moral, and spiritual values. But here, as assuredly as in the other prose and poetical works of the previous decade of his life as a frustrated careerist, Donne reveals his preoccupation with the sociopolitical world even as he abstracts himself from it devotionally.

Within the work, the contexts of Donne's allusions to secular political power are those of his desire for forgiveness and renewal and of his ambivalence about his future secular or ecclesiastical career choices. Treating his personal suffering (implicitly attributed to his poor fortunes in the public world) as the instrument of God's healing power,[265] Donne contemplates the possibility of a "Vocation . . . to serve God" (p. 71), works toward the *contemptus mundi* gesture of the final prayer section, yet, because of yet-unrenounced political ambitions, clearly expresses envy toward the politically successful and criticism of the political establishment. In a section dealing with God's justice, he asks a rhetorical question, for example, in which his envy of those who have benefited from royal patronage shows through:

. . .will any favorite, whom his Prince only for his appliableness to him, or some half-vertue, or his own glory, burdens with Honours and Fortunes every day, and destines to future Offices and Dignities, dispute or expostulate with his Prince, why he rather chose not another, how he will restore his Coffers; how he will quench his peoples murmurings, by whom this liberality is fed, or his Nobility, with whom he equalls new men; and will not rather repose himself gratefully in the wisdom, greatness and bounty of his Master? (p. 87).

At the end of the first decade of Jacobean rule, such a comment satirically alludes to some of the most powerful charges leveled at James by Parliamentarians, dissatisfied nobles, and the general populace.

In a section discussing miracles, Donne calls James's exercise of royal power into question through a particularly subversive use of the God/King analogy: "*Nature* is the *Common law* by which God governs us, and *Miracle* is his *Prerogative*. For Miracles are but so many *Non-Obstantes* upon Nature. And Miracle is not like prerogative in any thing more then in this, that no body can tell what it is" (p. 81). In the context of the Commons-Crown argument over the relative strengths of common law and royal prerogative, Donne expressed, at the least, a skeptical attitude toward the Jacobean expansion of the legal scope of kingly power. In this particular discussion, he finally obliterates the Nature-Miracle contrast by explaining that "Miracles . . . produced to day were determined and inserted into the body of the whole History of Nature . . . at the beginning, and are as infallible and certain, as the most Ordinary and customary things" (p. 81). This solution to the problem does not really do away with the suggestion he makes that royal prerogative constitutionally conflicts with a normative common law his contemporaries were trying to systematize, just as "*Miracle* is against the whole *Order* of Nature" (p. 81). Several pages later, he makes a comment that confirms this impression: " . . . multiplicity of laws . . . is not so burdenous as it is thought, except it be in a captious, and entangling, and needy State; or under a Prince too indulgent to his own Prerogative" (p. 94).

Donne earlier refers to earthly monarchs in the context of a discourse on "*Nothing*" (p. 27): "And, oh ye chief of men, ye Princes of the Earth . . . know ye by how few descents ye are derived from Nothing? you are the Children of the Lust and Excrements of your parents, they and theirs the Children of *Adam*, the child of durt, the child of Nothing" (p. 30). Or, again referring to kings, Donne asks:

"But alas, what are these our fellow-ants, our fellow-dirt, our fellow-nothings, compared to that God whom they make but their pattern?" (pp. 35–36). In the same place in the work, Donne's preoccupation with his poor sociopolitical status takes the form of a set of reflections just preceding the first prayer section, in which he seems to be in competition with royalty rather than in a stance of clientage:

A prince is Pilot of a great ship, a Kingdome; we of a pinnace, a family, or a less skiff, our selves: and howsoever we be tossed, we cannot perish; for our haven (if we will) is even in the midst of the Sea; and where we dy, our home meets us. If he be a lion and live by prey, and wast amongst Cedars and pines, and I a mole, and scratch out my bed in the ground, happy in this, that I cannot see him: If he be a butterfly, the son of a Silkworm, and I a *Scarab*, the seed of durt; If he go to the execution in a Chariot, and I in a Cart or by foot, where is the glorious advantage? If I can have (or if I can want) those things which the *Son of Sirach* calls principall, water, fire, and iron, salt and meal, wheat and hony, milk, and the blood of grapes, oyle, and clothing; If I can *prandere Olus*, and so need not Kings; Or can use Kings, and so need not *prandere Olus*: in one word, if I do not *frui* (which is, set my delight, and affections only due to God) but *Uti* the Creatures of this world, this world is mine; and to me belong those words, *Subdue the Earth and rule over all Creatures*; and as God is proprietary, I am *usufructuarius* of this Heaven and Earth which God created at the beginning. And here, because *Nemo silens placuit, multi brevitate*, shall be the end. (p. 36)

It is in the context of the kind of envy and dissatisfaction expressed in this passage that Donne in the *Essays* takes a *contemptus mundi* stance and portrays his conversion from secular to religious values.

Applying to his own life the meaning of the deliverance of the Israelites from Egypt, Donne interprets his personal suffering as God's schooling him through affliction to make a break with worldly values to which he was still, nonetheless, attached:

Thou hast delivered me, O God, from the Egypt of confidence and presumption, by interrupting my fortunes, and intercepting my hopes; And from the Egypt of despair by contemplation of thine abundant treasures, and my portion therein; from the Egypt of lust, by confining my affections; and from the monstrous and unnaturall Egypt of painfull and wearisome idleness, by the necessities of domestick and familiar cares and duties. Yet as an Eagle, though she enjoy her wing and beak, is wholly prisoner, if she be held by but one talon; so are we, though we could be delivered of all habit of sin, in bondage still, if Vanity hold us but by a silken thred. (p. 75)

That "silken thred" continued to keep the ambitious Donne connected to the world of secular preferment, even as he felt pushed toward the acceptance of the King's (if not also of his own) call to Church service.

The Religious Verse and Prose 265

The final gesture of rejecting worldly values toward which *Essays in Divinity* moves looks more like an act Donne would like to have made rather than one he actually felt ready to make with a full sense of new commitment:

> We renounce, O Lord, all our confidence in this world; for this world passeth away, and the lusts thereof: Wee renounce all our confidence in our own merits, for we have done nothing in respect of that which we might have done; neither could we ever have done any such thing, but that still we must have remained unprofitable servants to thee; we renounce all confidence, even in our own confessions, and accusations of our self . . . yea we renounce all confidence even in our repentances. . . . We have no confidence in this world, but in him who hath taken possession of the next world for us. (pp. 98–99)

This religious prose work records a stage in Donne's career in which he felt ambivalent both about his further search for courtly advancement and about the possibility of taking orders.

Donne no doubt used the occasion of writing the *Essays* to put his conflicted thoughts down on paper for his own benefit, but there are some signs that he intended the work to be read by a receptive, if quite limited, coterie audience also. Although he characterized the *Essays* as "solitary Meditations" (p. 41), or, as he put it elsewhere, "Sermons, that . . . have no Auditory" (p. 41), he suggests that he is writing "a Meta-theology, and super-divinity . . . but to my equals" (p. 59)—that is, composing a form of lay theology that metacommunicatively examines some of the premises and methods of the forms of theological and devotional discourse the work both enacts and parodies. In asking rhetorically, at one point, " . . . do not many among us study even the Scriptures only for ornament?" (p. 40), he seems to be addressing fellow men of fashion. The rationale he offers for God's allowing contradictions in Scripture is similar to the one implied by some of his own paradoxical coterie prose: "To make men sharpe and industrious in the inquisition of truth, he withdrawes it from present apprehension, and obviousness. For naturally great wits affect the reading of obscure books" (p. 56). Just as the *Paradoxes* and *Problems* were used by Donne as "alarums to truth" for a witty readership willing to work through intellectual perplexity, so too it is likely that Donne directed his *Essays in Divinity* to a similarly receptive coterie familiar with his "intemperance of scribbling" (*Letters*, p. 228).

In one of the final prayers, Donne suggests that he was composing the *Essays* in rural exile—possibly in the country house of one of his friends, if not in France during his Continental sojourn with Sir Robert Drury: "*And thou hast put me in my way towards thy land of prom-*

ise, thy Heavenly Canaan, by removing me from the Egypt of frequented and populous, glorious places, to a more solitary and desert retiredness, where I may more safely feed upon both thy Mannaes, thy self in thy Sacrament, and that other, which is true Angells food, contemplation of thee"* (p. 96).[266] At times, Donne implies the existence of an audience other than himself—in a phrase such as "let me observe to you" (p. 88), for example. He sometimes, especially in the formal prayer sections, utilizes the communal "we" for whom the writer speaks like a typical Protestant preacher: *"Behold us, O God, here gathered together in thy fear, according to thine ordinance, and in confidence of thy promise, that when two or three are gathered together in thy name, thou wilt be in the midst of them, and grant them their petitions"* (pp. 97–98). The work was clearly not intended for print, but Donne might have shown it to friends. It probably belonged to socioliterary circumstances similar to those of the religious lyric with which it seems to have intellectual and emotional affinities, "Goodfriday, 1613. Riding Westward."

Two related sets of terms are contrasted with one another in the Good Friday poem: 1) "Pleasure" and "businesse" (7) vs. the retreat from the secular world into the sphere of religious piety; 2) prideful rationality vs. humble intuitive faith. With regard to the first of these, the coterie context can help to focus the issues involved. If, as seems likely, "Goodfriday, 1613. Riding Westward" was composed en route from Sir Henry Goodyer's Polesworth estate to Sir Edward Herbert's Montgomerey Castle,[267] its circumstances of composition and of initial reception were properly incorporated thematically in the poem in specific ways. Given some of the values and interests Donne shared with both friends—in particular the courtly ambitions and fondness for witty intellectuality—the poem was particularly adjusted to the receptivities of a primary audience and its immediate circumstances, moving from a visit to one friend to enjoy the hospitality of another. One of the argumentative tasks Donne undertakes in this religious lyric is the reconciliation of worldly involvement with devotional obligations or of secular with religious goals. Initially the two orders are opposed: riding westward, in the specific metaphor of moral movement Donne employs, indicates a turning away from God toward the world that conflicts with the obligation to move eastward toward the theological Orient symbolized by the crucified Christ.[268] The speaker's strategy of splitting himself into a body riding westward on horseback and a soul bending devotionally toward the East is wittily presented as a rationalization that does not solve the problem posed by the conflict of allegiances. By the end of the poem, however, moving westward is redefined as a necessary condition of worldly existence that is a penitential preparation for facing that God whose bright image, according to traditional doctrine, can only be confronted in Heaven.

The solution Donne poses is based on an equation that is implicit also in the *Essays in Divinity*: worldly suffering = spiritual penance. Just as, in the *Essays in Divinity*, Donne interpreted his "idlenesse," his sociopolitical disappointments, and his consequent "despair" (p. 75) as the afflictions through which he could be redeemed, so, in the poem, he portrayed the fixation of his heart on worldly success (paradoxically) as the means by which he could turn toward God. What this redefinition of suffering permits, then, is the reconciliation of the two commitments opposed in the Good Friday poem. Moving westward becomes a penitential experience through which the man of the world makes himself available (here consciously, in Donne's life unconsciously or ironically) to God's loving, yet violent, ministrations. By having the speaker invite punishment, Donne imaginatively assumes control not only of what God will do to him to make him worthy of salvation, but also of what is happening and what has happened to cause him pain all along, all those griefs he has endured, especially in the decade prior to the poem's composition:

> I turne my backe to thee, but to receive
> Corrections, till thy mercies bid thee leave.
> O thinke me worth thine anger, punish me,
> Burne off my rusts, and my deformity,
> Restore thine Image, so much, by thy grace,
> That thou may'st know me, and I'll turne my face.
> (37–42)

The call for punishment is also, however, Donne's way of asking that some agency outside himself decide between a secular and a religious commitment for him. God's striking St. Paul off his horse to recruit him to His service seems a close analogue to Donne's request for divine action to change him (from an ambitious courtier to a devout Churchman).

The second contrast in the Good Friday poem—between rational and intuitive acts, or reason and faith—is related to the first: Reason is to worldly commitment as Faith is to spiritual commitment. As Donald Friedman has argued in his fine essay on this lyric:

The poem . . . illuminates a current of Donne's thought that became central to his sermon practice; it criticizes the rationalism that regards itself as self-sufficient, and demonstrates the rejection of that kind of devotion that believes it can comprehend the mysteries of faith by being 'reasonable.' Like many of the sermons the poem enacts a discovery of the inadequacy of such paltering mechanics of the mind; but it does this by transcending the concept-making skills of the intellect, not by discarding them.[269]

Friedman's analysis of the rhetorical development of the poem, especially his account of the function of its opening ten lines, is convincing: one can see how the speaker of the poem moves through intellectually strained conceitedness (1–10) and the recitation of smugly pat paradoxical formulae (11–14) to a more emotionally and imaginatively charged response to the crucifixion and his own sinfulness (15–34) and to an affectionately pious (if masochistic) colloquy.

Friedman notes that "'Goodfriday, 1613. Riding Westward' proceeds towards its spiritual discovery by way of mockery and self-parody,"[270] but such features characteristically mark it as a coterie work that is both a religious lyric and a metapoetic commentary on its poetic materials as well as on the implied relationship of poet and audience. The private agonizing over personal commitments figured in the poem is enacted for readers able to relate the lyric's self-reflexivity to the private and sociopolitical contexts in which it is set. Although I agree with the basic analysis of the poem's rhetorical development that Friedman offers, I think there is something wrong with his explanation of Donne's intentions. To say that this lyric was meant to serve as "a vehicle of conversion for Donne's audience"[271] is to ignore the poet's presentation of the crisis of commitment and the need for (violent) change as his own. In order to support his claim, Friedman has to argue that the poem "foreshadows both the purpose and the designs of many sermons Donne was to preach in later years."[272] The preacher-congregation situation, however, does not really fit a lyric in which, as in the *Anniversaries* and the *Essays in Divinity*, personal struggles and disappointments, doubts about the future, and a crisis of purpose are expressed through vexed intellectuality, emotional masochism, and idealistic yearning. In "Goodfriday, 1613" Donne was less confidently in control—intellectually, emotionally, rhetorically—than he was in his later sermons, and the instability or uncertainty of this lyric, like that of the *Holy Sonnets*, accounts for much of its power. All the biographical evidence suggests that at the time Donne composed this poem, he was still unable to accept the ecclesiastical service toward which the King had beckoned him. He was still unwilling to relinquish his aggressive pursuit of secular preferment: in the context of his actual behavior, the religious thematics of "Goodfriday, 1613" and of the other preordination religious and philosophical poetry were rendered deeply problematic, and would have been perceived as such by a knowing coterie readership.

THE FINAL SECULAR POEMS

The secular poems Donne wrote in the last years before his ordination were occasional works related directly or indirectly to his pursuit of patronage and preferment. Apart from the final verse letters to noblewomen, he composed "The Elegy on Prince Henry" (1613), the epithalamion celebrating the marriage of James's daughter Elizabeth to Count Palatine (1613), the eclogue/epithalamion for the Somerset marriage (1613), and the "Obsequies to the Lord Harrington, brother to the Countesse of Bedford" (1614)—the last of which announced his decision to cease writing poetry. All these works reflect Donne's involvement in courtly society, his need for secular advancement, and his wish to benefit from a complex system of patronage. Given the ambitions, the ambivalence about career pursuits, and the sociopolitical preoccupations expressed in the religious verse and prose he wrote in the seven or eight years before his ordination, it should not be surprising that he wrote poems, such as these, with a strong secular orientation.

The Prince Henry elegy is the one work that, by Donne's own words, he wrote in the context of coterie poetic competition: Jonson told Drummond that "Done said . . . he wrott that Epitaph on Prince Henry . . . to match Sir Ed: Herbert in obscurenesse."[273] Donne joined Herbert and a number of other former clients of the deceased Prince to mourn the royal patron's death in a collection of verse published finally for a wider audience.[274] This group included not only very close friends such as Sir Henry Goodyer, George Garrard, and Sir Christopher Brooke, but other members of Donne's extended social circle such as Hugh Holland and Sir William Cornwallis. Bald concludes from such evidence that "Donne's circle made a concerted effort to celebrate the Prince's memory" (*Life* p. 269). This was no doubt the case, but this was also a special set of coterie socioliterary circumstances in which very specific responses to a shared experience of loss could be rendered in a ceremonially generalized traditional language.

In her study of Donne's Prince Henry elegy in relation to the tradition of poetry in which it participates, Ruth Wallerstein gives an account of the poem that idealizes its historical situation. She contextualizes the work with remarks like the following: " . . . we have to remember how far men of that day still believed in the historical force of the great, good man, and how much real hope England set on Prince Henry. We must remember, too, that Donne believed implicitly in the hierarchy of the state and in the unction of its leaders, despite the mixture of personal disillusion and deep religious pessimism which made him so bitterly cynical of the actual court world and so contemptuous of its hypocrisy."[275] Apart from Wallerstein's problem in reconciling Donne's attitudes toward the Jacobean courtly establishment with his elegiac hyperboles, she is historically mistaken in her basic definition of the poem's coterie meaning. In arguing that "the central theme of Donne's elegy . . . appears to be the same as that treated by the other major elegists: the meaning of the death, the significance, for our view of the universe and of society, of the death of a young and noble man,"[276] she ignores the specific historical context of Donne's and of the other elegists' poems.

The politically active men who had waited upon Prince Henry in his separate courtly establishment responded to the death of the young heir to the throne in terms of the loss of particular hopes and aspirations. Having gravitated toward Prince Henry's court as a satellite center of power from which they could sometimes look critically on the main courtly establishment, they responded to the death of their patron with feelings of hopelessness and abandonment. Sir John Holles, for example, who was the comptroller of the Prince's household, wrote his friend Sir Robert Mansfield in November 1613 about the sorts of disappointment he and his fellows shared:

Virginia, the North West passage, all brave undertakings by sea or land for the honour and benefit of this nation, the reformation and care of a sick, diseased, home state by upholding religion, bettering the policy, moderating the "oligarchal" greatness of Court, of council, opening the passage to virtue with reward of merit to whosoever, in what sphere soever, is gone: our great Hercules hath taken up all these joys and many more up with him and as a worthless people hath left us to the jaws of the lion, the venom of the dragon, the insatiable rapine of the harpies, till the days of our misery be full answerable to our misgiving fears and the menacing prophecies of times past which, while we had him, we held as old wives' tales and ourselves rather in Paradise than in this wretched world.[277]

Aside from the Prince's encouragement of radical Protestantism,[278] his sponsorship of exploration, and his patronage of some of those who were not being advanced in his father's Court, he was associated by Holles with an ideal of preferment through merit. Holles's opposition to the "'oligarchal' greatness of Court, of council" sounds like Greville's contemporary complaint about the "oppressions of the grandees"[279]—the stance of the ambitious men of the gentry who longed for the power and status of successful aristocrats and who used the norm of advancement through merit as the egalitarian means by which they hoped to move upward socially.[280] Furthermore, since

Prince Henry's death occurred only a few months after the (even more politically significant) death of Robert Cecil, Earl of Salisbury,[281] whose demise left open major offices for which a number of candidates competed, the general sociopolitical context in which the elegies for Prince Henry were composed was one of both loss and opportunity.[282]

With its complex thematics and metaphoric virtuosity, Donne's elegy is more a witty metapoetic performance than a poetic memorial for the Prince. In indulging in a "contemplation of the Prince wee misse" (18), it addresses the special awareness and situation of its coterie audience of fellow mourners, men whose hopeful clientage was destroyed and who could understand lines like the following in terms of their sociopolitical loss: "'T were an ambition to desire to fall" (50) and " . . . wee/May saflier say, that wee are dead, then hee" (79–80). Such an audience would have understood Donne's strategy of simultaneously praising Prince Henry and King James in calling the former

> . . . his great father's greatest instrument,
> And activ'st spirit to convey and tye
> This soule of peace through Christianitie.
> (32–34)

Such language glosses over the contrast between James's pacific policies and the Prince's militant Protestantism even as it symbolically transforms the alienation the Prince's clients felt and expressed toward the King and the courtly establishment. Refusing to define the Prince, as they might have, as the kind of capable monarch they hoped would replace the unsatisfactory James, Donne and his fellows, in publishing their elegies, made their private disappointment into the King's and the country's loss—the politic thing to do. But such an unusual outpouring of poetic mourning had its politically subversive side.

Donne may have composed "An Epithalamion, or Marriage Song on the Lady Elizabeth, and Count Palatine being Married on St. Valentine's Day" because, as Bald suggests, he wished to atone for his patron Drury's indiscreet remarks about the man who married James I's daughter.[283] He may also have chosen the occasion for celebration because of Lady Bedford's association with the Princess through her parents, Lord and Lady Harrington, in whose charge the Lady Elizabeth was kept for some years at the beginning of the reign. Finally, Donne may simply have been calling attention to himself as an active courtier involved in the marriage festivities. In any event, there is a kind of sophisticated comic perception built into the poem that marks its author as a social participant in the elaborate courtly ceremonials rather

272 Social Exile and Jacobean Courtier

than as a poet composing deferential complimentary verse on the fringes of that social world.[284] Donne includes himself among the courtly all-night revelers—"we/As Satyres watch the Sunnes uprise" (103–4). He takes the social liberty of writing teasingly about the sexual consummation of the marriage, portraying the new husband's and wife's paying of their marriage "debt" (93) several times over on the wedding night. In depicting the ceremony of putting the bride to bed and greeting the couple the next morning, he refers to the peculiarly public character of wedding nights at the Jacobean court, from which the couple could only retreat by being behind the curtains of the bed.[285] The whole performance in which Donne engages in the poem is that of a man proclaiming his own right to participate in this royal event at a high level of courtly society. Whatever the poem's function as a gift, it is clear that it assumes an audience of equals.

So too, the Somerset eclogue/epithalamion advertises Donne's social connection both to his friend Sir Robert Ker and to that man's more powerful namesake and cousin, the Earl of Somerset, whom Donne served in a secretarial capacity replacing the imprisoned Sir Thomas Overbury.[286] The poem-within-a-poem format of the work, epithalamion text framed by eclogue dialogue, served Donne's purpose as a way of belatedly presenting a marriage poem to Somerset, whose wedding festivities he had missed. Representing himself and his friend Ker in the dialogue of "Idios" and "Allophanes" that begins and ends the work, he expressed his hope that the complimentary poem would be presented to those at Court (particularly Somerset) who could "prize" the poet's "devotion" (235) and thus, of course, reward him for his gift.

This work is unusually preoccupied with the Court as the place of (patronage) favor. The poet, whose retreat to "countries solitude" (2) is depicted as the "dead, and buried" (101) condition of the sociopolitically frustrated man, looks toward the Court as the attractive center of the society, a place where "The Princes favour is defus'd o'r all/From which all Fortunes, Names and Natures fall" (23–24). "Idios" characterizes a James whose secular generosity Donne still hoped to enjoy:

> Kings (as their patterne, God) are liberall
> Not onely'in fulnesse, but capacitie,
> Enlarging narrow men, to feele and see,
> And comprehend the blessings they bestow.
>   (44–47)

In portraying the Jacobean court as a place of "zeale and love" (37) free from "lust and envy" (35) and the monarch himself as the fount of

The Final Secular Poems 273

"Wisedome, and honour" (68), Donne went as far as he ever allowed himself to go in verse toward flattering idealization of the courtly establishment—desperate as he was to succeed finally in obtaining a respectable position in the government through the offices of his patron/employer Somerset. Though there are hints of a critical awareness beneath the surface compliment of this poem—in, for example, the mention of the word "divorce" (127) and the association of the adjective "falne" (207) with the hardly virginal Frances Howard—Donne did not allow his satirically analytical intelligence to operate freely in this work.[287] The wish of his fictional spokesman "Idios" to "burne" (227) rather than send the epithalamion might have been Donne's way of expressing his reservations about performing an act of such brazen poetic flattery, but he did transmit the poem as a gift and, in one letter to a close friend, even went a step further in proclaiming that he was willing to pen a prose defense of the scandalous Essex-Howard divorce that cleared the way for the marriage his poem celebrated.[288] Such behavior prompted R. C. Bald to remark that "Donne's life during his last eighteen months as a layman does not present a particularly edifying spectacle" (*Life*, p. 300).[289]

Through the sterile ingenuity of the "Obsequies to the Lord Harrington, brother to the Countesse of Bedford" Donne paid a final tribute to the woman who served as a patroness for some eight years before his ordination. On the verge of entering orders, Donne used the work as an occasion of announcing his abandonment of poetry and, therefore, of his suitorship to the woman whose help he needed one last time to help him settle his debts. The cover letter he sent Lady Bedford with the poem, however, denied its obvious economic intention: " . . . I do not . . . send this paper to your Ladyship, that you should thanke mee for it, or thinke that I thanke you in it; your favours and benefits to mee are so much above my merits, that they are even above my gratitude . . ." (Grierson, 1:270). When Lady Bedford could not offer Donne as much money as he had hoped, he was quite irritated, as he revealed to his friend Goodyer,[290] and it took some more maneuvering on his part to coerce the Countess into assisting him out of his difficulties.

In the midst of its intellectual and metaphoric preciosity, the poem itself contains clear suggestions that its author was leaving the secular for the religious life, a change he tried to portray in the most favorable light, especially since Lady Bedford thought his past life a poor background for the ministry. In surveying the vices of youth and maturity he seems to have been reflecting on his own liabilities as he bade farewell to the course he had been following for the previous twenty or so years:

> ... age endures
> His Torrid Zone at Court, and calentures
> Of hot ambitions, irreligions ice,
> Zeales agues, and hydroptique avarice,
> Infirmities which need the scale of truth,
> As well, as lust and ignorance of youth. . . .
>   (123–28)

Donne used the praise of the virtue of the deceased young brother of his patroness as an occasion for personal meditation, making it clear that he had his own imminent career change in mind and taking pains to portray secular activities as inferior to religious and ecclesiastical ones:

> Mee thinkes all Cities, now, but Anthills bee,
> Where, when the severall labourers I see,
> For children, house, provision, taking paine,
> They'are all but Ants, carrying eggs, straw, and grain;
> And Church-yards are our cities, unto which
> The most repair, that are in goodnesse rich.
> There is the best concourse, and confluence,
> There are the holy suburbs, and from thence
> Begins Gods City, New Jerusalem,
> Which doth extend her utmost gates to them.
>   (167–76)

Contrasting the worldly greatness Lord Harrington supposedly would have attained with the heavenly glory he is imagined to enjoy, Donne took the opportunity to distance himself morally from the pursuit of political success to which he had devoted himself and which he pretended to be forsaking as he entered the Church (see 183ff.). Donne may have been somewhat serious about his resolution to "interre" his "Muse" (256) in the grave of Lord Harrington, having proclaimed she "spoke her last" (258)—he may, in effect, have intended to write no more poetry—but it is clear that such a sacrifice, in the poem's autobiographical and socioliterary contexts, was bound up, at the time of his ordination, with the gesture of renouncing those secular ambitions with which both his encomiastic and nonencomiastic verse had been connected.[291]

Epilogue:
Donne's Last Poems

Donne took orders on 23 January 1615, formally entering the life of ecclesiastical service recommended for him years before by King James.[1] Although he had to wait close to seven years for a major appointment, some benefits came to him almost immediately. He was made one of the royal chaplains and, as a result of some kingly coercion, Cambridge granted him a Doctor of Divinity degree.[2] He preached at Court regularly in April of each year in his capacity as one of James's "Chaplains-in-Ordinary."[3] He was granted his first benefice by the King, the rectory of Keyston, approximately a year after his ordination, and the second one by Lord Ellesmere (Egerton) shortly after. In October 1616 he was chosen Reader in Divinity for Lincoln's Inn, a post he held until he became Dean of St. Paul's in 1621.[4]

In an Accession Day sermon preached at Paul's Cross on 24 March 1617, Donne expostulated upon the text "He that loveth pureness of heart, for the grace of his lips, the king shall be his friend" (Proverbs 22.11), defining royal "friendship," among other ways, in the context of the benefits he himself obviously hoped to continue enjoying, broadening the scope of the term "King" to refer not just to royal, but also to virtually every other kind of patronage:

. . . by the name of *King* both in the Scriptures, and in *Josephus*, and in many more prophane and secular Authors, are often designed such persons as were not truly of the rank and quality of Kings; but persons that lived in plentiful and abundant fortunes, and had all the temporal happinesses of this life, were called Kings. And in this sense, the Kings friendship that is promised here . . . is *utilis amicitia*, all such friends as may do him good. God promises, that to men thus endow'd and qualified belongs the love and assistance that men of plentiful fortunes can give; great Persons, great in Estate, great in Power and Authority, shall confer their favours upon such men, and not upon such as only serve to swell a train, always for *ostentation*, sometimes for *sedi-*

tion; much less shall they confer their favours upon *sycophants* and *buffoons*; least of all upon the servants of their vices and voluptuousness; but they whom God hath made Kings in that sense, (Masters of abundant fortunes) shall do good to them only who have this *pureness of heart*, and *grace of lips*. (*Sermons*, 1:211)

It is not difficult to detect in this passage Donne's own continuing desire for the rewards of patronage.[5] Especially in the period from his ordination to the time of his being made Dean of St. Paul's, he still continued to act on his strong ambitions: Bald remarks that "he appears as one who had mastered at last the arts of the courtier, and it is clear, even when he finally turned to the Church, that he did not intend to abandon those arts, but to rise by them" (*Life*, p. 301). The death of his wife in 1617 and his serious illness in 1623—the latter recorded in the beautifully self-scrutinizing *Devotions*—may mark turning points in which Donne's religious commitment deepened,[6] but, especially before his being appointed to the deanship, a position he won largely through the assistance of the infamous Duke of Buckingham,[7] he continued to seek advancement. He traveled to Germany in 1619 on the Doncaster embassy, serving the King's needs; he still cultivated friends in high places; and he preached regularly at Court, both in the late Jacobean and the early Caroline period. His *Sermons* and his *Devotions* reflect continuing political preoccupations.

After his ordination, Donne composed relatively little verse, some 700 lines, including the 390-line versification of Scripture, "The Lamentations of Jeremy, for the most part according to Tremelius."[8] Among the other pieces are a Latin poem to George Herbert, "To Mr. Tilman after he had taken orders," two or three late *Holy Sonnets*, "A Hymne to Christ, at the Authors last going into Germany," "A Hymne to God the Father," "Upon the translation of the Psalmes by Sir Philip Sidney, and the Countesse of Pembroke his Sister," "A Hymne to God my God, in my sicknesse," and "A Hymne to the Saints, and to Marquesse Hamylton." Some of these works reveal a mixture of worldly and spiritual motives; some demonstrate Donne's interest in politics and religiopolitical foreign affairs; some attest to continuing relations with friends and patrons. While particular poems seem to have been released to a kind of general manuscript circulation as the work of a man able to accept a limited role as a poet-priest, it is evident that Donne regarded his days of writing poetry as largely over and poetic composition as inappropriate for someone in his position, especially after he became Dean of St. Paul's.[9]

Apparently on the very day of his ordination, Donne wrote a

Latin poem to George Herbert, who was, at the time, a fellow of Trinity College, Cambridge, treating this younger brother of his friend Sir Edward Herbert as someone who appeared to be heading for the kind of secular success he had repeatedly failed to win for himself. This boundary poem stands paradoxically as both his gesture of valediction to the world and as a symptom of his reluctance to forsake secular ambitions. In "To Mr. George Herbert, with my Seal, of the Anchor and Christ," Donne explicates the symbolic meaning of his newly adopted seal—the image of Christ on an anchor/cross—portraying it as a sign of his shift to a career of ecclesiastical service. At the same time, however, he looked longingly at the secular sphere of activity as he wished Herbert well in his pursuit of worldly success, hoping for him the many royal bounties ("Plura . . . Regia . . . [21–22]) he himself still desired in some form. Both David Novarr and Helen Gardner note the appropriateness of this work to its primary coterie reader, a man who, in turn, replied to it with some lines of his own.[10] Gardner reads the first seven lines of Herbert's Latin poem "In Sacram Anchoram Piscatoris" as a formal reply to Donne's epistolary verse.[11] It is thus another example of a relationship of verse exchange in which Donne participated as a coterie author.

Novarr connects with George Herbert another of the poems expressing Donne's ambivalent feelings about his priestly calling, "To Mr. Tilman after he had taken orders," suggesting that "Herbert . . . called Donne's attention to Tilman's problem of choosing between the secular and religious life and to his poem, with his own [Donne's] situation very much in mind."[12] As Gardner has observed in analyzing the piece as a response to Tilman's verses, in this patently self-preoccupied poem Donne ignores the reason Tilman gave for being reluctant to enter the ministry ("personal unworthiness"), and "congratulates Tilman for triumphing over 'Lay-scornings of the Ministry'," thus revealing his own concern with the "unattractiveness of the clerical profession from a worldly point of view."[13] Although I agree with Gardner that Donne "writes in a high other-worldly strain, to glorify the priest's calling, which the foolish world 'disrespects'," I disagree with her definition of the tone and motivation of the lines: "There is an accent of warm sincerity . . . as in all Donne's references to his late-adopted profession."[14] Instead of "warm sincerity," I detect a kind of characteristic self-persuasive urgency rooted in Donne's uncomfortable mixture of secular and religious motives and his ambivalent feelings about his own vocation. Still inordinately concerned with status and place, Donne used the opportunity of answering the Tilman poem to engage, probably before a sympathetic and knowledgeable coterie reader such as George Herbert, in the kind of self-persuasion that would justify his own decision to take orders and present his actions in their best light:

> Why doth the foolish world scorne that profession,
> Whose joyes passe speech? Why do they think unfit
> That Gentry should joyne families with it;
> As if their day were onely to be spent
> In dressing, Mistressing and complement?
> (26–30)

As an ambitious courtier who had engaged in the very activities named in this last line, Donne argues a little too insistently that the ministry, that haven for prospectless younger brothers of the gentry, was a socially respectable profession:

> Let then the world thy calling disrespect,
> But goe thou on, and pitty their neglect.
> What function is so noble, as to bee
> Embassadour to God and destinee?
> (35–38)

His own ambition and self-esteem were at stake in such lines and his coterie reader would have understood this.[15]

Donne's wife Ann died at the age of thirty-three in 1617 of childbirth fever after delivering a stillborn baby in her tenth pregnancy. In three subsequent poems Donne seems to have connected his response to her death with his conflicted feelings about his still-active worldly aspirations: the sonnet "Since she whome I lovd, hath payd her last debt," "A Hymne to Christ, at the Authors last going into Germany," and "A Hymne to God the Father." In each work the languages of emotional loss and of renunciation bring together the two preoccupations.

The sonnet on the death of his wife clearly reveals a tension between Donne's spiritual motives and secular attachments. Donne explains that the death of his spouse, like her life, moved him to orient his desires toward heavenly, rather than worldly, ends:

> Since she whome I lovd, hath payd her last debt
>   To Nature, and to hers, and my good is dead,
> And her soule early'into heaven ravished,
> Wholy in heavenly things my mind is sett.
> Here the admyring her my mind did whett
> To seeke thee God. . . .
> (1–6)

The loss of a wife is made into an occasion for purifying the poet's motives. But this leads to an association of "more love" (11), the (potentially idolatrous) attachment to Ann More, with the realm of the secular—"the World, fleshe, [and] Devill" (14)—and, therefore, changes the deceased wife from a medium of contact with God into an obstacle in the way of a wholehearted religious commitment. Working through mourning in this way involves not simply coming to terms with the loss of a beloved spouse but also, somewhat cruelly, rejecting her along with the secular world with which the poem associates her.

Like the sonnet, "A Hymne to Christ, at the Authors last going into Germany" attempts to come to terms with Donne's deep ambivalence about rejecting worldly values and ambitions. As a "bill of . . . Divorce to All" (22), the hymn not only alludes to the poet's ties to a deceased wife and to living friends and family, but also to "Fame, Wit, Hopes" (25), the "false mistresses" (25) of "youth" (24) he had not yet really repudiated. The yearning for death, which (as Gardner notes)[16] Donne criticized in the first sermon he delivered on his return, seems both a way of continuing mourning as well as yet another request for a divine punishment that could rectify his motives. Like the Tilman poem and the (possibly) late *Holy Sonnets* "O to vex me," this hymn deals with the combination of secular and religious desires with which Donne lived at the time he wrote it.

There is a prose text parallel to this hymn that can serve as a gloss on some of the poem's themes—the "Sermon of Valediction"[17] Donne preached to his beloved Lincoln's Inn congregation. Associating parting with dying in the manner of the earlier valedictory lyrics, this work focuses on "repentance" (*Sermons*, 2:373) and "conversion and regeneration" (*Sermons*, 2:379)—that is, on the strengthening of the speaker's (and listeners') religious-devotional desires and commitments. Several elements in the sermon suggest that, in the circumstances of his imminent departure, Donne was deeply bothered by the worldly purposes of the journey. He makes a point of suggesting (generally of men, but particularly of himself) that the "heats of youth" become in "middle age" the sin of "Ambition" and in "old age" those of "covetousness" (*Sermons*, 2:385). He reminds himself and his congregation that "men fraught with honor and riches" have no "use" if "that lead them not to the honor and glory of the Creator" (*Sermons*, 2:385). He seems to have been trying to put James's general and particular favors to him in a moral perspective by stating: " . . . what purpose soever thy Parents or thy Prince have to make thee great, how had all these purposes been frustrated, if God had not made thee before? . . . soe what degrees or titles soever a man have in the world, the greatest of all is the first of all, that he had a being by Creation . . . " (*Sermons*, 2:387).

Donne's preoccupation with worldly "offices," including ecclesiastical ones, comes through in his meditation on the persistence of worldly "impressions" in the souls of the damned:

. . . those impressions which we have received from men, from nature, from the world, the image of a Lawyer, the image of a Lord, the image of a Bishop may all burne in hell, but they cannot be burnt out, not onely not those soules, but not those offices shall returne to nothing, but our condemnation shalbe everlastingly aggravated for the ill use of those offices. And therefore Remember thy Creator, who as he made thee of nothing shall hold thee still to his glory, though to thy confusion, in a state capable of his heaviest judgment; for the Court of God is not like other Courts, that after a surfett of pleasure or greatnes a man may retyre, after a surfett of sin there is no such retyring, as a dissolving of the Soule into nothing: and therefore remember that he made thee, thou wast nothing, and what he made thee, thou canst not be nothing againe. (*Sermons*, 2:388)

In the light of his misgivings about becoming a part of the luxurious Doncaster embassy, "one of the most opulent diplomatic expeditions to leave English shores since the Field of the Cloth of Gold" (in the words of one historian),[18] Donne preached to himself as much as to his listeners about the damnation awaiting the man more concerned with "offices" and "Courts" than with his own spiritual condition. As he prepared to depart for the Continent, Donne was clearly caught between two types of "courtiership"—worldly and religious.[19] The above passage immediately precedes his affectionately personal farewell to his congregation.

Some two weeks before his depature, Donne wrote Goodyer, expressing his emotional turmoil, feelings that were evidently a combination of regrets about leaving his motherless children, concern about his personal health, fears about exposing himself to Catholic enemies on the Continent, and, as in the hymn, guilt about his mixed religious and secular motives: "I leave a scattered flock of wretched children, and I carry an infirme and valetudinary body, and I goe into the mouth of such adversaries, as I cannot blame for hating me, the Jesuits, and yet I go. Though this be no service to my Lord: yet I shall never come nearer doing him a service, nor do any thing liker a service then this" (*Letters*, pp. 174–75). In poem, letter, and sermon, then, with various degrees of privacy and publicity, Donne dealt with the experience of leaving England as part of an ambassadorial mission. Novarr places "A Hymne to Christ, at the Authors last going into Germany" in a set of socioliterary circumstances halfway between Donne's usual situation of coterie poetic transmission and a more extensive (manuscript) transmission of verse:

> It is likely that he voluntarily wrote the hymn partly to express for himself and to dramatize for others the resolution of his apprehensions about departing for Germany and partly out of a feeling that it was entirely fitting that, in his role as chaplain, he give public expression to an attitude, unexceptional and orthodox but still stamped with his own characteristic mark, which he considered proper to inculcate in those for whose religious guidance he was responsible. The widespread availability of the hymn in manuscript is an indication that Donne was not averse to its being known.[20]

As Novarr suggests, Donne probably sent the hymn to Sir Robert Ker along with the large collection of verse he gave his friend in 1619. In this case, such a testamentary gesture would have fit in with the thematics of the poem itself. The poem was occasional just as the occasion was made poetic—metaphorized in both verse and prose.

Donne apparently expressed some willingness to be known to an extended manuscript audience as a minister-poet. "A Hymne to God the Father" represents his attempt to write liturgical verse, poetry suitable for singing in Church.[21] The appearance of this piece in so many manuscripts attests to its author's allowing it to travel beyond his usual coterie readership. But at the same time, the poem seems to express, by way of what Harry Morris has called the "terrifying pun"[22] on the deceased Ann More's name, some quite disturbing personal feelings. As in the sonnet on his wife's death and "A Hymne to Christ, at the Authors last going into Germany," Donne associates the purgation of his sins and of his baser worldly desires with the loss of his spouse—as though she had been a focus for a spiritual idolatry that encompassed all his faults: "that sinne where I begunne" (1), "those sinnes through which I runne" (3), "that sinne by which I'have wonne/ Others to sinne" (7–8), "that sinne which I did shunne/A yeare, or two: but wallowed in, a score" (9–10) and, finally, the "sinne of feare, that when I'have spunne/My last thred, I shall perish on the shore" (13–14). In its punning insistence on "done" and "more," the bases of all the poem's rhymes, Donne composes another poetic "bill of . . . Divorce," turning mourning into renunciation and self-hatred into religious *contemptus mundi*, setting emotionally intense private experience, as in the sermons, in a public mode of communication. The degree to which the poem's puns were heard or read as autobiographical utterances depended, of course, on the auditor or reader: what friends like Garrard and Goodyer could have perceived as personally expressive a more general audience might have understood as a conventional language of religious experience.

Two of Donne's other late poems reflect his interest in the plight of European (particularly German) Protestantism at the start of the Thirty Years' War. The sonnet "Show me deare Christ" and the biblical paraphrase "The Lamentations of Jeremy, for the most part according to Tremelius" both seem to have been written in the charged atmosphere of international crisis of the early 1620s. Gardner, for example, dates "Show me deare Christ" after the defeat of the Elector Palatine's Protestant forces in October 1620.[23]

Although "Show me deare Christ" mentions the Church that "rob'd and tore/Laments and mournes in Germany and here" (3–4), referring probably to the defeats German Protestants were suffering and to the sympathetic response of their English coreligionists (who grumbled with varying intensity at James's pacific policies), the sonnet seems less concerned with current events than with an issue Donne himself raised a number of times in his poetry and prose, that of Church unity. The rhetorical questions of the poem undermine sectarian certainty as Donne rejects both Protestant and Catholic claims to exclusive truth:

> Show me deare Christ, thy spouse, so bright and cleare.
>   What, is it she, which on the other shore
> Goes richly painted? or which rob'd and tore
> Laments and mourns in Germany and here?
> Sleepes she a thousand, then peepes up one yeare?
> Is she selfe truth and errs? now new, now'outwore?
> Doth she,'and did she, and shall she evermore
> On one, on seaven, or on no hill appeare?
> Dwells she with us, or like adventuring knights
> First travaile we to seeke and then make love?
>   (1–10)

Donne's poem may be expressing, as Gardner suggests, a typical "Anglican refusal to choose one of two mutually exclusive positions."[24] In the context of James's foreign policy and the calls for a holy war by more militant English Protestants who criticized the King's accommodations to Spain, however, Donne's emphasis on the need for a Universal Church might have been read as support for James's approach to European religious conflict.[25]

The sonnet is a problematical, witty, and, finally, shockingly indecorous poem. Its final conceit, as critics have noted, portrays the Church as an adulterous wife and Christ as a wittol:

> Betray kind husband thy spouse to our sights,
> And let myne amorous soule court thy mild Dove,
> Who is most trew, and pleasing to thee, then
> When she'is embrac'd and open to most men.
>
> (11-14)

Such sexual-religious metaphorizing, like that of the earlier sonnet, "Batter my heart," marks this poem as a highly self-conscious work appropriately directed to a very restricted audience: hence its unique appearance in the Westmoreland manuscript. Gardner speculates: "If Donne deliberately withheld it from publication, it might well be because he thought it was too witty a poem for a man of his profession to write."[26]

As a biblical paraphrase, the "Lamentations of Jeremy" is a more public and publicizable poem than the sonnet "Show me deare Christ." Gardner believes that Donne designed the work to be sung in church services "in penitential season."[27] It thus may represent another effort to enact the public role of minister-poet. Novarr substantially agrees with Gardner's conjecture, but adds that "the manuscripts . . . indicate that the poem did not circulate widely." He relates the poem to the political frustration the poet probably felt following the Doncaster mission, after which Donne hoped to "be rewarded by promotion to a higher office in the Church," assuming he wrote the work "either to distract himself, or to provide further evidence of his talents." Novarr explains its restriction of circulation by noting that Donne aggressively campaigned for the position of Dean of St. Paul's from August 1621 on, was chosen by the King in September and "put ["The Lamentations of Jeremy"] aside instead of circulating it widely when he threw himself into seeking active support wherever he might find it."[28]

The poem is an abortive attempt to comment, from an ecclesiastical vantage point, on current religious warfare. Gardner notes that, given the contemporary analogy between "the distress of the German Protestants" and "the captivity of Zion,"[29] Lamentations was an appropriate text for Donne to translate.[30] She notes that Donne preached a sermon on a text from Lamentations on 5 November 1622, an occasion for celebrating James's deliverance from the Gunpowder Plot. But the differences rather than the similarities between the two works are interesting and may partly explain Donne's restriction of the poem to a narrow coterie audience. The sermon is a strong pro-royalist political statement arguing that the weakening of monarchy spells doom for a state. It exculpates the King from the sins of his "inferiour instruments" (*Sermons*, 4:252), his corrupt officers, and attacks those Puritans who criticized James's foreign policy as they pretended only to "pray" (*Sermons*, 4:253) that he not decline into Catholicism. This sermon articulates the ideology of royal absolutism as it attacks those in Parliament and in the pulpit who blamed the King for an insufficiently strong anti-Catholic stance in foreign policy. In the light of what occurred in the Parliament of 1621 and what was transpiring between the King and the Spanish ambassador Gondomar, this panegyrical political sermon speaks with the kind of prophetic-priestly authority Donne felt able to exercise only *after* the King granted him the deanship of St. Paul's. It thus differs markedly in context and meaning from the poetic translation of the Lamentations passages. What would have been read in the poem as a call for more militant measures to combat (Spanish) Catholic forces is, in the sermon, a defense of James's pacific policies of accommodation and of limited response. Given the sensitivity of the public issue, it is no wonder the poem was not distributed widely.

In "The Lamentations of Jeremy" Donne seems to have been using Scripture in the simultaneous personal and public manner he practiced in the *Essays in Divinity*, *Devotions*, and *Sermons*.[31] It is hard to read a passage like the following apart from the kinds of comments Donne habitually made about his past life:

> I am the man which have affliction seene,
>   Under the rod of Gods wrath having beene,
> He hath led mee to darknesse, not to light,
> And against mee all day, his hand doth fight.
>   (177–180)

Lewalski has suggested that the poem was "an outgrowth of [Donne's] interest in the Sidney psalms,"[32] poems he probably liked for their fusion of private and public idioms, works, therefore, that would have served as models for the style Donne adopted in his personalized public rhetoric.

"Upon the translation of the Psalmes by Sir Philip Sidney, and the Countesse of Pembroke his Sister" evidently was used by Donne as patronage verse. Novarr connects its composition with the death of the Countess on 25 September 1621, with Donne's association with the Sidney-Pembroke circle, and with his pursuit of the deanship of

St. Paul's: "The death of the Countess gave him an opportunity to call himself to the attention of [William Herbert, 3rd Earl of] Pembroke in the hope that he might see fit to support him. . . . Here, more than in any other poem that he wrote after his ordination, Donne's motive was the motive behind his earlier poetry of patronage—self-advancement."[33] However seriously Donne took the instructive role of the psalm translators ("They tell us *why*, and teach us *how* to sing" [22]), Donne obviously intended the poem primarily as an encomiastic offering, like the verse letters to Lady Bedford, and demonstrated that he was not unwilling, before he won the ecclesiastical preferment he desired, to exercise himself in this mode.

In his role as Dean of St. Paul's, however, he felt an obvious reluctance to write poetry of this kind. When his good friend Sir Robert Ker asked him to compose an elegy commemorating the deceased Marquess Hamilton, Donne complied with an epicede, but felt that writing verse was inappropriate for someone of his station.[34] Donne was unwilling to risk the limited publicity even the restricted circulation of his poem brought, trying to prevent the kind of response he obviously did receive in John Chamberlain's comment on the verses: " . . . though they be reasonable wittie and well don yet I could wish a man of his yeares and place to give over versifying."[35] The time for encomiastic poetry had passed for Donne, even the time for the customary coterie circulation of his verse.

One other late poem deserves comment, "Hymne to God my God, in my sicknesse," one of Donne's finest lyrics. Written, apparently, during the same 1623 illnesss in which he composed the *Devotions*, this eloquent religious poem embodies in the public genre of the hymn the private, but religiously exemplary, self-scrutiny of the man trying to prepare himself for "holy dying."[36] The work deals with some expected themes—the faith in the Resurrection, the yearning for Heaven, and the redemptive nature of a suffering that participates in the meaning of Christ's Passion, but it also, in the light of Donne's other uses of religiopolitical language, ironically portrays death and exaltation as the attainment of a success missed in life:

> So, in his [Christ's] purple wrapp'd receive me Lord,
>   By these his thornes give me his other Crowne;
> And as to others soules I preach'd thy word,
>   Be this my Text, my Sermon to mine owne,
> Therefore that he may raise the Lord throws down.
>
> (26–30)

Some twenty years earlier, when he wrote he Lord Keeper who had dismissed him from service, hoping to be reinstated as secretary, Donne had used a similar language: "I have . . . no way before me; but must turn back to your Lordship, who knowes that redemtion was no less worke than creation" (*Selected Prose*, pp. 119–20). In the hymn, God is portrayed as the beneficient patron who dispenses a final, spiritual reward.

Eight years later, Donne, in effect, preached his own funeral sermon a few days before his death, but "Hymne to God my God, in my sicknesse" was a premature valedictory gesture, finally restricted in circulation after the poet recovered from his illness. Gardner notes that a copy of the poem was in the possession of Sir Julius Caesar, whom Donne may have known directly or through an old friend like Sir Lionel Cranfield.[37] It appears in only one other Group III manuscript, was first published in the 1635 edition of the poetry, and, thus, was quite restricted in its original circulation. Apart from the obvious impropriety of having a poetic farewell to the world circulate freely after his recovery, the wish to put strict limits on its transmission is consistent with Donne's reluctance to compose the elegy for the Marquess Hamilton. The poetical Dean wanted to be finished with poetry.

By this time, however, Donne was a practiced and successful writer of sermons, and, while he neither wished to compose more verse nor continue to transmit poetry to coterie audiences, he had been giving copies of some of his sermons to appreciative readers and considered the transmission of his religious prose in printed form. Evelyn Simpson notes that, after the first two of Donne's sermons were published in 1622, one by order of the King (since it defended his *Directions for Preachers*), the other at the behest of the Virginia Company, Donne's attitude toward publication changed:

Donne was evidently pleased, and anxious to distribute copies to his friends, and it is from this point that we can date his growing realization that some of his sermons might have a future life in print. Hitherto none of his sermons had been published, though it was nearly eight years since he had taken Holy Orders. A few of them, such as *A Sermon of Valediction*, and the sermon on *Matthew* 2.44, preached before the Countess of Montgomery, had circulated in handwritten copies among his friends, but these could reach very few readers, and their life would obviously be short. Now he began to realize the potentialities of the printed word. Another sermon . . . would be printed in 1623, and in 1624 he would hasten to print the *Devotions upon Emergent Occasions* which were composed during his sickness and convalescence. In the autumn of 1625 in his enforced seclusion at Chelsea he would revise and write out in full as many as eighty of his sermons, and so the way was prepared for the eventual publication of the three great Folios of his sermons. (*Sermons*, 4:36)

No longer regarded as a "stigma," then, print became for Dean Donne an extension of the public authority he exercised before King, Court, and the large congregrations before whom he preached. The coterie character of most of his earlier work had suited the conditions of his relative powerlessness. As a sanctioned religiopolitical spokesman, however, Dean Donne could freely publish his words in printed form.[38]

Notes
Index

Notes

PREFACE

1. Bald (*Life*, pp. 241–42) suggests that Donne might also have contemplated printing his poems in 1611.
2. Robert Krueger suggests, however, that this was not an unusual situation. He says of the poet Sir John Davies: "When Davies decided to publish his epigrams he may have been in the same position as Donne was upon his decision to publish—forced to ask friends for copies of his poems because he could not supply them all himself. If so, Davies may not have received all the epigrams. Or it may be he had most of his epigrams at hand and made no attempt to gather the remainder. The point is that an author could easily lack copies of his own poems" (*The Poems of Sir John Davies*, ed. Robert Krueger, with introduction and commentary by the editor and Ruby Nemser [Oxford: Clarendon Press, 1975], p. 122; citations of Davies's poetry are from this edition).
3. See Bald, *Life*, p. 296. Peter Beal (*Index of English Literary Manuscripts* [London and New York: Mansell Publishing Ltd., 1980], 1:245) suggests that the fall of the Earl of Somerset was also a factor.
4. See Geoffrey Keynes, *A Bibliography of Dr. John Donne, Dean of St. Paul's*, 4th ed. (Oxford: Clarendon Press, 1973), pp. 164–67, 173–78.
5. See J. W. Saunders, "Donne and Daniel," *Essays in Criticism* 3 (1953): 109–14. In another essay, Saunders calls Donne a "courtly satellite whose poetry was essential to his private life and thinking, but whose primary ambition was nonliterary and who therefore saw no justification in making poetry public" ("The Social Situation of Seventeenth-Century Poetry," in *Metaphysical Poetry*, ed. Malcolm Bradbury and David Palmer, Stratford-upon-Avon Studies, no. 11 [London: Edward Arnold and New York: St. Martin's Press, 1970], p. 250). Patricia Thomson argues that Donne "belonged with his own kind, with Sir Henry Wotton, Sir Henry Goodyer, Sir Thomas Roe, and his other courtier friends, and had his place in a scheme of social rather than literary patronage" ("Donne and the Poetry of Patronage: *The Verse Letters*," in *John Donne: Essays in Celebration*, ed. A. J. Smith [London: Methuen, 1972], p. 310). Cf. Arthur F. Marotti, "John Donne and the Rewards of Patronage," in *Patronage in the Renaissance*, ed. Guy Fitch Lytle and Stephen Orgel (Princeton, N.J.: Princeton University Press, 1982), pp. 207–34.

6. Listing Donne's friends, patrons, and patronesses in the three decades in which almost all of his poems were written (1593–1623) gives a sense of his various coterie audiences. In addition to those already named, the following individuals probably read some of the manuscript-circulated poetry (and/or prose) Donne composed: Samuel Brooke, Thomas Woodward, Beaupre Bell, Sir William Cornwallis, Ben Jonson, Sir Lionel Cranfield, Joseph Hall, Sir Thomas Roe, and Sir James Hay. Other friends and acquaintances perhaps also should be added, among them Hugh Holland, Richard Martin, John Pory, Sir Richard Baker, John Hoskins, Sir Francis Wooley, Sir Toby Mathew, Sir Francis Bacon, William Hakewill, Sir Julius Caesar, Sir Robert More, Sir Robert Cotton, Sir Maurice Berkeley, and the Earl of Northumberland. See Bald passim and the lists of names found in the following: Alan MacColl, "The Circulation of Donne's Poems in Manuscript," in *John Donne: Essays in Celebration*, ed. Smith, pp. 28–46, and A. Alvarez, *The School of Donne* (1961; repr. New York and Toronto: New American Library, 1967), pp. 143–48. Cf. Alexander Sackton, "Donne and the Privacy of Verse," *Studies in English Literature* 7 (1967): 67–82. Beal remarks that Donne's poems "were read, copied, and circulated in manuscript, within limited social groups, perhaps sharing some of Donne's values and assumptions, MSS themselves having a personal significance not possessed by printed books. Appropriately, if in a playful context, Donne himself testified to the special value which MSS might have, in his Latin poem to Dr Andrews, written when he had received from Andrews a MS copy of one of Donne's books which Andrews' children had torn up: 'sed quae scripta manu, sunt veneranda magis . . .'" (Grierson 1:397). The relevant passage has been translated by Edmund Blunden:

> What Printing-presses yield we think good store,
> But what is writ by hand we reverence more:
> A book that with this printing-blood is dyed
> On shelves for dust and moth is set aside,
> But if't be penned it wins a sacred grace
> And with the ancient Fathers takes its place. . . .
>
> (1:245)

7. Apparently the man with whom Donne shared lodgings in the early Jacobean period, George Garrard, also had access to much of Donne's verse (see Bald, *Life*, p. 159n) as did Rowland Woodward.

8. Quoted in W. Milgate, *Satires, Epigrams and Verse Letters*, p. lix.

9. See my essay "Countertransference, the Communication Process, and the Dimensions of Psychoanalytic Criticism," *Critical Inquiry* 4 (1978): 471–89. In it I use the work of recent "Object-Relations" psychoanalysts to emphasize the social dimension of individual psychology, arguing that the artist's or writer's "fantasies . . . are shaped by his personal way of internalizing his culture's symbolic code" (486).

10. I have used this book in its fourth edition: J. B. Leishman, *The Monarch of Wit: An Analytical and Comparative Study of the Poetry of John Donne*, 4th ed. (London: Hutchinson, 1959).

INTRODUCTION

1. See J. W. Saunders, "The Stigma of Print: A Note on the Social Bases of Tudor Poetry," *Essays in Criticism* 1 (1951): 139-64, and *The Profession of English Letters* (London: Routledge and Kegan Paul and Toronto: Univ. of Toronto Press, 1964), pp. 31-48.

2. Francis Meres, *Palladis Tamia* (1958) in *Elizabethan Critical Essays*, ed. with an introduction by G. Gregory Smith (London: Oxford Univ. Press, 1904), 2:317.

3. Quoted in Bruce Pattison, *Music and Poetry of the English Renaissance* (London: Methuen, 1948), p. 36.

4. *The Letters and Epigrams of Sir John Harington*, ed. Norman E. McClure (Philadelphia: Univ. of Pennsylvania Press, 1930), p. 320. Further citations are from this edition.

5. Although he printed his translation of Ariosto and the whimsical *Metamorphosis of Ajax*, Harington did not think of himself as a professional author and avoided printing his occasional verse.

6. Saunders, "Stigma of Print," p. 153.

7. Smith, *Elizabethan Critical Essays*, 2:224.

8. Preface to *Poly-Olbion*, in *Works*, ed. J. William Hebel (Oxford: Clarendon Press, 1961), 4:v. In the preface to his famous miscellany, the printer Richard Tottel complained about the "horders up" of poems who kept them from the general public (*Tottel's Miscellany* [1557-1587], ed. Hyder Rollins, 2nd ed., 2 vols. [Cambridge, Mass.: Harvard Univ. Press, 1965], 1:2). George (?) Puttenham praised the verse of "Courtly makers Noble men and Gentlemen of her Maiesties owne seruauntes, who haue written excellently well as it would appeare if their doings could be found out and made publicke . . . " (*The Arte of English Poesie, 1589* [facs. repr. Menston, England: The Scolar Press, 1968], p. 49).

9. *The Works of Thomas Campion*, ed. Walter R. Davis (Garden City, N.Y.: Doubleday, 1967), p. 55.

10. J. W. Saunders, "From Manuscript to Print: A Note on the Circulation of Poetic MSS. in the Sixteenth Century," *Proceedings of the Leeds Philosophical and Literary Society* 6.8 (1951): 513-14.

11. Saunders, "From Manuscript to Print," pp. 514-15.

12. Saunders, "From Manuscript to Print," p. 517. For a discussion of the practice of writing commendatory verse, see Franklin B. Williams, "Commendatory Verses: The Rise of the Art of Puffing," *Studies in Bibliography* 19 (1966): 1-14.

13. E. F. Hart, ("The Answer-Poem of the Early Seventeenth Century," *Review of English Studies* n.s. 7 [1956]: 19-29) distinguishes four kinds of answer poems: "the answer proper, in which the theme or arguments of a poem are criticized as a whole, or (more usually) refuted one by one" (22), "imitations" (24) such as the transformation of Pembroke's "Soules joy" into Herbert's "A Parodie," "extension poems [that] develop or amplify some idea, im-

age, or characteristic feature of rhythm or style of the original poem" (25), and "'Mock-songs'" (27). The custom of composing answer poems is a long-standing one by the seventeenth century.

14. Saunders, "Stigma of Print," p. 152.

15. Saunders, "From Manuscript to Print," p. 517.

16. J. B. Leishman, "'You Meaner Beauties of the Night,' A Study in Transmission and Transmogrification," *The Library*, 4th ser., vol. 26 (1945): 99–121.

17. For a discussion of this manuscript (BL Add. MS 17492), see Raymond Southall, *The Courtly Maker: An Essay on the Poetry of Wyatt and His Contemporaries* (New York: Barnes and Noble, 1964), pp. 16–21, and Richard Harrier, *The Canon of Sir Thomas Wyatt's Poetry* (Cambridge, Mass.: Harvard Univ. Press, 1975), pp. 23–29.

18. See *The Arundel Harington Manuscript of Tudor Poetry*, ed. Ruth Hughey, 2 vols. (Columbus: Ohio State Univ. Press, 1960).

19. This manuscript has been edited by Laurence Cummings as "John Finet's Miscellany" (Ph.D. diss., Washington Univ., St. Louis, Mo., 1960).

20. L. G. Black, "Studies in Some Related Manuscript Poetical Miscellanies of the 1580's," 2 vols. (D.Phil. thesis, Oxford, 1970), 1:50. Black's unpublished thesis, which concentrates on Bod. Rawl. Poet. MS 85, Cambr. Univ. Lib. MS Dd.5.75, Marsh Lib. MS Z.3.5.21, Folger MS V.a.89, BL Harl. MS 7392, is the best available study of sixteenth-century manuscript miscellanies.

21. See L. G. Black, "Manuscript Poetical Miscellanies," 1:55–59, and "Some Renaissance Children's Verse," *Review of English Studies* n.s. 24 (1973): 1–16. This manuscript has been edited by Steven May, "Henry Stanford's Anthology: An Edition of Cambridge U. Library MS Dd.5.75" (Ph.D. diss. Univ. of Chicago, 1968).

22. See *The Farmer-Chetham Manuscript*, ed. Alexander Grosart (Manchester: Chetham Society, vol. 89, 1873); James Lee Sanderson, "An Edition of an Early Seventeenth-Century Manuscript Collection of Poems (Rosenbach MS 186 [renumbered as 1083/15])" (Ph.D. diss. Univ. of Pennsylvania, 1960) and "Epigrames P[er] B[enjamin] R[udyerd] and Some More 'Stolen Feathers' of Henry Parrot," *Review of English Studies* n.s. 17 (1966): 241–55; and Robert Krueger, "Sir John Davies: *Orchestra* Complete, *Epigrams*, Unpublished Poems," *RES* n.s. 13 (1962): 17–124.

23. Black, "Manuscript Poetical Miscellanies," 1:247.

24. Black, "Manuscript Poetical Miscellanies," 1:22.

25. See William Bond, "The Cornwallis-Lysons Manuscript and the Poems of John Bentley," in *Joseph Quincy Adams Memorial Studies*, ed. James G. McManaway, Giles E. Dawson, and Edwin E. Willoughby (Washington, D.C.: The Folger Shakespeare Library, 1948), pp. 683–93.

26. Stephen Booth remarks that "Most readers and editors have agreed with George Steevens' inference (1780), that 'probably this sonnet was designed to accompany a present of a book consisting of blank paper,' a 'table book' like the one Hamlet mentions (I.v.98–107) . . . " (*Shakespeare's Sonnets*,

ed. with analytic commentary by Stephen Booth [New Haven and London: Yale Univ. Press, 1977], p. 267).

27. See Katharine K. Gottschalk, "Discoveries Concerning British Library MS Harley 6910," *Modern Philology* 77 (1979–80): 121–31.

28. Hughey, *Arundel Harington Manuscript* 1:66.

29. Rollins, *Tottel's Miscellany*, 2:92–93.

30. *The Paradise of Dainty Devices, 1576–1606*, ed. Hyder E. Rollins (Cambridge, Mass.: Harvard Univ. Press, 1927), p. xiii.

31. See the introductions to the following editions: *The Phoenix Nest, 1593*, ed. Hyder E. Rollins (Cambridge, Mass.: Harvard Univ. Press, 1931) and *A Poetical Rhapsody, 1602–1621*, ed. Hyder Edward Rollins, 2 vols. (Cambridge, Mass.: Harvard Univ. Press, 1931–32). Rollins (*Phoenix Nest*, p. xvii) notes that these miscellanies were the only published ones edited by gentlemen rather than printers.

32. For an excellent discussion of the idea of "laureateship," see Richard Helgerson, *Self-Crowned Laureates: Spenser, Jonson, Milton and the Literary System* (Berkeley, Los Angeles, London: Univ. of California Press, 1983).

33. George Gascoigne's A Hundreth Sundrie Flowres, ed. with an introduction and notes by C. T. Prouty, Univ. of Missouri Studies, 17. 2 (1942; repr. Columbia: Univ. of Missouri Press, 1970), p. 49. Further references are included in the text.

34. On the "setting of themes" in Renaissance schools, see Hoyt Hudson, *The English Epigram in the Renaissance* (Princeton, N.J.: Princeton Univ. Press, 1947), pp. 145–53. Douglas Peterson relates the practice to the poetic debate and to legal mooting. (*The English Lyric From Wyatt to Donne: A History of the Plain and Eloquent Styles* [Princton, N.J.: Princeton Univ. Press, 1967], pp. 72–73.

35. On the social custom of reading aloud, see William Nelson, "From 'Listen, Lordings' to 'Dear Reader,'" *University of Toronto Quarterly* 46 (1976–77): 110–24. Edward Doughtie remarks that "Most of the really vital literary forms of the sixteenth century were written with the possibility of oral performance in mind: sermons, plays, and song lyrics, of course—even romances and long poems were probably read aloud to small groups" (*Lyrics from English Airs, 1596–1622*, ed. Edward Doughtie [Cambridge, Mass.: Harvard Univ. Press, 1970], p. 36).

36. See Rudolph Gottfried, "Autobiography and Art: An Elizabethan Borderland," in *Literary Criticism and Historical Understanding*, ed. Phillip Damon, English Institute Essays (New York: Columbia Univ. Press, 1967), pp. 109–34. If one looks at the kinds of "titles" used in works like Tottel's *Miscellany*, one discovers an attempt to recreate, if in general form, some sense of social context for the poems. The practice of situating verse biographically and socially goes back to the appended "vidas" and "razos" of troubadour verse (see Maurice Valency, *In Praise of Love: An Introduction to the Love-Poetry of the Renaissance* [New York: Macmillan, 1958], pp. 90–91 and Paul Zumthor, *Langue, Texte, Énigme* [Paris: Seuil, 1975], p. 178) and to the tradition, in Petrarch commentaries, of presenting a quasi-narrative account of the situations

of particular poems. Vellutello, for example, makes the relationship of lovers in the *Canzoniere* into a romantic narrative (see Luigi Baldacci, *Il Petrarchismo Italiano Nel Cinquecento* [Milan and Naples: Riccardo Ricciardi, 1957], p. 52).

37. See my discussion of Sidney in "'Love is not love': Elizabethan Sonnet Sequences and the Social Order," *ELH* 49 (1982): 399–406.

38. For a discussion of Sidney's situation see James M. Osborn, *Young Philip Sidney, 1572–1577* (New Haven and London: Yale Univ. Press, 1972), especially pp. 496–509 and *The Poems of Sir Philip Sidney*, ed. William Ringler (Oxford: Clarendon Press, 1962), pp. 435–47 (citations of the poetry are from this edition.). Cf. Richard Lanham, "Sidney: The Ornament of His Age," *Southern Review* 2 (1967): 319–40.

39. See Patricia Thomson, *Sir Thomas Wyatt and His Background* (Stanford, Calif.: Stanford Univ. Press, 1964) and Stephen Greenblatt, *Renaissance Self-Fashioning: From More to Shakespeare* (Chicago and London: Univ. of Chicago Press, 1980), pp. 115–56.

40. Jonathan Kamholtz, "Thomas Wyatt's Poetry: The Politics of Love," *Criticism* 20 (1978): 349–65.

41. Rollins, *Poetical Rhapsody*, 2:166.

42. The Farmer-Chetham MS, for example, opens with a larger number of prose selections, from the description of the arraignment of the Earl of Essex on charges of treason through letters by Essex, Lady Rich, and others, including Ralegh.

43. *The Poems of Sir Arthur Gorges*, ed. Helen Sandison (Oxford: Clarendon Press, 1953), p. xxxvi. Cf. Rollins, *Phoenix Nest*, pp. 76–85, and Michael Rudick, "The 'Raleigh Group' in *The Phoenix Nest*," *Studies in Bibliography* 24 (1971): 131–37.

44. Rosenbach MS 243/4, p. 73.

45. Cf. Maria Corti's discussion of "desemiotization" in *An Introduction to Literary Semiotics*, trans. Margherita Bogat and Allen Mandelbaum (Bloomington and London: Indiana Univ. Press, 1978), p. 19.

46. Michel Foucault, "What Is an Author?", in *Textual Strategies: Perspectives in Post-Structuralist Criticism*, ed. with an introduction by Josué V. Harari (Ithaca, N.Y.: Cornell Univ. Press, 1979), pp. 141–60.

47. See Grierson, 2:lxxix–cliii, and Gardner, *Elegies and Songs and Sonnets*, pp. lxii–xcix, and *Divine Poems*, pp. lvi–cxviii.

48. *Divine Poems* p. lxiv.

49. Margaret Crum, "Notes on the Physical Characteristics of Some Manuscripts of the Poems of Donne and of Henry King," *The Library* 16 (1961): 132.

50. Alan MacColl, "The New Edition of Donne's Love Poems," *Essays in Criticism* 17 (1967): 258–63.

51. The manuscripts that Alan MacColl discusses in "The Circulation of Donne's Poems in Manuscript" (in *John Donne: Essays in Celebration*, ed. Smith, pp. 28–46) belong mainly to times some ten to twenty-five years after the poems' original time of composition. The presence or absence of titles in manuscripts and manuscript groups probably indicate the closeness or distance from original circumstances of coterie circulation. Gardner notes that

the Group I manuscripts associated with Donne's attempt in 1614 to gather his verse for publication generally lack titles for individual poems (showing signs of Donne's only having begun the job of providing them), while the Group II manuscripts contain more titled pieces probably because Donne felt the need, in giving his work to Ker in 1619, to include them since the poems were far removed from their original socioliterary circumstances. Significantly, the Westmoreland manuscript, associated with a close friend of the poet, lacks titles entirely ("The Titles of Donne's Poems," in *Friendship's Garland: Essays Presented to Mario Praz on His Seventieth Birthday* [Rome: Edizioni di Storia e Letteratura, 1966], 1:189–207). Manuscript-circulated verse and poems in manuscript miscellanies usually lack titles (and often authors' names), their original social contexts having served to frame them.

52. *Elegies and Songs and Sonnets*, p. lxxii.

53. See Peters, *Paradoxes and Problems*, pp. lxxi and lxxix.

54. Beal (Index, 1:247) notes that the "Conway Papers" contain copies of this poem, the Somerset Epithalamion, and "Goodfriday, 1613. Riding Westward" in the hand of Donne's close friend Sir Henry Goodyer.

55. See MacColl, "Circulation of Donne's Poems," pp. 41–42; Crum, "Physical Characteristics," pp. 131–32; Gardner, *Elegies and Songs and Sonnets*, p. lxxxii.

56. See Jonson's epigram, "To Lucy, Countesse of Bedford, with Mr. Donnes Satyres," in *The Complete Poetry of Ben Jonson*, ed. William B. Hunter, Jr. (1963; New York: Norton, 1968), p. 42. (Jonson's poetry is cited in this edition.)

57. See Milgate, *Satires, Epigrams and Verse Letters*, pp. xlii–lxi.

58. *Elegies and Songs and Sonnets*, p. lxxxii. MacColl states that "the only apparent mention of the *Songs and Sonnets* during Donne's lifetime is the entry 'Thone Dones lyriques' in a list of books read by William Drummond in 1613" ("Circulation of Donne's Poems," p. 31).

59. *Elegies and Songs and Sonnets*, p. lxxxii.

60. Gardner's translation, aided by John Sparrow, quoted by Helen Gardner, "'A Nocturnall upon St. Lucy's Day, being the shortest day'," in *Poetic Traditions of the English Renaissance*, ed. Maynard Mack and George deForest Lord (New Haven and London: Yale Univ. Press, 1982), p. 188.

61. Quoted in Milgate, *Satires, Epigrams and Verse Letters*, p. lix.

62. Robert A. Bryan ("John Donne's Poems in Seventeenth-Century Commonplace Books," *English Studies* 43 [1962]: 170–74) notes that the following lyrics do not appear in the nineteen commonplace books he examined in the United States: "A Nocturnall upon S. Lucies Day," "The Blossom," "The Primrose," "The Relique," "The Dissolution," "A Jeat Ring Sent," "Negative Love," and "Farewell to Love." Gardner (*Elegies and Songs and Sonnets*, p. lxv) notes that there are nine lyrics missing from the Group I manuscripts: "A Nocturnall upon S. Lucies Day," "The Dissolution," "Farewell to Love," "Witchcraft by a Picture," "A Jeat Ring Sent," "Negative Love," "The Expiration," "The Computation," and "The Paradox." Of these, five were pieces that, I believe, Donne "loosely scattered in [his] youth" ("A Jeat Ring Sent,"

"Farewell to Love," "Witchcraft by a Picture," "The Expiration," and "The Computation")—poems that he didn't get back into his possession in 1614 when he was gathering in his verse. Of the others, "The Dissolution," "Negative Love," and "The Paradox" strike me as exchange/competition poems associated with Donne's relationship with someone like Sir Edward Herbert. "A Nocturnall upon S. Lucies Day," the scarcest of all the lyrics in the manuscripts, may have been Donne's most private poem.

63. Crum, "Physical Characteristics," p. 131.
64. See Krueger/Nemser, *John Davies*, p. 389.
65. See Grierson, 2:ciii–iv, and Gardner, *Elegies and Songs and Sonnets*, pp. lxv–vii.
66. See Grierson, 2:civ–v, and Gardner, *Elegies and Songs and Sonnets*, pp. lxviii–ix.
67. *Elegies and Songs and Sonnets*, p. lxxvi.
68. Grierson, 2:cvii.
69. Crum, "Physical Characteristics," p. 127; cf. Grierson, 2:cvii and Gardner, *Elegies and Songs and Sonnets* pp. lxxviii–ix.
70. For the former, see Milgate, *Satires, Epigrams and Verse Letters*, pp. li–ii. For the latter, see Alan MacColl, "A New Manuscript of Donne's Poems," *Review of English Studies*, n.s. 19 (1968): 293–95.
71. See Beal, *Index*, 1:256 and 561–62 for a discussion of this manuscript that, for many years, was believed to have been destroyed. Grierson says that "The chief interest of the collection is that is comes from the commonplace book of Sir Henry Wotton, and therefore presumably represents the work of the group of wits to which Donne, Bacon, and Wotton belonged" (2:267–68). Grierson (1:437–43) prints a number of poems from this manuscript written by authors other than Donne.
72. MacColl ("Circulation of Donne's Poems," p. 29) estimates that Donne's poems appear in some 100 extant manuscripts. The fullest list of these is to be found in *The Complete Poetry of John Donne*, ed. with an introduction, notes, and variants by John Shawcross (Garden City, N.Y.: Doubleday, 1967), pp. 422–27.
73. For a more recent discussion of the authorship of "The Expostulation" and some of the other "dubious" elegies, see D. Heywood Brock, "Jonson and Donne: Structural Fingerprinting and the Attribution of Elegies XXXVIII–XLI," *Papers of the Bibliographical Society of America* 72 (1978): 519–27.
74. See Gardner's discussion of these works in *Elegies and Songs and Sonnets*, pp. xxxi–xlix.
75. This term is used by John Stevens (*Music and Poetry in the Early Tudor Court* [Lincoln: Univ. of Nebraska Press, 1961], p. 206) to define the kind of aesthetic transaction that took place in courtly coterie verse. Cf. Thomas O. Sloan's discussion of the "transactional" rhetoric of Donne's poem to the Earl of Dorset ("The Crossing of Rhetoric and Poetry in the English Renaissance," in *The Rhetoric of Renaissance Poetry From Wyatt to Milton*, ed. Thomas O. Sloan and Raymond B. Waddington (Berkeley, Los Angeles, London: Univ. of California Press, 1974), pp. 223–25. What Joan Webber has said of Donne the

preacher applies, I believe, to Donne the poet as well—that "the building of an audience into the work itself is characteristic of Donne. He often looks past himself in the mirror to see who is looking on, and then recognizes that his own poise is accordingly affected. . . . He constantly imagines himself under observation, imagines a complexity of reaction on the part of the observer" (*The Eloquent 'I': Style and Self in Seventeenth-Century Prose* [Madison: Univ. of Wisconsin Press, 1968], p. 25).

76. E. H. Gombrich (*Meditations on a Hobby Horse*, 2nd ed. [London and New York: Phaedon, 1971], p. 37) says that the game in sophisticated art from the Renaissance onward "presupposes the trained response of the connoisseur, who repeats the artist's imaginative performance in his own mind."

77. Cf. the Preface to the Reader of *The Alchemist*, in *Ben Jonson*, ed. C. H. Herford, Percy and Evelyn Simpson, 11 vols. (Oxford: Clarendon Press, 1925–52), 5:291. Except for the poetry, all citations of Jonson's works are from this edition.

78. *Ben Jonson*, 1:138.

79. Lewis Theobald, Preface, *The Works of Shakespeare* (1733), in *John Donne: The Critical Heritage*, ed. A. J. Smith (London and Boston: Routledge and Kegan Paul, 1975), p. 197.

80. John Dryden, *A Discourse Concerning the Original and Progress of Satire* (1693), in Smith, *Donne: Critical Heritage*, p. 151.

81. Gregory Bateson, "A Theory of Play and Fantasy," in *Steps to an Ecology of Mind* (New York: Ballantine Books, 1972), p. 178.

82. Gregory Bateson, "Information and Codification: A Philosophical Approach," in Gregory Bateson and Jurgen Ruesch, *Communication: The Social Matrix of Psychiatry* (New York: Norton, 1951), p. 209.

83. What Roman Jakobson has said of poetry in general pertains particularly to coterie verse: "Virtually any poetic message is a quasi-quoted discourse with all those peculiar, intricate problems which 'speech within speech' offers to the linguist" ("Linguistics and Poetics," in *The Structuralists: From Marx to Levi-Strauss*, ed. Richard and Fernande De George [New York: Doubleday, 1972], p. 112). Cf. Umberto Eco on the poem as a "metasemiotic statement" in *A Theory of Semiotics* (Bloomington and London: Indiana Univ. Press, 1976), p. 261.

84. Stanley Fish, *Self-Consuming Artifacts: The Experience of Seventeenth-Century Literature* (Berkeley, Los Angeles, London: Univ. of California Press, 1972), passim. Recently this phenomenon has been discussed in Tillotama Rajan, "'Nothing Sooner Broke': Donne's *Songs and Sonnets* as Self-Consuming Artifacts," *ELH* 49 (1982): 805–28.

85. See Joan Webber, *Contrary Music: The Prose Style of John Donne* (Madison: Univ. of Wisconsin Press, 1963), p. 12 and passim and Donald Friedman, "Memory and the Art of Salvation in Donne's Good Friday Poem," *English Literary Renaissance* 3 (1973): 421.

86. Rosalie L. Colie has suggested that this was Donne's method in *Biathanatos* (*Paradoxica Epidemica: The Renaissance Tradition of Paradox* [Princeton, N.J.: Princeton Univ. Press, 1966], p. 501n).

87. Thomas Carew, "An Elegie upon the death of the Dean of Paul's, Dr Iohn Donne," in Smith, *John Donne: Critical Heritage*, p. 95.

88. Jasper Mayne, "On Dr Donnes death," in Smith, *John Donne: Critical Heritage*, pp. 97–98.

89. The relationship of Donne's poems to their different social circumstances is suggested, however, by the title used in the 1719 edition, *Poems on Several Occasions* . . . (Grierson, 2:lxxiv).

CHAPTER ONE

1. In the "Conversations with Drummond," *Ben Jonson*, 1:135.

2. For a discussion of the Inns as law schools and as social environments, see Philip Finkelpearl, *John Marston of the Middle Temple: An Elizabethan Dramatist in his Social Setting* (Cambridge, Mass., Harvard University Press, 1969), pp. 3–80, and Wilfrid R. Prest, *The Inns of Court Under Elizabeth I and the Early Stuarts* (London: Longman, 1972).

3. Those who did not have the status of gentlemen, of course, could use the Inns as a means of elevating their social standing. In satirizing such social climbing, Joseph Hall wrote of the commoner's son who was sent for social polishing to the

> . . . Ins of Court of the Chancerie:
> There to learn law, and courtly carriage,
> To make amends for his meane parentage,
> Where he vnknowne and ruffling as he can,
> Goes current each-where for a Gentleman. . . .

(*Virgedemiarum*, IV.2.54–58 in *The Collected Poems of Joseph Hall*, ed. Arnold Davenport [Liverpool: Liverpool Univ. Press, 1949], p. 56).

4. See Bald, *Life*, pp. 50–52, and Dennis Flynn, "Donne's First Portrait: Some Biographical Clues?", *Bulletin of Research in the Humanities* 82 (1979): 7–17.

5. "Amoretto" of *The Second Part of the Return from Parnassus*, in *The Three Parnassus Plays (1598–1601)*, ed. with an introduction and commentary by J. B. Leishman (London: Ivor Nicholson & Watson, 1949).

6. See Leishman's discussion of these plays in relation to their literary and social contexts (*Three Parnassus Plays*, pp. 24–92).

7. John Hoskins, *Directions for Speech and Style*, ed. Hoyt H. Hudson (Princeton, N.J.: Princeton Univ. Press, 1935), p. 11. Subsequent citations are to this edition, by page number.

8. See Lawrence Stone, "The Educational Revolution in England, 1560–1640," *Past and Present* 28 (1964): 41–80, and "Social Mobility in England, 1500–1700," *Past and Present* 33 (1966): 16–55. Cf. Wallace MacCaffrey, "Place and Patronage in Elizabethan Politics," in *Elizabethan Government and Society:*

Essays Presented to Sir John Neale, ed. S. T. Bindoff, J. Hurstfield, and C. H. Williams (London: Althone Press, 1961), pp. 95–126.

9. *The Works of Francis Bacon*, ed. James Spedding, Robert Ellis, and Douglas Heath, 14 vols. (London: Longman, 1857–74), 8:108. Subsequent citations of Bacon's work are to this edition, cited as *Works*, by volume and page number.

10. Lawrence Stone has recently observed that "'my friends' . . . before the eighteenth century always meant no more than 'my advisors, associates and backers.' This category often indicated a relative, particularly a parent or an uncle by blood or marriage. But it could also include . . . a person of high status and influence with whom there was acquaintance and from whom there was hope of patronage" (*The Family, Sex, and Marriage in England, 1500–1800* [New York: Harper & Row, 1977], p. 97).

11. *Gabriel Harvey's Marginalia*, ed. G. C. Moore Smith (Stratford-upon-Avon: Shakespeare Head Press, 1913), p. 87.

12. See Finkelpearl, *Marston*, pp. 178–94.

13. See Kenneth Charlton, "Liberal Education and the Inns of Court in the Sixteenth Century," *British Journal of Educational Studies* 9 (1960–61): 25–38. John Stow (*A Survey of London*, reprinted from the text of 1603 with introduction and notes by Charles L. Kingsford [Oxford: Clarendon Press, 1908], 1:75–76) mentions the public lectures in surgery, mathematics, divinity, astronomy, music, geometry, civil law, medicine, and rhetoric available at the beginning of the seventeenth century in London.

14. See Finkelpearl, *Marston*, pp. 19–31.

15. In the dedication to *Every Man Out of His Humour* (*Ben Jonson*, 3:421). Cf. Finkelpearl, *Marston*, pp. 70–80.

16. Prest, *Inns of Court*, p. 41.

17. Quoted in Bald, *Life*, p. 72.

18. *Gesta Grayorum*, ed. Desmond Bland (Liverpool: Liverpool Univ. Press, 1968), p. 6.

19. Finkelpearl, *Marston*, p. 36.

20. *Gesta Grayorum*, p. 53. Marie Axton has observed: "By these Christmas king-games the Inns of Court men prepared themselves for government service. Their revels kingdom differed in one crucial aspect from its model; while England was ruled successively by a boy and two women, the lawyers always chose a king. When they took their plays and masks to Greenwich or Whitehall to entertain Elizabeth, their Christmas Prince rode in triumph through London with all the pomp appropriate to a monarch. The lawyers' hierarchy affirmed a 'god-given,' male-dominated, power structure broken by the death of Henry VIII . . . " ("The Tudor Mask and Elizabethan Court Drama," in *English Drama: Forms and Development, Essays in Honour of Muriel Clara Bradbrook*, ed. Marie Axton and Raymond Williams [Cambridge: Cambridge Univ. Press, 1977], p. 32).

21. See Spedding's comment in *Works*, 8:342–43.

22. Finkelpearl remarks: "It seemed to have been a natural function—it was at any rate their self-appointed task in the sixteenth and seventeenth cen-

turies—for the lawyers of the Inns of Court to 'instruct' their governors on their proper duties and responsibilities" (*Marston*, p. 22).

23. *Gesta Grayorum*, p. 82.

24. Finkelpearl, *Marston*, p. 41.

25. *Gesta Grayorum*, p. 58.

26. For a good discussion on the Inns as a literary milieu, see Robert Ellrodt, *L'Inspiration Personnelle et L'Esprit du Temps chez Les Poètes Métaphysiques Anglais*, (Seconde Partie) *Les origines Sociales, Psychologiques et Littéraires de la Poésie Métaphysiques au Tournant du Siècle* (Paris: Corti, 1960), pp. 13–42, 185–92, 284–91, and passim.

27. Clarendon, quoted in Prest, *Inns of Court*, p. 223.

28. See Prest, *Inns of Court*, pp. 153–58.

29. Mark Curtis, "The Alienated Intellectuals of Early Stuart England," *Past and Present* 23 (1962): 25–41.

30. Finkelpearl, *Marston*, pp. 67–69.

31. Louise Brown Osborn, *The Life, Letters, and Writings of John Hoskyns, 1566–1638* (1937; repr. Hamden, Conn.: Archon Books, 1973), p. 71.

32. In one of his private memoranda in the early Jacobean period, Bacon noted that he should "corresp[ond] wth Salis.[bury] in a habite of naturall but nowayes perilous boldness" (*Works*, 11:52). Donne's employer, Sir Thomas Egerton, wrote in just such a style to Sir Robert Cecil in 1599, remarking "I am sparing of verbal professions and trust you like me not the worse for it" (*HMC Salisbury*, 9:119).

33. John Marston, *The Fawn*, ed. Gerald A. Smith [Lincoln: Univ. of Nebraska Press, 1965), p. 24.

34. Logan Pearsall Smith, *The Life and Letters of Sir Henry Wotton*, 2 vols. (Oxford: Clarendon Press, 1907), 1:307.

35. See Bald, *Life*, pp. 45–46. John Carey emphasizes the importance of Donne's Catholicism and apostasy in his recent study (*John Donne: Life, Mind and Art* [New York: Oxford Univ. Press, 1981], especially pp. 15–59).

36. Bald writes that "At Thavies Inn in 1591 Donne was not only a Catholic, influenced and guided by Catholic tutors, but also in contact with the most active Catholic proselytizers in England" (*Life*, p. 63). For a discussion of Donne's Inns-of-Court period, see Bald, *Life*, pp. 53–79.

37. Donne wrote his friend George Garrard in 1612 of his somewhat casual attitude toward the law: "I ever thought the study of it my best entertainment and pastime . . . " (*Letters*, p. 255).

38. Ellrodt (*L'Inspiration*, p. 23) mentions satire, epigram, the philosophical poem, the Ovidian elegy, verse epistles, lyrics in the new manner, and the prose paradox, essay, and character as forms that flourished in the Inns environment. Cf. Finkelpearl, *Marston*, pp. 19–31.

39. For provocative discussions of the topic of the mixing of genres, see Rosalie Colie, *The Resources of Kind: Genre-Theory in the Renaissance*, ed. Barbara K. Lewalski (Berkeley, Los Angeles, London: Univ. of California Press, 1973), and *Shakespeare's Living Art* (Princeton, N.J.: Princeton Univ. Press, 1974), pp. 68–134. Cf. Corti, *Literary Semiotics*, pp. 115–43.

40. See D. J. Palmer, "The Verse Epistle," in Bradbury and Palmer, *Metaphysical Poetry*, pp. 73–99.

41. See also R. C. Bald, "Donne's Early Verse Letters," *Huntington Library Quarterly* 15 (1952): 283–89.

42. Finkelpearl, *Marston*, p. 30.

43. Printed in Milgate, *Satires, Epigrams and Verse Letters*, p. 212.

44. For the preceding poems, see the notes in Milgate, *Satires, Epigrams and Verse Letters*, pp. 210–22.

45. Grierson (2:111) makes this suggestion on the basis of the note by Drummond "After C. B. Coppy," but Milgate (*Satires, Epigrams and Verse Letters*, p. 128) believes the evidence is weak.

46. Milgate (*Satires, Epigrams and Verse Letters*, pp. 117, 127) dates the first satire 1593 and the second sometime shortly after the appearance of the atrocious sonnet-sequence *Zepheria* (1594).

47. The valuable, recent monograph by M. Thomas Hester (*Kinde Pitty and Brave Scorn: John Donne's Satyres* [Durham, N.C.: Duke Univ. Press, 1982]), says little about the immediate social contexts of the poems.

48. John Webster, *The Duchess of Malfi*, ed. John Russell Brown (Cambridge, Mass.: Harvard Univ. Press, 1964), p. 10.

49. See O. J. Campbell, *Comicall Satyre and Shakespeare's "Troilus and Cressida"* (San Marino, Calif.: Huntington Library, 1938), pp. 59–61.

50. In *The Second Part of The Return from Parnassus* this character comes onstage reading Juvenal and expressing admiration for "truth telling *Aretine*" (Leishman, *Parnassus Plays*, pp. 225–26).

51. Harington, *Letters and Epigrams*, p. 66.

52. John Wilcox ("Informal Publication of Late Sixteenth-Century Verse Satire," *Huntington Library Quarterly* 13 [1950]: 191–200) has argued that writers like Donne, Harington, Davies, and Hall composed satire to draw the attention and patronage of the Court rather than simply to criticize the age for its corruption.

53. Isaac Walton, "The Life of Dr. John Donne," in John Donne, *Devotions* (Ann Arbor: Univ. of Michigan Press, 1959), p. xxxiv.

54. See Prest, *Inns of Court*, pp. 40–41.

55. See Brian Gibbons, *Jacobean City Comedy: A Study of the Satiric Plays by Jonson, Marston and Middleton* (Cambridge, Mass.: Harvard Univ. Press, 1968), pp. 32–49.

56. See the discussion in Hester, *Kinde Pitty*, pp. 54–72. See also Sister M. Geraldine, "John Donne and the Mindes Indeavours," *Studies in English Literature* 5 (1965): 115–31; Thomas V. Moore, "Donne's Use of Uncertainty as a Vital Force in *Satyre III*," *Modern Philology* 67 (1969): 41–49; Camille Slights, *The Casuistical Tradition in Shakespeare, Donne, Herbert, and Milton* (Princeton, N.J.: Princeton Univ. Press, 1981), pp. 160–67; and Thomas Sloan, "The Persona as Rhetor: An Interpretation of Donne's *Satyre III*," *Quarterly Journal of Speech* 51 (1965): 14–27.

57. Milgate (*Satires, Epigrams and Verse Letters*, pp. 139–40) dates the poem sometime in 1594 or 1595, that is, at a time Donne was probably moving away

from his Catholicism, but had not yet embraced the established Church. Paul Sellin's recent attempt at dating the poem in 1620 ("The Proper Dating of John Donne's 'Satyre III'," *Huntington Library Quarterly* 43 [1980]: 275–312) is not likely to win much support.

58. See the copy of the Bishops' order of 1599 printed in *Joseph Hall*, ed. Davenport, pp. 293–94.

59. Milgate notes (*Satires, Epigrams and Verse Letters*, p. 135) that these lines were omitted by the editor of the 1633 edition of Donne as politically dangerous.

60. Slights (*Casuistical Tradition*, p. 164) observes that this attitude toward human authority is a typical casuistic stance.

61. See Robert Southwell, *An Humble Supplication to her Majestie*, ed. R. C. Bald (Cambridge: Cambridge Univ. Press, 1953). Southwell's work, in the context of the anti-Catholic legislation of the 1590s (see J. E. Neale, *Elizabeth I and Her Parliaments*, 2 vols. [London: Cape, 1953–57] 2:280–97), is an impassioned plea to lessen the persecution of his coreligionists. In it, he assures Queen Elizabeth of the patriotic loyalty of her Catholic subjects, but he objects to the requirement that they attend Protestant services. He characterizes Catholic priests as missionaries facing martyrdom rather than as seditious traitors posing a danger to the state. Finally, at a time when England was still at war with Spain, Southwell claims that one of the Protestants' chief polemical adversaries, the Jesuit Robert Parsons, was responsible for the courteous treatment of the English, including English prisoners-of-war, by the Spaniards.

62. See John Phillips, *The Reformation of Images: Destruction of Art in England, 1535–1660* (Berkeley, Los Angeles, London: Univ. of California Press, 1973), p. 205.

63. See Prest, *Inns of Court*, p. 159 and Krueger/Nemser, *John Davies*, pp. xxx–xxxi.

64. Gardner states: "The evidence of the manuscripts suggests that Donne's *Elegies*, like his *Satires*, circulated as a set of poems, and that there was probably a 'book of Elegies' as there was a 'book of Satires'" (*Elegies and Songs and Sonnets*, p. xxxi). She suggests that the publication in 1595 of Campion's elegies in *Poemata* (a book Donne owned and annotated) might have prompted Donne to "put together his own Book of Elegies, making it up by including, among poems modelled on Ovid and rehandlings of Ovidian themes, some Verse-Paradoxes composed independently" (*Elegies and Songs and Sonnets*, p. xxxiii). The compilation of a "book" of elegies, then, if it took place at all, would have come at a stage after the initial composition and circulation of at least some of the poems. I agree with Roma Gill's belief that "Donne's scattering of poems [cannot] be viewed as a projected collection, a 'book of Elegies' such as Ovid and Propertius have left" ("*Musa Iocosa Mea*: Thoughts on the *Elegies*," in Smith, *John Donne: Essays in Celebration*, p. 50).

The canon of the *Elegies* is unclear. I shall deal with the fourteen poems Gardner prints in her edition (the thirteen elegies of the Group I MSS plus "A Funeral Elegy") in addition to "The Autumnal," which she lists separately. I think it makes sense to regard "Image of her whom I love," as Gardner does, as a lyric, and to put "The Expostulation," "Julia," "A Tale of a Citizen and his Wife," "Variety," the heroical epistle "Sappho to Philaenis" and "His Parting from Her" in the category of "Dubia" (See *Elegies and Songs and Sonnets*, pp. xxxi–xlvi). The last of these, a remarkably uneven work stylistically, might have been the result of "composite authorship" (*Elegies and Songs and Sonnets*, p. xlii).

65. "'Blanda Elegeia': The Background to Donne's 'Elegies'," *Modern Language Review* 61 (1966): 357–68. Cf. Leishman, *Monarch of Wit*, pp. 52–106, and Alan Armstrong, "The Apprenticeship of John Donne: Ovid and the *Elegies*," *ELH* 44 (1977): 419–42.

66. John Carey has remarked: "To the young man . . . at the turn of the sixteenth century who wished to write outrageous or shocking love-poetry, Ovid, the Ovid of the *Ars* and the *Amores* was the obvious model. At School he would have seen enough of these works to whet his appetite and, to whet it further, detailed study of it was forbidden. They were anathema for Puritan and moral writers, and their concentration on the hard facts of money and sex, along with their bright, brittle cynicism, gave them an irresistibly modern ring" ("The Ovidian Love Elegy in England," D.Phil. thesis, Oxford Univ., 1960 [pp. 125–26]). Carey's excellent unpublished study is the finest treatment of its subject to date, surveying the English love elegy in the contexts of both European (Neo-Latin and vernacular) writing and English literary history.

67. *Works of Thomas Campion*, p. 403.

68. Carey observes that the "recognition . . . of similarity between the two metropolitan cultures, Augustan Rome and late-Elizabethan London, is of the utmost importance in the development of the love-elegy fashion" ("Ovidian Love Elegy," p. 135).

69. In his "Elegie upon the death of . . . Donne," Carew refers to the almost total absence of mythological material from Donne's verse:

> . . . the goodly exil'd traine
> Of gods and goddesses . . . in thy just raigne
> Were banish'd nobler Poems.
> (Grierson, 1:379)

70. Donne also pointedly excluded such other features of the traditional love-elegy as the formal (nondramatic) monologue, the *lena* and *dives amator* figures, the *exclusus amator* theme, the emotional brutality represented by a work like Ovid's poem on Corinna's abortion (*Amores* II.13), and the high degree of explicit literary self-consciousness exemplified in the repeated use of the eternizing conceit.

71. Donne and Marston both helped to reinvent formal satire, Davies and Donne composed vernacular epigrams, Campion and Donne composed elegies, and Lodge boasted of his verse letters: "For my Epistles, they are in that kind, wherein no Englishman of our time hath publiquely written" (Address to the "Gentleman Readers" of *A Fig for Momus* [1595], quoted in Palmer, "Verse Epistle," p. 76).

72. Gill, "*Elegies*," p. 47.

73. "Elegiacs . . . more especially erotic elegy, and hendecasyllables . . . should be entirely banished, if possible, [from a school curriculum]; if not absolutely banished, they should be reserved for pupils of a less impressionable age" (*The Institutio Oratoria of Quintilian*, trans. H. E. Butler, Loeb Classical Library [London: Heinemann and New York: Putnam, 1921], 1:149).

74. Bald (*Life*, p. 47) believes that Donne probably came across Marlowe's translation of the *Amores* while he was at Cambridge.

75. Some of these works are prurient or pornographic. See, for example, the poem in Rosenbach 1083/15 beginning "Nay pish: nay pue: nay fayth" (Sanderson, "Edition," pp. 9–10), a bawdy dramatic monologue found in a large number of manuscripts. This same commonplace-book anthology also includes Marlowe's translation of *Amores* I.5 (Sanderson, "Edition," p. 209), the classical source of Donne's "Going to Bed."

76. Thomas Nashe, *The Anatomie of Absurditie*, in *The Works of Thomas Nashe*, ed. Ronald B. McKerrow, reprinted with corrections, ed. F. P. Wilson (Oxford: Basil Blackwell, 1958), 1:30.

77. See W. Leonard Grant, *Neo-Latin Literature and the Pastoral* (Chapel Hill: Univ. of North Carolina Press, 1965), pp. 38–43, and Carey, "Ovidian Love Elegy," pp. 30–53 and 99–110 for discussions of the Neo-Latin amorous elegy. Humanist writers, using the Latin language for male audiences, felt free to compose more explicitly erotic, if not prurient, verse than was possible in the vernacular. Donne and others claimed the same freedom for their vernacular love elegies.

78. For the young gentlemen of the Inns of Court, erotic adventurism, at least the pretense of it, was a way of imitating the greater sexual freedom of the nobility and, at the same time, a means of attacking the Puritan morality of the London citizenry. See Lawrence Stone, *The Crisis of the Aristocracy, 1558–1641* (Oxford: Oxford Univ. Press, 1965), pp. 662–68.

79. Carey, "Ovidian Love Elegy" p. 197.

80. On the tradition of paradoxy, see Colie, *Paradoxica Epidemica*, passim; Peters, *Paradoxes and Problems*, pp. xvi–xxvii; and Henry Knight Miller, "The Paradoxical Encomium with Special Reference to its Vogue in England, 1600–1800," *Modern Philology* 53 (1956): 145–78.

81. See, for example, Leishman, *Monarch of Wit*, pp. 74–81, and Wilbur Sanders, *John Donne's Poetry* (Cambridge: Cambridge Univ. Press, 1971), pp. 27–43.

82. *The Diary of John Manningham of the Middle Temple, 1602–1603*, ed. Robert Parker Sorlien (Hanover, N.H.: The University Press of New England, 1976), pp. 191–92.

83. See Peters, *Paradoxes and Problems*, p. xxi, and R. E. Bennett, "Four Paradoxes by Sir William Cornwallis, The Younger," *Harvard Studies and Notes in Philology and Literature* 13 (1931): 219–40.

84. Peters, (*Paradoxes and Problems*, p. lxvi) argues that this piece, usually attributed to Donne, was not written by him.

85. See Paradox 3 (pp. 4–6); in Paradox 8, Donne mocks, in passing, "sely old mens exclayming agaynst our tymes and extolling ther owne" (p. 17).

86. See Paradoxes, 2, 8, and 10.

87. Donne observes of himself and his fellows in Paradox 7, " . . . now when our superstitious civility of manners is become but a mutuall tickling flattery of one another, allmost every man affects an humor of jeasting, and is content to deject, and deforme himself, yea to become foole, to none other end that I can spy, but to give his wise companions occasions to laughe, and to shew themselves wise" (p. 16).

88. In the light of his own religious struggles, it is interesting to note that, in this paradox, Donne remarks that "Controversies in religion" can increase "Religion it selfe. For in a troubled misery men are allwayes more religious then in a secure peace" (p. 20).

89. In commenting on Donne's letter about his own Paradoxes, Colie emphasizes the fact that "paradoxes flourish in a period with many competitive 'truths'" (*Paradoxica Epidemica*, p. 37), serving as the means to question orthodoxies even as they wittily undo themselves as artifacts.

90. On the literary background of this elegy, see Gardner, *Elegies and Songs and Sonnets*, p. 138, and Leishman, *Monarch of Wit*, pp. 74–81.

91. Leishman says that "Donne flings moderation to the winds and overwhelms us with a continuous fire of short analogical or syllogistic arguments which follow one another so rapidly that we have scarcely time to detect or to protest against their fallaciousness" (*Monarch of Wit*, p. 80).

92. Gabriel Harvey (*Marginalia*, p. 232) notes the contemporary popularity of Shakespeare's erotic Ovidian poem *Venus and Adonis*. For a discussion of such verse, see William Keach, *Elizabethan Erotic Narratives* (New Brunswick, N.J.: Rutgers Univ. Press, 1977).

93. See the comic antiblazon from the *Old Arcadia*, printed in Ringler, *Sidney*, p. 12. Cf. the idealizing blazon of Mira (Ringler, *Sidney*, pp. 85–90).

94. See Stone, *Family, Sex, and Marriage*, p. 550, and passim. The author of "A Fantasticke Innes of Court Man" remarks: "For his recreation he had rather goe to a Citizens wife, then a Bawdy-house, only to save charges" (in *The Overburian Characters*, ed. W. J. Paylor, Percy Reprints, 13 [Oxford: Basil Blackwell, 1936], pp. 45–46).

95. N. J. C. Andreasen claims that this poem has "an anti-Ovidian thesis about the progress of love-making," since it flies in the face of Ovid's contention in the *Ars Amatoria* (717–28) that "much of the pleasure of sexual consummation derives from putting it off as long as possible" (*John Donne, Conservative Revolutionary* [Princeton, N.J.: Princeton Univ. Press, 1967], p. 118).

96. See Leonard Tennenhouse, "The Counterfeit Order of *The Merchant of Venice*," in *Representing Shakespeare*, ed. Murray M. Schwartz and Coppelia Kahn (Baltimore and London: Johns Hopkins Univ. Press, 1980), pp. 54–69.

97. Raymond Southall, *Literature and the Rise of Capitalism: Critical Essays Mainly on the Sixteenth and Seventeenth Centuries* (London: Lawrence and Wishart, 1973), pp. 21–85.

98. Armstrong argues that "the larger purpose of the relentless succession of witty and deceitful arguments is to disarm the audience" (p. 439). See his discussion of the poem ("Apprenticeship of Donne," pp. 435–39).

99. See, for example, Gardner, *Elegies and Songs and Sonnets*, pp. 252–54.

100. Gardner, *Elegies and Songs and Sonnets*, p. 148.

101. The elegy "Change" might be grouped along with the verse paradoxes, since it argues paradoxically that change is better than constancy, but it also incorporates some of the features of the dramatic elegies. Its rhetorical situation is somewhat confusing: after initially addressing a woman with whom he has been having an affair (1–4), the speaker turns to the kind of sympathetic male audience that would be receptive to libertine arguments, switching back (21–25) to the dramatically present mistress before returning to the male audience for the remaining eleven and one-half lines of the poem. This elegy handles the ironic predicament of the libertine who finds himself in love with a woman who demands freedom in love—one that Donne handles more subtly in his other elegies and lyrics—and treats it as a witty problem. Reaching a strange compromise between libertinism and the felt need for emotional commitment, the speaker decides to be a libertine in moderation, a nonsensical conclusion. The work seems to come apart intellectually and emotionally as well as rhetorically (cf. William Rockett, "John Donne: The Ethical Argument of Elegy III," *Studies in English Literature* 15 [1975]: 57–69; Andreasen, *Donne, Conservative*, pp. 100–16; and Sanders, *Donne's Poetry*, p. 41).

102. Carey, "Ovidian Love Elegy" p. 370. As Carey has noted, the antifeminist devaluation of woman, particularly of the rich citizen woman of the elegies, is a sign of the economic and social vulnerability of Inns-of-Court gentlemen-amorists. He is right to see in "the affectation of patronizing masculine superiority, of insolent self-assertion, of a purely physical interest in women . . . a sort of defense response" (p. 371). One can detect the basic social and economic insecurities of Inns men in a "libel against some Grayes Inns gentlemen & Revellers" associated with the 1594–95 *Gesta Grayorum* (included in Rosenbach MS 1083/15—Sanderson, "Edition," pp. 335–46). The poem satirizes: 1. the impecuniousness of Inns men—"Lambert" and "Glascock" both frequent pawnshops; 2. unflattering social backgrounds—"Grimes," the crude son of a candlemaker, when he danced with Lady Howard, conducted himself like one raised at a "Butchers stall" (80); "Baldwin," formerly the butler rewarded for his service with admission to the Inns, is depicted as an intruder; and "Belly" has as his "pedygree" "a baudy doctor & a byshopps spawne"; 3. wealth derived from disrespectable means—"Fleetwood" is the son of a man who amassed a fortune through usury and "Bing" is the son of a judge of the "baudy court" who got gold from whores and knaves; 4. mindless fashionmongering—"Claxton" is a "Mongrell student youth" who "coming from his studdy to a wench / he straight begann to court her in law french" and "Tonstall" and "Anderton" insist on hiring a coach and using cosmetics and other French fashions.

A recurrent motif is phallic frustration: one man is "wounded in the tayle" in a duel; the foolish amorist Claxton masturbates after being turned down by the woman he ineptly wooes ("when he could not his sute prevaile / went home & studdyed cases in the tayle"). The one titled gentleman of the group, "William Humberston," is a foolish stammerer who is regarded as a disgrace to gentility. Class consciousness, economic need, the aping of current sophisticated modes of behavior, sexual adventurism all figure in this satiric libel as they do in Davies's epigrams on Donne's satires and elegies.

103. Rosenbach MS 239/18 has an interesting title for this elegy, "Uppon one whom J. D. taught to loue and complement" (f.51a), one that highlights the class issue.

104. Carey, "Ovidian Love Elegy" p. 207. Cf. his discussion of the poem in *John Donne: Life, Mind, and Art*, pp. 104–8 and Clay Hunt, *Donne's Poetry: Essays in Literary Analysis* (New Haven and London: Yale Univ. Press, 1954), pp. 18–31.

105. See Finkelpearl, *Marston*, pp. 95–104.

106. For a discussion of the young men's attraction to military service, see Anthony Esler, *The Aspiring Mind of the Elizabethan Younger Generation* (Durham, N.C.: Duke Univ. Press, 1966), pp. 99–104. It is possible that Donne, who posed for a portrait at eighteen in the garb of a soldier, served in the Earl of Essex's unauthorized expedition to Spain and Portugal in 1589 (see Bald, *Life*, p. 51). Gardner (*Elegies and Songs and Sonnets*, p. 128) suggests 1594 as a date for the poem. For a good discussion of this elegy, see Armstrong, "Apprenticeship of Donne," pp. 421–26.

107. Stone, *Crisis of Aristocracy*, p. 458.

108. Harvey, *Marginalia*, p. 191.

109. J. E. Neale has said of the situation in late Elizabethan England: "The wars were diverting the impecunious younger sons of the squierarchy from 'the gentlemanly profession of serving-men' into that of soldiering. And this new party of gilded youth—'men of action'—found a leader after their own heart in the dashing young court-favorite, Essex" (*Queen Elizabeth I: A Biography* [1934; repr. Garden City, N.Y.: Doubleday, 1957], p. 334).

110. This poem, in effect, returns to an earlier Renaissance definition of the elegy as a love-complaint; see Francis Weitzmann, "Notes on the Elizabethan *Elegie*," *Publications of the Modern Language Association* 50 (1935): 435–43.

111. For example, "suck, smack, and embrace" (16).

112. In terms of its poetic strategies, the epigrammatic elegy "His Picture" belongs in this group, but, since I believe it makes sense to read it in the context of Donne's leaving England on one of the two naval expeditions in 1596 and 1597, I discuss it in the next chapter.

113. Leishman, *Monarch of Wit*, p. 71.

114. LaBranche, "Donne's 'Elegies'," p. 359.

115. Leishman, *Monarch of Wit*, p. 59.

116. Sir Richard Baker (quoted in Bald, *Life*, p. 72) called Donne a "great frequenter of Playes."

117. Ellrodt, *L'Inspiration*, 2:305 and passim.

118. See *Renaissance Self-Fashioning*, passim and *Sir Walter Ralegh: The Renaissance Man and His Roles* (New Haven, Conn.: Yale Univ. Press, 1973).

119. Armstrong, "Apprenticeship of Donne," p. 431.

120. Earl Miner's useful distinction of the three typical audiences of a "Metaphysical poem," "the speaker himself as audience; the 'dramatic' audience of another person in the poem; and the vicarious audience of the reader, to whom the poem is in some sense related" (*The Metaphysical Mode from Donne to Cowley* [Princeton, N.J.: Princeton Univ. Press, 1969], p. 15) is incomplete because it omits the actual author, who is part of the literary transaction,

especially in situations where he addresses a known audience who can appreciate the witty fictionalizing of personal and group experience. What Frederick Goldin has said of the Medieval courtier-poet applies well to a coterie poet like Donne: "As an author he is a real man well known to his peers, who are his audience; but as hero he assumes a fictional identity, an imaginary 'I' whom he endows with his own name and quality but who has no existence outside the confines of the lyric. This double identity . . . is the source of the greatest value of his song" (*The Mirror of Narcissus in the Courtly Love Lyric* [Ithaca, N.Y.: Cornell Univ. Press, 1967], p. 107).

121. Gordon Williams's analysis of the art of Roman lyric poets like Catullus applies as well to someone like Donne:

The technique is to compose in the form of a monologue, avoiding narrative accompaniment, and to leave it to the reader to construct the dramatic setting from apparently random clues casually dropped by the speaker: the result varies from a riddle at one end of the scale to a highly complex and involved drama at the other. The motive for its application was to exploit the poetic pleasure to be found in the mysterious, the difficult and the obscure, which gives the imagination something to work on, involves the reader in the poet's creation, and makes him work in cooperation with the poet.

(*Tradition and Originality in Roman Poetry* [Oxford: Oxford Univ. Press, 1968], p. 220). Of course, an audience in the habit of attending plays would more easily imagine lyric scenes of a dramatic character. For a discussion of the impact on Donne of the theatrical depiction of love, see H. M. Richmond, "Donne's Master: The Young Shakespeare," *Criticism* 15 (1973): 126–44.

122. In *Elizabethan Critical Essays*, ed. Smith, 2:223.
123. "Conversations with Drummond," in *Ben Jonson*, 1:135.
124. See Rockett ("Ethical Argument," p. 513) for a discussion of the "expeditio" trope in these lines.
125. Rockett, "Ethical Argument," p. 516.
126. Rockett, "Ethical Argument," p. 515.
127. See Propertius, IV.5; Tibullus, II.6; and Ovid, I.8.
128. See Bald, *Life*, pp. 59, 81.
129. Rockett, "Ethical Argument," p. 516.
130. Carey, "Ovidian Love Elegy," p. 200.
131. In the Oxford commonplace-book poetic anthology (Rosenbach MS 1083/16) these lines appear as a separate poem entitled "One proving false" (pp. 303–4), thus illustrating one way this section of "The Perfume" could be read as words addressed to a woman who has betrayed her lover.
132. Miner (*Metaphysical Mode*, p. 228) notices the rhetorical ambiguity of the poem's final section but misses its point.
133. Weitzmann ("Elizabethan *Elegie*," pp. 435–43) demonstrates that the elegy was a relatively open form, used for epistolary poetry, love-complaints and compliments, didactic verse, lamentation and mourning, as well as for some of the purposes for which Donne employed it.
134. Walton, "Life of Donne," p. xxviii.

Notes to Pages 67–70   311

135. *The English Works of Giles Fletcher, the Elder*, ed. Lloyd E. Berry (Madison: Univ. of Wisconsin Press, 1964), p. 79.

136. "Manuscript Poetic Miscellanies," 1:55–59 and passim, and "Some Renaissance Children's Verse," pp. 1–16.

137. The printer's letter to the Reader of Gascoigne's *A Hundreth Sundrie Flowres* refers to the collection of works as "pleasant Pamphlets" (p. 47), expressing a casual attitude toward printed works characteristic of editors presenting such literature to a genteel readership.

138. *Essays by William Cornwallis, the Younger*, ed. Don Cameron Allen (Baltimore: Johns Hopkins Press, 1946), p. 20.

139. See Roy Strong, *The English Icon, Elizabethan and Jacobean Portraiture* (London: Routledge & Kegan Paul, 1969), p. 353. Strong remarks of this and of similar paintings: "People when they sit for their portraits in the 1590s are beginning to want to see themselves depicted less as symbols and more as vehicles of human emotion and feeling" (p. 36). This is, of course, consistent with the way Donne's self-dramatization in his poetry is a means of exploring emotional nuances and complexities.

140. Keynes, *Bibliography of Donne*, p. 374.

141. Finkelpearl, *Marston*, p. 60.

142. For a discussion of this manuscript see Robert Krueger, "Sir John Davies: *Orchestra* Complete, *Epigrams*, Unpublished Poems," *Review of English Studies* n.s. 13 (1962): 2–29 and 113–24.

143. *Works of Thomas Campion*, p. 15.

144. See Doughtie's discussion of the differences between madrigals and airs (*Lyrics*, pp. 2–9). Campion, five years Donne's senior, composed poetry while he was at Gray's Inn and it was well enough known to be included among the additional verse of the 1591 edition of Sidney's *Astrophil and Stella*.

145. Colie, *Resources of Kind*, p. 75. Since, as Maria Corti has pointed out, "the choice of a genre on the part of the writer implies his choice of a certain interpretive model of reality" (*Literary Semiotics*, p. 117) and since both individual genres and the literary system of hierarchically arranged genres are ideologized, the mixing of genres has social implications.

146. In Smith, *Donne: Critical Heritage*, p. 73.

147. In Smith, *Donne: Critical Heritage*, p. 196.

148. Paula Johnson, *Form and Transformation in Music and Poetry of the English Renaissance* (New Haven and London: Yale Univ. Press, 1972), p. 82 and passim.

149. Michael McCanles, "Mythos and Dianoia: A Dialectical Methodology of Literary Form," in *Literary Monographs* 9, ed. Eric Rothstein (Madison: Univ. of Wisconsin Press, 1971), p. 35.

150. Quoted in Charlton, "Liberal Education," p. 34. Alvarez writes of Donne's coterie readers: "The pleasure they got from his and from each other's poetry was the same kind of enjoyment that one of the circle, Sir Richard Baker, found in Tacitus: '[His] very obscurity is pleasing to whosoever by labouring about it, findes out the true meaning; for then he counts it an issue of his own braine, and taking occasion from these sentences to goe

further than the thing he reads, and that without being deceived, he takes the like pleasure as men are wont to take from hearing metaphors, finding the meaning of him that useth them.' It was the coterie pleasure of recognizing one another's wit, almost as though the readers were let in on a secret. The style presumed on the fact that both poets and audience had had the same kind of training, done much the same reading and shared the same taste for the sceptical, paradoxical and, above all, the dialectical" (*School of Donne*, pp. 36–37). See the discussion of Donne's skepticism in John Carey, *John Donne: Life, Mind, and Art*, pp. 231–60.

151. Quoted in Sanderson, "*Epigrames P[er] B[enjamin] R[udyerd]* and Some More 'Stolen Feathers' of Henry Parrot," p. 244. Robert Jones, *The Second Booke of Songs and Ayres* (1601) (in Doughtie, *Lyrics*, pp. 147–66), a volume in which the editor says are collected "the private contentments of diuers Gentlemen" (p. 149), includes many bawdy poems. In *Virgedemiarum* 1:9, Joseph Hall specifically attacks the taste for such obscene verse (see *The Poems of Joseph Hall*, pp. 19–20).

152. See poems 7, 55, and 176 in Sanderson, "Edition," pp. 9–12, 91–100, 305–6.

153. Sanderson, "Edition," p. 96.

154. *The Autobiography of Thomas Whythorne*, Modern Spelling Edition, ed. James M. Osborn [Oxford: Clarendon Press, 1962], p. 29. Cf. David R. Shore, "The *Autobiography* of Thomas Whythorne: An Early Elizabethan Context for Poetry," *Renaissance and Reformation* n.s. 5 (1981): 72–86.

155. In the *Gesta Grayorum*, weak male lovers are satirized, those who

shall have any Charge, Occasion, Chance, Opportunity, or possible Means to entertain, serve, recreate, delight, or discourse with any vertuous or honourable Lady or Gentlewoman, Matron, or Maid, publickly, privately, or familiarly, and shall faint, fail, or be deemed to faint or fail in Courage, or Countenance, Semblance, Gesture, Voice, Speech, or Attempt, or in Act or Adventure, or in any other Matter, Thing, Manner, Mystery, or Accomplishment, due, decent, or appertinent to her or their Honour, Dignity, Desert, Expectation, Desire, Affection, Inclination, Allowance, or Acceptance; to be daunted, dismayed, or to stand mute, idle, frivolous, or defective, or otherwise dull, contrary, sullen, malecontent, melancholy, or different from the Profession, Practice, and Perfection of a compleat and consummate Gentleman or Courtier. (pp. 23–24).

156. See Andreasen, *Donne, Conservative*, pp. 31–53.

157. See the discussion of both poems in William Rockett, "Donne's Libertine Rhetoric," *English Studies* 52 (1971): 507–18.

158. Arnold Stein, *John Donne's Lyrics: The Eloquence of Action* (Minneapolis: Univ. of Minn. Press, 1962), p. 103.

159. See the discussions of the poem in Stein, *Donne's Lyrics*, pp. 115–20; Hunt, *Donne's Poetry*, pp. 1–15; and Miner, *Metaphysical Mode*, pp. 15–18.

160. Gardner (*Elegies and Songs and Sonnets*, p. 165) points to Ovid, *Amores*

II.4, as a source for the first stanza. See Harington's translation of this poem in Hughey, *Arundel Harington Manuscript* 1:253–54.

161. In Marston's *Metamorphosis of Pygmalion's Image*, Venus is called "Queene of sportiue dallying" (133) (*The Poems of John Marston*, ed. Arnold Davenport [Liverpool: Liverpool Univ. Press, 1961], p. 57). Citations of Marston's poetry are from this edition.

162. Hunt, *Donne's Poetry*, pp. 2–10.

163. A poem, possibly by John Hoskins, entitled "Impossibilities" is found in the fifth edition of Camden's *Remaines* (1637) (printed in Osborn, *John Hoskyns*, p. 299).

164. Apparently this poem circulated by itself (see Gardner, *Elegies and Songs and Sonnets*, p. lxxxii).

165. See Gardner, *Elegies and Songs and Sonnets*, p. 163, and Robert A. Bryan, "John Donne's Use of the Anathema," *Journal of English and Germanic Philology* 41 (162): 305–12.

166. See Gardner, *Elegies and Songs and Sonnets*, p. 164.

167. Black, for example, comments on the contents of BL Harl. 7392: "The poems in MS Harl. 7392 have moved out of the world of the college into that of the court, from student ribaldry and Ovidian imitation to the elaborately mannered graces and protestations of the Petrarchan situation, with its hints of actual liaisons veiled by the standard love conceits. They give the appearance of poems by young men about town with connections at court, imitating the courtly makers of the day" (1:353–54).

168. John Marston, *The Scourge of Villainy*, Satire 8, in *The Poems of John Marston*, pp. 151–52.

169. These are the first poems included in the Inns-of-Court Farmer-Chetham MS.

170. See my discussion of this topic in "'Love is not Love'," pp. 398–99 and passim. Cf. Leonard Forster, *The Icy Fire: Five Studies in European Petrarchism* (Cambridge: Cambridge Univ. Press, 1969), pp. 122–47; Roy Strong, *The Cult of Elizabeth: Elizabethan Portraiture and Pageantry* (London: Thames and Hudson, 1977); and Louis A. Montrose, "Celebration and Insinuation: Sir Philip Sidney and the Motives of Elizabethan Courtship," *Renaissance Drama* n.s. 8 (1977): 3–35.

171. See Krueger/Nemser, *John Davies*, p. 191.

172. BL MS Harl. 6910, for example, includes some 374 ring posies. See Joan Evans, *English Posies and Posy Rings* (Oxford: Oxford Univ. Press, 1931).

173. The short lyric, "The Token," included by Gardner among the "Dubia," enumerates some of the conventional kinds of love tokens exchanged by lovers. These include not only ribbons, rings, bracelets, and pictures (the last three of which Donne metaphorizes in his verse), but also poems or "witty Lines" (15).

174. See Krueger/Nemser, *John Davies*, p. 354.

175. Rosenbach MS 1083/15 (Sanderson, "Edition," pp. 288–301) includes both Marlowe's poem and Sir Walter Ralegh's answer poem, as does the

printed miscellany, *England's Helicon* (1600). See R. S. Forsythe, "The Passionate Shepherd and English Poetry," *Publications of the Modern Language Association* 40 (1925), 692–742.

176. Quoted in Gardner, *Elegies and Songs and Sonnets*, p. 156.

177. Andreas Capellanus related *amor* and *amus* (hook) etymologically in *The Art of Courtly Love* (translated, with introduction and notes by John Jay Parry [1941; repr. New York: Ungar, 1959], p. 31).

178. See II.iv. 78–87 in *The Complete Plays and Poems of William Shakespeare*, ed. William Neilson and Charles Hill (Cambridge, Mass.: Houghton Mifflin, 1942). Further citations are from this edition.

179. This work, edited by Sir Benjamin Rudyerd, was published in 1660. The text is included in J. A. Manning, *Memorials of Sir Benjamin Rudyerd* (London: T. & W. Boone, 1841), pp. 9–18.

180. Gardner, *Elegies and Songs and Sonnets*, p. 161.

181. Printed in Gardner, *Elegies and Songs and Sonnets*, p. 161.

182. See Colie (*Paradoxica Epidemica*, p. 119–20) who discusses this poem as a version of the "liar paradox."

183. In "The Legacie," another poem probably written in this period, Donne connects the language of love, with its rhetorical colors, with the "colours" (18) or deceptions and lies lovers practice on one another, as he converts a courtly Petrarchan lyric of compliment into a poem of satiric accusation.

184. "Breake of Day," for example, appears in William Corkine's *The Second Book of Ayres* (1612) (Doughtie, *Lyrics*, p. 389) and "The Expiration" in Alfonso Ferrabosco's *Ayres* (1609) (Doughtie, *Lyrics*, pp. 294–95).

185. The Group II manuscripts identify "The Message," "Song: Sweetest love," and "The Baite" as poems composed "to certain airs which were made before" (see MacColl, "Circulation of Donne's Poems," p. 34). MacColl notes that the Dolau Cothi manuscript also lists "Communitie," "Confined Love," and "Song: Goe and catche" (p. 34).

186. See Doughtie, *Lyrics*, pp. 8–30.

187. See Keach, *Elizabethan Erotic Narratives*, p. 36.

188. Keach, *Elizabethan Erotic Narratives*, p. 49.

189. Quoted in A. L. Rowse, *Simon Forman: Sex and Society in Shakespeare's Age* (London: Weidenfeld and Nicolson, 1974), p. 20. Cf. the perceptive discussion of this passage in Louis A. Montrose, "'Shaping Fantasies': Figurations of Gender and Power in Elizabethan Culture," *Representations* 1 (1983): 62–64.

190. From an anonymous piece found in Rosenbach 1083/15 (Sanderson, "Edition," p. 520).

191. *Sir Philip Sidney: Rebellion in Arcadia* (New Brunswick, N.J.: Rutgers Univ. Press, 1979), p. 195.

192. This is the point of Ralegh's "The Advice," a poem supposedly written for a young woman newly arrived at Court (see *The Poems of Sir Walter Ralegh*, ed. with an introduction by Agnes M. C. Latham [Cambridge, Mass.: Harvard Univ. Press, 1951], p. 14).

193. Cf. the twelfth song from Campion's first book of airs, "Thou art not faire, for all thy red and white" (in *The Works of Thomas Campion*, p. 34).
194. For the bawdy meaning of the word "heart" (15) see Eric Partridge, *Shakespeare's Bawdy*, 2nd ed. (New York: Dutton, 1969), p. 119.
195. The poem beginning "Image of her whom I love," which Gardner reclassifies among the lyrics rather than among the elegies, bears some resemblance to "The Dreame." It similarly assumes that there is a conflict between polite courtly loving that forbids sexual union and that kind of love that can be enjoyed in fantasy, if denied in reality, a love that finds sexual "fruition" (17). But, instead of settling on the latter, the speaker prefers to keep the affectionate relationship with his beloved, even though it involves sexual frustration, being "Mad with much heart" (26).
196. Donald Guss, *John Donne, Petrarchist: Italianate Conceits and Love Theory in* The Songs and Sonets [Detroit: Wayne State Univ. Press, 1966], p. 53. Although Guss offers much useful information from literary tradition (see pp. 53–60), I disagree with his Petrarchist interpretation of this poem. The Petrarchan theme that Samuel Daniel handles in a straightforward manner in *Delia* 33 (in *Poems and a Defence of Ryme*, ed. Arthur Colby Sprague [1930; repr. Chicago and London: Univ. of Chicago Press, 1965], p. 27) Donne perversely transforms in order to write an erotic seduction lyric.
197. See Gardner, *Elegies and Songs and Sonnets*, p. 174, and H. David Brumble III, "John Donne's 'The Flea': Some Implications of the Encyclopedic and Poetic Flea Traditions," *Critical Quarterly* 15 (1973): 147–54.

CHAPTER TWO

1. Bald says that "He was evidently mature enough, or prosperous enough, or dandified enough, to want to have a boy to attend on him" (*Life*, p. 77).
2. Bald writes: "No doubt he had been living extravagantly and his inheritance was dwindling, so that hopes of booty could not be ignored" (*Life*, p. 81).
3. In one of his letters to Donne, Henry Wotton refers to "your mistress, than whom the world doth possess nothing more virtuous" (Smith, *Life and Letters of Sir Henry Wotton*, 1:306).
4. What Shakespeare calls in *King Lear* the "complement of leave-taking" (I.i.297) was a ceremony that often involved the bestowing or exchanging of symbolic gifts. Proteus and Julia in *The Two Gentlemen of Verona* (II.i) exchange rings as part of a formal farewell; when Posthumus parts from Imogen in *Cymbeline* (I.i), he gives her a bracelet and she gives a diamond ring to him. John Buxton (*Elizabethan Taste* [New York: St. Martin's Press, 1965], pp. 120–22) discusses the fashion of wearing a miniature around the neck as a me-

mento. In Marlowe's *Edward II*, Edward and Gaveston exchange such pictures at parting. Ralegh wrote his half-brother Sir Humphrey Gilbert about Queen Elizabeth's request for a picture of him for her to have while he was at sea (quoted in Walter Oakeshott, *The Queen and the Poet* [London: Faber and Faber, 1960], p. 25).

5. For the tradition of this verse, see Peter Dronke, *The Medieval Lyric* (London: Hutchinson, 1968), pp. 127–31. The *chanson de croisade* provides a model for later military farewells in lyrics, dramas, and fictions. In the revised *Arcadia* Sidney's portrayal of the farewell scene between (the married) Argalus and Parthenia (Book III, Ch. 12) is in this tradition.

6. The Venetian ambassador refers to the Earl of Essex's change in appearance after the Cadiz raid: "The Earl is a great favorite of the Queen; he is about twenty-six years of age, fair-skinned, tall, but wiry; on this last voyage he began to grow a beard, which he used not to wear. He is a right modest, courteous, and humane gentleman" (*CSP Venetian*, 9:238).

7. For an account of the attraction of young Elizabethans to military adventure, see Esler, *Aspiring Mind*, pp. 87–124.

8. See Gardner, *Elegies and Songs and Sonnets*, pp. 144–45.

9. Donne's "Song: Sweetest Love" is a lyric of the same kind. For another example of a contemporary sophisticated courtly valediction, see Robert Sidney's fifth song (in Katherine Duncan-Jones, "'Rosis and Lysa': Selections from the Poems of Sir Robert Sidney," *English Literary Renaissance* 9 (1979): 247–48).

10. Guss (*Donne, Petrarchist*, p. 69) discusses the influence of Serafino on Donne's use of the tear conceit.

11. In discussing long absence as a cause of jealousy, Robert Burton remarks: "[those who] make frivolous impertinent journeys, tarry long abroad to no purpose, lie out, and are gadding still, upon small occasions, it must needs yield matter of suspicion" (*The Anatomy of Melancholy*, ed. Floyd Dell and Paul Jordan-Smith [New York: Tudor Publishing Co., 1955], p. 830).

12. See Bald, *Life*, pp. 83–84.

13. Bald (*Life*, p. 86) suggests Donne wrote the poem shortly after the Cadiz expedition; Milgate (*Satires, Epigrams and Verse Letters*, p. 148) places its composition between March and September of 1597. For a discussion of this work and Donne's Catholic background, see Hester, *Donne's Satyres*, pp. 73–97.

14. Milgate (*Satires, Epigrams and Verse Letters*, p. 148) says Donne probably made his first appearance at Court between the Cadiz and Islands expeditions.

15. Two of Wotton's letters to Donne written from Ireland in 1599 suggest the point of view of this group: see Smith, *Life and Letters of Sir Henry Wotton*, 1:308–10.

16. Cf. Andreasen, *Donne, Conservative*, pp. 135–39.

17. See Rosemond Tuve, *Elizabethan and Metaphysical Imagery: Renaissance Poetic and Twentieth-Century Critics* (Chicago: Univ. of Chicago Press, 1947), pp. 423–24.

18. See John Carey, "Donne and Coins," in *English Renaissance Studies*

Presented to Dame Helen Gardner in Honor of Her Seventieth Birthday (Oxford: Clarendon Press, 1980), pp. 151–63.

19. Cf. the discussion of this lyric in Stein, *Donne's Lyrics*, pp. 130–35.

20. Clay Hunt remarks that this "was evidently written as a personal poem . . . to a particular lady . . . on a particular occasion . . . the end of a visit with the lady" (p. 44). I basically agree with his interpretation (*Donne's Poetry*, pp. 44–50), but not with the identification of the woman with Mrs. Herbert.

21. See Hunt, *Donne's Poetry*, p. 46.

22. As Hunt notes (*Donne's Poetry*, pp. 46–47), Donne reshapes the conventional debate of the body and soul. On the Medieval background of such verse, see F. J. E. Raby, *A History of Secular Latin Poetry in the Middle Ages*, 2nd ed. (Oxford: Clarendon Press, 1957), 2:282–308.

23. Hunt, *Donne's Poetry*, pp. 48–49.

24. From *Hekatompathia*, reprinted in Rollins, ed., *A Poetical Rhapsody*, 1:279. The same miscellany also contains Walter Davison's "A dialogue betweene him and his Hart" (1:110–111) and the anonymous poem "To his Heart" (1:117).

25. A. J. Smith, "The Dismissal of Love," in Smith, *John Donne: Essays in Celebration*, p. 123.

26. *The Phoenix Nest* (ed. Rollins) contains a palinode called "A Counterlove" (p. 80).

27. See the discussion of this poem in Hunt, *Donne's Poetry*, pp. 33–41.

28. For a discussion of Spenser's use of the figure of the *donna angelicata*, see O. B. Hardison, Jr., "*Amoretti* and the *Dolce Stil Novo*," *English Literary Renaissance* 2 (1972): 208–16.

29. This is one of the rarest of Donne's lyrics in the manuscripts. As Gardner notes (*Elegies and Songs and Sonnets*, p. 212), it appears in only three manuscripts and one manuscript miscellany, two of the four having probably been copied from the printed version. It is reasonable to conclude that Donne kept this poem quite close.

30. See Smith, "Dismissal of Love," pp. 89–131.

31. Instead of Gardner's reading ("had, indammage") I adopt Grierson's (1:71).

32. Smith, "Dismissal of Love," p. 121.

33. Milgate believes that 1597 is "a likely date" (*Satires, Epigrams and Verse Letters*, p. 223) for this poem. See the discussion of the epistle in Allen Barry Cameron, "Donne's Deliberate Verse Epistles," *English Literary Renaissance* 6 (1976): 393–98.

34. Donne's classification of his amorous verse as "love-song weeds" expresses the patronizing attitude toward love poetry characteristic of serious men of affairs who regarded such work as an idle indulgence of youth. Writing from Court to Sir Robert Sidney, who had composed some love poetry as polite recreations, Rowland Whyte reported on his efforts to get the Earl of Nottingham and Lady Warwick to help his master to win advancement: "Both his Lordship and she did assure me, that they never found her Majestie to

haue a better Opinion of you then at this Present; and that she said, *Now all your youthfull Toyes were out of your Brain, you wold proue an honest Man. My Lord, I observe that the least Toy, is here made powerfull to hinder Preferment; and therefore you, and all that stand for Advancements, ought to shunne every small Occasion that may hurt*" (*Letters and Memorials of State*, ed. Arthur Collins [1746; repr. New York: AMS Press, 1973], 2:168). The ambitious Donne had reason to disparage his own poetry.

35. See the collection of Donne's statements about poetry found in Leah Jonas, *The Divine Science: The Aesthetic of Some Representative Seventeenth-Century English Poets* (New York: Columbia Univ. Press, 1940), pp. 273–79.

36. See the discussions of these poems in B. F. Nellist, "Donne's 'Storm' and 'Calm' and the Descriptive Tradition," *Modern Language Review* 59 (1964): 511–15; Palmer, "Verse Epistle," in Bradbury and Palmer, eds., *Metaphysical Poetry*, pp. 85–86; and Milgate, *Satires, Epigrams and Verse Letters*, pp. xxxiv–xxxv, 203–10.

37. For an excellent discussion of the biblical and moral thematics of this poem and of Donne's creative use of literary tradition see Clayton D. Lein, "Donne's 'The Storme': The Poem and the Tradition," *English Literary Renaissance* 4 (1974): 137–63.

38. As Bald (*Life*, pp. 88–89) explains, after the storm had forced the fleet back into port, both Essex and Ralegh tried to argue Elizabeth into letting them attack the Spanish treasure fleet in the West Indies instead of in the Azores. Donne's epigram "Cales and Guyana" refers to this possibility, but the succeeding epistle to Woodward ("If, as mine is, thy life a slumber be"), as Bald indicates, refers to the failure of the proposal. In this verse letter, Donne uses friendship and the shared devotion to "Almightie Vertue" (27) as the recourse of the man with "discontinued hopes" (26).

39. Carey observes of these lines: " . . . though Donne was in new and exotic circumstances—becalmed off the Azores—his head . . . was still full of London life: the court, the playhouse, the second-hand clothes shops ('fripperies')" (*Donne: Life, Mind, and Art*, p. 68).

40. Quoted in Bald, *Life*, p. 87.

41. Bald remarks: "Egerton's secretaries could expect promotion either in the service of the state or in the courts of law" (*Life*, pp. 97–98). See A. G. R. Smith's study of the prosperous careers of the secretaries who served Lord Burghley and his son, "The Secretariats of the Cecils, circa 1580–1612," *English Historical Review* 83 (1968): 481–504. Cf. Richard C. Barnett, *Place, Profit, and Power: A Study of the Servants of William Cecil, Elizabethan Statesman* (Chapel Hill: Univ. of North Carolina Press, 1969).

42. See Walton, "Life of Donne," p. ix.

43. See Bald, *Life*, pp. 100–1; Milgate, *Satires, Epigrams and Verse Letters*, p. 165; and Hester, *Donne's Satyres*, pp. 98–99.

44. Hester (*Donne's Satyres*, pp. 100–16) discusses the address to the suitor(s) in relation to Donne's imitation of Juvenal's thirteenth satire.

45. I. A. Shapiro, "The Date of a Donne Elegy, and Its Implications," in *English Renaissance Studies Presented to Dame Helen Gardner*, pp. 141–50.

46. See Shapiro, "Donne Elegy," p. 145.

47. Bald remarks that "Donne and Wotton constantly expressed themselves in the terms and phraseology of Senecan ideals" (*Life*, p. 123). For a contemporary critique of the Stoical stance, see the remarks of Jonson's Asper/Macilente in *Everyman Out of His Humour*:

> I am no such pild *Cinique*, to beleeue
> That beggary is the onely happinesse;
> Or (with a number of these patient fooles)
> To sing: *My minde to me a kingdome is*,
> When the lanke hungrie belly barkes for foode.
> (I.i.11–14 in *Ben Jonson*, 3:442)

48. See H. J. C. Grierson, "Bacon's Poem, 'The World': Its Date and Relation to Certain Other Poems," *Modern Language Review* 6 (1911): 145–56; R. C. Bald, "Donne's Early Verse Letters," *Huntington Library Quarterly* 15 (1952): 283–89; Allen Barry Cameron, "Donne's Deliberative Verse Epistles," pp. 375–81; Milgate, *Satires, Epigrams and Verse Letters*, pp. 225–30; and Bald, *Life*, pp. 119–21.

49. Text printed in *Elizabethan Lyrics from the Original Texts*, chosen, edited, and arranged by Norman Ault, 3rd ed. (New York: William Sloane, 1949), p. 248.

50. The text of Wotton's poem to Donne is printed in Grierson, 2:141.

51. See Bald, *Life*, pp. 122–23. Carey (*Donne: Life, Mind, and Art*, p. 60) points to two passages from Donne's prose that express a preference for involvement and activity over withdrawal and contemplative passivity: "Any Artificer is a better part of a state, then any retired or contemplative man" (*Sermons*, 3:329); "Wee are not sent into this world to Suffer, but to Doe" (*Pseudo-Martyr*, "Preface," sig. E1ᵛ).

52. See Cameron, "Verse Epistles," pp. 381–82.

53. See Milgate, *Satires, Epigrams and Verse Letters*, p. 230.

54. For an account of Essex's rise and fall, see J. E. Neale, *Queen Elizabeth I*, pp. 331–91. In 1591 Wotton himself had written to Lord Zouche, referring to Essex and Sir Charles Blount as "the only two gentlemen whom the younger brothers, that were not students, did follow for preferment" (Smith, *Life and Letters of Sir Henry Wotton*, 1:259). About the time Donne wrote this verse letter, Lord Grey wrote Lord Cobham about the Earl's forcing him to declare allegiance to him and to dissociate himself from enemies (like Cecil), referring to Essex as "this great patron of the wars" (*HMC Salisbury*, 8:269).

55. See, for example, the letter from Sir Robert Sidney to Essex of 28 March 1599 (*HMC Salisbury*, 8:132–33) complaining about the slow progress of his career (which the Earl was assisting).

56. See Neale, *Queen Elizabeth I*, pp. 365–68.

57. See the description of the latter incident in Rowland Whyte's letter to Sir Robert Sidney in Collins, *Letters and Memorials*, 2:127–28.

58. On the danger of letters' miscarrying, see Smith, *Life and Letters of Sir Henry Wotton*, 1:306 ff.

59. In Smith, *Life and Letters of Sir Henry Wotton*, 1:308.
60. See Bald, *Life*, pp. 107–10.
61. Smith (*Life and Letters of Sir Henry Wotton*, 1:34) notes that Wotton accompanied Essex on his return from Ireland with the disgraceful treaty the Earl had made with the Earl of Tyrone.
62. See Neale, *Queen Elizabeth I*, pp. 378–79.
63. Peters (*Paradoxes and Problems*, p. xxvii) reports that I. A. Shapiro believes this letter to have been addressed to someone other than Wotton.
64. In the Proem to Book IV of *The Faerie Queene*, Spenser mentions Burghley's objection to the amorous subject matter of the first three (already published) books of the poem.
65. This order not only ordered the confiscation and destruction of Marston's, Hall's, Guilpin's satires, "Davyes *Epigrams* with Marlowes *Elegyes*," "all Nasshes books and Doctor Harvey's," and prohibited the publication of new "*Satyres* or *Epigrams*," but also specifically directed that "noe Englishe historyes be printed excepte they bee allowed by some of her maiesties privie Counsell" (*Works of Joseph Hall*, p. 293). This last regulation probably was the immediate consequence of Heywood's dedication to Essex of his *Henry IV*, a work regarded as a politically subversive document by a Queen fearful of being overthrown in her old age by the popular Earl.
66. Bald (*Life*, p. 125) agrees with Evelyn Simpson's suggestion that Donne composed his prose paradoxes at this time.
67. Bald calls *Metempsychosis* a "savage satire directed at court and public life" (*Life*, p. 124). For a discussion of the poem as a piece of witty paradoxy, see Robert J. Corthell, "Donne's *Metempsychosis*: An 'Alarum to Truth'," *Studies in English Literature*, 21 (1981): 97–110.
68. See D. C. Allen, "The Double Journey of John Donne," in *A Tribute to George Coffin Taylor*, ed. Arnold Williams (Chapel Hill: Univ. of North Carolina Press, 1952), pp. 83–99; Milgate, *Satires, Epigrams and Verse Letters* pp. 171–91; Janel M. Mueller, "Donne's Epic Venture in the *Metempsychosis*," *Modern Philology* 70 (1972): 109–37; and M. van Wyk Smith, "John Donne's *Metempsychosis*," *Review of English Studies* n.s. 24 (1973): 17–25.
69. See Mueller, "Donne's Epic Venture," pp. 111–22.
70. See, for example, M. Mahood, *Poetry and Humanism* (London: Jonathan Cape, 1950), pp. 104–6; Helen Gardner, "The 'Metempsychosis' of John Donne," *Times Literary Supplement* [29 December 1972], pp. 1587–88.
71. Van Wyk Smith, "Donne's *Metempsychosis*," pp. 141–52. In a letter to Goodyer written after Cecil's death, when a number of people were writing bad libels against this politician, Donne justified the composition of libels written while their object was alive: "I dare say to you, where I am not easily misinterpreted, that there may be cases where one may do his Countrey good service, by libelling against a live man, For, where a man is either too great, or his Vices too generall, to be brought under a judiciary accusation, there is no way, but this extraordinary accusing, which we call Libelling" (*Letters*, pp. 90–91).
72. HMC *De L'Isle and Dudley*, 2:240.

73. See van Wyk Smith, "Donne's *Metempsychosis*," pp. 148–50.
74. See van Wyk Smith, "Donne's *Metempsychosis*," pp. 150–51.
75. *Satires, Epigrams and Verse Letters*, pp. xxx–xxxi.
76. See Richard E. Hughes, *The Progress of the Soul: The Interior Career of John Donne* (New York: William Morrow, 1968), pp. 72–79 and Milgate, *Satires, Epigrams and Verse Letters*, p. 190.
77. See Bald, *Life*, p. 96.
78. Gosse (1:95–96) claims Ann stayed on in York House after Lady Egerton's death to manage the household, returning to her father at Loseley in October, when the Lord Keeper remarried.
79. Letter quoted in Bald, *Life*, p. 161.
80. For this and for the other type of spousal (*per verba de futuro*), see Stone, *Family, Sex, and Marriage*, p. 32.
81. Walton, "Life of Donne," pp. ix–x.
82. As Bald points out (*Life*, p. 128) we do not know when Donne actually moved out of York House to take separate lodgings for himself, but the arrival of Egerton's new wife, the Dowager Countess of Derby, and her daughters in October 1600 was probably the latest date he would have done so.
83. Walton, "Life of Donne," p. xii.
84. Bald, *Life*, p. 130.
85. "Love seeks for two persons who are bound together by a mutual trust and an identity of desires, . . . if the parties concerned marry, love is violently put to flight, as is clearly shown by the teaching of certain lovers" (Andreas Capellanus, *Art of Courtly Love*, p. 156).
86. *Gesta Grayorum*, p. 39.
87. Stone, *Family, Sex, and Marriage*, p. 272.
88. See note in Gardner, *Elegies and Songs and Sonnets*, p. 188.
89. Leishman, *Monarch of Wit*, p. 175. I would agree with Leishman that "A Nocturnall upon S. Lucies Day," "The Dissolution," "The Good Morrow," "The Sunne Rising," "The Canonization," "Loves Infiniteness," "The Anniversarie," "A Valediction: of Weeping," "The Broken Heart," "A Valediction: forbidding Mourning," and "A Lecture upon the Shadow" were connected with Donne's relationship with Ann More, but I would add "Loves Growth" to his list and delete from Leishman's group "A Feaver" and "Aire and Angels," both probably poems of compliment, as well as "The Dreame," "The Prohibition," "The Expiration," "The Computation," "The Paradox," and "The Token."
90. See *Elegies and Songs and Sonnets*, pp. liii–lxii.
91. Harry Morris, "John Donne's Terrifying Pun," *Papers on Language and Literature* 9 (1973): 128–37. I disagree with Morris's suggestion that Donne punned on "More" in "Witchcraft by a Picture," "The Will," and "Going to Bed," but I would add "The Dissolution" to his list of lyrics.
92. The erotic dream poem "Image of her whom I love" may also belong in this group: in lines 1, 8, 19, and 20 Donne may be employing the "more" pun.
93. For the Petrarchan material of this poem, see Guss, *Donne, Petrarchist*, pp. 118–20.

94. *Elegies and Songs and Sonnets*, p. 168.

95. For Bacon's discussion in the 1601 Parliament of the relationship of royal prerogative and *non-obstante* clauses, see *The Tudor Constitution: Documents and Commentary*, ed. and with introduction by G. R. Elton (Cambridge: Cambridge Univ. Press, 1965), pp. 25–26. This Parliament, in which Donne served, met from 27 October to 19 December. Bald states that "Donne neither took part in any of the debates, nor served on any committees" (*Life*, 115).

96. Leishman, *Monarch of Wit*, p. 181. Cf. the excellent discussion of this poem in Sanders, *Donne's Poetry*, pp. 76–82.

97. Sanders detects a "passing reference to some social complication which prevents [the couple's] ever being husband and wife" (*Donne's Poetry*, p. 79).

98. Hunt, *Donne's Poetry*, p. 53. In his discussion of the poem (*Donne's Poetry*, pp. 53–69), Hunt treats it as a lyric Donne wrote to Ann after they were married. Cf. the treatment of the poem in Stein, *Donne's Lyrics*, pp. 65–77.

99. See A. J. Smith, "The Metaphysic of Love," in *Discussions of John Donne*, ed. with an introduction by Frank Kermode (Boston: Heath, 1962), pp. 150–60.

100. Conrad Russell (*The Crisis of Parliaments: English History, 1509–1660* [London and New York: Oxford Univ. Press, 1971], p. 245) points out that the 1601 Parliament voted four subsidies to raise money to fight the Spanish.

101. See L. C. Knights, "All or Nothing: A Theme in John Donne," in *William Empson: The Man and His Work*, ed. Roma Gill (London and Boston: Routledge & Kegan Paul, 1974), pp. 109–16.

102. Peter Beal (Index, 1:247) has noted that a copy of this poem survives in the hand of Sir Henry Goodyer. This suggests that Donne was quite willing (at least some time after the time of composition) to transmit some of the poems he wrote for the woman he married to close friends.

103. Louis Martz, *The Wit of Love: Donne, Carew, Crashaw, Marvell* (Notre Dame and London: Univ. of Notre Dame Press, 1969), p. 54.

104. Guss remarks that as "A series of conceits upon so unpromising a subject as a window" this poem "resembles a sequence of strambotti" (*Donne, Petrarchist*, p. 69) in the manner of Serafino.

105. *Elegies and Songs and Sonnets*, p. 64.

106. Frances Yates, *The Art of Memory* (Chicago: Univ. of Chicago Press, 1966), p. 155.

107. Eric Jacobsen, *Translation: A Traditional Craft* (Copenhagen: Gyldendal, 1958), p. 113. Rosemary Freeman alludes to the Elizabethan custom behind Donne's poem: " . . . it was natural and intelligible for a man to scratch an emblematic poem on his friend's window pane, taking the brittleness of the glass for his 'picture' and his theme" (*English Emblem Books* [London: Chatto and Windus, 1948], p. 5).

108. Carey, I believe, is right about the last stanza of the poem when he says that it "returns us to reality and firm substantial love. The brusque recantation surmounts fears. Yet fears have been voiced and will not go away. Trying to ignore them only makes their menace clearer. As the final stanza coun-

teracts the rest of the poem, so the rest of the poem counteracts the final stanza, making its briskness seem blustering" (*Donne: Life, Mind, and Art*, p. 196).

CHAPTER THREE

1. Bald points out that there were tenements in this former hospital leased by "people of fashion," but also that "The precincts of the hospital were . . . a 'liberty,' free from the ordinary civil and ecclesiastical jurisdiction, and the chapel was notorious later in the century for its clandestine marriages" (*Life*, pp. 128–29).

2. Bald finds no evidence on Donne's connection with the Earl, but does note that "Northumberland was on friendly terms with Sir George More" (*Life*, p. 134). Furthermore, Northumberland owned the Leconfield MS of Donne's poems.

3. This is quite evident in the manuscript copies of the letters to More (Folger MS L.b.526–29).

4. See Bald, *Life*, pp. 135–40.

5. Walton, "Life of Donne," p. xi.

6. *Diary of John Manningham*, ed. Sorlien, p. 150.

7. "Certain Precepts for the Well ordering of a Man's Life," in *Advice to a Son: Precepts of Lord Burghley, Sir Walter Raleigh, and Francis Osborne*, ed. Louis B. Wright (Ithaca, N.Y.: Cornell Univ. Press, 1962), p. 9.

8. Quoted in Bald, *Life*, p. 161.

9. Quoted in Bald, *Life*, pp. 138–39.

10. For a discussion of the classical propempticon, see Kenneth Quinn, *Latin Explorations: Critical Studies in Roman Literature* (London: Routledge & Kegan Paul, 1963), pp. 239–73.

11. For Wotton, who managed to move from his politically tainted service to the Earl of Essex to becoming Sir Robert Cecil's client, the ambassadorship to Venice was a sign of great success. Cf. his letter of 23 May 1603 to Cecil requesting patronage (Smith, *Life and Letters of Sir Henry Wotton*, 1:317–18).

12. See Bald, *Life*, pp. 146–47.

13. I use the term *narcissistic injury* in the psychoanalytic sense. See Heinz Kohut, *The Analysis of the Self: A Systematic Approach to the Psychoanalytic Treatment of Narcissistic Personality Disorders* (New York: International Universities Press, 1971), pp. 11–13 and passim.

14. Given Donne's recent relationship with both Egerton and his father-in-law, this witty formulation is not surprising. Jonathan Saville (*The Medieval Erotic Alba: Structure as Meaning* [New York: Columbia Univ. Press, 1972], pp. 146–47) notes the Oedipal potential of the erotic dawn poem.

15. A. J. Smith, *John Donne: The Songs and Sonnets* (London: Edward Arnold, 1964), p. 55.

16. Miner, *Metaphysical Mode*, p. 28.

17. Cleanth Brooks, "The Language of Paradox," in *John Donne's Poetry: Authoritative Texts, Criticism*, ed. A. L. Clements (New York: Norton, 1966), p. 179.

18. Andreasen, *Donne, Conservative*, p. 168.

19. Recently Carey (*Donne: Life, Mind and Art*, p. 43) has discussed the religious imagery, emphasizing the relationship of this poem to Donne's apostasy.

20. The 1633 edition, as Gardner notes (*Elegies and Songs and Sonnets*, p. 203), follows Cambridge Univ. Add. MS. 5778 and the Leconfield MS in printing "more" for "man" in this line, but I would not call this reading "less vivid," as Gardner does, since it preserves the pun on Donne's wife's name.

21. *Propertius*, with an English translation by H. E. Butler, The Loeb Classical Library (Cambridge, Mass.: Harvard Univ. Press and London: Heinemann, 1912), pp. 12-13.

22. See Valency, *In Praise of Love*, pp. 171-72.

23. See Marotti, "'Love is not Love'," pp. 405-06.

24. In the Pembroke-Rudyerd collection, there is a poem of a similar sort using the reactions of a critic-friend as a poetic opportunity: "Of his Mistress, of his Friends Opinion of her, and his answer to his Friend's Objections, with his constancy toward her" (*Poems Written by the Right Honorable William Earl of Pembroke. . . . Whereof Many of which are answered by way of Reparetee, by Sr Benjamin Ruddier, Knight. With several Distinct Poems, written by them Occasionally, and Apart* [London, 1660], pp. 50-52).

25. Quoted in Bald, *Life*, p. 144.

26. The most likely reader of a poem like "The Canonization" was Sir Henry Goodyer, who was active at the Jacobean Court. *HMC Salisbury*, 16:240 summarizes a letter from Goodyer to Cecil offering his services and requesting economic assistance. Goodyer, a Gentleman of the Privy Chamber, danced in the Court masque at Christmas 1603 (see Dudley Carleton's letter to John Chamberlain in *Dudley Carleton to John Chamberlain, 1603-1624, Jacobean Letters*, ed. with an introduction by Maurice Lee, Jr. [New Brunswick, N.J.: Rutgers Univ. Press, 1972], p. 54).

27. Keynes (*Bibliography of Donne*, p. 260) points out that the line is from Petrarch, *Canzoniere* 19, st. 7, l. 1.

28. See Duncan-Jones, "'Rosis and Lysa': Selections from the Poems of Sir Robert Sidney," 245.

29. Gardner (*Elegies and Songs and Sonnets*, pp. 202-3) refers to Ovid (*Amores*, II.10) as literary background to Donne's poem.

30. Although Gardner (*Elegies and Songs and Sonnets*, p. 203) claims this reference is no sure way of dating the poem, the 1603-4 plague would have been the most likely object of Donne's allusion.

31. In "A Litanie," for example, Donne himself called the plague God's "Angell" (194) or messenger.

32. Guss, *Donne, Petrarchist*, pp. 159-60.

33. "The Fly in Donne's 'Canonization'," *Journal of English and Germanic Philology* 65 (1966): 253-55.

34. *Palladis Tamia*, ed. D. C. Allen (New York: Scholars' Facsimiles and Reprints, 1938), p. 42.
35. Chambers, "Fly," p. 254.
36. Gardner, *Elegies and Songs and Sonnets*, p. 204.
37. See, for example, Thomas Lodge, "Praise of Rosalind" (in *Lyrics from the Dramatists of the Elizabethan Age*, ed. A. H. Bullen [London: Bullen, 1901], p. 269): "Of all proud birds the eagle pleaseth Jove,/Of pretty fowls Venus likes the dove" (9–10).
38. Colie, *Paradoxia Epidemica*, p. 130.
39. Equicola, quoted in Guss, *Donne, Petrarchist*, p. 158.
40. Guss, *Donne, Petrarchist*, p. 158.
41. Albert C. Labriola, "Donne's 'The Canonization': Its Theological Context and Its Religious Imagery," *Huntington Library Quarterly* 36 (1973): 337.
42. Labriola, "'Canonization'," p. 332.
43. Guss, *Donne, Petrarchist*, p. 158.
44. Donne himself used the phoenix in "An Epithalamion, or Mariage Song on the Lady Elizabeth, and Count Palatine being married on St. Valentine's Day" (99–102) as a symbol of both the sexual consummation of the marriage and of the marriage itself.
45. *The Phoenix Nest* was dedicated to the memory of Sidney and, as William Matchett (The Phoenix and the Turtle: *Shakespeare's Poem and Chester's Loves Martyr* [The Hague: Mouton, 1965]) has argued, *Loves Martyr* connects the phoenix with the deceased Essex. Matchett (pp. 158–59) detects echoes of *Loves Martyr* in "The Canonization."
46. See Horst S. Meller, "The Phoenix and the Well-Wrought Urn," *Times Literary Supplement* [22 April 1965], p. 320. The woodcut shows a funeral urn on which are the images of Petrarch and Laura beneath the figure of the phoenix and the motto "Semper Eadem."
47. For the hermaphrodite as a symbol of marriage see Barptolemaeus Anulus, *Picta Poesis* (1552), p. S14f, in *Emblemata: Handbuch Für Sinnibildkunst des XVI. und XVII. Jahrhunderts*, ed. Arthur Henkel and Albricht Schone (Stuttgart: J. B. Metzler, 1967), col. 1631. For a discussion of the Neoplatonic dimension of the image, see A. R. Cirillo, "The Fair Hermaphrodite: Love-Union in the Poetry of Donne and Spenser," *Studies in English Literature* 9 (1969): 61–95.
48. Michael McCanles observes: "The plot of the poem reverses itself neatly in the third stanza, where the persona, like Erasmus's Stultitia, first accepts his critic's categories of dispraise in order to turn them into categories of approbation" (*Dialectical Criticism and Renaissance Literature* [Berkeley, Los Angeles, London: Univ. of California Press, 1975], p. 64).
49. Barbara Kiefer Lewalski, *Donne's Anniversaries and the Poetry of Praise: The Creation of a Symbolic Mode* (Princeton, N.J.: Princeton Univ. Press, 1973), pp. 23–24.
50. Donne uses this word in his *Sermons* to mean both example and model: "God proceeds by example, by pattern" (*Sermons*, 4:98); "thy *Idaea*, thy Pattern, thine Original" (*Sermons*, 4:99).
51. I quote the text of the Giolito poem (which I discovered before read-

ing Meller's article) from *Il Petrarcha, con l'espositione d'Allesandro Vellutello* (Venice: Appresso Gabriel Gioli di Ferrarii, 1544), p. Aiii:

> Laura, ch'un Sol fu tra le Donne in terra,
> Hor tien del cielo il piu sublime honore:
> Merce di quella penna; il cui valore,
> Fa, che mai non sara spenta o sotterra
> Mentre facendo al tempo illustre guerra,
> Con dolce foco di celeste amore
> Accende e infiamma ogni gelato core;
> Le sue reliquie il piccol marmo serra:
> Et le ceneri elette accoglie anchora
> Di lui; che seco ne i stellanti seggi
> Fra Dante et Bice il terzo ciel congiunse.
> Tu, che l'un miri; e i bassi accenti leggi;
> A lor t'inchina; e'l sacro Vaso honora,
> Che le sante reliquie insieme aggiunse.

52. A. J. Smith ("The Phoenix and the Urn," *Times Literary Supplement* [13 May 1965], p. 376) is right, I believe, when he observes that Donne writes in a different spirit from that of the Giolito woodcut and poem, but this does not mean that he did not use the Italian material for ironic purposes. Donne, who usually avoided the eternizing conceit in his verse, employs it ironically in the last part of "The Canonization," partly in response to the tradition represented by the Giolito treatment of the deceased Petrarch and Laura.

53. Meaning "6b" in the OED defines *rage* as "Violent desire; sexual passion, heat" and cites *Hamlet* III.iii.89, "When he is drunk asleep or in his rage."

54. Gosse was right, I believe, to see "The Canonization" as "an index to the feelings of indignant and irritated impatience with which [Donne] regarded the obstacles set in the way of his happiness" (1:117) in the early part of his marriage. Carey states: "To proclaim the all-sufficiency of the woman for whom he had sacrificed his career may have been the defiant response with which Donne's imagination faced worldly disaster. And it may have been made more defiant by the realization that she did not, after all, mean everything to him" (*Donne: Life, Mind, and Art*, p. 75).

55. See the 1605 letter to Goodyer in which he bids his friend farewell as he goes abroad to find "a course" (*Letters*, p. 94) by which to be advanced.

56. See Bald, *Life*, p. 148.

57. HMC *De L'Isle and Dudley*, 2:145.

58. Stone (*Family, Sex, and Marriage*, p. 226) identifies the love letter (along with the self-revelatory diary and the autobiography) as a new genre in late-sixteenth-century England. See, for example, the letters that the Earl of Southampton wrote his wife, both from Ireland and, after the Essex revolt, from prison (e.g., HMC *Salisbury*, 11:35 and 4:175–76) and the letters of John Hoskins to his wife (Osborn, *John Hoskyns*, pp. 63–90).

59. See Stone, *Family, Sex, and Marriage*, chapter 8 and passim.

60. Walton, "Life of Donne," p. xxvii.

61. Bacon wrote, in the 1612 version of one of his *Essays*, "Hee that hath wife and children hath giuen hostages to fortune. For they are impediments to great enterprises, either of vertue or mischief" (*Works*, 6:547).

62. In *Biathanatos* Donne justifies the stronger penalties for wife-killing than for matricide, reasoning "not that the fault is greater, but that otherwise more would commit it" (p. 47).

63. Leishman, *Monarch of Wit*, pp. 180-81.

64. There is a possible autobiographical reference in the fifth stanza, in which the efforts of lawyers to discover "by what title Mistresses are ours" (38) might refer to Donne's legal battle with his father-in-law to keep his marriage from being annulled (see Bald, *Life*, pp. 137-39).

65. Johan Huizinga, *Homo Ludens: A Study of the Play Element in Culture* (Boston: Beacon Press, 1955), p. 155.

66. Richard Hughes connects this poem with Donne's interests in the 1598-1605 period in "esoterica: Neoplatonism, cabalism, Hermeticism, the occultism of transcendent philosophy" (*Progress of Soul*, p. 98). Guss (*Donne, Petrarchist*, p. 145) cites Guido Casoni's *Della magia d'amore* as a source for the poem.

67. Andreas Capellanus, *Art of Courtly Love*, p. 154.

68. Hugh M. Richmond ("Donne's Master: The Young Shakespeare," 132) points to the similarity of the opening of this poem and *Loves Labours Lost* IV.iii.22-30 as well as *Two Gentlemen of Verona* II.ii.9-12, 14-15.

69. Morris ("Donne's Terrifying Pun," p. 131) identifies this pun.

70. Guss (*Donne, Petrarchist*, p. 73) notes the similarity of this final formulation and the conceit in Guarino's Madrigal 69.

71. In a letter to Goodyer sent as Donne was about to leave for France in 1611, a similar formulation appears: "I speak to you at this time of departing, as I should do at my last upon my death-bed; and I desire to deliver into your hands a heart and affections, as innocent towards you, as I shall to deliver my soul into Gods hands then" (*Letters*, p. 93).

72. Sidney's "A Farewell" was published in the 1598 edition of his poems, a volume of which Donne undoubtedly was aware:

> Oft have I musde, but now at length I finde,
> Why those that die, men say they do depart:
> Depart, a word so gentle to my minde,
> Weakely did seeme to paint death's ougly dart.
>
> But now the starres with their strange course do binde
> Me to leave, with whome I leave my hart.
> I heare a crye of spirits faint and blinde,
> That parting thus my chiefest part I part.
>
> Part of my life, the loathed part to me,
> Lives to impart my wearier clay some breath.
> But that good part, wherein all comforts be,

> Now dead, doth shew departure is a death.
> Yea worse then death, death parts both woe and joy,
> From joy I part still living in annoy.
> (*Poems*, p. 148)

Lord Herbert's 1608 valediction ("I must depart" in *The Poems English and Latin of Edward, Lord Herbert of Cherbury*, ed. G. C. Moore Smith [Oxford: Clarendon Press, 1923], p. 17—further citations of Herbert are of this edition) looks like an imitation not only of the same Sidney poem, but also of Donne's valediction.

73. John Freccero, "Donne's 'Valediction: Forbidding Mourning'," *ELH* 30 (1963): 335–76.

74. David Novarr comments on "A Valediction: forbidding Mourning": "If the appeal to souls seems rarefied, that to geometry seems totally lacking in humanity" (*The Disinterred Muse: Donne's Texts and Contexts* [Ithaca, N.Y., and London: Cornell Univ. Press, 1980], p. 56).

75. Walton, "Life of Donne," p. xiv.

76. Bald quotes from a letter of Garrard's to Viscount Wentworth enclosing some of Donne's poetry, "Verses made in the Progress. I that never had Patience in all my Life to transcribe Poems, except they were very transcendent, such as Dean *Donn* writ in his younger Days, did these with some Pain" (*The Earl of Strafforde's Letters and Dispatches*, 1:338 in Bald, *Life*, p. 159n). When Donne wrote Garrard from France in 1611, he sent greetings "to all those Gentlemen whom I had the honour to serve at our lodging" (*Letters*, p. 265), referring to the group to which he and Garrard belonged (one probably considerably less prestigious in social rank than Walton's remarks suggest).

77. Godfrey Goodman concludes *The Court of King James the First* (ed. John Brewer, 2 vols. [London: Richard Bentley, 1839] with a "Parallel Between the Times of Queen Elizabeth and King James" (1:413–21) complimentary to the latter, having earlier criticized Elizabeth's parsimony: " . . . the queen . . . was ever hard of access, and grew to be very covetous in her old days: so that whatsoever she undertook, she did it to the halves only, to save charge; that suits were very hardly gotten, and in effect more spent in expectation and attendance than the suit could any way countervail; that the court was very much neglected, and in effect the people were very generally weary of an old woman's government" (1:96–97). Sir Roger Wilbraham praises both Elizabeth and James in comparing their different styles (*The Journal of Sir Roger Wilbraham*, ed. Harold Spencer Scott, *Camden Miscellany*, vol. 10 [London: Royal Historical Society, 1902], pp. 59ff.]). See the collection of comments on James I in *James I by his Contemporaries*, ed. and with an introduction by Robert Ashton (London: Hutchinson, 1969), and the valuable discussion of this monarch and his style in Jonathan Goldberg, *James I and the Politics of Literature* (Baltimore and London: Johns Hopkins Univ. Press, 1983).

78. See, for example, the summary of Jacobean political issues in Conrad Russell, *Crisis of Parliaments*, pp. 256–99.

79. *The Political Works of James I*, ed. with an introduction by Charles

Howard McIlwain [Cambridge, Mass.: Harvard Univ. Press, and London: Oxford Univ. Press, 1918] 1:295. Further citations of James's prose are from this edition.

80. Franklin Williams, *Index of Dedications and Commendatory Verses in English Books Before 1641* (London: Bibliographical Society, 1962).

81. King James thought of himself as a serious scholar, a skillful writer, and a connoisseur of wit. Having been told by Lord Thomas Howard that his "learning may somewhat prove worthy" (*Nugae Antiquae*, ed. Henry Harington [1779; repr. Hildesheim: Georg Olms, 1968], 1:275) at Court, Sir John Harington was granted a private interview in the course of which the King wandered from intellectually serious to intellectually eccentric and trivial topics. As Harington described the meeting to Sir Amias Paulet:

. . . he enquyrede muche of lernynge, and showede me his owne in suche sorte, as made me remember my examiner at Cambridge aforetyme. He soughte muche to knowe my advances in philosophie, and utterede profounde sentences of Aristotle, and such lyke wryters, whiche I had never reade, and which some are bolde enoughe to saye, others do not understand: but this I must passe by. . . . He asked me 'what I thoughte pure witte was made of; and whome it did best become? Whether a Kynge shoulde not be the beste clerke in his owne countrie; and, if this lande did not entertayne goode opinion of his lerynge and good wisdome?' His Majestie did much presse for my opinion touchinge the power of Satan in matter of witchcraft; and askede me, with muche gravitie,—'If I did trulie understande, why the devil did worke more with anciente women than others?' I did not refraine from a scurvey jeste, and even saide (notwithstandinge to whome it was saide) that— 'we were taught hereof in scripture, where it is tolde, that the devil walketh in dry places.' His Majestie, moreover, was peasede to saie much, and favouredelye, of my good report for merth and good conceite: to which I did covertlie answer; as not willinge a subjecte shoulde be wiser than his Prince, nor even appeare so. (*Letters and Epigrams*, p. 110)

James could have given no clearer signal of his preference for philosophical (and religious) poetry than the way he received Sir John Davies in Scotland (according to Anthony Wood): " . . . the king straitway asked, whether he was *Nosce Teipsum*? and being answered that he was the same, he graciously embraced him, and thenceforth had so great a favour for him, that soon after he made him his solicitor and then his attorney-general in Ireland" (quoted in Kreuger/Nemser, *John Davies*, p. xliv).

82. Marotti, "'Love is not Love'," pp. 420–22.

83. I include such other literary forms as libels and epigrams as well as more informal performances such as "table talk" in this list of literary types.

84. Donne's connection with Dean Morton is the subject of much speculation. Bald (*Life*, pp. 210–11) is reluctant to argue that Donne and Morton collaborated on polemical works, but Timothy Healy, in an appendix to his edition of *Ignatius His Conclave* (pp. 168–73) offers a good argument for this collaboration.

85. See, for example, *Letters*, pp. 137–38.

86. In two essays ("The Originals of Donne's Overburian Characters," *Bulletin of the New York Public Library* 77 [1973]: 63–69, and "Three Unnoticed Companion Essays to Donne's 'An Essay on Valour'," *Bulletin of the New York Public Library* 73 [1969]: 424–39), Dennis Flynn has argued that Donne wrote not only "The True Character of a Dunce," "The Character of a Scot at the First Sight," and "An Essay of Valour" but also the three short essays printed in *Cottoni Posthuma* under the heading "Sir Francis Walsingham's Anatomizing of Honesty, Ambition, and Fortitude." Although she does not offer strong reasons for rejecting their authenticity, Helen Peters (*Paradoxes and Problems*, p. xlviii) places the first four of these works among the Dubia in her edition of Donne's short prose works.

87. For a list of the individuals with whom Donne was associated through his membership in one or more groups that regularly dined together at such places as the Mermaid and Mitre Taverns, see I. A. Shapiro, "The 'Mermaid Club'," *Modern Language Review* 45 (1950): 6–17, 58–63, and Bald, *Life*, pp. 193–95. Donne was in close social contact not only with good friends like Christopher Brooke and Sir Henry Goodyer, but also with prominent Parliamentarians like Richard Martin, Sir Robert Phelps, and William Hakewill, and financiers like Arthur Ingram and Sir Lionel Cranfield. He developed his friendship with Sir Robert Cotton whom Bald (*Life*, p. 117) says Donne met during his secretaryship and whose antiquarian research served both Court and Parliament in the early Stuart period (see Kevin Sharpe, *Sir Robert Cotton, 1586–1631: History and Politics in Early Modern England* [Oxford: Oxford Univ. Press, 1979]). He was also associated with John Hoskins, Richard Connock, John West, Sir Henry Neville, and Inigo Jones.

88. See *The "Conceited Newes" of Sir Thomas Overbury and His Friends*, a Facsimile Reproduction of the Ninth Impression of 1616 of *Sir Thomas Ouerbury His Wife*, with a commentary and textual notes on the "Newes" by James E. Savage (Gainesville, Fla.: Scholars' Facsimiles & Reprints, 1968).

89. See, for example, the edition and discussion of the "Parliament Fart" poem in Sanderson, "Edition," pp. 529–54.

90. Wallace Notestein (*The House of Commons, 1604–1610* [New Haven, Conn. and London: Yale Univ. Press, 1971], p. 434) places Martin among the half-dozen or so true leaders of the 1604–1610 Parliament.

91. It has been argued recently by Linda Levy Peck (*Northampton: Patronage and Policy at the Court of James I* [London: George Allen & Unwin, 1982], pp. 208–10) that Hoskins's "Sicilian Vespers" speech (which landed him in the Tower) was not directly tied to a conspiracy by his patron, the Earl of Northampton, to force James to prorogue the 1614 Parliament. Its witty iconoclasm was consistent with Hoskins's style and represented some of his genuine political sentiments.

92. Notestein has argued (*House of Commons*, pp. 500–1) that there was a marked difference between the late Elizabethan and early Jacobean Parliaments on the very subject of freedom of speech.

93. Lawrence Stone (*The Causes of the English Revolution, 1529–1642* [New

York: Harper & Row, 1972], pp. 103–5) lists the Common Law as one of the four main intellectual bases of the English Revolution. He quotes James's comment that "ever since his coming to the Crown the popular sort of lawyers have been the men that most affrontedly in all Parliaments have trodden upon his Prerogative" (p. 104). Notestein cites the 1604 comment of the Venetian ambassador about the behavior of the M.P.s: "The Parliament is full of seditious subjects, turbulent and bold, who talk freely and loudly about the independence and the authority of Parliament, in virtue of its ancient privileges, which have fallen into disuse, but may be revived, and this will prove a diminution . . . of the royal prerogative" (*House of Commons*, p. 129).

94. When, however, there was a debate at Cambridge on the relative merits of elective and hereditary monarchies, James did not regard the event as a harmless academic exercise: see *The Letters of John Chamberlain*, ed. Norman E. McClure, 2 vols. (Philadelphia: American Philosophical Society, 1939), 1:440.

95. For a useful corrective to the "democratic reform" school of Parliamentary history (which includes Notestein), see *Faction and Parliament: Essays on Early Stuart History*, ed. Kevin Sharpe (Oxford: Clarendon Press, 1978), especially Kevin Sharpe, "Introduction: Parliamentary History, 1603–1629: In or Out of Perspective" (pp. 1–42), R. C. Munden, "James I and 'the growth of mutual distrust'" (pp. 43–72) and R. W. K. Hinton, "The Decline of Parliamentary Government Under Elizabeth I and the Early Stuarts" (pp. 116–32). Responding to such analyses, however, as an overcorrection of the anachronistic Whig conception of early Stuart Parliamentary history, J. H. Hexter has recently reminded us that "what was ultimately at stake in England in the early decades of the seventeenth century was liberty, not only the liberty of seventeenth-century Englishmen but our own liberty, and . . . failure to keep this firmly in mind has bound able historians to the futile and stultifying labor of trying to build an arch of explanation without a keystone" (*Reappraisals in History: New Views on History and Society in Early Modern Europe*, 2nd ed. [Chicago and London: Univ. of Chicago Press, 1979], p. 215).

96. Peters, *Paradoxes and Problems* (pp. 92–93) suggests that this was written against Sir Walter Ralegh.

97. See *Pseudo-Martyr*, pp. 47–48.

98. In *Ignatius His Conclave* (pp. 41, 43) Donne depicts the preferment of men through homosexual favoritism by evil Italian ecclesiastical authorities, a dangerously topical allusion to the association of sodomy and advancement at the Jacobean Court.

99. See the chapter on "State Secrets" in Goldberg, *James I*, pp. 55–112.

100. The expression is used by Jonson in *Epicoene* (I.i.80).

101. See *The Courtier's Library*, p. 48.

102. Bacon was implicated in the charges of "undertaking" in the 1614 Parliament and finally became the victim of the revived powers of impeachment in 1621.

103. See Goldberg, *James I*, pp. 1–17.

104. Donne also joined a number of his friends in composing mock-commendatory poems for the edition of Thomas Coryat's *Crudities* (see Bald,

Life, pp. 192-93). For the tradition of verse Donne and his associates mocked, see Williams, "Commendatory Verses," pp. 1-14.

105. See *Letters*, p. 34.

106. See A. Alvarez, *The Savage God: A Study of Suicide* (New York: Random House, 1970), pp. 153-61, and Carey, *Donne: Life, Mind, and Art*, p. 209. Webber (*Contrary Music*, p. 11) makes a similar comment. Slights argues that "Donne avoids treating the personal problem directly, but it is always there as a disrupting pressure on the logical consistency of the argument" (*Casuistical Tradition*, p. 143).

107. A number of critics have dealt with *Biathanatos* in terms of Donne's libertine skepticism and subversive paradoxical strategies: see, for example, George Williamson, "The Libertine Donne," *Philological Quarterly* 13 (1934): 276-91; A. E. Malloch, "The Techniques and Function of the Renaissance Paradox," 53 (1956): 191-203; and Colie, *Paradoxica Epidemica*, pp. 497-507. Scholars have noted the importance of the casuistical tradition for this work, but have disagreed about Donne's argumentative purpose in this long prose paradox. Although Rudick and Battin offer much useful information in the extensive introduction to their edition (pp. ix-xcvi), I cannot accept their conclusion that *Biathanatos* is a coherent argument in favor of altruistic religious suicide and that Donne withheld the work from the general public because he feared it would have persuaded people to kill themselves. In the context of Donne's habitual relationship with his coterie audience, I find this highly problematic treatise (which heavily uses various forms of one of Donne's favorite words, "perplexity") a self-subverting work—one that, as Webber (*Contrary Music*, p. 5) and Slights (*Casuistical Tradition*, pp. 139-44) claim, satirizes casuistry even as it makes use of casuistical methods.

108. I agree with Carey's statement that "If we seek, among the slippery turns of Donne's thought, for the emotional heart of *Biathanatos*, we find it in his defiance of law and his assertion of individual autonomy" (*Donne: Life, Mind, and Art*, p. 205).

109. See *Biathanatos*, pp. 84-86.

110. Goldberg (*James I*, pp. 113-63) suggests that James could be quite obtuse on occasion.

111. Cecil had recently failed to rescue the King's finances by means of getting the Parliament to accept the "Great Contract," his scheme for putting royal income on a stable basis.

112. See the discussions of Donne's letter-writing in E. N. S. Thompson, *Literary Bypaths of the Renaissance* (New Haven, Conn.: Yale Univ. Press, 1924), pp. 91-126; Simpson, *Prose*, pp. 291-336; Martin Seymour-Smith, *Poets through Their Letters: From the Tudors to Coleridge* (New York: Holt, Rinehart and Winston, 1969), pp. 84-122; John Carey, "John Donne's Newsless Letters," *Essays and Studies* 34 (1981), ed. Anne Barton (London: John Murray, 1981): 45-65; and Annabel Patterson, "Misinterpretable Donne: The Testimony of the Letters," *John Donne Journal* 1 (1982): 39-53. The particular letters Donne composed while abroad with Sir Robert Drury are examined in R. E. Bennett,

"Donne's Letters from the Continent in 1611–12," *Philological Quarterly* 19 (1940): 66–78.

113. Carey calls this verse epistle "the noblest of Donne's poems" (*Donne: Life, Mind, and Art*, p. 77).

114. Bald (*Life*, pp. 165–66), citing I. A. Shapiro, points to Goodyer's financial difficulties as the real reason Donne urged his friend to make a break with his current way of life. Milgate (*Satires, Epigrams and Verse Letters*, p. 236) dates the poem before a trip Goodyer probably took in 1609.

115. Bald (*Life*, p. 184) cannot date Donne's first acquaintance with Herbert, but he notes that the younger man was the ward of Donne's father-in-law until 1603. Having been an M.P. in the 1601 Parliament, in which Donne also served, he was also part of the 1604–10 Parliament, although he traveled on the Continent in 1608. Knighted at the beginning James's reign, Herbert remained an active courtier enjoying a measure of royal rewards: in 1605 he was made chief forester of Snowden Forest, constable of Conway Castle, Steward of the King's lands in the Monastery of Badsey, and Sheriff for Montgomeryshire, where from 1607 on he worked to make his Montgomery Castle fit for residence (see Amy Charles, *A Life of George Herbert* [Ithaca, N.Y., and London: Cornell Univ. Press, 1977], pp. 49–54). Herbert joined the force besieging Juliers in 1610, lived in England from 1611 to 1614, was rescued from prison in France in 1614, and was made Ambassador to France in 1619. Cf. the introduction to G. C. Moore Smith's edition of Herbert's poetry (pp. ix–xv) and *The Autobiography of Edward, Lord Herbert of Cherbury*, ed. with an introduction by J. M. Shuttleworth (London, New York, Toronto: Oxford Univ. Press, 1976).

116. Herbert composed the proto-deistic *De Veritate* as well as a number of other philosophical and religious works.

117. See Bald, *Life*, pp. 180–84.

118. "Conversations with Drummond," in *Ben Jonson*, 1:136.

119. Donne wrote two elegies, "Death I recant" and "Language thou art too narrow"; Herbert composed an epitaph, "Methinks Death like one laughing lyes" (*Poems*, pp. 20–21).

120. Bald says that "Donne . . . possessed a number of Pembroke's poems in manuscript" (*Life*, p. 351) and that the Hawthornden MS, William Drummond's transcription of a commonplace book of Donne's, contains several of the Earl's poems mixed in with Donne's own lyrics. One seventeenth-century manuscript poetical miscellany, Rosenbach MS 240/2, actually presents a Pembroke-Rudyerd lyric exchange as a poem-and-answer set by Wotton and Donne (See Grierson, 1:430–32).

121. "The Relique" might also have belonged to this group.

122. See Gardner, *Elegies and Songs and Sonnets*, p. 256, and George Williamson, "The Convention of *The Extasie*," in *Seventeenth Century Contexts* (Chicago: Univ. of Chicago Press, 1961), pp. 63–77. See my longer discussion of this lyric in "Donne and 'The Extasie'," in Sloan and Waddington, eds., *Rhetoric of Renaissance Poetry*, pp. 141–73, portions of which are repeated here.

123. Ezra Pound, *The ABC of Reading* (1934; repr. Norfolk, Conn.: New Directions, 1951), p. 218.
124. See Hughes, *Progress of Soul*, pp. 84-86.
125. I discuss the marriage symbolism and autobiographical allusiveness of the poem in "Donne and 'The Extasie'," in Sloan and Waddington, eds., *Rhetoric of Renaissance Poetry*, pp. 158-73.
126. Walton, "Life of Donne," p. xxvii.
127. See Bald, *Life*, p. 183.
128. *Elegies and Songs and Sonnets*, p. 256.
129. *Elegies and Songs and Sonnets*, pp. 219-20.
130. For a discussion of five as a marriage number, see Alastair Fowler, *Triumphal Forms: Structural Patterns in Elizabethan Poetry* (Cambridge: Cambridge Univ. Press, 1970), p. 74.
131. See Gardner, "Titles," p. 202.
132. Herbert, *Autobiography*, p. 112.
133. Herbert, *Autobiography*, p. 42.
134. T. J. Kelly remarks that "Far from being a celebration of Platonic love, the poem is aware of tension and cost, and finally exultant in the realization of quite unplatonic possibilities. One suspects that Donne's coterie readers were quicker on the uptake than some of his most earnest modern admirers" ("Donne's 'Firme Substantiall Love'," *The Critical Review* 13 [Melbourne, 1970]: 102).
135. Some manuscripts entitle this poem "The Nothing." See Gardner, *Elegies and Songs and Sonnets*, p. 56.
136. See Don A. Keister, "Donne and Herbert of Cherbury: An Exchange of Verses," *Modern Language Quarterly* 8 (1947): 430-34, and Milgate, *Satires, Epigrams and Verse Letters*, pp. 238-42.
137. *The Life of the Renowned Sr. Philip Sidney*, in *The Works in Verse and Prose Complete*, ed. Alexander Grosart (1870; repr. New York: AMS, 1966), 4:70.
138. Milgate makes this point when he says that "Donne's letter pays compliment to his friend . . . in respecting his tastes for philosophy and for congested meaning in poetry" (*Satires, Epigrams and Verse Letters*, p. 239).
139. For Donne's relationship with this patroness, see, in particular, Bald, *Life*, pp. 170-79, 275-76, and passim; Gardner, *Elegies and Songs and Sonnets*, pp. 248-51; Milgate, *Satires, Epigrams and Verse Letters*, p. 253; Patricia Thomson, "John Donne and the Countess of Bedford," *Modern Language Review* 44 (1949): 329-40; and Margaret Maurer, "The Real Presence of Lucy Russell, Countess of Bedford, and the Terms of John Donne's 'Honour is so sublime perfection'," *ELH* 47 (1980): 205-34. For other biographical information about the Countess, see also J. H. Wiffen, *Historical Memoirs of the House of Russell* (London: Longman, 1833), 2:74-123; Ian Grimble, *The Harington Family* (London: Jonathan Cape, 1957), pp. 165-76; and Bernard Newdigate, *Michael Drayton and his Circle* (Oxford: Shakespeare Head Press, 1961), pp. 56-69.
140. In the contemporary *Problem* 7 Donne joked about the power of in-

fluential women at Court in asking "doe wee . . . in this dignifying them, flatter Princes and great Personages that are so much governd by them?" (p. 29). Donne's friend the Earl of Northumberland remarked in his *Advice to His Son* (ed. G. B. Harrison [London: Benn, 1930]): "Of great use I have known my mistresses in a court when either a lady governed all, or ladies ruled them that ruled all, and so as instruments to collude, or as spies, they are advantageous often" (p. 98).

141. See *Letters*, pp. 22–24, 67–68. More letters, no doubt, were written to her and have not survived.

142. For the difference between Donne's situation and that of the professional writers Lady Bedford helped with her artistic patronage, see Patricia Thomson, "Donne and the Poetry of Patronage: *The Verse Letters*," in Smith, *John Donne: Essays in Celebration*, pp. 310–11. The Countess served as patroness for such other authors as John Florio and Michael Drayton (see *Ben Jonson*, 11:14). John Dowland, John Davies of Herford, and George Chapman dedicated works to her (see Williams, *Index*, p. 161). See Jonson's *Epigrams* 76, 84, and 94, which are addressed to her, and the twelfth poem of *The Forrest*, which has a dozen lines of praise for her in an epistle to the Countess of Rutland. For a discussion of Daniel's epistles to her, see Margaret Maurer, "Samuel Daniel's Poetical Epistles, Especially Those to Sir Thomas Egerton and Lucy, Countess of Bedford," *Studies in Philology* 74 (1977): 418–44.

143. See Bald, *Life*, p. 158.

144. Jonson similarly praised her for having "a learned, and manly soule" (*Epigrams* 76.13) and Daniel called her a "learned Lady" (in his epistle "To The Ladie Lucie, Countesse of Bedford," 1.33 in *Poems*, p. 117). Wallace Notestein ("The English Woman, 1580–1650," in *Studies in Social History: A Tribute to G. M. Trevelyan*, ed. J. H. Plumb [London: Longmans, 1955], p. 100) points to the praise of a woman's intellect as a new phenomenon in the late Renaissance. Thomson states that "Perhaps the subtlest part of [Donne's] complimentary addresses to the Countess of Bedford lies not in his 'Petrarchan' divinisation of her, but in his assumption that, on his level, she could follow the intricacies of . . . ingenious arguments" ("Donne and the Poetry of Patronage," p. 316), but I agree with John Buxton, who suggests that "by the verse letters to her she may have been as much bewildered as flattered" (*Sir Philip Sidney and the English Renaissance*, 2nd ed. [London: Macmillan and New York: St. Martin's Press, 1964], p. 230). Evelyn Simpson notes that Donne's "prose works show that he despised the intellectual powers of women, and that he never regarded them as the equals and comrades of men" (*Prose*, p. 71).

145. For information about Cecilia Bulstrode, see Milgate, *Epithalamions, Anniversaries, and Epicedes*, pp. 182–83. Sir Thomas Roe was Cecilia Bulstrode's lover (see Alvaro Ribeiro, "Sir John Roe: Ben Jonson's Friend," *Review of English Studies* n.s. 24 [1973]: 161). John Chamberlain (*Letters*, 1:285) refers to Meautis's relationship with Donne's friend George Garrard. For Lady Bedford's later correspondence with Jane Meautis, see *The Private Correspondence of Jane Lady Cornwallis, 1613–1644* (London: Bentley, Wilson, & Fley, 1842). For a discussion of all three women, see Bald, *Life*, pp. 176–79.

146. *The Diary of the Lady Anne Clifford*, ed. Victoria Sackville-West (New York: George Duran, n.d.), pp. 16–17.
147. Quoted in *Ben Jonson*, 10:448.
148. Stone, *Crisis*, p. 664.
149. Quoted in E. K. Chambers, *The Elizabethan Stage* (Oxford: Clarendon Press, 1923), 1:54.
150. Jonson, "Conversations with Drummond," *Ben Jonson*, 1:150.
151. Savage, ed., "Conceited Newes," pp. lvi–lxii.
152. I cite the text printed in Peters's *Paradoxes and Problems*, even though she places the piece (for no especially compelling reason) among the Dubia. In the section of the expanded edition of Overbury's *The Wife* in which the "Newes" game is printed, the collection of pieces is described as being "occasioned by diuers Essayes, and priuate passages of Wit, between sundrie Gentlemen" (Savage, ed., *Conceited Newes*, p. 223), the product, therefore, of a game of coterie competition.
153. We know that Lady Arabella Stuart objected to *Epicoene* because she felt that she was an object of satire in it: see *CSP Venetian*, 11:427 quoted in Ben Jonson, *Epicoene or the Silent Woman*, ed. L. A. Beurline (Lincoln: Univ. of Nebraska Press, 1966), p. xiii.
154. See Thomson, "Donne and the Countess of Bedford," p. 330.
155. David Aers and Gunther Kress, "'Darke Texts Need Notes': Versions of Self in Donne's Verse Epistles," *Literature and History* 8 (Autumn 1978): 138–58.
156. Maurer ("Real Presence," pp. 215–22) discusses this important aspect of Lady Bedford's courtly activities.
157. Maurer, "Real Presence," p. 212.
158. Cf. "Aire and Angels," and the second epistle to the Countess of Huntington ("Man to Gods image"), especially 17–20.
159. The O'Flahery MS entitles the poem "Twitnam: To the Countess of B."
160. Aers and Kress argue, however, that Donne suggests in this poem that (in the context of patronage) Lady Bedford "is not inherently valuable" since "her worthiness is a product of contingent social circumstances" ("'Darke Texts'," p. 139).
161. Milgate, *Satires, Epigrams and Verse Letters*, p. 235. For a similar poem see "*Sir* Henry Wotton, and *Serjeant* Hoskins, *riding on the way*" (in Osborn, *John Hoskyns*, pp. 211–12).
162. See Milgate, *Epithalamions, Anniversaries, and Epicedes*, pp. 235–37.
163. See "Verses made by the earle of Oxforde and Mrs Ann Vauesor" ("Sittinge alone vpon my thoughte in melancholy moode") in *Bodleian Rawlinson Poetical MS 85*, ed. Cummings, p. 197, and the discussion of an exchange of verse between Ralegh and Elizabeth in L. G. Black, "A Lost Poem by Queen Elizabeth I," *Times Literary Supplement* (23 May 1968), p. 535.
164. For information about the Countess of Huntington and about Donne's relationship to her, see Milgate, *Satires, Epigrams and Verse Letters*,

pp. 242–43; Bald, *Life*, pp. 110–11, 179–80; and John Yoklavich, "Donne and the Countess of Huntington," *Philological Quarterly* 43 (1964): 283–88.

165. In one of his sermons, Donne remarks that "A familiar and assiduous conversation with women will hardly be without tentation and scandal" (*Sermons*, 1:201).

166. See Smith, *John Donne: The Songs and Sonnets*, p. 51. For a contemporary song on the same theme, see John Danyel's "Now the earth, the skies, the Aire" in Doughtie, *Lyrics*, pp. 268–69.

167. Andreasen, *Donne, Conservative*, p. 151.

168. Philip Martin, "Donne in Twicknam Garden," *Critical Survey* 4 (1970): 174.

169. On the relationship of this poem to Lady Bedford, see Bald, *Life*, pp. 175–76 and Gardner, *Elegies and Songs and Sonnets*, pp. 250–51.

170. I follow Grierson's (1:28) reading of this word, which has the support of both the 1633 edition and a number of manuscripts. Gardner's choice of "grow," which has less textual support, has been criticized by Mark Roberts, "If It Were done When 'Tis Done," *Essays in Criticism* 16 (1966): 315–16.

171. Guss, *Donne, Petrarchist*, p. 87.

172. See D. C. Allen, "Donne on the Mandrake," *Modern Language Notes* 74 (1959): 393–97.

173. There is an interesting marginal note in Ben Jonson's copy of the 1619 edition of Martial referring to Lady Bedford's behavior. Beside the title of Martial's *Epigrams* IX.37, "In Gallam," which David McPherson notes is "the epigram [in which] the speaker insultingly refuses the lascivious advances of an aging lady" (*Ben Jonson's Library and Marginalia: An Annotated Catalogue, Studies in Philology* 71, Texts and Studies [1974], 22), Jonson has written what appears to be "a nasty allusion to Lucy, Countess of Bedford . . . 'vel Lu.Cu.B.'" (p. 11). One of Dudley Carleton's letters to John Chamberlain, written in 1606, refers to the disorderly festivities during the visit to the English Court of Queen Anne's brother, King Christian of Denmark, and seems to allude to an affair that Lady Bedford had with the Duke of Holstein: "My lady of Bedford had the grace to be sent for one day to the court; and she had not the grace but to come, where she was openly laughed at by the queen as she began to dance, and all she said to her (not having seen her since her discourting) was that her brother of Denmark was as handsome a man as the duke of Holstein" (*Dudley Carleton to John Chamberlain*, ed. Lee, p. 90).

174. Leishman, *Monarch of Wit*, p. 170.

175. See Guss, *Donne, Petrarchist*, pp. 61–62. For evidence connecting "The Funeral" with Lady Bedford, see C. M. Armitage, "Donne's Poems in Huntington Manuscript 198: New Light on 'The Funeral'," *Studies in Philology* 63 (1966): 697–707.

176. The alternate possibilities of "have" and "save" found in the manuscripts probably reflect revision for different audiences, the former reading being the emphatically bawdy one.

177. I disagree, however, with Wesley Milgate ("'Aire and Angels' and

the Discrimination of Experience," in *Just So Much Honour: Essays Commemorating the Four-Hundredth Anniversary of the Birth of John Donne*, ed. Peter Amadeus Fiore [University Park and London: Pennsylvania State Univ. Press, 1972], pp. 149–76), who tries to make the poem more straightforwardly complimentary than it really is. A. J. Smith, who reads the lyric as a witty performance, is right to notice that the "complimentary love-plot on which the poem is threaded" is "slight" ("New Bearings in Donne: 'Air and Angels'," in *John Donne: A Collection of Critical Essays*, ed. Helen Gardner [Englewood Cliffs, N.J.: Prentice-Hall, 1962], p. 176).

178. Cf. "Loves Deitie," 11–12.

179. See the Duke's speech to Viola/Cesario on the differences between men's and women's love, II.iv.96–106.

180. See, for example, the letters to Bridget White (*Letters*, pp. 1–6).

181. Guss, *Donne, Petrarchist*, p. 90. For a near-contemporary poem on the same topic, see Henry Constable's "*Complaynt of his Ladies sickness*" (in *The Poems of Henry Constable*, ed. Joan Grundy [Liverpool: Liverpool Univ. Press, 1960], p. 163). Jonson's poem "To Sicknesse" (*The Forrest*, 8) looks like it belongs either to the same or to a similar occasion as Donne's "A Feaver." Jonson begins the piece with the question "Why, *Disease*, does thou molest Ladies? and of them the best?" (1–2), possibly referring to the Countess of Bedford. As a satiric epigram, the poem concentrates on the debased world from which the complimented woman is set apart by her "Daintinesse . . . sleeked limmes, and finest blood" (22–23).

182. *Satires, Epigrams and Verse Letters*, p. 260.

183. Thomson ("John Donne and the Countess of Bedford," pp. 331–35) argues that the Countess's illness in 1612 and her conversion to a more serious piety by the Puritan Dr. Burgess alienated her somewhat from Donne, but there are signs on Donne's part of his impatience and disappointment with the relationship.

184. For the possible bawdy pun in this word, see the listing in Partridge, *Shakespeare's Bawdy*, p. 86.

185. Margaret Maurer ("John Donne's Verse Letters," *Modern Language Quarterly* 37 [1976]: 256) argues for a connection between the satiric elements in this epistle and Lady Bedford's interest in Donne's *Satires*.

186. There is only one first-person-plural pronoun (66).

187. *Satires, Epigrams and Verse Letters*, p. 266.

188. *Satires, Epigrams and Verse Letters*, p. 267.

189. Maurer, "Real Presence," p. 212.

190. Maurer, "Real Presence," p. 205.

191. Maurer, "Real Presence," p. 223. In discussing, in the *Essays in Divinity*, that part of practical judgment he terms "Discretion," Donne says that it operates "when we consider not so much the thing which we then do, as the whole frame and machine of the businesse, as it is complexioned and circumstanced with time, and place, and beholders" (p. 90). He demonstrates a sensitivity to context that applies as well to the situations of his verse.

192. See Jakobson, "Linguistics and Poetics," p. 92.

193. Aers and Kress, "'Darke Texts'," p. 139.

194. *Satires, Epigrams and Verse Letters*, p. 272.

195. Donne wrote Goodyer, however, that he wanted to keep Lady Bedford's favor while he was abroad with Drury (see *Letters*, pp. 95–96) and he seems to have written at least one prose letter to her from France (*Letters*, pp. 244–45).

196. Cf. Jonson, *Epigrams* 65.15–16: "Who e're is rais'd,/For worth he has not, He is tax'd, not prais'd."

197. Bald (*Life*, p. 248) says that their brother, Sir Robert Rich, who visited Donne at Amiens, probably suggested that he write them a complimentary piece.

198. See *Letters*, pp. 259–61, and Milgate, *Satires, Epigrams and Verse Letters*, p. 277.

199. In the second epistle to the Countess of Huntington ("Man to Gods image") Donne allowed himself to be lively, playful, and teasingly familiar with the addressee. What comes through in this verse letter is an affectionate cordiality missing from the other epistles to women of station. He felt free enough to joke easily and metapoetically about the "flatteries" (49) expressed in encomiastic verse. A similar mode of communication is found in Jonson's epistle to Lady Aubigny (*The Forrest* 13), a noblewoman in whose house he resided some five years.

200. Donne was painfully conscious that, in his encomiastic verse, he risked turning himself into a mere artistic client, something he wished to avoid. In replying in 1609 to Goodyer's suggestion that he write verse to someone other than Lady Bedford, he said he wished to be thought of as pursuing "a graver course, then [that] of a Poet, into which (that I may also keep my dignity) I would not seem to relapse. The Spanish proverb informes me, that he is a fool which cannot make one Sonnet, and he is mad which makes two" (*Letters*, pp. 103–4).

201. Frank Kermode, *John Donne*, British Council and National Book League, Writers and Their Work, no. 86 (London: Longmans, 1957), p. 20.

202. "'A Nocturnall upon St. Lucy's Day, being the shortest day'," pp. 181–201. Gardner accepts the suggestion made by Louis Martz (in both *The Poetry of Meditation*, 2nd ed. [New Haven, Conn., and London: Yale Univ. Press, 1962], p. 215, and in *The Poem of the Mind* [New York: Oxford Univ. Press, 1966], pp. 17–20) that the poem was written as a response to Ann's death. The original suggestion of this dating was made in W. A. Murray, "Donne and Paracelsus," *Review of English Studies* 25 (1949): 115–23.

203. "'The Dissolution': Donne's Twofold Elegy," *ELH* 28 (1961): 301–15.

204. For the poem's liturgical materials, see Clarence H. Miller, "Donne's 'A Nocturnall upon S. Lucies Day' and the Nocturns of Matins," *Studies in English Literature* 6 (1966): 77–86. Miller (p. 80), incidentally, associates the poem with the *La Corona* sonnets and, thus, with an early (1608) date.

205. See Edgar Hill Duncan, "Donne's Alchemical figures," *ELH* 9 (1942): 257–85; Murray, "Donne and Paracelsus," pp. 115–23; Joseph A. Mazzeo, "Donne's Alchemical Imagery," in *Renaissance and Seventeenth Century Studies*

(New York: Columbia Univ. Press, 1964), pp. 60–89; and Eluned Crawshaw, "Hermetic Elements in Donne's Poetic Vision," in Smith, *Donne: Essays in Celebration*, pp. 324–48.

206. Gunther Kress, "Poetry as Anti-language: A Reconsideration of Donne's 'Nocturnall Upon S. Lucies Day'," *PTL: A Journal for Descriptive Poetics and Theory of Literature* 3 (1978): 327–44.

207. Kress, "Poetry as Anti-language," p. 336.

208. On the dates of composition, see Milgate, *Epithalamions, Anniversaries, and Epicedes*, pp. xxx–xxxi. For an account of Donne's relationship with Sir Robert Drury, see R. C. Bald, *Donne and the Drurys* (Cambridge: Cambridge Univ. Press, 1959) and *Life*, pp. 237–71.

209. See Bald, *Life*, p. 240.

210. For a good discussion of the conflation of genres in these poems, see Rosalie Colie, "'All in Peeces': Problems of Interpretation in Donne's Anniversary Poems," in Fiore, *Just So Much Honor*, pp. 189–218.

211. "Conversations with Drummond," *Ben Jonson*, 1:133.

212. For example, the "shee" of the poem has been identified as Queen Elizabeth (Marjorie Nicolson, *The Breaking of the Circle: Studies in the Effect of the 'New Science' upon Seventeenth Century Poetry* [Evanston, Ill.: Northwestern Univ. Press, 1950], p. 88), Astraea (George Williamson, "The Design of Donne's *Anniversaries*," in *Milton and Others* [Chicago: Univ. of Chicago Press, 1970]), the Roman Catholic Church (Marius Bewley, "Religious Cynicism in Donne's Poetry," *Kenyon Review* 14 [1952]: 619–46), and Wisdom (*John Donne: The Anniversaries*, ed. with an introduction and commentary by Frank Manley [Baltimore: Johns Hopkins Press, 1963], p. 18).

213. These poems have been read primarily in the contexts of intellectual and literary history. Their most elaborate treatment is found in Lewalski's *Donne's Anniversaries*, a work that, in some ways, answers the classic interpretation of the poem found in Louis Martz's *The Poetry of Meditation*, pp. 211–48.

214. On this particular combination of attitudes, see Harold Searles, "Scorn, Disillusionment and Adoration in the Psychotherapy of Schizophrenia," in *Collected Papers on Schizophrenia and Related Subjects* (London: Hogarth Press, 1965), pp. 605–25.

215. "Conversations with Drummond," *Ben Jonson*, 1:133.

216. The term *occasion* is used in the long title of each of the two long poems.

217. One of the authors included in this miscellany subscribes his poems with the motto "My lucke is losse."

218. This famous lyric was probably composed by the Earl of Oxford. See Steven W. May, "The Authorship of 'My Mind to Me a Kingdom Is'," *Review of English Studies* n.s. 26 (1975): 385–94.

219. In *The Poems of Sir Walter Ralegh*, p. 11.

220. *The Life of Fulke Greville, First Lord Brooke* (Oxford: Clarendon Press, 1971), p. 213.

221. Donne wrote George Garrard in August 1612: " . . . my Fortune

hath still that spitefull constancy, to bring me near my desires, and intercept me" (*Letter*, p. 251). Bald says of Drury that "he never obtained the appointments which he sought" (*Life*, p. 238). Samuel Calvert wrote William Trumbull on 25 July 1610 about Drury's traveling to France: "Sir Robert Drury goes thither with his lady from the Spa, because he can purchase no other employment for all his bravadoes, only to spend time" (*HMC Downshire*, 2:328).

222. On this, see Michael Macklem, *The Anatomy of the World: Relations between Natural and Moral Law from Donne to Pope* (Minneapolis: Univ. of Minnesota Press, 1958), pp. 3–19.

223. See Milgate's note in *Epithalamions, Anniversaries, and Epicedes*, p. 148.

224. Manley, pp. 159–60, cites Donne's *Sermons*, 9:64–66.

225. Donne refers to his "course lines" (*First Anniv.*, 446).

226. For discussion of this poem as a transition between the two *Anniversaries*, see Paul Parrish, "Donne's 'A Funeral Elegie'," *Papers on Language and Literature* 11 (1975): 83–87.

227. See Colie, "'All in Peeces'," pp. 206–13.

228. See Donne's letters to Goodyer and Garrard discussing the *Anniversaries* (*Letters*, pp. 73–78, 237–39, 253–57).

229. When it became clear to Donne that those who read the printed versions of the poems misinterpreted them, or took exception to their hyperbolic praise, he strongly regretted their publication. He wrote Goodyer from France:

I hear from *England* of many censures of my book, of M^{ris} *Drury*; if any of those censures do but pardon me of my descent in Printing any thing in verse, (which if they do, they are more charitable then my self; for I do not pardon my self, but confesse that I did it against my conscience, that is, against my own opinion, that I should not have done so) I doubt not but they will soon give over that other part of that indictment, which is that I have said so much . . . it became me to say, not what I was sure was just truth, but the best that I could conceive; for that had been a new weaknesse in me, to have praised any body in printed verses, that had not been capable of the best praise that I could give. (*Letters*, pp. 74–75).

Donne expresses his characteristic aversion to becoming a publishing poet and defends the symbolic use he made of Elizabeth Drury in the poems. One of the letters to Garrard indicates that particular "Ladies" (*Letters*, p. 239), including, perhaps, Lady Bedford, objected to the fulsome praise of the deceased girl.

230. Lewalski, *Donne's* Anniversaries, pp. 312–17.

231. Garrard, who shared lodgings with Donne at the time he composed many of the religious poems, probably had some of this verse in mind when he referred to the "very transcendent" poems of Donne he had read in manuscript and copied out for his own use.

232. See Gardner, *Divine Poems*, pp. xlviii–ix. The Earl, who succeeded to the title in Feburary 1609, was hastily married to Lady Anne Clifford (with whom Donne was acquainted through Lady Bedford) two days before his fa-

ther's death to avoid becoming a ward to the Duke of Lennox. He was one of the biggest spenders among the aristocracy (see Stone, *Crisis*, pp. 213, 582–83), someone to whom authors could look for patronage.

233. See Greenblatt (*Renaissance Self-Fashioning*, pp. 115–56) for a discussion of Wyatt's penitential psalms in relation to their political context. The Elizabethan and Jacobean courtier Sir John Harington, who composed in his last years a treatise based on Petrarch's *Life of Solitude*, *The Prayse of Private Life*, wrote of the futility of his own courtly striving: "I have spent my time, my fortune, and almoste my honestie, to buy false hope, false friends, and shallow praise;—and be it rememberd, that he who castethe up this reckoning of a cowrtlie minion, will set his summe like a foole at the ende, for not being a knave at the beginninge. Oh, that i coud boaste with chaunter Davide, *In te speravi Domine*" (*Nugae Antiquae*, 2:212).

234. Since these poems were not printed until the nineteenth century, Donne knew them in manuscript and composed his late poem about them, "Upon the translation of the Psalmes by Sir Philip Sidney, and the Countesse of Pembroke his Sister."

235. Like Donne, Greville was out of office from about 1604–1614. The poems in the last part of *Caelica* (82, 84–109), an anthology of philosophical and religious verse, were probably composed in this period. Some of them express his political frustration and resentment over the success of others. *Caelica* 91, for example, demystifies the honors and titles dispensed by royalty, referring to "*Nobilitie*" as "*Powers golden fetter*" (7) and expressing a hatred of "subiection" (8). *Caelica* 95 is preoccupied with the forces responsible for "scornfull wrong or . . . suppressing merit" (9).

236. In the Preface to *Pseudo-Martyr*, Donne explained to the King the composition of the work in the following way: "The influence of those your Maiesties Bookes, as the Sunne, which penetrates all corners, hath wrought vppon me, and drawen vp, and exhaled from my poore Meditations, these discourses: Which with all reuerence and deuotion, I present to your Maiestie" (p. A3ʳ). In his sixth Problem, with the Jacobean context in mind, Donne clearly attributed secular motives to an intellectual interest in theology, suggesting that "perchance when wee study it by mingling humane respects, it is not divinity" (p. 28). In the account of his meeting with James (quoted above), it is not surprising to learn that Sir John Harington made a point of trying to talk theology with the King.

237. King James, of course, was well known as a religious poet himself. He translated DuBartas's *Uranie* into English, invited the author to visit him in Scotland in 1587, translated Psalms (that were published posthumously), and wrote other religious verse: see the discussion in Lily B. Campbell, *Divine Poetry and Drama in Sixteenth-Century England* (Cambridge: Cambridge Univ. Press and Berkeley and Los Angeles: Univ. of California Press, 1959), pp. 74–83. Campbell says of the religious sonnet sequence of Henry Lok, who came to the Scottish Court as Elizabeth's secret agent, that it was "literary work which would win favour with the Scottish King, who was probably in a simi-

lar exercise himself" (p. 131). She notes also that "Sir John Harington . . . during the reign of King James undertook to translate the Psalms and sent them to the King for criticism" (p. 54). It is not surprising that Ben Jonson began the collection of largely secular poems in *Under-wood* with three religious lyrics.

238. In the context of the "cult of Elizabeth," which had appropriated to itself both the language of Petrarchan amorousness and some of the features of Catholic Mariolotry, Southwell's elevation of religious over secular poetry (a traditional gesture on the part of a sacred poet) and Constable's choice of the Virgin Mary rather than the sonnet mistress or the Queen as the object of praise are both indirect forms of political protest.

239. See, for example, *La Corona* 5.

240. See, for example, *Letters*, pp. 48–54, 137–39.

241. I refer by number to the twelve sonnets printed as a set by Gardner, but use "1635-HS" to designate the four additional sonnets printed in the 1635 edition and "W-HS" to refer to the three poems found in the Westmoreland MS.

242. Gardner (*Divine Poems*, p. 81) suggests the autumn of 1608 as a date of composition.

243. Barbara Kiefer Lewalski, *Protestant Poetics and the Seventeenth-Century Religious Lyric* (Princeton, N.J.: Princeton Univ. Press, 1979), p. 260.

244. See, for example, the 1608 letter to Lord Hay (quoted in Bald, *Life*, pp. 161–62).

245. See my discussion of these topics in "'Love is not Love'," pp. 407–18.

246. Carey, *Donne: Life, Mind, and Art*, pp. 15–59.

247. In a letter to Goodyer, Donne described her reaction to his announcement that he intended to take orders: " . . . she had more suspicion of my calling, a better memory of my past life, then I had thought her nobility could have admitted" (*Letters*, p. 218).

248. Gardner (*Divine Poems*, p. 152) suggests 1608 as the year of composition, while Novarr estimates "late in 1608 or early in 1609" (*Disinterred Muse*, p. 93).

249. For Donne's relationship with Mrs. Herbert, see Gardner, *Elegies and Songs and Sonnets*, pp. 251–55; Bald, *Life*, pp. 180–84; H. W. Garrod, "Donne and Mrs. Herbert," *Review of English Studies* 21 (1945): 161–73; and the four letters printed in Gosse, 1:164–67. In describing Mrs. Herbert's household at Charing Cross, where she generously entertained many friends, Amy Charles uses Donne's funeral sermon for her to emphasize the piety that was mixed with her hospitality: "Not only did Mrs. Herbert see to it that prayers were conducted morning and evening in her home, but Donne tells us, she herself went to church for daily offices: 'From this I testifie her holy *cheerfulnesse*, and a *Religious alacrity*, (one of the best *evidences* of a *good conscience*) that as shee came to this place, God's house of *Prayer*, duly not onely every *Sabbath* . . . but even in those *weeke-dayes*'" (*George Herbert*, p. 42). The verse letter Donne sent Mrs. Herbert in 1608 (before her second marriage, to the much

younger Sir John Danvers), bespeaks an easy social familiarity. In it, Donne uses encomiastic topoi in a comically teasing manner. He humorously alludes to his own clientage (in which he vied with, as well as enjoyed the company of, other "noble'ambitious wits" [35] who gathered socially about Mrs. Herbert in her "Cabinet" [34]). He contrasts this healthy vying for her favor with the vicious competition of the larger world. In this smaller context, she is like a "Prince" (11) but lacks princely "faults" (11); she "dares preferre" "Truth" (12), rather than evil men—the kinds of "wicked" (8) political scramblers for "great place" (6) whose success Donne resented. The speaker's feigned envy of her fiancé, whose writings are portrayed as competing with his and others' for her affectionate attention, finally turns into a compliment as the poem's speaker declares "so much I doe love her choyce, that I/Would faine love him that shall be lov'd of her" (51–52). The poems Donne sent to her to read might have included such occasional pieces as "The Crosse" and "Upon the Annunciation and Passion falling upon one day. 1608." The former poem, identified by Gardner as a work that seems "more like a Verse-Letter than a Divine Poem" (*Divine Poems*, p. 92), defends the cross as a religious artifact against the kind of radical Protestant criticism to which King James responded in the 1603 Hampton Court Conference (Gardner, *Divine Poems*, p. 92), but, despite the public issue involved, Donne probably used the work to express his own belief in the legitimacy of using the cross for devotional purposes, communicating this attitude to someone who, like Mrs. Herbert, would have agreed with him.

250. Gardner dates the first six *Holy Sonnets* between February and August of 1609 (*Divine Poems*, p. xlix) and the second six, along with the four penitential sonnets between 1609 and the writing of *The Second Anniversarie* (*Divine Poems*, p. 1). Of the Westmoreland sonnets, the first two ("Since she whome I lov'd" and "Show me deare Christ") seem clearly to have been written after Donne's ordination, and the third ("Oh, to vex me, contraryes meete in one") probably belongs to the same period.

251. Roy Schafer, "The Loving and Beloved Superego in Freud's Structural Theory," *The Psychoanalytic Study of the Child* 15 (1960): 163–88.

252. Donne lost his real father at the age of four and he grew up with Dr. John Syminges as a stepfather (see Bald, *Life*, pp. 36–38).

253. Carey, *Donne: Life, Mind, and Art*, pp. 122–25.

254. I agree with the analysis of these twelve poems as the enactment of a process of discovery in Carol Marks Sicherman, "Donne's Discoveries," *Studies in English Literature* 11 (1971): 84–87.

255. See the discussion of the *Holy Sonnets* in Lewalski, *Protestant Poetics*, pp. 264–75.

256. Lewalski, *Protestant Poetics*, p. 270.

257. William Kerrigan, "The Fearful Accommodations of John Donne," *English Literary Renaissance* 4 (1974): 337–63.

258. See, for example, Murray Roston, *The Soul of Wit: A Study of John Donne* (Oxford: Clarendon Press, 1974), pp. 163–84.

259. Kerrigan, "Fearful Accommodations," pp. 351–56.
260. Lewalski (*Donne's* Anniversaries, p. 105) uses this term.
261. Earl Miner is right, but only in a limited sense, when he says of the religious poems: " . . . there is almost none of that antagonism of the secular poems against his audience" (*Metaphysical Mode*, p. 173).
262. By now the emphasis on the importance of Ignatian meditation for Donne's religious poetry found in Martz's *Poetry of Meditation* (for the *Holy Sonnets*, see pp. 43–56), has been corrected by a counteremphasis on Augustinian Protestantism: see especially William Halewood, *The Poetry of Grace: Reformation Themes and Structures in Seventeenth-Century English Poetry* (New Haven, Conn., and London: Yale Univ. Press, 1970) and Lewalski's *Protestant Poetics*.
263. I include Donne's service to Dean Morton in the years preceding the composition of his own polemical works.
264. In the introduction to her edition, Evelyn Simpson calls the *Essays* "essentially private meditations" (p. x), while Joan Webber says they are "closet sermons" (*Contrary Music* p. 16). Bald cites an undated letter to Goodyer in which Donne refers to his preparation for Communion by solitary "arraignment of my self" in which practice he "digested some meditations of mine, and apparelled them (as I use) in the form of a Sermon" confessing "I have not yet utterly delivered my self from this intemperance of scribbling" (*Letters*, p. 228, quoted in Bald, *Life*, p. 299).
265. Donne writes of the biblical Israelites that all their sufferings "were . . . as Physick, and had only a medicinall bitternesse in them" (p. 90).
266. Bald (*Life*, pp. 298–99) believes the reference to *"desart retiredness"* points to Donne's Mitcham years, but it is as likely that the *Essays* were written on a visit to a place like Sir Edward Herbert's Montgomerey Castle or while Donne was in France.
267. Beal (*Index* 1:247) points out a manuscript copy of the poem in Goodyer's hand. British Library Add. MS. 25707 entitles the piece "M[r] J. Dunne goeinge from S[r] H G: on good fryday sent him back this Meditacion on the waye" while British Library Harl. MS. 4955 has "Riding to S[r] Edward Herbert in wales" (See Gardner, *Divine Poems*, p. 98). See Bald, *Life*, pp. 269–71. Some four days after Donne arrived at Montgomery Castle he wrote the following socially complimentary letter to an ill Sir Robert Harley:

I could almost be content to be desperate of seeinge you while I am in thys contry if I might hope well of your health. The conversation of thys noble gentleman, who refuses me not in hys house, recompences the want of any company; but my sensiblenes of any frind's sicknes ys encreased by the healthfullnes of thys place; for I thinke if Bellarmine knew what immortality dwells here, he would looke that hys Enoch and Elias should come out of thys castle to fight against hys Antichrist. But, Sir, as I was willinge to make thys paper a little bigger than a physician's receit lest that representation should take your stomach from yt, so I wyll avoyd to make it very longe or busy, least your patient would have done. It shall, therefore, onlely say that which if I were goinge to my grace should be the honorablest peice of my epitaph, that I am your humble and affectionate servant. (*HMC Portland*, 3:6)

268. On the symbolism of movement in the poem, see A. B. Chambers, "Goodfriday, 1613. Riding Westward: The Poem and the Tradition," *ELH* 28 (1961): 31–53.

269. Donald Friedman, "Memory and the Art of Salvation in Donne's Good Friday Poem," *English Literary Renaissance* 3 (1973): 421. Cf. Sicherman, "Donne's Discoveries," pp. 68–74.

270. Friedman, "Memory and Salvation," p. 430.

271. Friedman, "Memory and Salvation," p. 424.

272. Friedman, "Memory and Salvation," p. 441.

273. "Conversations with Drummond," *Ben Jonson*, 1:136. For a discussion of this work as particularly addressed to Herbert and Sir Henry Goodyer, see Terry G. Sherwood, "Reason, Faith, and Just Augustinian Lamentation in Donne's Elegy on Prince Henry," *Studies in English Literature* 13 (1973): 53–67.

274. As Milgate (*Epithalamions, Anniversaries, and Epicedes*, p. 190) notes, the poem was printed in the third edition of Joshua Sylvester's *Lachrymae Lachrymarum, or The Spirit of Tears distilled from the untimely death of the Incomparable Prince Panaretus* (1613), but the identity of some of the amateur poets was protected by anonymity.

275. Ruth Wallerstein, *Studies in Seventeenth-Century Poetic* (Madison: Univ. of Wisconsin Press, 1951), p. 68.

276. Wallerstein, *Studies*, p. 69.

277. *HMC Portland*, 9:35–36.

278. Sir John Harington, writing to Sir Thomas Challenor on 6 September 1607, reported a preacher's saying of the Prince: "Henry the 8 pulled down abbeys and cells,/But Henry the 9 will pull down bishops and bells" (*HMC Salisbury*, 19:242).

279. Fulke Greville, *The Life of the Renowned Sr. Philip Sidney*, p. 70.

280. Elkin Calhoun Wilson (*Prince Henry and English Literature* [Ithaca, N.Y.: Cornell Univ. Press, 1946], p. 50) points out that by 1610 there were some 500 people in Prince Henry's Court. Sir John Holles's social aspirations were later satisfied when he became the Earl of Clare.

281. Cecil died 24 May 1612 and the Prince on 6 November 1612.

282. See John Chamberlain's letters of 12 May, 11 June, and 17 June 1612 about the competition for the deceased Cecil's offices (1:350–61). One of the major candidates was Sir Henry Wotton, a man whose help Bald (*Life*, p. 271) claims would have ensured Donne's success at Court. He is named by Chamberlain (1:359) as the favored candidate of the Queen and, before his death, of Prince Henry.

283. Bald, *Donne and the Drurys*, pp. 102–3.

284. This was the situation of, for example, George Wither and John Taylor the Water Poet. For the circumstances of the poem, see Milgate, *Epithalamions, Anniversaries, and Epicedes*, pp. 113–14.

285. See Stone, *Family, Sex, and Marriage*, p. 334.
286. See Bald, *Life*, pp. 272–74.
287. Margaret M. McGowan claims that "Donne is careful to write into his work references to the distasteful circumstances surrounding this particular wedding with the words 'unjust opinion' in stanza 2; and he dwells strangely on wisdom and honour (in stanza 7). It is as if he wants the reader to recognize that he himself is conscious that an extraordinarily difficult feat of persuasion is being undertaken, and that he is capable of accomplishing it" ("'As Through a Looking-glass': Donne's Epithalamia and their Courtly Context," in Smith, *John Donne: Essays in Celebration*, pp. 214–15). Goldberg (*James I*, pp. 131–33) offers a sensitive reading of the poem's courtly duplicities. Gardner (*Divine Poems*, p. lxxvii) notes that the Conway Papers (British Library, Add. MS. 23229) contain a copy of part of this poem in Sir Henry Goodyer's hand.
288. See *Letters* pp. 180–81. In one of his sermons, Donne later might have had such behavior in mind when he remarked: "By the benefit of this light [of reason], men see through the darkest and most impervious places, that are, that is, *Courts of Princes*, and the greatest *Officers* in Courts; and can submit themselves to second, and to advance the humours of men in great place, and so make their profit of the weaknesses which they have discovered in these great men" (*Sermons*, 3:360).
289. Six months before his ordination, Donne wrote his brother-in-law, Sir Robert More, "no man attends Court Fortunes with more impatience than I do" (Gosse, 2:46). He served in the 1614 ("Addled") Parliament, apparently being careful not to offend his courtly patrons (see Bald, *Life*, p. 289). Bald says that "Soon after the dissolution of Parliament Donne made his supreme and final effort to secure state employment" (*Life*, p. 289) through the Earl of Somerset and, only after the King made it clear that he would grant him only ecclesiastical, not secular, preferment, did Donne decide to enter the ministry.
290. See *Letters*, pp. 218–20.
291. In many ways, Donne's farewell to his Muse is the same gesture Sir John Harington conspicuously performed in sending the last of his epigrams to King James in 1603 at a time he thought it ripe to appeal to his new monarch for preferment (*Letters and Epigrams*, pp. 321–22).

EPILOGUE

1. Walton (*Life of Donne*, p. xix) notes that James's response to Donne's *Pseudo-Martyr* was to try to persuade him to enter the ministry (in 1610).
2. Bald (*Life*, pp. 307–8) notes that, at first, Cambridge was unwilling to comply with the King's request and only did so after an official royal mandate.
3. Bald observes that "He seems quite early to have gained James's favour as a preacher, and in many years he preached two sermons at Court

during his month. . . . In addition he became a regular preacher at Court during Lent" (*Life*, p. 313).
  4. For a discussion of Donne's first two years of ecclesiastical service, see Bald, *Life*, pp. 302–19.
  5. For Donne's continual preoccupation with patronage, see Marotti, "Donne and Rewards of Patronage," pp. 207–34.
  6. Bald (*Life*, p. 328) argues this for the former occasion.
  7. See Bald, *Life*, p. 375. Before Donne obtained the deanship, Chamberlain gossiped about him in much the same way he did about political opportunists: see the letters of 20 March 1620 and 13 October 1621 (2:296, 399).
  8. These statistics are noted by Novarr (*Disinterred Muse*, p. 94) to whose chapter on the postordination poems (pp. 94–205) I am indebted.
  9. In the "Conversations with Drummond" Jonson remarked that "now since he was made Doctor [Donne] repenteth highlie & seeketh to destroy all his poems" (*Ben Jonson*, 1:136). Considering, however, that Donne gave a manuscript of his poetry to Ker in 1619, we should not take Jonson's remark too seriously.
  10. See the discussion of this poem in Novarr (*Disinterred Muse*, pp. 103–7). He remarks that "Donne's verses to Herbert are tailored for their recipient beyond their wit and their Latin . . . Donne was familiar with Herbert's ambitions for a career at court and recognized in Herbert a younger version of himself and of the ambitions and pulls he still felt, though, as a last resort, he had taken orders" (p. 106).
  11. *Divine Poems*, p. 145. See Gardner's discussion of the two poems in *Divine Poems*, pp. 138–47.
  12. Novarr, *Disinterred Muse*, p. 113.
  13. *Divine Poems*, p. 129.
  14. *Divine Poems*, p. 132.
  15. See the discussion of the Tilman poem in Cameron, "Donne's Deliberative Verse Epistles," pp. 398–99.
  16. *Divine Poems*, p. 107.
  17. I cite this sermon in the early text printed by Potter and Simpson as an appendix in *Sermons*, 2:373–90.
  18. Robert Zaller, *The Parliament of 1621: A Study in Constitutional Conflict* (Berkeley, Los Angeles, London: Univ. of California Press), p. 9. For a discussion of Donne's service on the Doncaster embassy, see Bald, *Life*, pp. 338–65 and Paul Sellin, "John Donne: The Poet as Diplomat and Divine," *Huntington Library Quarterly* 39 (1976): 267–75.
  19. Referring to the poem, Carey remarks that "The struggle between the ambitious careerist and the lofty scorner of the world's rewards is . . . quite naked" (*Donne: Life, Mind, and Art*, p. 218).
  20. Novarr, *Disinterred Muse*, p. 130.
  21. Novarr remarks that "the evidence of the manuscripts . . . reveals that the poem circulated widely" (*Disinterred Muse*, p. 174) and that it was composed because Donne "was interested in writing verse to be used as part of a Church service" (*Disinterred Muse*, p. 192).

22. See his discussion of this poem ("Donne's Terrifying Pun," pp. 129–30, 136–37). The pun is also noted in David Leigh, S.J., "Donne's 'A Hymne to God the Father': New Dimensions," *Studies in Philology* 75 (1978), 84–92.
23. *Divine Poems*, p. 124. See Gardner's discussion of this poem (pp. 121–27).
24. *Divine Poems*, p. 126.
25. On James's handling of this foreign-policy crisis, see Zaller, *Parliament of 1621*, pp. 6–18.
26. *Divine Poems*, p. 123. Novarr (*Disinterred Muse*, p. 140), however, suggests that the political sensitivity of the poem's issues caused Donne to restrict its circulation.
27. *Divine Poems*, p. 104.
28. Novarr, *Disinterred Muse*, pp. 143–45.
29. *Divine Poems*, p. 104.
30. Lamentations was, however, a favorite scriptural text for religious poets to translate and paraphrase (see Lily B. Campbell, *Divine Poetry*, p. 73).
31. Brian Morris ("Not, Siren-like to tempt: Donne and the Composers," in Smith, *Donne: Essays in Celebration*, pp. 240–41 and 252–58) discusses the Court musician Thomas Ford's setting of the first two stanzas of Donne's paraphrase of Lamentations, speculating about a connection between Donne and Ford through the Killigrew musical circle with which Donne was affiliated.
32. Lewalski, *Protestant Poetics*, p. 276.
33. Novarr, *Disinterred Muse*, p. 157.
34. See Milgate, *Epithalamions, Anniversaries, and Epicedes*, p. 209.
35. Chamberlain, *Letters*, 2:613, quoted by Milgate, *Epithalamions, Anniversaries, and Epicedes*, p. 209.
36. See the interpretation of this poem by Hunt (*Donne's Poetry*, pp. 96–117).
37. *Divine Poems*, pp. 132–35. Gardner remarks, in arguing for the 1623 date for the poem, that "if it was written in 1623, a good reason can be suggested for Donne's not wishing it to circulate. The Hymn is a solemn poem, written in expectation of death. He might well have been unwilling to publish a poem written in an expectation which had been falsified by the event" (*Divine Poems*, p. 135). Cf. the discussion of the poem in Novarr, *Disinterred Muse*, pp. 175–84.
38. When Donne published his *Devotions* in 1623, he dedicated the work to Prince Charles and, as Bald (*Life*, p. 455) notes, sent complimentary copies to Princess Elizabeth, to one of her court ladies, to the Duke of Buckingham, and to an anonymous lord (possibly the Earl of Dorset). He thus used a work of private religious exercise as sociopolitical currency, possibly as part of a campaign for a bishopric. For a good discussion of some of the political dimensions of this prose work, see Robert M. Cooper, "The Political Implications of Donne's *Devotions*," in *New Essays on Donne*, ed. Gary A. Stringer (Salzburg: Institut für Englishe Sprache und Literatur, Universitat Salzburg, 1977), pp. 192–210.

Index

Adam (in D's *First Anniversarie*), 239
Adversarius, 159, 197
Aers, David, 207, 228, 336, 339
Alexander, Sir William: *Darius*, 180
Allen, D. C., 311, 320, 325, 337
Alvarez, A., 292, 311, 332
Amiens, 339
Anacreontic poetry, 68, 69
Anderton (in "libel against some Grayes Inns gentlemen & Revellers"), 308
Andreas Capellanus, 135, 172, 314, 327
Andreasen, N. J. C., 73, 157, 214, 307, 308, 312, 316, 324, 337
Andrews, Launcelot, Bishop, 292
Anne, Queen, consort of James I, 135, 181, 186, 202, 203, 205, 209, 337
Answer poem, the, 5, 13, 85, 293, 313, 333
Antipholus of Syracuse (in Shakespeare's *The Comedy of Errors*), 49
Anulus, Barptolemaeus, 325
Arcana imperii, 187
Aretino, Pietro, 68, 193, 303
Argalus (in Sidney's *Arcadia*), 316
Aristotle, 11, 70, 329
Armitage, C. M., 337
Armstrong, Alan, 58, 305, 307, 309
Ashton, Robert, 328
Asper/Macilente (in Jonson's *Everyman Out of His Humour*), 319
Astraea, 340
Aubigny, Lady, 339
Ault, Norman, 319

Authority, poetic, 246
Authority, religious, 260
Axton, Marie, 301
Azores, 318

Bacon, Francis, Viscount St. Albans, 32, 34, 123–24, 188, 191, 292, 298, 301, 302, 322; *The Advancement of Learning*, 27, 180; *Essays*, 27–29, 135, 168, 327; letters, 27; "The World's a Bubble," 119, 319
Badsey, Monastery of, 333
Baker, Sir Richard, 30, 100, 155, 292, 309, 311
Bald, R. C.: *Donne and the Drurys*, 340, 346; *John Donne: A Life*, 36, 97, 102, 127, 135, 166, 178, 181–82, 269, 271, 273, 276, 291, 292, 301, 302, 304, 306, 309, 310, 315, 316, 318, 319, 320, 321, 322, 323, 324, 326, 333, 334, 335, 337, 340, 341, 343, 345, 346, 347, 347–48, 348, 349; on D's early verse letters, 303
Balducci, Luigi, 296
Baldwin (in "libel against some Grayes Inns gentlemen & Revellers"), 308
Bannister, Edward, of Putney, 6
Barnett, Richard C., 318
Barton, Ann, 332
Bateson, Gregory, 20–21, 299
Battin, M. Pabst, 332
Beal, Peter, 291, 292, 297, 298, 322, 345
Beatrice (Dante's), 326
Beatrice (in Shakespeare's *Much Ado About Nothing*), 59

Beaumont, Sir John, 17, 128
Bell, Beaupré, 292
Bellarmine, Robert, Cardinal, 345
Benedick (in Shakespeare's *Much Ado About Nothing*), 59
Bennett, R. E., 306, 332
Bentley, John, 294
Berkeley, Sir Maurice, 292
Berkeley family, 6
Berry, Lloyd E., 311
Beurline, L. A., 336
Bewley, Marius, 340
Bindoff, S. T., 301
Bishops' Order (1599), 128, 304
Black, L. G., 6, 67, 294, 313, 336
Bland, Desmond, 301
Blazon, 47–48
Blount, Charles, Lord Montjoy, 1st Earl of Devonshire, 126, 319
Blunden, Sir Edmund, 292
Bogat, Margherita, 296
Boleyn, Anne, 11
Bond, William, 294
Booth, Stephen, 294–95
Bosola (in Webster's *The Duchess of Malfi*), 39
Bradbrook, Muriel Clara, 301
Bradbury, Malcom, 291, 303
Breton, Nicholas, 180
Brewer, John, 328
Brock, D. Heywood, 298
Brooke, Christopher, x, 15, 19, 37, 96, 97, 114, 269, 330
Brooke, Henry, Lord Cobham, 319
Brooke, Samuel, 36, 292
Brooks, Cleanth, 157, 324
Brown, John Russell, 303
Brumble, H. David, III, 315
Bryan, Robert A., 297, 313
Buchanan, George, 188
Bullen, A. H., 325
Bulstrode, Cecilia, 184, 196, 203, 204–5, 211, 222, 242, 335
Burghley, Lord. *See* Cecil, Sir William
Burton, Robert, 316

Butler, H. E., 306, 324
Buxton, John, 315, 335

Cabbalistic thought, 128
Cadiz Expedition (1598), 97, 102, 316; raid on Cadiz, 102, 115, 316
Caesar, 11
Caesar, Sir Julius, 286, 292
Cain (in D's *Metempsychosis*), 131, 132
Calvert, Samuel, 341
Calvin, John, 70, 190
Cambridge, University of: 6, 34, 44, 189, 306, 329, 331, 347; awards Donne a D.D. degree, 275; St. John's College, 26; Trinity College, 277
Camden, William, 180; *Remaines*, 313
Cameron, Allen Barry, 317, 319, 348
Campbell, Lily B., 342, 349
Campbell, O. J., 303
Campion, Thomas, 4–5, 17, 45, 69, 305, 311; airs, 3, 315; *Booke of Ayres* (1601), 68; book of elegies, 44; *Poemata*, 304
Carew, Thomas, 23; "An Elegie upon the death of the Dean of Paul's," 300, 305
Carey, John, 45, 52, 53, 61, 251, 254, 302, 305, 306, 308, 309, 310, 312, 316, 318, 322, 324, 326, 332, 343, 344, 348
Carleton, Sir Dudley, 1st Viscount Dorchester, 193, 203, 324, 337
Casoni, Guido, 327
Catholics, English, 190, 304
Catullus, 5, 310
Cecil, Sir Robert, Earl of Salisbury, 6, 34, 129, 131, 179, 188, 192, 270, 302, 319, 323, 324, 346
Cecil, Sir William, Lord Burghley, 27, 28, 31, 127, 129, 131, 154, 318
Celestine, Pope, 126
Challenor, Sir Thomas, 346
Chamberlain, John, 193, 285, 324, 335, 337, 346, 349
Chambers, A. B., 162, 325, 346

Index 353

Chambers, E. K., 336
Chambers, Sir Robert: *Palestina*, 180
Chanson de croisade, 316
Chapman, George, 128, 335
Character, the, 181, 193
Charing Cross, 343
Charles I, King, 6; as Prince of Wales, 349
Charles II, King, 203
Charles, Amy, 333, 343
Charlton, Kenneth, 301, 311
Christian, King, of Denmark, 337
Chute, Sir Walter, 34, 155, 166
Circe (in D's *Satire* 4), 104
Cirillo, A. R., 325
Civil War, English, period leading up to, 184
Clara (in Rudyerd's epigrams), 72
Clarendon, Earl of. *See* Hyde, Sir Edward
Claxton (in "libel against some Grayes Inns gentlemen & Revellers"), 308
Clements, A. J., 324
Clifford, Lady Ann, Countess of Dorset, Countess of Montgomery, 203, 336, 341
Cobham, Lord. *See* Brooke, Henry
Coffin, Charles Monroe, 199
Coke, Sir Edward, 70, 123
Colie, Rosalie, 47, 68, 69, 299, 302, 306, 307, 311, 314, 325, 332, 340, 341
Collins, Arthur, 318, 319
Colman, Morgan, 181
Common lawyers: in Parliament, 184
Commonplace book anthologies of poetry. *See* Miscellanies, manuscript poetical
Congé d'amour, 99
Connock, Richard, 330
Connoisseurship, 20
Constable, Henry, 251, 343; poems, 247; "Complaynt of his Ladies sickness," 338
Constitution, English, 185

Contemptus mundi, 119, 164, 236, 262, 264, 281
Conway Castle, 333
Conway Papers. *See* Donne, John, manuscripts of poetry, BL Add. MS. 23229
Cooper, Robert M., 349
Corinna (in Ovid's *Amores*), 54, 60, 305
Corkine, Sir William, 314
Cornwallis, Ann, 6
Cornwallis, Sir William, 269, 292, 306; essays, 67; paradoxes, 46
Corthell, Robert J., 320
Corti, Maria, 296, 302, 311
Coryat, Thomas: *Crudities*, 331
Coscus (in D's *Satire* 2), 41–42
Cotton, Sir Robert, 292, 330; *Cottoni Posthuma*, 330
"A Counterlove" (Anon.), 317
Court of Wards, 124
Craig, A.: *The poetical essays of A. Craig Scotobritane*, 180
Cranfield, Sir Lionel, 1st Earl of Middlesex, 286, 292, 330
Crawshaw, Eluned, 340
Crum, Margaret, 14, 17, 18, 296, 297, 298
Cummings, Laurence, 294, 336
Curtis, Mark, 33, 302
Cynthia (in Propertius' elegies), 60

Damon, Philip, 295
Daniel, Samuel, 202, 211; *Delia*, 315; epistles to the Countess of Bedford, 335; *Vision of the Twelve Goddesses*, 203; *Works*, 180
Dante, 126, 177, 326
Danvers, Sir John, 344
Danyel, John, 337
Davenport, Arnold, 300, 313
David, the Psalmist, 342
Davies, John, of Hereford, 335; *Microcosmos*, 180
Davies, Sir John, 32, 69, 291, 294, 303, 305, 313, 329; *Epigrams*, 17,

354 Index

Davies, Sir John (*continued*) 39–40, 49, 50, 308, 320; "Gulling Sonnets," 83; *Hymnes to Astraea*, 84; *Nosce Teipsum*, 329; "Sonnets to Philomel," 83–84
Davis, Walter R., 29
Davison, Francis, xi, 7, 16
Davison, Walter: "A dialogue betweene him and his Hart," 317
Dawson, Giles, 294
"Dear Love, continue nice and chaste" (Anon.), 19
De George, Fernande, 299
De George, Richard, 299
Delia (in Tibullus' elegies), 60
De L'Isle and Dudley, HMC, 326
Dell, Floyd, 316
Derby, Countess of. *See* Spencer, Alice
De Vere, Edward, 17th Earl of Oxford, 3, 113, 340; poems, 18, 212; "My mind to me a kingdom is," 237; "Verses made by the earle of Oxforde and Mrs Ann Vauesor," 336
Devereux, Penelope, Lady Rich, Countess of Devonshire, 11, 296
Devereux, Robert, 2nd Earl of Essex, 12, 33, 59, 97, 100, 119, 120, 122–23, 124, 125, 126, 129, 131, 163, 188, 206, 309, 316, 319, 320, 323; clients of, 102, 123
Dipsas (in Ovid's *Amores*), 60
Dives amator, 148, 305
Doncaster, Viscount. *See* Hay, James
Doncaster embassy (1619), 276, 280–81, 283, 348
Donna angelicata, 111, 209, 219, 317
Donne, Ann (More), xi, 96, 98, 133–78 *passim*, 278–79, 321; as primary audience for some poems, 139; death of, 138, 232, 278, 339
Donne, John: appointed Reader in Divinity at Lincoln's Inn, 275; appointed royal chaplain, 275; Catholicism and Catholic background, 97, 116, 302, 304; collects poetry for possible publication, ix–x; Dean of St. Paul's, 276, 283, 285; service in Parliament (1601), 141, 152; service in Parliament (1614), 186; travels, 1605–6, 148, 166, 168, 169, 177, 181; travels, 1611–12, 169, 229, 235, 265; travels, 1619, 276

POETRY

Anniversaries, ix, 16, 23, 118, 181, 182, 222, 227, 230, 231, 232, 233, 234, 235–45, 262, 268, 340, 341; *The First Anniversarie*, 23, 201, 224, 236–42, 243; "A Funeral Elegie," 235, 242–43, 341; *The Second Anniversarie*, 237, 238, 243–44, 344

Divine Poems:
  La Corona, 15, 17, 182, 246–48, 252–53, 339, 343; "To Mrs. Magdalen Herbert: of St. Mary Magdalen," 247, 252–53; *La Corona* 1, 253; *La Corona* 3, 253; *La Corona* 4, 253; *La Corona* 5, 253; *La Corona* 7, 248
  "The Crosse," 344
  "Goodfriday, 1613. Riding Westward," 24, 261, 266–68, 297
  Holy Sonnets, 15, 17, 182, 245, 247, 251, 253–61, 268, 344; "To E. of D. with six holy Sonnets," 245; *Holy Sonnet* 1, 255; *Holy Sonnet* 2, 254, 256; *Holy Sonnet* 3, 254, 256, 256–57, 276; *Holy Sonnet* 4, 248, 255–56; *Holy Sonnet* 5, 254, 256; *Holy Sonnet* 6, 248, 257; *Holy Sonnet* 7, 254, 256, 257; *Holy Sonnet* 9, 251, 254, 258; *Holy Sonnet* 10, 259; *Holy Sonnet* 1635–3 ("O might those sighes"), 248; *Holy Sonnet* Westmoreland–1 ("Since she whom I lov'd"), 138, 177, 278–79; *Holy Sonnet* Westmoreland–2 ("Show me deare Christ"), 282–83; *Holy*

Sonnet Westmoreland-3 ("Oh, to vex me"), 248, 251, 279
"A Hymne to Christ, at the Authors last going into Germany," 138, 276, 278, 279, 281–82
"Hymn to God, my God, in my sicknesse," 21, 276, 285–86
"A Hymne to God the Father," 138, 248, 276, 278, 281, 349
"The Lamentations of Jeremy, for the most part according to Tremelius," 276, 283–84
"A Litanie," 245, 248–50, 324
"To Mr. George Herbert, with my Seal, of the Anchor and Christ," 276–77
"To Mr. Tilman after he had taken orders," 115, 276, 277–78, 279, 348
"Upon the Annunciation and Passion falling upon one day. 1608," 344
"Upon the translation of the Psalmes by Sir Philip Sidney, and the Countess of Pembroke his Sister," 276, 284–85, 342
Elegies, xii, 15, 16, 17, 44–66, 127, 245, 304, 305, 308
"The Anagram," 45, 47–48, 50
"The Autumnal," 45, 51–52, 304
"The Bracelet," 45, 57, 59–62, 66
"Change," 45, 308
"The Comparison," 45, 48–50
"A Funeral Elegy," 118–19, 304
"His Picture," 44, 45, 83, 98–100, 101, 169, 309
"Jealosie," 45, 55, 57
"Loves Progress," 45, 50–51, 74
"Loves Warre," 45, 55–56, 99
"Natures lay Ideot," 44, 45, 53
"Oh, let mee not serve so," 44, 56–57, 213
"On his Mistris," 44, 45, 57, 64–66, 178
"The Perfume," 45, 57, 62–64, 66, 94, 100, 178, 310

"To his Mistris Going to Bed," 45, 53–55, 57, 92, 306, 321
Epicedes and Obsequies:
"Elegie on M^{ris} Boulstred," 196, 223, 242, 333
"Elegie on Prince Henry," x, 196, 199, 269–71
"Elegie on the Lady Markham," 223, 242, 333
"An Hymne to the Saints, and to Marquesse Hamylton," 276, 285, 286
"Obsequies to the Lord Harrington, brother to the Countess of Bedford," 112, 118, 208, 233, 261, 269, 273–74
Epithalamions:
"Epithalamion at the Marriage of the Earl of Somerset," 269, 272–73, 297
"Epithalamion made at Lincolnes Inne," 30, 52
"An Epithalamion, or Marriage Song on the Lady Elizabeth, and Count Palatine being married on St. Valentine's Day," 174, 269, 271–72
Epigrams, 17, 102
"A Burnt Ship," 102
"Cales and Guyana," 318
"Sir John Wingfield," 102
Satires, xii, 15, 16, 17, 37–43, 45, 46, 127, 128, 206, 209, 245, 308, 338
Metempsychosis ("The Progresse of the Soule"), 20, 24, 128–33, 192, 320, 321
Satire 1, 39–40, 105, 118
Satire 2, 38, 40–42, 105, 118
Satire 3, 41–43, 70, 254, 303, 304
Satire 4, 102–5, 110, 111, 118
Satire 5, 116–18, 123
Songs and Sonnets, xii, 15, 16
"Aire and Angels," 211, 218, 219–22, 321, 336, 338
"The Anniversarie," 139, 141, 142–43, 146, 148, 165, 178, 321

356 Index

Songs and Sonnets *(continued)*
"The Apparition," 88, 90, 92–93
"The Baite," 84–85, 87, 314
"The Blossome," 106, 108–10, 297
"Breake of Day," 13, 16, 314
"The Broken Heart," 137, 138, 139, 141–42, 321
"The Canonization," 21, 36, 56, 137, 138, 139, 147, 157–65, 170, 171, 172, 176, 198, 201, 216, 233, 321, 324, 325, 326
"Communitie," 73–74, 79, 87
"The Computation," 297, 298, 321
"Confined Love," 74, 79, 87
"The Curse," 15, 79, 80–81, 82
"The Dampe," 88, 91
"The Dissolution," 17, 137, 138, 139, 232, 297, 298, 321
"The Dreame," 88, 90, 91–92, 315, 321
"The Expiration," 88, 175, 247, 298, 321
"The Extasie," 15, 24, 139, 147, 157, 171, 175, 196–99, 200, 201
"Farewell to Love," 17, 112–13, 297, 298
"A Feaver," 211, 218, 222–23, 321, 338
"The Flea," 88, 93–94, 315
"The Funeral," 211, 218–19
"The Good-Morrow," 139, 143–44, 321
"Image of her whom I love," 304–5, 315, 321
"The Indifferent," 21, 24, 76–79, 82
"A Jeat Ring Sent," 15, 16, 83–84, 297
"A Lecture upon the Shadow," 139, 147–48, 178, 321
"The Legacie," 314
"Loves Alchymie," 111–12, 132
"Loves Deitie," 106–7, 135, 338
"Loves Diet," 79, 81–82
"Loves Exchange," 83, 139–40
"Loves Growth," 137, 138, 139, 148, 321

"Loves Infiniteness," 15, 137, 138, 139, 144–47, 321
"Loves Usury," 74–76
"The Message," 13, 16, 87, 88, 314
"Negative Love," 17, 196, 200–201, 297, 298
"A Nocturnall upon S. Lucies Day, being the shortest day," 17, 87, 177, 222, 232–35, 236, 297, 298, 321, 339
"The Paradox," 85–87, 297, 298, 321
"The Primrose," 17, 196, 199, 297
"The Prohibition," 88, 90, 321
"The Relique," 17, 83, 297, 333
"Song: Goe, and catche a falling starre," 79–80, 87
"Song: Sweetest love, I do not goe," 16, 87, 176, 314, 316
"The Sunne Rising," 139, 147, 156–57, 164, 165, 178, 201, 321
"The Triple Foole," 17, 87–88
"Twicknam Garden," 15, 24, 107, 211, 214–18
"The Undertaking," 199–200
"A Valediction: forbidding Mourning," 137, 149, 168–69, 175–78, 229, 321, 328
"A Valediction: of my Name in the Window," 137, 138, 139, 148–50, 170
"A Valediction: of the Booke," 168, 169–72, 197
"A Valediction: of Weeping," 137, 138, 168, 169, 172–75, 321
"The Will," 83, 106, 107–8, 321
"Witchcraft by a Picture," 100–102, 297, 298, 321
"Womans Constancy," 74, 79
Verse Letters: xii, 16, 36–38
"The Calme," 15, 17, 38, 97–98, 99, 114, 115
"Epitaph on Himselfe: *To the Countesse of Bedford*," 229
H. W. in Hiber. Bellegranti, 124

"A Letter to the Lady Carey, and Mrs Essex Rich," 230
"A Letter written by Sir H. G. and J. D. *alternis vicibus*," 211
"The Storme," 15, 17, 19, 21, 38, 114–15, 318
"To the Countess of Bedford At New-yeares Tide" ("This twilight of two yeares"), 225–27
"To the Countess of Bedford" ("Honour is so sublime"), 227–29
"To the Countess of Bedford" ("Reason is our Soules left hand"), 208–9, 219
"To the Countess of Bedford" ("T'have written then"), 223
"To the Countess of Bedford" ("Though I be *dead*"), 229–30
"To the Countess of Bedford" ("You have refin'd mee"), 209–11
"To the Countess of Huntington" ("Man to Gods image"), 231, 336, 339
"To the Countess of Huntington" ("That unripe side of earth"), 212–14, 231
"To the Countess of Salisbury," 230–31
To Dr. Andrews, Latin poem, 292
"To the Lady Bedford" ("You that are she and you"), 223–25
To Mr. C. B. ("Thy friend, whom thy deserts"), 36, 37
To Mr. E. G. ("Even as lame things"), 36
To Mr. I. L. ("Blest are your North parts"), 36, 37
To Mr. I. L. ("Of that short Roll of friends"), 36
To Mr Rowland Woodward ("Like one who'in her third widdowhood"), 113–14
To Mr. R. W. ("If, as mine is, thy life"), 318

To Mr. R. W. ("Zealously my Muse"), 37
To Mr. S. B. ("O thou which to search"), 36
To Mr. T. W. ("All haile sweet Poet"), 36, 37
To Mr. T. W. ("At once, from hence"), 37
To Mr. T. W. ("Hast thee harsh verse"), 37
To Mr. T. W. ("Pregnant again with th'old twins"), 36
"To Mrs M. H." ("Mad paper stay"), xi, 217, 343–44
"To Sir Edward Herbert, at Julyers," 201–2
"To Sir Henry Goodyere" ("Who makes the Past"), 195–96, 226
"To Sir Henry Wotton, at his going Ambassador to Venice," 155
To Sir Henry Wotton ("Here's no more newes"), 122–23
To Sir Henry Wotton ("Sir, more then kisses"), 80, 119–22
Dubia, xiii, 18
"The Expostulation," 18, 298
"His Parting from Her," 18, 305
"Julia," 18, 305
"Sapho to Philaenis," 18, 305
"Self Love," 18
"Song: Stay, O sweet, and do not rise," 18
"A Tale of a Citizen and his Wife," 18, 305
"The Token," 18, 313, 321
"Variety," 18, 305
Editions of poetry: 1633, xii, 24, 325; 1635, 286; 1719, 300
Manuscripts of poetry: Group I, 14, 199, 232, 297, 304; Group II, 15, 297, 314; Group III, 286; Bod. Rawl. Poet. MS 31, 17; BL Add. MS 23229 (Conway Papers), 297, 347; BL Add. MS 25707, 18, 345; BL Harl. MS 4064, 17; BL Harl. MS 4955, 345; BL Lansdowne 740,

358   Index

Manuscripts of poetry (*continued*) 17, 19; Cambridge Univ. Add. MS 5778, 324; Dolau Cothi, 341; Haslewood-Kingsborough (Hunt. Lib. MS. HM 198), 18; Hawthornden MS (National Library of Scotland MS 2067), 18, 333; Leconfield MS, 323, 324; O'Flaherty MS, 336; Stephens MS, 52; Wedderburn MS (National Library of Scotland MS 6504), 18; Westmoreland MS, 15, 16, 17, 36–37, 46, 56, 102, 122, 245, 283, 297, 343

PROSE

Biathanatos, ix, 181, 182, 183, 189–90, 191, 262, 327, 332
Catalogus Librorum Aulicorum (*The Courtier's Library*), 84, 183, 188, 189, 331
Devotions upon Emergent Occasions, 276, 284, 286, 349
Essays in Divinity, 121, 182, 230, 249, 261–66, 267, 268, 284, 345
Ignatius His Conclave, 181, 182, 183, 187, 190, 191–92, 262, 329, 331
Letters, 186, 192–95, 332–33, 339, 343, 347; to the Countess of Bedford, 211–12, 335; to George Garrard, 230, 244, 340, 341; to Lady Susan Vere, Countess of Montgomery, 22; to Magdalen Herbert, 252, 343; to Sir Henry Goodyer, ix–x, 14, 21, 30, 161, 187, 190–91, 193–95, 202, 206, 218, 244, 247, 248, 251–52, 265, 280, 327, 343, 345; to Sir George More, 98, 134–35; to Sir Henry Wotton, 121–22, 124–27; to Sir James Hay, 343; to Sir Robert Harley, 345–46; to Sir Robert Ker, Earl of Ancrum, ix; to Sir Thomas Egerton, 154, 286; to unknown correspondents, xi, 41, 46–47, 102, 121, 165, 168; Folger MS L. b. 526–29, 323
Paradoxes, 46–47, 127, 128, 262, 265, 306–7; Paradox 2, 46, 306; Paradox 3, 306; Paradox 7, 46, 307; Paradox 8, 306; Paradox 9, 46; Paradox 10, 306
Problems, 15, 181, 182, 183–84, 186–88, 189, 260, 262, 265, 334–35, 342
Pseudo-Martyr, 43, 181, 182, 183, 190, 191, 259, 262, 319, 331, 342, 347
Sermons, 22, 69, 70–71, 121, 135, 138, 188, 204, 254, 255, 258, 276, 283–84, 319, 325, 337, 347, 348; at Lincoln's Inn, 30, 31, 38, 67, 279–80, 286; at Paul's Cross, 275–76
Dubia
"A Defence of Womens Inconstancy," 46, 52
"The Description of a Scot at first sight," 188, 330
"An Essay of Valour," 183, 188, 189
"Newes from the Very Country," 205
"Sir Francis Walsingham's Anatomizing of Honesty, Ambition, and Fortitude," 330
"The True Character of a Dunce," 330
Donne, John, Jr., 196, 314
Donne, Nicholas, son of John and Ann, 168
Dorset, Earl of. *See* Sackville, Sir Edward
Doughtie, Edward, 295, 311, 312, 314
Dowland, John, 335
Downshire, HMC, 341
Drayton, Michael, 4, 211, 335; *Poly-Olbion*, 293
Dromio (in Shakespeare's *The Comedy of Errors*), 49
Drummond, William, of Hawthornden, 69, 269, 297, 303, 333
Drury, Elizabeth, 118, 230, 236, 341
Drury, Sir Robert, x, 137, 229, 235, 242, 244, 271, 332, 339, 340, 341

Dryden, John, 299; on Donne's
  poetry, 20
Du Bartas, Guillaume: *Uranie*, 342
Dudley, Robert, 1st Earl of Leicester,
  11, 90
Duessa (in Spenser's *The Faerie
  Queene*), 50
Duke (in Shakespeare's *Twelfth
  Night*), 338
Duncan, Edgar Hill, 339
Duncan-Jones, Katherine, 316, 324
Dyer, Sir Edward, 3, 4, 10; "The
  lowest trees have topps," 12

Eco, Umberto, 299
Edwards, Richard, 7
Egerton, Lady Elizabeth, 133, 148,
  155, 321
Egerton, Sir Thomas, Lord Ellesmere, Viscount Brackley, xi, xii,
  35, 96, 106, 113, 116, 117, 118, 119,
  128, 153, 154, 161, 187, 275, 286,
  302, 318, 321, 323; as client of the
  Earl of Essex, 116; marriage to the
  Dowager Countess of Derby, 134
Egerton, Thomas, Jr., 116, 118
Egypt (in D's *Essays in Divinity*), 264
Elias, 345
Elizabeth I, Queen, 6, 8, 12, 28, 29,
  31, 42–43, 50, 56, 57, 73, 84, 89,
  97, 103, 105, 116, 117, 122, 124,
  127, 128, 129, 167, 180, 184, 212,
  300, 301, 304, 309, 316, 318, 319,
  320, 336, 342, 343
Elizabeth, Princess, Queen of
  Bohemia, 271, 349
Ellis, Robert, 301
Ellrodt, Robert, 58, 302, 309
Elton, G. R., 322
Empson, William, 322
England's Helicon, 314
Enoch, 345
Epyllia, erotic, 88, 89, 93
Equicola, 325
Erasmus, Desiderius, 325
Esler, Anthony, 90, 309, 316

Essay, the, 181, 193
Essex-Howard divorce, 273
Essex Revolt, 128, 326
Eve (in D's *First Anniversarie*), 239
Exclusus amator, 305

"A Fantasticke Innes of Court Man"
  (Anon.), 307
Ferrabosco, Alfonso, 314
Ficino, Marsilio, 198
Finet, John, 6, 12, 294
Finkelpearl, Philip, 31–32, 34, 68,
  300, 301, 301–2, 303, 309, 311
Fiore, Peter Amadeus, 338, 340
Fish, Stanley, 299
Fleetwood (in "libel against some
  Grayes Inns gentlemen & Revellers"), 308
Fletcher, Giles, the Elder, 311; *Licia*,
  67
Florio, John, 335
Flynn, Dennis, 300, 330
Ford, Thomas, 349
Forman, Simon, 89, 314; dream of
  Queen Elizabeth, 89–90
Forster, Leonard, 313
Foucault, Michel, 13, 296
Fowler, Alastair, 334
France, 61, 229, 244, 327, 328, 333,
  339, 341, 345; ambassador to, 333
Freccero, John, 176–77, 328
Freedom, political, 184
Freeman, Rosemary, 322
Friedman, Donald, 22, 267–68, 299,
  346

Galileo, 240; *Siderius Nuntius*, 199
Gardner, Dame Helen, 14, 15, 16,
  17–18, 85, 137, 140, 199, 232, 261,
  277, 282, 283, 296, 297, 298, 304,
  307, 309, 312, 313, 314, 315, 316,
  317, 320, 321, 324, 325, 334, 341,
  343, 344, 345, 347, 348, 349
Garrard, George, x, 178, 193, 203,
  230, 244, 245, 260, 269, 282, 292,
  302, 328, 335, 340

Garrod, H. W., 343
Gascoigne, George, 3, 8–10, 113; *The Adventures of Master F. J.*, 92; "Hemetes the Hermit," 8; *A Hundreth Sundrie Flowres*, 8–10, 295, 311; *The Posies*, 8
Gaveston (in Marlowe's *Edward II*), 316
Gella (in Davies's *Epigrams*), 49
Genres, mixing of, 71, 261
Geraldine, Sister M., 303
Gesta Grayorum, 31–32, 49, 68, 136, 301, 302, 308, 321
Gibbons, Brian, 303
Gilbert, Sir Humphrey, 316
Gill, Roma, 44, 304, 305, 322
Gioli, Gabriel: editions of Petrarch, 163, 164, 325, 326
Glascock (in "libel against some Grayes Inns gentlemen & Revellers"), 308
Gnosticism, 128
Goldberg, Jonathan, 328, 331, 332, 347
Goldin, Frederick, 310
Gombrich, E. H., 299
Gondomar, Conde de (Don Diego de Sarmiento), 284
Goodman, Godfrey, 328
Goodman-Hakewell Controversy, 240
Goodyer, Sir Henry, ix, x, xi, 17, 21, 127, 155, 156, 171, 182, 186, 187, 189, 193, 202, 203, 206, 211, 226, 244, 245, 260, 266, 269, 273, 282, 291, 297, 322, 324, 326, 330, 333, 347
Gorges, Sir Arthur, 12, 113, 296
Gosse, Edmund, 321, 326, 343
Gottfried, Rudolph, 295
Gottschalk, Katherine, 295
Grant, W. Leonard, 306
Gray's Inn, 7, 9, 25, 27, 308, 311
Great Contract, The, 332
Greek Anthology, The, 68
Greenblatt, Stephen, 11, 58, 296, 342

Greenwich Palace, 301
Greville, Sir Fulke, Lord Brooke, 4, 10, 160, 201, 246, 270; *Caelica*, 342; *Life of Sidney*, 237, 346
Grey de Wilton, Arthur, Lord, 319
Grierson, Sir Herbert, 14, 18, 119, 129, 206, 233, 296, 298, 300, 303, 305, 319
Grimble, Ian, 334
Grimes (in "libel against some Grayes Inns gentlemen & Revellers"), 308
Grosart, Alexander, 294
Grundy, Joan, 338
Grymes, Sir Thomas, 135
Guarino, 327
Guilpin, Everard, 320
Gunpowder Plot, The, (1605), 179, 180, 283
Guss, Donald, 93, 162, 163, 223, 315, 316, 321, 322, 324, 325, 327, 337

Hakewill, William, 183, 292, 330
Halewood, William, 345
Hall, Joseph, 235, 244, 292, 303, 304, 312, 320; *Virgedemiarum*, 300
Hamilton, James, 2nd Marquess of, 285
Hampton Court Conference (1603), 344
Harari, Josué, 296
Hardison, O. B., Jr., 317
Harington, Henry, 327
Harington, Sir John, 4, 6, 293, 303, 313, 329, 346; *Epigrams*, 4, 17, 167, 203–4, 347; *The Metamorphosis of Ajax*, 39, 293; *The Prayse of Private Life*, 342
Harington, Sir John, of Stepney, 6, 7
Harley, Sir Robert, 345
Harrier, Richard, 294
Harrington, Bridget, Lady Markham, 203, 211, 242
Harrington, Lady. *See* Kelway, Anne
Harrington, Lucy, Countess of Bed-

ford, ix, x, 15, 17, 182, 195, 202–32 *passim*, 234, 251, 271, 273–74, 285, 334, 335, 337, 338, 339, 341; "Death be not proud, thy hand gave not this blow," 19
Harrington, Sir John, 1st Lord of Exton, 271, 274
Harrison, G. B., 335
Hart, E. F., 293
Harvey, Gabriel, 56, 320; *Marginalia*, 301, 307, 309
Hatton, Sir Christopher, 28, 126
Hay, James, Lord, Viscount Doncaster, Earl of Carlisle, ix, 183, 186, 195, 276, 292, 343
Healy, Timothy, S.J., 329
Heath, Douglas, 301
Hebel, J. William, 293
Helgerson, Richard, 295
Henkel, Arthur, 325
Henry VIII, King, 11, 236, 301, 346
Henry, Prince, 179, 271, 346; court of, 245, 270, 346; death of, 269; elegies to mourn the death of, 245
Herbert, George, 277, 278, 303, 348; poems, 255, 256; "In Sacram Anchoram Piscatoris," 277; "A Parodie," 293
Herbert, Magdalen, Lady Danvers, x, 51, 196, 199, 245, 252, 260, 317, 343, 344
Herbert, Sir Edward, Lord Herbert of Cherbury, x, 17, 155, 182, 196–202 *passim*, 266, 269, 277, 298, 333, 346; *Autobiography*, 200, 334; *De Veritate*, 333; "I must depart," 328; "Methinks Death like one laughing lyes," 333; "Ode upon a Question Moved," 196; "Platonick Love," 197, 199; "The State Progress of Ill," 196, 201
Herbert, William, 3rd Earl of Pembroke, 90, 196, 285; poems, 18; "Soules joy," 293; "Who so termes love a fire," 85–86
Hercules, 270

Hester, M. Thomas, 303, 318
Hexter, J. H., 331
Heywood, Thomas: *Henry IV*, 320
Hill, Charles, 314
Hilliard, Nicholas, 19
Hinton, R. W. K., 331
Hoby, Sir Edward, 189
Holland, Hugh, 269, 292; *Pancharis*, 180
Holles, Sir John, Earl of Clare, 270, 346
Holstein, Duke of, 337
Holy Spirit, 163
Horace (in Jonson's *The Poetaster*), 26
Hoskins, John, 12, 184, 292, 302, 326, 330; *Directions for Speech and Style*, 26, 33; 300; poems, 6, 18; "Absence," 19; "Impossibilities," 313; "Sicilian Vespers" speech, 330
Howard, Charles, Admiral, 28, 100
Howard, Lady (in "libel against some Grayes Inns gentlemen & Revellers"), 308
Howard, Lady Frances, Countess of Essex, Countess of Somerset, 230, 273
Howard, Lord Henry, 1st Earl of Northampton, 330
Howard, Lord Thomas, 329
Howard family, 6
Hudson, Hoyt, 295, 300
Hughes, Richard, 321, 327, 334
Hughey, Ruth, 7, 294, 295, 313
Huizinga, Johan, 170, 327
Humberston, William (in "libel against some Grayes Inns gentlemen & Revellers"), 308
Hunt, Clay, 79, 110, 143, 309, 312, 313, 317, 322, 349
Hunter, William B., 297
Huntington, Countess of. *See* Stanley, Elizabeth
Hurstfield, J., 301
Hyde, Sir Edward, 1st Earl of Clarendon, 302

362 Index

Ignatius (in D's *Ignatius His Conclave*), 191–92
Imogen (in Shakespeare's *Cymbeline*), 315
Ingenioso (in the *Parnassus* plays), 39
Ingram, Arthur, 330
Inner Temple, 25
Ireland, 125
Irish Expedition, 124
Ironmonger's Company, The, 26
Islands Expedition (1597), 97, 102, 114, 115, 119, 316
Israelites, 345

Jacobsen, Eric, 150, 322
Jakobson, Roman, 299, 338
James I, King, 6, 34, 155, 156, 160, 167, 179–81, 184, 186–92, 203, 205, 243, 244, 245, 248, 249, 250, 254, 264, 268, 271, 275, 282, 285, 329, 342, 343, 347, 349; addresses to Parliament, 185–86; *Directions for Preachers*, 286; poems, 246–47, 251, 342; *Political Works*, 179, 185–86, 328–29
Johnson, Paula, 311
Jones, Inigo, 330
Jones, Leah, 318
Jones, Robert, 312
Jonson, Benjamin, 20, 23, 50, 166, 196, 202, 211, 292, 295, 298, 337; on Donne's poetry, 25; on Inns of Court, 30; poems, 17, 18; "Conversations with Drummond," 59, 235, 269, 300, 310, 336, 340, 346, 348; *Cynthia's Revels*, 32, 110; *Epicoene*, 188, 204, 206, 331, 336; *Epigrams*, 206, 222, 247, 335, 339; "An Epigram on the Court Pucell," 204–5; "To Lucy, Countesse of Bedford, with Mr. Donnes Satyres," 297; *Everyman Out of His Humour*, 26, 301, 319; *The Forrest*, 335, 339; "To Sicknesse," 338; *Hymenaei*, 203; *The Masque of Beauty*, 203; *The Masque of Blackness*, 203; *The Masque of Queenes*, 203; *Under-wood*, 343; *The Works of Beniamin Jonson* (1616), 5
Jordan-Smith, Paul, 316
Josephus (in D's *Sermons*), 275
Julia (in Shakespeare's *The Two Gentlemen of Verona*), 315
Juliers, 201, 333
Juliet (in Shakespeare's *Romeo and Juliet*), 60, 142
Juvenal, 318

Kahn, Coppelia, 307
Kamholtz, Jonathan, 12, 296
Keach, William, 89, 307, 314
Keister, Don A., 334
Kelly, T. J., 334
Kelway, Anne, Lady Harrington, 271
Ker, Sir Robert, Earl of Ancrum, x, 15, 272, 281, 285; Donne sends poems and *Biathanatos* to, ix, xi, 15, 195, 281, 348
Ker, Sir Robert, Earl of Somerset, Lord Chamberlain, ix, x, 179, 183, 186, 192, 231, 272–73, 291
Kermode, Frank, 232, 322, 339
Kerrigan, William, 257–58, 259, 344, 345
Keynes, Sir Geoffrey, 68, 291, 311, 324
Keyston, Rectory of, 275
King, Henry, 296
Kingsford, Charles L., 301
Kinwelmarshe, Francis, 9
Knights, L. C., 322
Kohut, Heinz, 323
Kress, Gunther, 207, 228, 234–35, 336, 339, 340
Krueger, Robert, 291, 304, 311

La Branche, Anthony, 44, 58, 309
La Briola, Albert C., 325
Lambert (in "libel against some Grayes Inns gentlemen & Revellers"), 308
Lamentations, 283, 349

Lanham, Richard, 296
Latham, Agnes M. C., 314
Laura (Petrarch's), 163, 164, 325, 326
Law, Civil, 189
Law, Common, 140, 185, 189, 263, 331
Leicester, Earl of. *See* Dudley, Robert; Sidney, Sir Robert
Leicester estate, 10–11
Leigh, David, S.J., 349
Lein, Clayton, 318
Leishman, J. B., xiii, 5, 58, 137, 142, 169, 218, 292, 294, 300, 303, 305, 306, 307, 321, 322, 327, 337
Lena, 305
Lennox, Duke of. *See* Richmond, Lodowick Stuart
Levine, Jay, 232
Levi-Strauss, Claude, 299
Lewalski, Barbara, 164, 245, 248, 257, 261, 284, 302, 323, 340, 343, 344, 345, 349
"libel against some Grayes Inns gentlemen & Revellers" (Anon.), 308
Lincoln's Inn, 25, 85, 89, 97, 114, 275
Livy, 180
Lodge, Thomas: *A Fig for Momus*, 305; "Praise of Rosalind," 325; *Scillas Metamorphosis*, 89
Lord, George deForest, 297
Loseley, Surrey, 134, 150, 165, 321
Losengier, 160
Low Countries, 61, 166
Loves Martyr, 197, 325
Luce (in Shakespeare's *The Comedy of Errors*), 49
Luciana (in Shakespeare's *the Comedy of Errors*), 49
Lucifer (in D's *Ignatius His Conclave*), 192
Lucio (in Shakespeare's *Measure for Measure*), 50
Lytle, Guy Fitch, 291

MacCaffrey, Wallace, 300
McCanles, Michael, 70, 311, 325

McClure, Norman E., 293, 331
MacColl, Alan, 14–15, 292, 296, 297, 298, 314
McCoy, Richard, 90
McGowan, Margaret M., 347
Machabees (in D's *Satire* 4), 105
Machiavelli (in D's *Ignatius His Conclave*), 191–92
McIlwain, Charles Howard, 328–29
Mack, Maynard, 297
McKerrow, Ronald B., 306
Macklem, Michael, 341
McManaway, James, 294
McPherson, David, 337
Mahood, M., 320
Maids of Honor, Elizabethan, 90
Malloch, A. E., 332
Mandelbaum, Allen, 296
Manley, Frank, 340, 341
Manning, J. A., 314
Manningham, John, 323; *Dairy*, 46, 153
Mansfield, Sir Robert, 270
Markham, Lady. *See* Harrington, Bridget
Marlowe, Christopher, 26; *Edward II*, 316; "The Passionate Shepherd to his Love," 84, 313; translation of Ovid's *Amores*, 44–45, 306, 320
Marotti, Arthur F., 291, 292, 296, 324, 329, 343, 348
Marston, John, 32, 128, 300, 303, 305, 320; *The Fawn*, 34, 302; *The Metamorphosis of Pygmalion's Image*, 54, 313; *The Scourge of Villainy*, 313
Martial, 5, 68, 337
Martin, Philip, 337
Martin, Richard, 34, 84, 183, 292, 330
Martz, Louis, 148, 261, 322, 339, 340, 345
Marx, Karl, 299
Mary, Queen of Scots, 189
Mary Magdalen, 247
Matchett, William, 325
Mathew, Sir Toby, 292

364 Index

Maurer, Margaret, 204, 208, 227, 228, 334, 335, 336, 338
May, Stephen, 294, 340
Mayne, Jasper, 23; "On Dr Donnes death," 300
Mazzeo, Joseph A., 339
Meautis, Jane, Lady Cornwallis, 203, 335
Medwall, Henry: *Fulgens and Lucres*, 136
Melanchton, 70
Meller, Horst, 164, 325–26
Memory, art of, 149–50
Meres, Francis: *Palladis Tamia*, 162, 293
Mermaid Tavern, 182, 330; social circle associated with, 184, 189
Metacommunication, 20–22, 23, 193, 195, 257, 265, 268
Middle Temple, 25, 31, 84; 1610 Revels, 46
Middleton, Thomas, 303
Milgate, Wesley, 131, 223, 226, 227, 292, 297, 298, 303, 304, 316, 317, 321, 323, 333, 334, 335, 336, 337, 340, 341, 346
Miller, Clarence H., 339
Miller, Henry Knight, 306
Milton, John, 295, 303; *Paradise Lost*, 262
Miner, Earl, 157, 309, 310, 312, 324, 345
Mira (in Sidney's *Arcadia*), 307
Miscellanies, manuscript poetical, 5–7, 12–13, 297; custom of compiling, 82; erotic elegies in, 45; Arundel-Harington MS, 7, 294; Bod. Add. MS B.97, 6, 68; Bod. Rawl. Poet. MS 85, 6, 12, 294, 336; Bod. Rawl. Poet. MS 172, 6; BL Add. MS 28253, 6; BL Harl. MS 6910, 7, 295, 313; BL Harl. MS 7392, 6, 294, 313; Burley MS, 18; Cambr. Univ. Lib. MS Dd.5.75, 6, 294; Devonshire MS 6; Farmer-Chetham MS 6, 18, 68, 294, 313; Folger MS V.a.89, 6; Marsh Lib. MS 3.5.21, 294; Rosenbach MS 186, 294; Rosenbach MS 239/18, 309; Rosenbach MS 240/2, 333; Rosenbach MS 243/4, 13; Rosenbach MS 1083/15, 6, 18, 68, 308, 310, 313, 314
—printed, 5; *England's Helicon*, 314; *The Paradise of Dainty Devices*, 7, 236; *The Phoenix Nest*, 7, 317, 325; *A Poetical Rhapsody*, xi, 7, 295, 317; Tottel's *Miscellany*, 7, 293, 295
Mitcham, 178, 182, 205, 345
Mitre Tavern, 182, 330; social circle associated with, 184, 189
Montaigne, Michel de, 193
Montgomery Castle, 266, 333, 345
Montgomery, Countess of. *See* Vere, Lady Susan
Montgomeryshire, 333
Montrose, Louis A., 313, 314
Moore, Thomas V., 303
Mopsa (in Sidney's *Arcadia*), 49
More, Ann. *See* Donne, Ann
More, Sir George, 133–35, 147, 150, 152–53, 166, 323
More, Sir Robert, 292, 347
Morris, Brian, 349
Morris, Harry, 137, 281, 321, 327
Morton, Thomas, Bishop, 329, 345
Mueller, Janel M., 320
Munden, R. C., 331
Murray, W. A., 339

Narcissistic injury, 156, 236, 323
Nashe, Thomas, 4, 26, 39; *The Anatomie of Absurditie*, 306; "The Choice of Valentines," 50, 72; defense of erotic elegies, 45; introduction to Sidney's *Astrophil and Stella*, 58
"Nay pish: nay pue: nay faith" (Anon.), 306
Neale, J. E., 304, 309, 319, 320

Neilson, William, 314
Nellist, B. F., 318
Nelson, William, 295
Nemser, Ruby, 291, 304
Neo-Latin poetry, 45
Neville, Sir Henry, 330
Newdigate, Bernard, 334
Nicholson, Marjorie, 340
Non-obstante clauses, in letters patent, 140–41, 322
Norris, Captain John, 28
Northampton, Earl of. *See* Howard, Lord Henry
Notestein, Wallace, 184, 330, 331, 335
Nottingham, Earl of, 317
Novarr, David, 277, 281, 283, 284, 328, 343, 348, 349
Nurse (in Shakespeare's *Romeo and Juliet*), 60

Oakeshott, Walter, 316
Oath of Allegiance, Elizabethan, 42–43
—Jacobean, 180, 191
Oglander, Sir John, 135
Orgel, Stephen, 291
Osborn, James M., 296, 312
Osborn, Louise B., 302, 313, 326, 336
Overbury, Sir Thomas, 272, 330; poems, 18; social circle of, 189; *The Wife*, 336
Ovid, 148, 304, 305; *Amores*, 44, 54, 60, 72, 76, 305, 312–13, 324; *Ars Amatoria*, 305, 307; *Remedia Amoris*, 50, 57
Ovid (in Jonson's *the Poetaster*), 26
Ovidianism, fashion for prurient, 48, 71–72
Oxford, Earl of. *See* De Vere, Edward
Oxford, University of, 34, 189, 310

Paget family, 6
Palinode, the, 110–13, 317

Palmer, David, 291, 303, 305, 318
Paracelsan medicine, 239
Paracelsus, 339
Paradise of Dainty Devices, The, 7, 236
Paradoxes, verse, 45, 47–52
Parliament, English, 179, 184–86; conflicts with Crown, 179, 184, 188; history of, 331; House of Commons, 184, 201, 330; House of Commons, Speaker of, 186; House of Lords, 188; of 1597–98, 140; of 1601, 140–41, 152, 322, 333; of 1604–10, 180, 184, 330, 333; of 1614 ("Addled"), 34, 184, 186, 330, 331, 347; of 1621, 284, 348
Parliament, Scottish, 184
Parliamentarians, 182
"The Parliament Fart" (anon.), 330
Parnassus plays, 26, 68, 300; *The Second Part of the Return from Parnassus*, 303
Parrish, Paul, 341
Parrot, Henry, 294
Parry, John Jay, 314
Parry, Sir Thomas, 7
Parsons, Robert, S.J., 304
Parthenia (in Sidney's *Arcadia*), 316
Partridge, Eric, 315
Patronage, 136, 154, 187, 202–32, 235, 259, 286, 337; artistic, 251; royal, 187
Patterson, Annabel, 332
Pattison, Bruce, 293
Paulet, Sir Amias, 329
Paylor, W. J., 307
Peck, Linda Levy, 330
Pembroke, Earl of. *See* Herbert, William
Penshurst, Estate of Sir Robert Sidney, 166
Percy, Henry, 9th Earl of Northumberland, 152, 292, 323; *Advice to His Son*, 335
Persuasion to love, the, 68, 88–95

366 Index

Peters, Helen, 297, 306, 320, 330, 331, 336
Peterson, Douglas, 295
Petrarch, 12, 157, 161, 163, 164, 177, 325, 326; commentaries on the work of, 13, 295–96; *The Life of Solitude*, 342; "Zefiro torna," 214
Phatic utterance, 228
Phelips, Sir Edward, Master of the Rolls, 186
Phelips, Sir Robert, 330
Phillips, John, 304
Phoenix Nest, The, 7, 12, 317, 325
Piggot, 185
Plato, 70
Plumb, J. H., 335
Plutarch, 180; *Moralia*, 180
Poetical Rhapsody, A, xi, 7, 295, 317
Polesworth, 211, 266
Portland, HMC, 346
Portugal, 309
Pory, John, 292
Posthumus (in Shakespeare's *Cymbeline*), 315
Potter, George, 348
Pound, Ezra, 197, 334
Powle, Stephen, 12, 46
Praeceptor amoris, 44
Praz, Mario, 297
Prerogative, royal, 140, 188, 190, 322, 331
Prest, Wilfrid, 30, 300, 301, 302, 303, 304
Prince D'Amour, Middle Temple Revels, 31, 68, 86
Privy Council, 186, 188; Elizabethan, 124; members in House of Commons, 184
Propempticon, 155
Propertius, 60, 148, 304, 324; elegies, 159, 310
Protestants, German, 283
Proteus (in Shakespeare's *The Two Gentlemen of Verona*), 315
Prouty, C. T., 295
Puritans, 61, 179, 184

Puttenham, George (?), 293
Pyrford, Surrey, 155, 165
Pythagorean thought, 128

Quaestio amoris, 148
Quinn, Kenneth, 323
Quintilian: *Institutio Oratoria*, 44, 306

Raby, F. J. E., 317
Rajan, Tillotoma, 299
Ralegh, Sir Walter, 3, 12, 13, 14, 28, 90, 100, 113, 296, 316, 318, 331, 336; poems, 18, 85, 212, 313, 340; "The Advice," 314; "Like to a hermit poor," 237; poem put into Lady Laiton's pocket, 9
Rebholz, Ronald, 237
Remedia amoris, 112
Revolution, English, 331
Ribeiro, Alvaro, 335
Richmond, H. M., 310, 327
Richmond, Lodowick Stuart, 1st Duke of Lennox, 342
Ringler, William, 296, 307
Roberts, Mark, 337
Rockett, William, 61, 308, 310, 312
Roe, Sir John: poems, 18; epistles to Ben Jonson, 18, 187; "Sleep, next Society," 15, 19
Roe, Sir Thomas, 12, 155, 193, 203, 291, 292, 335; poems, 18
Rollins, Hyder, 7, 293, 295, 296, 317
Romeo (in Shakespeare's *Romeo and Juliet*), 142
Rosseter, Philip, 3
Roston, Murray, 344
Rothstein, Eric, 311
Rowse, A. L., 314
Rudick, Michael, 296, 332
Rudyerd, Sir Benjamin, 196, 294, 314, 324; epigrams, 72; poems, 85, 333
Ruesch, Jurgen, 299
Russell, Conrad, 322, 328
Russell, Edward, 3rd Earl of Bedford, 206

Index 367

Rutland, Countess of, 335

Sackton, Alexander, 292
Sackville, Sir Edward, 3rd Earl of Dorset, 233, 245, 260, 298, 341, 349
Sackville-West, Victoria, 336
St. Paul, 190, 267
St. Paul's Cathedral, Deanship of, 284
Salisbury, HMC, 302, 319, 326
Sanders, Wilbur, 306, 322
Sanderson, James, 294, 306, 308, 312, 313, 314, 330
Sandison, Helen, 12, 296
San Felipe, the Spanish galleon, 102
Satan, 329
Saunders, J. W., 3, 4–5, 5, 291, 293, 294
Savage, James, 205, 330, 336
Saville, Jonathan, 323
Savoy, The, 152
Schafer, Roy, 254, 344
Schone, Albricht, 325
Schwartz, Murray, 307
Scott, Harold Spencer, 328
Searles, Harold, 340
Segar, Sir William: *Honor, Military and Civil*, 180
"Self-consuming artifacts," 71
Sellin, Paul, 304, 348
Senecan ideals, 126
Serafino, 316, 322
Seth (in D's *Metempsychosis*), 131, 132
Seymour-Smith, Martin, 332
Shakespeare, William, 23, 64, 69, 302, 303; romantic comedies, 59, 78, 83, 136; *All's Well That Ends Well*, 97; *As You Like It*, 85; *The Comedy of Errors*, 49; *Cymbeline*, 315; *Hamlet*, 165, 294; *King Lear*, 315; *Loves Labours Lost*, 327; *Measure for Measure*, 50, 94; *The Merchant of Venice*, 50, 134, 307; *Much Ado About Nothing*, 59; *Romeo and Juliet*, 60, 63, 94; *Sonnets*, 3, 7, 69, 108, 259, 294–95; *The Tempest*, the tempest in, 114; *Troilus and Cressida*, 303; *Twelfth Night*, 222, 338; *The Two Gentlemen of Verona*, 315, 327; *Venus and Adonis*, 93, 307
Shapiro, I. A., 118, 318, 319, 320, 330, 332
Sharpe, Kevin, 330, 331
Shawcross, John, 298
Sherwood, Terry G., 346
Shore, David R., 312
Shrewsbury, Earl of, 204
Shuttleworth, J. M., 333
Sicherman, Carol Marks, 344, 346
Sidney, Mary, Countess of Pembroke, 284; with Sir Philip Sidney, translation of Psalms, 246, 284
Sidney, Sir Philip, 3, 4, 11, 12, 13, 14, 33, 163, 166, 296, 313, 325; *Arcadia*, 49, 92, 316; *Old Arcadia*, 90, 307; poems, 18, 316; *Astrophil and Stella*, 3, 4, 10–11, 58, 90, 101, 136, 139, 160, 197, 311; "A Farewell," 327–28; with Mary Sidney, Countess of Pembroke, translation of Psalms, 246, 284
Sidney, Sir Robert, Lord Lisle, 2nd Earl of Leicester, 129, 161, 166, 167, 317, 319
Simpson, Evelyn, 189, 286, 299, 320, 332, 335, 345, 348
Simpson, Percy, 299
Siphatecia (in D's *Metempsychosis*), 132
Slights, Camille, 303, 304, 332
Sloan, Thomas O., 298, 303, 333, 334
Smith, A. G. R., 318
Smith, A. J., 110, 112–13, 157, 291, 296, 299, 300, 304, 311, 317, 322, 323, 326, 335, 337, 338, 340, 347, 349
Smith, G. C. Moore, 301, 328, 333
Smith, Gerald A., 302
Smith, G. Gregory, 293
Smith, Logan Pearsall, 302, 315, 316, 319, 320, 323

Snowden Forrest, 333
Somerset, Edward, Earl of Worcester, 204
Somerset, Protector, 6
Song of Solomon, 162
Sorlien, Robert Parker, 306
Southall, Raymond, 51, 294, 307
Southampton, Earl of. See Wriothesley, Henry
Southwell, Robert, S.J., 343; poems, 247; *An Humble Supplication to Her Majestie*, 42, 304
Spain, 61, 179, 282, 304, 309
Sparrow, John, 297
Spedding, James, 301
Speech, free, 184, 330
Spence, Joseph, 69
Spencer, Alice, Countess of Derby, Lady Egerton, 134, 321
Spenser, Edmund, 23, 295, 325; *Amoretti*, 111, 135, 317; *The Faerie Queene*, 50, 320
Sprague, Arthur Colby, 315
Stanford, Henry, 6, 294
Stanley, Elizabeth, Countess of Huntington, 213–14, 336, 339
Steevens, George, 294
Stein, Arnold, 74, 312, 317
Stella (in Sidney's *Astrophil and Stella*), 11
Stevens, John, 298
Stoicism, Christian, 68, 119
Stoicism, Senecan, 114, 319
Stone, Lawrence, 27, 56, 136, 203, 300, 301, 306, 307, 309, 321, 326, 330–31, 336, 342, 347
Stow, John, *A Survey of London*, 301
Strand, The, 178
Stringer, Gary, 349
Strong, Roy, 311, 313
Stuart, Lady Arabella, 336
Surrey, Earl of, 3
Sylvester, Joshua: translation of Du Bartas, 180; *Lachrymae Lachrymarum*, 346
Syminges, Dr. John, 344

Table book, 7
Table talk, 329
Tacitus, 311
Tasso, Torquato, 180
Taylor, John, the Water Poet, 346
Tennenhouse, Leonard, 307
Thavies Inn, Inn of Chancery, 34–35
Themech (in D's *Metempsychosis*), 132
Theoblad, Lewis, 20, 299
Thompson, E. N. S., 332
Thomson, Patricia, 11, 291, 296, 334, 335, 336, 338
Throckmorton, Nicholas, 135
Tibullus, 60; elegies, 310
Tilman, Rev. Edward, 277
"To his Heart" (Anon.), 317
Tonstall (in "libel against some Grayes Inns gentlemen & Revellers"), 308
Tottel, Richard, 7, 13, 293
Tottel's *Miscellany*, 7, 12, 293
Trattati d'amore, 143
Trumbull, William, 341
Tuve, Rosemond, 316
Twickenham, 209, 211, 214–18 *passim*
Tyrone, Earl of, 320

Union, proposed, of England and Scotland, 180, 184, 185, 189

Valency, Maurice, 295, 324
Van Wyk Smith, M., 129, 320, 321
Vavasour, Ann, 212, 336
Vellutello, 296
Venetian ambassador, 316, 321
Venice, ambassadorship to, 186, 323
Venice, CSP, 316, 336
Venus (in D's "The Indifferent"), 77
Venus (in Marston's *Metamorphosis of Pygmalion's Image*), 313
Venus (in Shakespeare's *Venus and Adonis*), 77
Vere, Lady Susan, Countess of Montgomery, 22, 286
Via negativa, 200

Villiers, George, Duke of Buckingham, 179, 276, 349
Viola/Cesario (in Shakespeare's *Twelfth Night*), 338
Virgil (in Jonson's *The Poetaster*), 26
Virginia Company, The, 186, 286
Virgin Mary, 343

Waddington, Raymond, 298, 333, 334
Wales, 345
Wallerstein, Ruth, 269–70, 346
Walsingham, Sir Francis, 28, 380
Walton, Sir Isaac: *Life of Donne*, 39, 67, 84, 116, 134, 135, 137, 153, 168, 177, 178, 182, 199, 303, 310, 318, 321, 327, 328, 334, 347
Warwick, Earl of, estate of, 11
Warwick, Lady, 317
Watson, Thomas: "A Dialogue betweene the Louer and his heart," 110; *Hekatompathia*, 317
Webber, Joan, 22, 298, 299, 332, 345
Webster, John: *The Duchess of Malfi*, 39, 303, 309
Weitzmann, Francis, 310
Wentworth, Sir Thomas, Viscount; Earl of Stratford, 328
West, John, 330
Whig conception of history, 331
White, Bridget, 338
Whitehall, Palace of, 178, 301
Whyte, Rowland, 129, 167, 317–18, 319
Whythorne, Thomas: *Autobiography*, 73, 312
Wiffen, J. H., 334
Wilbraham, Sir Roger, 328
Wilcox, John, 303
William of Orange, 201
Williams, Arnold, 320
Williams, C. H., 301
Williams, Franklin B., 180, 293, 329, 332, 335

Williams, Gordon, 310
Williams, Raymond, 301
Williamson, George, 332, 333, 340
Willoughby, Edwin E., 294
Wilson, Elkin Calhoun, 346
Wilson, F. P., 306
Wither, George, 346
Wood, Anthony, 329
Woodward, Rowland, x, 15, 16, 102, 114, 245, 292
Woodward, Thomas, 292; "Thou sendst me prose & rimes," 37
Wooley, Sir Francis, 155, 292
Wooleys, The, 166
Worcester, Earl of. *See* Somerset, Edward
Wotton, Sir Henry, x, 12, 17, 96, 97, 114, 119–20, 123, 124, 128, 131, 155, 166, 196, 291, 298, 302, 315, 316, 319, 320, 323, 346; appointed ambassador to Venice, 155; as ambassador to Venice, 166; Burley MS, commonplace book of, 18; letter to Robert Cecil, 34; poems, 18, 120, 319
Wright, Louis B., 323
Wriothesley, Henry, 3rd Earl of Southampton, 90, 326
Wyatt, Sir Thomas, 3, 6, 11, 14, 296; poems, 11, 12, 110; Penitential Psalms, 246, 342

Yates, Frances, 149, 322
Yoklavich, John, 336
York House, 118, 125, 133, 212, 321

Zaller, Robert, 348, 349
Zepheria (Anon.), 303
Zion, captivity of, 283
Zouche, Edward La, Lord (11th Baron), 319
Zumthor, Paul, 295